"PHILOSOPHERS HAVE OFFERED VARIOUS INTERPRETATIONS OF THE WORLD . . . OUR BUSINESS IS TO CHANGE IT."

Thus Karl Marx stated the animating spirit of Communism. The changes he prophesied have been swift in coming. Today thirty-nine countries, containing over half the human race, proclaim themselves Communist.

Yet this great philosophy of change itself has not been immune to change, often dramatic, sometimes violent. In the past as in the present, Communism has meant very different things to very different men. To define it, understand it, answer it, means listening not to one view but to many.

This volume is designed to fill this vital need—to give the total spectrum of ideas, ideals, and prescriptions for action that have come together under the red flag of revolution.

SIGNET and MENTOR Titles of Related Interest

Communism:
BASIC WRITINGS

Edited by

ANNE FREMANTLE

A MENTOR BOOK from
NEW AMERICAN LIBRARY
TIMES MIRROR
New York and Toronto
The New English Library Limited, London

ACKNOWLEDGMENTS

Selections from THE ABC OF COMMUNISM, by N. I. Bukharin. Reprinted by permission of Penguin Books Ltd.

Selections from MARX & ENGELS: BASIC WRITINGS ON POLITICS & PHILOSOPHY, edited by Lewis S. Feuer, Doubleday & Company, Inc. 1959. Reprinted by permission of the editor.

Selections from KARL MARX: SELECTED WRITINGS IN SOCIOLOGY & SOCIAL PHILOSOPHY, edited by T. B. Bottomore. Copyright © 1956 C. A. Watts & Co. Ltd., London. Used with permission of McGraw-Hill Book Company and C. A. Watts & Co. Ltd.

Selections from DIDEROT: INTERPRETER OF NATURE, translated by Jonathan Kemp. Reprinted by permission of International Publishers Co., Inc.

Selections from THE DICTATORSHIP OF THE PROLETARIAT, by Karl Kautsky. Reprinted by permission of The University of Michigan Press and George Allen & Unwin Ltd.

Selections from FUNDAMENTAL PROBLEMS OF MARXISM, by G. V. Plekhanov, edited by Ryazonov. Reprinted by permission of International Publishers Co., Inc.

Selections from TERRORISM AND COMMUNISM, by Leon Trotsky. Reprinted by permission of The University of Michigan Press.

Selections from THE MODERN PRINCE by Antonio Gramsci. Reprinted by permission of International Publishers Co., Inc.

Selections from HO CHI MINH: ON REVOLUTION. Reprinted by permission of Frederick A. Praeger, Inc., and Pall Mall Press Ltd.

Excerpt from "Socialist Humanism" by Herbert Marcuse from SOCIALIST HUMANISM, edited by Erich Fromm. Copyright © 1965 by Doubleday & Company, Inc. Reprinted by permission of the publisher.

Excerpts from THE WRETCHED OF THE EARTH, by Frantz Fanon. Translated from the French by Constance Farrington. Preface by Jean-Paul Sartre. Reprinted by permission of Grove Press, Inc., and MacGibbon & Kee Ltd. Copyright © 1963 by Bresence Africaine.

"History Will Absolve Me." Published in CUBA: ANATOMY OF A REVOLUTION, by Leo Huberman and Paul M. Sweezy, 1960. Reprinted by permission of Monthly Review Press, 116 W. 14th St., N. Y. Copyright © by Leo Huberman and Paul M. Sweezy.

(The following page constitutes an extension of this copyright page.)

MENTOR TRADEMARK REG. U.S. PAT. OFF. AND FOREIGN COUNTRIES
REGISTERED TRADEMARK—MARCA REGISTRADA
HECHO EN CHICAGO, U.S.A.

SIGNET, SIGNET CLASSICS, SIGNETTE, MENTOR AND PLUME BOOKS
are published *in the United States* by
The New American Library, Inc.,
1301 Avenue of the Americas, New York, New York 10019,
in Canada by The New American Library of Canada Limited,
295 King Street East, Toronto 2, Ontario,
in the United Kingdom by The New English Library Limited,
Barnard's Inn, Holborn, London, E.C.1, England

FIRST PRINTING, DECEMBER, 1970

PRINTED IN THE UNITED STATES OF AMERICA

Revolution, Mr. Frazer thought, is no opium. Revolution is a catharsis; an ecstasy which can only be prolonged by tyranny. The opiums are for before and after . . .

—Ernest Hemingway,
The Gambler, the Nun and the Radio

ACKNOWLEDGMENTS

My profound thanks are due to Sir Isaiah Berlin, to Dr. Leonard Shapiro, and to Mr. Boris Souvarine, who helped me so much, and without whom this book could never have been compiled. I am also grateful to Mrs. Samuel Anderson, who took great pains with the typing and preparation of the manuscript.

—ANNE FREMANTLE

CONTENTS

INTRODUCTION

PART ONE

What is communism?

"Communism," states J. Edgar Hoover, "is more than an economic, political, or social-philosophical doctrine. It is a way of life."

It is *the* way of life for the 45,500,000 people in eighty-eight countries who are Communist Party members, and it is the political theory by which thirty-nine countries, containing more than half the human race, are governed. In this anthology, it is proposed to give extracts from basic communist writings, illustrating the philosophy and the economic, political, and social doctrines of communism, as well as the various deviations therefrom and revisions thereto, up to 1970.

Communism is generally equated with Marxist-Leninism, that is, with a system of ideas propounded by Karl Marx (1818–1883), a German, elaborated by Friedrich Engels (1820–1895), another German, and expounded by Nicolas Lenin, a Russian (1870–1924). But ideas, because they are created by people, have antecedents like people: parents, grandparents, and great grandparents. Thus communist ideas existed long before Marx and have developed in many directions since his death. Communists claim a long heritage for their ideas, starting with the Greek philosopher Heraclitus (6th–5th century B.C.), who first declared that all things flow, all change, that it is impossible to enter twice into one and the same stream. At one moment things are in process of stabilization; at another, of decomposition. Everything develops by virtue of the strife of opposites. Existence and non-existence are two poles between which all phenomena continuously move, the parts of creation are divided into two halves, each one opposed to the other, as the earth is divided into mountains and plains or water into fresh and salt. Heraclitus expounded three basic communist ideas: dialectical materialism, the disclosure of essential opposites, and the negation of negation. These ideas will reappear constantly in this anthology. Other

Greeks, such as Democritus (5th–4th century B.C.), declared things were determined only by their use: "By use there is sweet, by use there is bitter, by use there is warm and by use there is cold." This is another basic communist tenet.

Just as the philosophical ideas of communism can be traced to the Greeks, so some of their economic ideas, for example, the abolition of private property, can be traced back to early Christian sources. In the New Testament it is written: "No one said that any of the things which he possessed was his own, but they had everything in common. . . . There was not a needy person among them, for as many as were possessors of lands or houses sold them, and brought the proceeds of what was sold and laid it at the apostle's feet, and distribution was made to each as had any need."[1] This curiously anticipates the Communist phrase: "From each according to his ability, to each according to his need."

But in spite of many passages in the Church Fathers which adumbrate the communist attitude to private property (as also to the specially privileged status of the poor) and the communist thesis that labor is the only criterion of value, and in spite, too, of obvious analogies between most forms of Christian monastic life and communist theory, it was during the upheavals that accompanied the Reformation that communism was first preached and practiced by laymen and in public, rather than by priests or monks in their private enclosures.

During the Peasants War (about which Martin Luther's comment was that God Himself had called him to shed the peasants' blood), Thomas Münzer (1489–1525) led the first serious literate people's uprising that took place on a European scale. Both Friedrich Engels and the contemporary East German writer Ernst Bloch, have commented on Münzer. Almost contemporary with Münzer's rebellion was John Ball's revolt in England, with its marching doggerel that has come down to us:

> When Adam delved and Eve span
> Where was then the gentleman?

Both these movements ended badly, in the total obliteration of almost all the participants. But they inspired others, such as, for example, a century later that of John Lilburne (1614?–1657) and the Levellers in England, and in France such movements as the Jacquerie.

[1] Acts IV, 32-34. Revised Version.

The Reformation, the Peasants War, the English Civil War, the French Revolution—for communists these are all giant steps forward of humanity on the march. But since Marx and Engels were Germans, it was not the Frenchmen of the Enlightenment—Jean Jacques Rousseau (1712–1778) or Denis Diderot (1713–1784)—who most influenced them, but rather the German philosophers, Immanuel Kant (1724–1804), Johann Fichte (1762–1814), and Georg Hegel (1770–1831). "Had there not previously existed German idealistic philosophy, above all that of Hegel, scientific socialism would never have been founded," Engels wrote, and added, "We German socialists are proud to take our origins also from Kant, Fichte and Hegel."[2] Engels also said that Marx "read Hegel and stood him on his head." Sir Isaiah Berlin, Regius Professor of Political Science at Oxford, sees Marx's ideas as having a fourfold source: from the basic concepts of Hegel; from the dynamic principles of the French Saint-Simon (1760–1825); from the belief in the primacy of matter of the German Ludwig Feuerbach (1804–1872), and, finally, from the French communist tradition. From this last Marx obtained his view of the sacred mission of the proletariat. Sir Isaiah adds, "Marx's achievements in turning paradoxes into truisms have been necessarily ignored in proportion as their effects have become part of the permanent background of civilized thought."[3]

In fact, most communist ideas, philosophical or economic, so revolutionary in the nineteenth century, today appear commonplace, while the dialectical is now the classical scientific method, than which there is indeed no other. Only communist *political ideas* still seem challenging to many people, who agree with Sir Isaiah Berlin that "communism is the doctrine of humanitarianism driven to an extreme in the pursuit of offensive and defensive methods."[4] But as the strongly anticommunist Walter Kolarz declared in his *Communism and Colonialism*, "The strength of communism has always been the weakness of its opponents, not so much their material weakness but their moral and intellectual inadequacy, their failure to understand the signs of the times and their inability to cope resolutely with political, social and economic problems. Those who uphold racial inequality, suppress civil liberties

[2] Friedrich Engels, *The Peasant War in Germany*, New York, 1941, p. 23.
[3] Sir Isaiah Berlin, *Marx*, London, 1963, p. 158.
[4] *Foreign Affairs* (New York, April 1950), p. 364.

or obstruct social reforms, help communism . . . however loudly they may proclaim their anti-communist convictions."[5]

And for its devotees, as R. N. C. Hunt wrote, "Communism has the *value* of a religion in so far as it is felt to provide a complete explanation of reality and of man as a part of reality and at the same time to give life, as does religion, a sense of purpose."[6]

Finally, President Nixon, returning to the White House in August, 1969, after his world tour, which included a visit to communist Rumania, declared: "Deep differences in political philosophy cannot permanently divide the peoples of the world." May all who study those differences help to make these words come true!

PART TWO

Communist philosophy is based on dialectical materialism.

What is dialectic?

Dialectics is the study of things in their relationships and in their processes of development and change. Dialectics, therefore, is not an abstract system of logic which men are asked to accept. It is dialectical to look for the special characteristics of anything in every new set of relations and then adapt one's thought to the new form which reality has taken. Dialectics foresees no final scientific laws and tries to avoid dogmatic finality. Dialectical thought allows for the concept of matter to change from one evolutionary level to the next. For example, at one level matter is mindless, at the next it is "minded." It is matter itself which *thinks* when it is organized into a brain.

What is dialectical materialism?

Dialectical materialism believes that in the evolution of the universe the nonliving preceded the living. At a specific time, there was no mind. Mind is a characteristic of matter at a high stage of development. Dialectical materialism believes matter evolves from level to level, and recognizes the emergence of new qualities—such as mind and spiritual values—at different levels. It does not believe that emer-

[5] Macmillan, London, 1964, p. 1.
[6] *The Theory and Practice of Communism*, London, Pelican, 1968, p. 29.

gence means the emerging qualities were always there existing in suspension or in imperceptible degrees: it believes
that they appeared for the first time at a definite period in
the history of matter, as the result of specific causes, and
that they are the inevitable consequence of certain material
patterns. "Consciousness is a characteristic of some facts
of organic behaviour," as Everett Dean Martin has said.
"Of course there is life out there," said rocket designer
Werner von Braun about outer space. Engels expressed the
view of the universe held by dialectical materialists as
follows:

> Matter moves in an eternal cycle, completing its trajectory
> in a period so vast that in comparison with it our earthly
> year is as nothing; in a cycle in which the period of highest
> development, namely the period of organic life with its
> crowning achievement, self-consciousness, is a space just as
> comparatively minute in the history of life and of self-
> consciousness; in a cycle in which every particular form of
> the existence of matter—be it the sun or a nebula, a par-
> ticular animal or animal species, a chemical combination
> or decomposition—is equally in transition; in a cycle in
> which nothing is eternal, except eternally changing, eter-
> nally moving matter and the laws of its movement and
> change. But however often and pitilessly this cycle may be
> accomplished in time and space, however many countless
> suns and earths may arise and fall, however long it may be
> necessary to wait until in some solar system, on some
> planet, appear conditions suitable for organic life, however
> many countless beings may fall and rise before, out of their
> midst, develop animals with a thinking brain that find an
> environment that permits them to live, be it even only for
> a short period, we are, nevertheless, assured that matter in
> all its changes remains eternally one and the same, that not
> one of its attributes may perish, and that that same iron
> necessity which compels the destruction of the highest
> earthly bloom of matter—the thinking spirit—also neces-
> sitates its rebirth at some other place, at some other time.[7]

Dialectically evolving matter is thus seen to be the initial
point in communist philosophy. Thinking individuals and
the social history that develops around them find their
origin and explanation in the dialectic of the development
of material actuality. The conditions necessary for the
emergence of organic life and of thinking human beings
from organic life include socially controlled production,
when organic life is no longer subject to the mindless
processes of cause and effect but comes under conscious

[7] *Dialectic of Nature*, translated by Foreign Languages Publishing
House, Moscow, 1950, p. 125.

social control. Social knowledge emerges when every new
generation receives from its predecessor not only the heritage of productive forces but the sum of inherited and
experienced knowledge. Experience is the sum, the result,
of social practice, and of all the earlier developments of
historic practice as contained in the experience of every
epoch.

But the development of the productive process actually
changes the objects of material nature. When Engels
wrote, organic compounds were unknown things for chem-
ists of the first half of the nineteenth century; but today
they are more and more being made by means of the synthesis of chemical elements and with no recourse to organic
process. Thus the objective material world is revealed by
practice. Indeed, for the dialectical materialist, practice is
the key to knowledge of the external world. "The question
whether objective truth can be attributed to human thinking
is not a question of theory but is a practical question. Any
dispute over the reality or nonreality of thinking isolated
from practice is a purely scholastic question," Marx wrote
in his second thesis on Feuerbach; and Engels notes, "The
success of our actions proves the agreement of our per-
ceptions with the apprehensible objective truth of things.
However conditional and imperfect knowledge at any stage
may be, it reflects objective material reality approximating
to absolute truth. Practice turns knowledge into actual existing objects of production, and changes material actuality."

From the point of view of dialectical materialism, Lenin
said, every ideology is historically conditioned, but to
every scientific ideology there corresponds objective truth,
for absolute nature is unconditioned. So even Marx's doctrine on capitalist society, or Lenin's doctrine on imperialism, are not, by communists, held to be absolute truths, but
as being capable of further development, since they contain
in themselves moments of relativism. The materialist view
of history was modified by Marx through his historical
conception of matter: the material world today is, he
affirms, what centuries of men have made it. It is "the
result and product of the action of a succession of generations." "It is possible," Marx wrote in his *German Ideology*,
"to distinguish men from animals by conscience, religion,
by anything one chooses. They begin to distinguish themselves from animals the moment they begin to produce their
own means of existence."[8] Marx's whole view of life is thus
seen as activity; his most fundamental theory is of the

[8] Translated and edited by S. Ryazanskaya, London, 1965, p. 56.

indissoluble unity of theory and practice: man only *is* when
he *acts*. And since history does not move backwards or in
cyclical movements, all its conquests are final and irrevo-
cable. As Sir Isaiah Berlin wrote, "the only real rights are
those conferred by history, the right to act the part historically imposed upon one's class."[9] For, Sir Isaiah goes on to
explain, Marx thought that if man does not identify himself
with the direction of the world process he encompasses his
own certain destruction. To choose to do so deliberately
is to behave irrationally. Only a wholly rational being is
wholly free to choose between alternatives. Where one of
these irresistibly leads man to his own destruction, he cannot
choose it freely, because to say that an act is free is to deny
that it is contrary to freedom. Thus the path to freedom
entails the knowledge of historical necessity. (Compare
St. Bernard "Where necessity is, there is not free-will.")[10]

The notion of the causal connection of phenomena arose
from the fact of man's active changing of nature by his
activity. Thus theory and practice inter-react: the instruments man makes—microscope, telescope—lead to a widening of his field of vision. That which in human knowledge
"depends neither on the subject, nor on man, nor on society" Marx called "objective truth," whose source, according to Lenin, is "the aggregate of all the aspects of a
phenomenon, their actuality and mutual dependence." For
what is basic to materialism is the recognition of the objective existence of material objects. Yet even this is temporary,
for "dialectical philosophy dissolves all conception of final,
absolute truth, and of a final, absolute, sacred truth. It reveals the transitory character of everything and in everything: nothing can endure before it except the uninterrupted
process of becoming and of passing away, of endless ascendancy from the lower to the higher."[11]

How does dialectical materialism lead to socialism?

Social practice emerges in a quite definite form at each
given historical stage of social development. Every social
class has its own determinate criterion of practice, changed
in every historical epoch, as the class develops its historical
role. "In class society there cannot be extra-class practice.
The criterion of truth in class society is the practice of the
given class." So for a primitive society, feudal practice was

[9] Berlin, *Marx*, p. 152.
[10] See *The Age of Belief*, edited by Anne Fremantle, New York,
1954, pp. 104–105.
[11] Friedrich Engels, *Ludwig Feuerbach*, New York, 1966, p. 22.

the criterion of progessive knowledge; in feudal society capitalist practice was the criterion. So too, when human society is really understood, capitalism is revealed as one of its *necessary* forms of development, and the class struggle is recognized as the basis of progress from capitalism to the proletarian dictatorship.

And when the dictatorship of the proletariat has come about (as in Soviet Russia), then what?

Josef Stalin, speaking at the Sixteenth Communist Party Congress, described how the strengthening of the proletarian state is necessary for it to progress to its own ultimate extinction, which is its objective:

> We are for the withering away of the State. And yet we also believe in the proletarian dictatorship, which represents the strongest and mightiest form of State power that has hitherto existed. To keep on developing State power in order to prepare the condition for the withering away of State power—that is the Marxist formula. Is it "contradictory"? Yes, "contradictory." But the contradiction is vital, and wholly reflects Marxist dialectic.

For contradiction is a fundamental of dialectical materialism. As Lenin put it, "the unity (coincidence, identity, resultant force) of opposites is conditional, temporary, transitory and relative. The struggle of the mutually exclusive opposites is absolute, as movement and evolution are."[12] Marxists regard development as a "unity of opposites—the division of the one into mutually exclusive opposites and their reciprocal correlation."[13] To these two fundamental laws of dialectics must be added the third: the negation of the negation. This is based upon the fact that between the different phases of a contradictory development there exists a profound internal connection, since every phase, by overcoming the specific form of the contradiction of its predecessor, by *negating* it, brings forth the form of contradiction that belongs to it and thus prepares its own negation. This double contradiction shows how the "synthesis" negates and overcomes both "thesis" and "antithesis" but reproduces features of the original thesis. Thus it was in the beginning, is now, and ever will be.

It is thus in the emergence of contradictions and their resolution that "here we are back again," as Engels wrote, "back at the conceptions of the great founders of Greek philosophy, namely that all nature, from its smallest particular to its greatest bodies, from a grain of sand to the

12, 13 *The Collected Works of N. Lenin*, Vol. XIII, London, pp. 324, 323.

sun, is in eternal emergence and annihilation, in incessant movement and change." It is obvious then that for the Marxist, dialectical materialism is not one philosophy like another, but is the total awareness of the meaning of history, whose measure is man, man the conglomerate of all his social relationships. So all other ideologies—nationalistic, religious, economic—as Marx declared, are "forms of collective self-deception," for "philosophers have offered various interpretations of the world."

And he went on: *"Our* business is to change it."

How?

In the following pages, communist thinkers ask and answer this question.

CHRONOLOGY

1750   Beginning of the Industrial Revolution in England; widespread misery.

1776   American Declaration of Independence.

1789   French Revolution, followed by Napoleonic wars.

1792   Tom Paine publishes *The Rights of Man*.

1794   Prime Minister Pitt (1759–1806) suspends *Habeas Corpus* Act.

1807   Georg Wilhelm Friedrich Hegel's *Phenomenology of the Spirit*.

1815   Corn Laws passed in England. Food riots follow. Beginning of British Socialism with Robert Owen (1771–1858).

1817   First hunger march to London. Massacre of unarmed workers at Peterloo.
        David Ricardo (1772–1823) publishes *Principles of Political Economy*.
        William Cobbett (1763–1835) flees to United States.

1819   First Factory Act, England, forbids children 9–16 to work more than 13½ hours.

1823   Stockton-Darlington railway opens. Beginning of railroad boom.

1829   France: Charles Fourier (1772–1837) publishes *The New Industrial World*.

1830   France: July revolt.

1831   Workers revolt at Lyons, France.

1832   First Reform Bill passed in England. Electorate in population of 4,000,000 increased from 220,000 to 670,000.

1837   England: First People's Charter, demanding adult suffrage, free elections, etc., signed by 1¼-million, rejected. Chartist leaders jailed.

1840   England: Petition of National Chartist Association signed by more than half the adult male population. Rejected by Parliament 1842.

1844   Karl Marx (1818–1883) writes *The Jewish Question, Economico-Philosophic Mss., Introduction to Hegel's Philosophy of Law* (all published posthumously).

1845   Marx, expelled from Paris, moves to Brussels. Publishes *The Holy Family* in collaboration with Friedrich Engels (1820–1895).

1848 Rising in Paris, proclamation of Second Republic. Revolts in Germany, Austria, and Italy.

1849 Marx, expelled from Belgium, moves to London, where he remains until his death.

1851 Napoleon III takes over in France.
T'ai Ping revolt in China begins (continues until 1864).

1855 Alexander II of Russia, a liberal, succeeds to the throne.

1857 Worldwide economic crisis.

1861 American Civil War breaks out.
Emancipation of serfs in Russia by Alexander II.

1863 Ferdinand Lassalle (1825–1864) founds German General Workers Association.

1864 International Working Men's Association (First International) founded.

1866 London Working Men's Association founded.

1867 Marx publishes Vol. I of *Capital*.
Universal manhood suffrage granted in Germany by Bismarck.

1868 Michael Bakunin (1814–1876) creates anarchistic Social Democratic Alliance. International Working Men's Association founded in England.

1870 Franco-Prussian War. Flight of Napoleon III, proclamation of Third Republic in France.

1871 Paris Commune.

1872 Bakunin and anarchists thrown out of First International at Hague Conference.

1876 End of First International.

1880 Henry George publishes *Progress and Poverty* in England.

1881 Alexander II assassinated.

1883 Death of Marx. Georgii Plekhanov (1857–1918) creates Marxist group in Russia.

1884 England: Foundation of Social Democratic Federation (H. M. Hyndman, Tom Mann, John Burns, William Morris, Karl Marx's daughter Eleanor Aveling, and husband).
Foundation of Fabian Society (George Bernard Shaw, Sidney Webb, et al.).

1886 Foundation of American Federation of Labor.

1889 Second International convenes in Brussels, meets every three years; May Day chosen as Workers Day.

1891 At Erfurt Congress in Germany, German Social Democratic Party, under Karl Kautsky (1854–1938), adopts Marxist program.

1894 France: Sadi-Carnot assassinated. Russia: repression by Nicholas II.

1899 France: Second International holds congress in Paris. Germany: Edward Bernstein (1850–1932) attacked by August Bebel (1840–1913). Russia: Vladimir Ilyich Lenin (1870–1924) publishes first book. Development of capitalism in Russia.

1900 Lenin founds magazine *Iskra* in Switzerland with Plekhanov.
China: Boxer revolt.

1901 Jean Jaurès founds French socialist party.

1903 Split at Russian Social Democratic Party Congress between Bolshevik majority (Lenin) and Mensheviks (Plekhanov).

1904 Foundation in Paris of daily *Humanité* by Jaurès.

1905 Revolutionary outbreak in Russia following defeat of Russia by Japan; *Potemkin* naval mutiny; formation of Petersburg Soviet under Leon Trotsky (1879–1940).
China: revolutionary manifesto of Sun Yat-sen (1866–1925).

1906 First two *Dumas* in Russia. Twenty-nine Labour Members elected to British Parliament. Trade Disputes Act reverses Taff Vale decision.

1907 German Social Democratic party wins 3¼-million votes in election.

1908 British Labour Party joins Socialist International. George Sorel publishes his *Reflections on Violence*.

1911 Revolution in China. Proclamation of Chinese Republic. Sun Yat-sen founds Kuomintang. Young Turk revolution.

1914 Russia: Bolshevist deputies deported.
Assassination of Jaurès.
Assassination of Archduke Francis Ferdinand at Sarajevo. Outbreak of World War I. All European socialist parties support war.

1915 Nicolas Bukharin (1888–1938) attacks Lenin's support of national self-determination as "Utopian and harmful" at Stockholm.

1917 February Revolution in Russia (Petersburg); abdication of the Tsar; Lenin and Trotsky return to Russia from Zurich in sealed train.
United States enters war.
France: mutinies, strikes.
October Revolution in Russia: proclamation of Socialist Republic. Lenin head of People's Com-

missars, Trotsky, foreign affairs and war; creation of Cheka (secret police).

Germany: Kautsky founds Social-Democratic Party.

China: Sun Yat-sen founds government in Canton.

1918   Treaty of Brest–Litovsk between Soviet Russia and Germany; abdication of German Kaiser. German Republic founded. Armistice between Allies and Central powers.

1919   Germany: Spartacus (Communist) coup fails; Karl Liebknecht and Rosa Luxemburg assassinated; Weimar Constitution signed.

Russia: Foundation of Third International (Comintern). Red Army defeats White Generals Denikin, Wrangel, Youdeni, and Koltchak.

Hungary: Communist regime of Bela Kun.

Treaty of Versailles signed in France.

1920   Germany: Social-Democratic Party defeated; Communist Party formed.

1921   Russia: Revolt of *Kronstadt* sailors.

China: Communist Party founded.

Italy: Communist Party founded.

1922   Russia: Creation of Union of Soviet Socialist Republics (USSR).

Treaty of Rapallo between USSR and Germany.

Benito Mussolini (1883–1945) marches on Rome and becomes President.

1923   USSR: Death of Lenin. Trotsky denounces suppression of democratic rights within Russian Communist Party.

China: Kuomintang reorganized with Soviet help.

Communist coups fail in Germany and Bulgaria.

1924   First Labour Party government in England.

1925   USSR: Break between Zinoviev, Kamenev, and Joseph Stalin (1879–1953).

China: Chiang Kai-shek unites China after death of Sun Yat-sen.

1926   Chinese Communist Party obliged to disarm and enter Kuomintang.

1927   Trotsky thrown out of USSR Communist Party.

China: Chiang Kai-shek turns against communists and kills 4,000 workers in Shanghai.

1928   USSR: First Five-Year Plan.

1929   Stalin turns against Bukharin. Beginning of Terror (until 1939).

Depression in the United States, later worldwide.

1931 Japan takes Manchuria.
Mao Tse-tung (1893–   ) forms Communist Republic in Kiangsi (South China).

1932 Five million unemployed in Germany; two million in Britain.

1933 Adolf Hitler (1889–1945) elected. Beginning of Nazi terror (until 1945).
China: Mao Tse-tung's Long March to Shensi in north.

1934 Japanese enter China.
France: Popular Front adopted by Seventh Congress of Communist International.

1935 Anglo-German Naval Agreement gives Hitler British support for German rearmament.
Italy conquers Abyssinia.

1936 Spanish Civil War (until 1939).

1937 Japan conquers most of Mainland China.

1938 Germany takes Austria (Anschluss).
Munich Pact which concedes Sudetenland to Germany.

1939 Franco triumphs in Spain.
Soviet-German (Hitler–Stalin) Nonaggression Pact.
Germany marches into Poland.
World War II starts.
USSR occupies part of Poland and marches into Finland.

1941 Germany attacks USSR.

1942 Communist successes in Yugoslavia and Greece.

1943 Siege of Stalingrad lifted; Germans retreat.

1944 Tito comes to power in Yugoslavia.
German anti-Nazi plot to kill Hitler fails.

1945 Yalta Conference with Churchill, Roosevelt, and Stalin.
German surrender.
First atom bomb on Hiroshima; Japan surrender follows.
Communist governments in Poland, Rumania, Hungary, Czechoslovakia, Bulgaria, Yugoslavia, Albania. Civil War in China between communists and Kuomintang (until 1949).

1946 Civil war in Greece.
Vietnam Revolutionary war against French occupation.

1947 Marshall Plan.

1948   Tito breaks with USSR.
       Greece: civil war ends with right-wing victory.

1949   Communist victory in China. Mao Tse-tung becomes chairman.

1950   Korean War (ends 1953).

1953   Stalin's death. Execution of Lavrenti Beria (chief of USSR police).

1954   Communist victory in Vietnam; Ho Chi Minh becomes president of People's Republic of North Vietnam. Geneva Treaty Agreement dividing Vietnam signed by United Kingdom, France, China, USSR, Cambodia, Laos, Vietnam, Vietminh.

1955   Fall of Georgi Malenkov in USSR. Nikita Khrushchev (1894–   ) becomes Party Chief.
       Kao Kang, pro-Soviet Chinese leader, thrown out of Chinese Communist Party and commits suicide.
       Bandung Conference.

1956   Tenth Communist Party Congress in Moscow, Denunciation by Khrushchev of Stalin's crimes; Stalin's corpse is disinterred from Kremlin.
       Poland: Poznan revolt; Wladyslaw Gomulka (1906–   ), National Communist, comes to power.
       Hungary: revolt against Matyas Rakosi (1892–1963); Communist Party collapses; USSR sends in troops and suppresses revolt.
       Albania: pro-Soviet elements retreat.

1957   China: Thousand Flowers campaign; Great Leap Forward.

1958   Sino-Soviet conflict flares.

1959   West Germany: Communist Party outlawed.

1960   USSR stops all aid to China; recalls its experts.

1961   Berlin Wall built.

1962   Bay of Pigs invasion (Cuba).

1963   Open Sino-Soviet conflict; Albania in Chinese camp.

1964   Fall of Khrushchev.

1968   Czechoslovakia: USSR sends troops to quell revolt.

1969   Twenty-first Communist Party Congress reveals deep rifts.
       Sino-Soviet armed clashes in Siberia.

1970   United States invades Cambodia.
       Roger Garaudy expelled from French Communist Party.

I.

CLASSICAL
COMMUNISM

Karl Marx
(1818–1883)

German philosopher and socialist economist, Marx was born at Trèves. The Communist Manifesto, which he wrote with his friend and benefactor Friedrich Engels (1820–1895), has been described by Sir Isaiah Berlin as "the greatest of all social pamphlets . . . a document of prodigious dramatic force . . . written in prose which has the lyrical quality of a great revolutionary hymn, whose effect, powerful even now, was probably greater at the time . . . its effect upon succeeding generations is unparalleled outside of religious history: had its author written nothing else, it would have ensured his lasting fame."[1]

Karl Marx founded in 1864 the First International, which altered radically the character, the objectives, and the course of European socialism. The ideas of Marx called the Communist Party into existence, although the name "Communist" came from the followers of Robert Owen and was first printed in a cooperative magazine in 1827. Until 1848 Marx himself called his followers social democrats and his creed socialism.

Marx emigrated first to Belgium and then to Germany, from which he was expelled in 1845. He then settled in London for the rest of his life and there worked daily in the British Museum, living on an income provided by Engels. He aided William Liebknecht in founding the German Social Democratic Party, and published the first volume of his great work, Capital, in 1867.

After his death, Engels completed and published this work. During his lifetime Marx quarreled with many of his fellow socialists, and after the dissolution of the First International both Marx and Engels lost contact with the working-class movement, which led to the rise of the revisionists. Revisionism differed from orthodox Marxism in that the revisionists did not in general think that the passage from capitalism to socialism must of necessity be violent.

Orthodox Marxists, however, particularly in the USSR, consider that the ideas of Marx and Engels, which called

[1] Berlin, *Marx*, p. 164.

the Communist Party into existence, have continued and should continue to guide and guard it throughout its existence. Herewith follows a selection of orthodox classic Marxist documents.

The Communist Manifesto

A specter is haunting Europe—the specter of communism. All the powers of old Europe have entered into a holy alliance to hunt down and exorcise this specter: Pope and Tsar, Metternich and Guizot, French Radicals and German police-spies.

Where is the party in opposition that has not been denounced as communistic by its opponents in power? Where the opposition that has not hurled back the branding reproach of communism against the more advanced opposition parties, as well as against its reactionary adversaries?

Two things result from this fact:

I. Communism is already acknowledged by all European powers to be itself a *power*.

II. It is high time that Communists should openly, in the face of the whole world, publish their views, their aims, their tendencies, and meet this nursery tale of the *specter of communism* with a manifesto of the party itself.

To this end, Communists of various nationalities have assembled in London and sketched the following *Manifesto*, to be published in the English, French, German, Italian, Flemish, and Danish languages.

I
BOURGEOIS AND PROLETARIANS

The history of all hitherto existing society is the history of class struggles.

Freeman and slave, patrician and plebeian, lord and serf,

From *The Communist Manifesto*, edited by Joseph Katz, New York, 1966.

guildmaster[1] and journeyman, in a word, oppressor and
oppressed, stood in constant opposition to one another, carried on an uninterrupted, now hidden, now open fight, a
fight that each time ended, either in a revolutionary recon-
stitution of society at large, or in the common ruin of the
struggling classes.

In the earlier epochs of history, we find almost everywhere a complicated arrangement of society into various
orders, a manifold gradation of social rank. In ancient
Rome we have patricians, knights, plebeians, slaves; in the
Middle Ages, feudal lords, vassals, guildmasters, journey-
men, apprentices, serfs; and in almost all of these particular
classes, again, other subordinate gradations.

The modern bourgeois society that has sprouted from the
ruins of feudal society has not done away with class antagonisms. It has only established new classes, new conditions
of oppression, new forms of struggle in place of the old
ones.

Our epoch, the epoch of the bourgeoisie, shows, however,
this distinctive feature: it has simplified the class antagonisms. Society as a whole is more and more splitting up
into two great hostile camps, into two great classes directly
facing each other: *bourgeoisie* and *proletariat*.

From the serfs of the Middle Ages sprang the chartered
burghers of the earliest towns. From these burghers the
first elements of the bourgeoisie were developed.

The discovery of America, the rounding of the Cape,
opened up fresh ground for the rising bourgeoisie. The
East-Indian and Chinese markets, the colonization of
America, trade with the colonies, the increase in the means
of exchange and in commodities generally, gave to commerce, to navigation, to industry, an impulse never before
known, and thereby, to the revolutionary element in the
tottering feudal society, a rapid development.

The feudal system of industry, under which industrial
production was monopolized by closed guilds, now no longer
sufficed for the growing wants of the new markets. The
manufacturing system took its place. The guildmasters
were pushed on one side by the manufacturing middle
class; division of labor between the different corporate
guilds vanished in the face of division of labor in each
single workshop.

Meanwhile the markets kept on growing; demand went
on rising. Manufacturing no longer was able to keep up

[1] Guildmaster, that is, a full member of a guild, a master within,
not a head of a guild.

with this growth. Then, steam and machinery revolutionized industrial production. The place of manufacture was
taken by the giant, *modern industry;* the place of the industrial middle class, by industrial millionaires, the leaders of
whole industrial armies, the modern bourgeois.

Modern industry has established the world market, for
which the discovery of America paved the way. This
market has given an immense development to commerce,
to navigation, to communication by land. This development
has, in its turn, reacted on the extension of industry; and
in proportion as industry, commerce, navigation, railways
extended, in the same proportion the bourgeoisie developed,
increased its capital, and pushed into the background every
class handed down from the Middle Ages.

We see, therefore, how the modern bourgeoisie is itself
the product of a long course of development, of a series of
revolutions in the modes of production and of exchange.

Each step in the development of the bourgeoisie was
accompanied by a corresponding political advance of that
class. An oppressed class under the sway of the feudal
nobility, an armed and self-governing association in the
medieval commune:[2] here an independent urban republic
(as in Italy and Germany); there taxable "third estate" of
the monarchy (as in France); afterward, in the period of
manufacturing proper, serving either the semi-feudal or the
absolute monarchy as a counterpoise against the nobility,
and, in fact, a cornerstone of the great monarchies in general, the bourgeoisie has at last, since the establishment of
modern industry and of the world market, conquered for
itself, in the modern representative state, exclusive political
sway. The executive of the modern state is but a committee
for managing the common affairs of the whole bourgeoisie.

The bourgeoisie, historically, has played a most revolutionary part.

The bourgeoisie, wherever it has got the upper hand, has
put an end to all feudal, patriarchal, idyllic relations. It
has pitilessly torn asunder the motley feudal ties that bound
man to his "natural superiors," and has left remaining no

[2] "Commune" was the name taken, in France, by the nascent
towns even before they had wrested from their feudal lords and
masters local self-government and political rights as the "Third
Estate." Generally speaking, for the economical development of
the bourgeoisie, England is here taken as the typical country; for
its political development, France.
This was the name given their urban communities by the towns-
men of Italy and France, after they had purchased or wrested their
initial rights of self-government from their feudal lords.

other bond between man and man than naked self-interest and callous "cash payment." It has drowned the most heavenly ecstasies of religious fervor, of chivalrous enthusiasm, of philistine sentimentalism, in the icy water of egotistical calculation. It has resolved personal worth into exchange value, and in place of the numberless indefeasible chartered freedoms, has set up that single, unconscionable freedom—free trade. In one word, for exploitation, veiled by religious and political illusions, it has substituted naked, shameless, direct, brutal exploitation.

The bourgeoisie has stripped of its halo every occupation hitherto honored and looked up to with reverent awe. It has converted the physician, the lawyer, the priest, the poet, the man of science, into its paid wage laborers.

The bourgeoisie has torn away from the family its sentimental veil, and has reduced the family relation to a mere money relation.

The bourgeoisie has disclosed how it came to pass that the brutal display of vigor in the Middle Ages, which reactionaries so much admire, found its fitting complement in the laziest indolence. It has been the first to show what man's activity can bring about. It has accomplished wonders far surpassing Egyptian pyramids, Roman aqueducts, and Gothic cathedrals; it has conducted expeditions that put to shame all former Exoduses of nations and crusades.

The bourgeoisie cannot exist without constantly revolutionizing the instruments of production, and thereby the relations of production, and with them the whole relations of society. Conservation of the old modes of production in unaltered form, was, on the contrary, the first condition of existence for all earlier industrial classes. Constant revolutionizing of production, uninterrupted disturbance of all social conditions, everlasting uncertainty and agitation, distinguish the bourgeois epoch from all earlier ones. All fixed, fast-frozen relations, with their train of ancient and venerable prejudices and opinions are swept away, all newformed ones become antiquated before they can ossify. All that is solid melts into air, all that is holy is profaned, and man is at last compelled to face his real conditions of life, and his mutual relations with sober eye.

The need of a constantly expanding market for its products chases the bourgeoisie over the whole surface of the globe. It must nestle everywhere, settle everywhere, establish connections everywhere.

The bourgeoisie has through its exploitation of the world market given a cosmopolitan character to production and consumption in every country. To the great chagrin of reactionaries, it has drawn from under the feet of industry the national ground on which it stood. All old-established national industries have been destroyed or are daily being destroyed. They are dislodged by new industries, whose introduction becomes a life and death question for all civilized nations, by industries that no longer work up indigenous raw material, but raw material drawn from the remotest zones; industries whose products are consumed, not only at home, but in every quarter of the globe. In place of the old wants, satisfied by the productions of the country, we find new wants, requiring for their satisfaction the products of distant lands and climates. In place of the old local and national seclusion and self-sufficiency, we have intercourse in every direction, universal interdependence of nations. And as in material, so also in intellectual production. The intellectual creations of individual nations become common property. National one-sidedness and narrow-mindedness become more and more impossible, and from the numerous national and local literatures, there emerges a world literature.

The bourgeoisie, by the rapid improvement of all instruments of production, by the immensely facilitated means of communication, draws all, even the most backward, nations into civilization. The cheap prices of its commodities are the heavy artillery with which it batters down all Chinese walls, with which it forces the underdeveloped nations' intensely obstinate hatred of foreigners to capitulate. It compels all nations, on pain of extinction, to adopt the bourgeois mode of production; it compels them to introduce what it calls civilization into their midst, i.e., to become bourgeois themselves. In one word, it creates a world in its own image.

The bourgeoisie has subjected rural areas to the rule of cities. It has created enormous cities, has greatly increased the urban population as compared with the rural, and has thus rescued a considerable part of the population from the idiocy of rural life. Just as it has made the country dependent on the cities, so has it made barbarian and semi-underdeveloped countries dependent on the civilized ones, nations of peasants on nations of bourgeois, the East on the West.

The bourgeoisie more and more keeps doing away with the scattered state of the population, of the means of production, and of property. It has agglomerated population, centralized means of production, and has concentrated property in a few hands. The necessary consequence of this was political centralization. Independent, or but loosely connected, provinces with separate interests, laws, governments, and systems of taxation became lumped together into one nation, with one government, one code of laws, one national class-interest, one frontier, and one customs-tariff.

The bourgeoisie, during its rule of scarcely one hundred years, has created more massive and more colossal productive forces than have all preceding generations together. Subjection of Nature's forces to man, machinery, application of chemistry to industry and agriculture, steam-navigation, railways, electric telegraphs, clearing of whole continents for cultivation, canalization of rivers, whole populations conjured out of the ground—what earlier century had even a presentiment that such productive forces slumbered in the lap of social labor?

We see then: the means of production and of exchange, on whose foundation the bourgeoisie built itself up, were generated in feudal society. At a certain stage in the development of these means of production and of exchange, the conditions under which feudal society produced and exchanged, the feudal organization of agriculture and manufacturing industry, in one word, the feudal relations of property became no longer compatible with the already developed productive forces; they became so many fetters. They had to be burst asunder; they were burst asunder.

Into their place stepped free competition, accompanied by a social and political constitution adapted to it, and by the economical and political sway of the bourgeois class.

A similar movement is going on before our own eyes. Modern bourgeois society with its relations of production, of exchange and of property, a society that has conjured up such gigantic means of production and of exchange, is like the sorcerer, who is no longer able to control the powers of the subterranean world which he has called up by his spells. For many decades now the history of industry and commerce has been but the history of the revolt of modern productive forces against modern conditions of production, against the property relations that are the conditions for the existence of the bourgeoisie and of its rule. It is enough to mention the commercial crises that by their periodical return put on trial, each time more threateningly, the existence of the entire bourgeois society. In these crises a great part not only of the existing products, but also of the previously created productive forces, are periodically destroyed. In these crises there breaks out an epidemic that, in all earlier epochs, would have seemed an absurdity—the epidemic of over-production. Society suddenly finds itself put back into a state of momentary barbarism; it appears as if a famine, a universal war of devastation had cut off the supply of every means of subsistence; industry and commerce seem to be destroyed; and why? Because there is too much civilization, too much means of subsistence, too much industry, too much commerce. The productive forces at the disposal of society no longer tend to further the development of the conditions of bourgeois property; on the contrary, they have become too powerful for these conditions, by which they are fettered, and so soon as they overcome these fetters, they bring disorder into the whole of bourgeois society, endanger the existence of bourgeois property. The conditions of bourgeois society are too narrow to comprise the wealth created by them. And how does the bourgeoisie get over these crises? On the one hand by enforced destruction of a mass of productive forces; on the other, by the conquest of new markets, and by the more thorough exploitation of the old ones. That is to say, by paving the way for more extensive and more destructive crises, and by diminishing the means whereby crises are prevented.

The weapons with which the bourgeoisie felled feudalism to the ground are now turned against the bourgeoisie itself.

But not only has the bourgeoisie forged the weapons that bring death to itself; it has also called into existence the men who are to wield those weapons—the modern working class—the proletarians.

In proportion as the bourgeoisie, i.e., capital, is developed, in the same proportion is the proletariat, the modern working class, developed—a class of laborers, who live only so long as they find work, and who find work only so long as their labor increases capital. These laborers, who must sell themselves piecemeal, are a commodity, like every other article of commerce, and are consequently exposed to all the vicissitudes of competition, to all the fluctuations of the market.

Owing to the extensive use of machinery and to division of labor, the work of the proletarians has lost all individual character, and, consequently, all charm for the workman. He becomes an appendage of the machine, and it is only the most simple, most monotonous, and most easily acquired knack that is required of him. Hence, the cost of production of a workman is restricted, almost entirely, to the means of subsistence that he requires for his maintenance, and for the propagation of his race. But the price of a commodity, and therefore also of labor, is equal to its cost of production. In proportion, therefore, as the repulsiveness of the work increases, the wage decreases. What is more, in proportion as the use of machinery and division of labor increases, in the same proportion the burden of toil also increases, whether by prolongation of the working hours, by increase of the work exacted in a given time or by increased speed of the machinery, etc.

Modern industry has converted the little workshop of the patriarchal master into the great factory of the industrial capitalist. Masses of laborers, crowded into the factory, are organized like soldiers. As privates of the industrial army they are placed under the command of a perfect hierarchy of officers and sergeants. Not only are they slaves of the bourgeois class, and of the bourgeois state; they are daily and hourly enslaved by the machine, by the foreman, and, above all, by the individual bourgeois manufacturer himself. The more openly this despotism proclaims gain to be its end and aim, the more petty, the more hateful, and the more embittering it is.

The less the skill and exertion of strength implied in manual labor, in other words, the more modern industry becomes developed, the more is the labor of men superseded by that of women. Differences in age and sex have no longer any distinctive social validity for the working class. All are instruments of labor, more or less expensive to use, according to their age and sex.

No sooner is the exploitation of the laborer by the manufacturer, so far, at an end, that he receives his wages in cash, than he is set upon by the other portions of the bourgeoisie, the landlord, the shopkeeper, the pawnbroker, etc.

The lower strata of the middle class—the small tradespeople, shopkeepers, and retired tradesmen generally, the handicraftsmen, and farmers—all these sink gradually into the proletariat, partly because their diminutive capital does not suffice for the scale on which modern industry is carried on, and is swamped in the competition with large capitalists, partly because their specialized skill is rendered worthless by new methods of production. Thus the proletariat is recruited from all classes of the population.

The proletariat goes through various stages of development. With its birth begins its struggle with the bourgeoisie. At first the contest is carried on by individual laborers, then by the workers of a factory, then by the members of one trade, in one locality, against the individual bourgeois who directly exploits them. They direct their attacks not against the bourgeois conditions of production, but against the instruments of production themselves; they destroy imported wares that compete with their labor, they smash machinery to pieces, they set factories ablaze, they seek to restore by force the vanished status of the workman of the Middle Ages.

At this stage the laborers still form an incoherent mass scattered over the whole country, and broken up by their mutual competition. If the workers unite at all this is not yet the consequence of their own initiative, but of the union of the bourgeoisie, which class, in order to attain its own political ends, is compelled to set the whole proletariat in motion, and is moreover still able to do so. At this stage, therefore, the proletarians do not fight their enemies, but the enemies of their enemies, the remnants of absolute monarchy, the landowners, the nonindustrial bourgeoisie, the petty bourgeoisie. Thus the whole historical movement is concentrated in the hands of the bourgeoisie; every victory so obtained is a victory for the bourgeoisie.

But with the development of industry the proletariat not only increases in number; it becomes concentrated in greater masses, its strength grows, and it feels that strength more. The various interests and conditions of life within the ranks of the proletariat are more and more equalized, in proportion as machinery obliterates all distinctions of labor, and nearly everywhere reduces wages to the same low level. The growing competition among the bourgeoisie, and the resulting commercial crises, make the wages of the workers ever more fluctuating. The unceasing improvement of machinery, ever more rapidly developing, makes their livelihood more and more precarious; the collisions between individual workmen and individual bourgeoisie take more and more the character of collisions between two classes. Thereupon the workers begin to form combinations (trade unions) against the bourgeoisie; they club together in order to keep up the rate of wages; they found permanent associations in order to make provision beforehand for these occasional revolts. Here and there the contest breaks out into riots.

From time to time the workers are victorious, but only for a time. The real fruit of their battles lies not in the immediate result, but in the ever-expanding union of the workers. This union is helped by the improved means of communication that are created by modern industry and that place the workers of different localities in contact with one another. It was just this contact that was needed to centralize the numerous local struggles, all of the same character, into one national struggle between classes. But every class struggle is a political struggle. And that union, to attain which the burghers of the Middle Ages, with their miserable highways, required centuries, the modern proletarians, thanks to railways, achieve in a few years.

This organization of the proletarians into a class, and consequently into a political party, is continually being upset again by the competition among the workers themselves. But it constantly rises up again, stronger, firmer, mightier. It compels legislative recognition of particular interests of the workers, by taking advantage of the divisions among the bourgeoisie itself. Thus was the ten-hours' bill in England carried.

Moreover, collisions between the classes of the old society advance, in many ways, the course of development of the proletariat. The bourgeoisie finds itself involved in a constant battle. At first with the aristocracy; later on, with those portions of the bourgeoisie itself, whose interests have become antagonistic to the progress of industry; at all times, with the bourgeoisie of foreign countries. In all these battles it sees itself compelled to appeal to the proletariat, to ask for its help, and thus, to drag it into the political arena. The bourgeoisie itself, therefore, supplies the proletariat with its own elements of political and general education, in other words, it furnishes the proletariat with weapons for fighting the bourgeoisie.

Further, as we have already seen, entire sections of the ruling classes are, by the advance of industry, precipitated into the proletariat, or are at least threatened in their conditions of existence. These also supply the proletariat with fresh elements of enlightenment and progress.

Finally, in times when the class struggle nears the decisive hour, the process of dissolution going on within the ruling class, in fact within the whole range of old society, assumes such a violent, glaring character, that a small section of the ruling class cuts itself adrift, and joins the revolutionary class, the class that holds the future in its hands. Just as, therefore, at an earlier period, a section of the nobility went over to the bourgeoisie, so now a portion of the bourgeoisie goes over to the proletariat, and in particular, a portion of the bourgeois ideologists, who have raised themselves to the level of comprehending theoretically the historical movement as a whole.

Of all the classes that stand face to face with the bourgeoisie today, the proletariat alone is a really revolutionary class. The other classes decay and finally disappear in the face of modern industry; the proletariat is its special and essential product.

The lower middle class, the small manufacturer, the shopkeeper, the artisan, the peasant, all these fight against the bourgeoisie, to save from extinction their existence as fractions of the middle class. They are therefore not revolutionary, but conservative. What is more, they are reactionary, for they try to roll back the wheel of history. If by chance they are revolutionary, they are so only in view of their impending transfer into the proletariat, they thus defend not their present, but their future interests, they desert their own standpoint to place themselves at that of the proletariat.

The "dangerous class," the social scum, that passively rotting mass thrown off by the lowest layers of old society, may, here and there, be swept into the movement by a proletarian revolution; its conditions of life, however, prepare it far more for the part of a bribed tool of reactionary intrigue.

The living conditions of the old society at large are already virtually swamped by the living conditions of the proletariat. The proletarian is without property; his relation to his wife and children has no longer anything in common with the bourgeois family relations; modern industrial labor, modern subjection to capital, the same in England as in France, in America as in Germany, has stripped him of every trace of national character. Law, morality, religion, are to him so many bourgeois prejudices, behind which lurk in ambush just as many bourgeois interests.

All the preceding classes that got the upper hand sought to fortify their already acquired status by subjecting society at large to their conditions of appropriation. The proletarians cannot become masters of the productive forces of society, except by abolishing their own previous mode of appropriation, and thereby also every other previous mode of appropriation. They have nothing of their own to secure and to fortify; their mission is to destroy all previous securities for, and insurances of, individual property.

All previous historical movements were movements of minorities, or in the interest of minorities. The proletarian movement is the self-conscious, independent movement of the immense majority, in the interest of the immense majority. The proletariat, the lowest stratum of our present society, cannot stir, cannot raise itself up, without the whole super-incumbent strata of official society being sprung into the air.

Though not in substance, yet in form, the struggle of the proletariat with the bourgeoisie is at first a national struggle. The proletariat of each country must, of course, first of all settle matters with its own bourgeoisie.

In depicting the most general phases of the development of the proletariat, we traced the more or less veiled civil war, raging within existing society, up to the point where that war breaks out into open revolution, and where the violent overthrow of the bourgeoisie lays the foundation for the sway of the proletariat.

Hitherto, every form of society has been based, as we have already seen, on the antagonism of oppressing and oppressed classes. But in order to oppress a class, certain conditions must be assured to it under which it can, at least, continue its slavish existence. The serf, in the period of serfdom, raised himself to membership in the commune, just as the petty bourgeois, under the yoke of feudal absolutism, managed to develop into a bourgeois. The modern laborer, on the contrary, instead of rising with the progress of industry, sinks deeper and deeper below the conditions of existence of his own class. He becomes a pauper, and pauperism develops more rapidly than population and wealth. And here it becomes evident that the bourgeoisie is unfit any longer to be the ruling class in society, and to impose its conditions of existence upon society as an overriding law. It is unfit to rule because it is incompetent to assure an existence to its slave within his slavery, because it cannot help letting him sink into such a state, that it has to feed him, instead of being fed by him. Society can no longer live under this bourgeoisie, in other words, its existence is no longer compatible with society.

The essential condition for the existence, and for the sway of the bourgeois class, is the formation and augmentation of capital; the condition for capital is wage labor. Wage labor rests exclusively on competition between the laborers. The advance of industry, whose involuntary promoter is the bourgeoisie, replaces the isolation of the laborers, due to competition, by their revolutionary combination, due to association. The development of modern industry, therefore, cuts from under its feet the very foundation on which the bourgeoisie produces and appropriates products. What the bourgeoisie, therefore, produces, above all, is its own grave-diggers. Its fall and the victory of the proletariat are equally inevitable.

II
PROLETARIANS AND COMMUNISTS

In what relation do the Communists stand to the proletarians as a whole?

The Communists do not form a separate party opposed to other working-class parties.

They have no interests separate and apart from those of the proletariat as a whole.

They do not set up any sectarian principles of their own, by which to shape and mold the proletarian movement.

The Communists are distinguished from the other working-class parties by this only: 1. In the national struggles of the proletarians of the different countries, they point out and bring to the front the common interests of the entire proletariat, independently of all nationality. 2. In the various stages of development that the struggle of the working class against the bourgeoisie has to pass through, they always and everywhere represent the interests of the movement as a whole.

The Communists, therefore, are on the one hand, practically, the most advanced and resolute section of the working-class parties of every country, that section which pushes forward all others; on the other hand, theoretically, they have over the great mass of the proletariat the advantage of clearly understanding the line of march, the conditions, and the ultimate general results of the proletarian movement.

The immediate aim of the Communists is the same as that of all the other proletarian parties: formation of the proletariat into a class, overthrow of the bourgeois supremacy, conquest of political power by the proletariat.

The theoretical conclusions of the Communists are in no way based on ideas or principles that have been invented, or discovered, by this or that would-be universal reformer. They merely express, in general terms, actual relations springing from an existing class struggle, from a historical movement going on under our very eyes. The abolition of existing property relations is not at all a distinctive feature of communism.

All property relations in the past have continually been subject to historical change consequent upon the change in historical conditions.

The French Revolution, for example, abolished feudal property in favor of bourgeois property.

The distinguishing feature of communism is not the abolition of property generally, but the abolition of bourgeois property. But modern bourgeois private property is the final and most complete expression of the system of producing and appropriating products that is based on class antagonisms, on the exploitation of the many by the few.

In this sense, the theory of the Communists may be summed up in the single phrase: Abolition of private property.

We Communists have been reproached with the desire of abolishing the right of personally acquiring property as the fruit of a man's own labor, which property is alleged to be the groundwork of all personal freedom, activity, and independence.

Hard-won, self-acquired, self-earned property! Do you mean the property of the petty artisan and of the small peasant, a form of property that preceded the bourgeois form? There is no need to abolish that; the development of industry has to a great extent already destroyed it, and is still destroying it daily.

Or do you mean modern bourgeois private property?

But does wage labor create any property for the laborer? Not a bit. It creates capital, i.e., that kind of property that exploits wage labor, and that cannot increase except upon condition of begetting a new supply of wage labor for fresh exploitation. Property, in its present form, is based on the antagonism of capital and wage labor. Let us examine both sides of this antagonism.

To be a capitalist, is to have not only a purely personal, but a social *status* in production. Capital is a collective product, and only by the united action of many members, nay, in the last resort, only by the united action of all members of society, can it be set in motion.

Capital is, therefore, not a personal, it is a social power.

When, therefore, capital is converted into common property, into the property of all members of society, personal property is not thereby transformed into social property. It is only the social character of the property that is changed. It loses its class character.

Let us now take wage labor.

The average price of wage labor is the minimum wage, i.e., that quantum of the means of subsistence, which is absolutely requisite to keep the laborer in bare existence as a laborer. What, therefore, the wage laborer appropriates by means of his labor, merely suffices to prolong and reproduce a bare existence. We by no means intend to abolish this personal appropriation of the products of labor, an appropriation that is made for the maintenance and reproduction of human life, and that leaves no surplus wherewith to command the labor of others. All that we want to do away with is the miserable character of this appropriation, under which the laborer lives merely to increase capital, and is allowed to live only in so far as the interest of the ruling class requires it.

In bourgeois society, living labor is but a means to increase accumulated labor. In communist society, accumulated labor is but a means to widen, to enrich, to promote the existence of the laborer.

In bourgeois society, therefore, the past dominates the present; in communist society, the present dominates the past. In bourgeois society capital is independent and has individuality, while the living person is dependent and has no individuality.

And the abolition of this state of things is called by the bourgeoisie, abolition of individuality and freedom! And rightly so. The abolition of bourgeois individuality, bourgeois independence, and bourgeois freedom is undoubtedly aimed at.

By freedom is meant, under the present bourgeois conditions of production, free trade, free selling and buying.

But if selling and buying disappears, free selling and buying disappears also. This talk about free selling and buying, and all the other "brave words" of our bourgeoisie about freedom in general, have a meaning, if any, only in contrast with restricted selling and buying, with the fettered traders of the Middle Ages, but have no meaning when opposed to the communistic abolition of buying and selling, of the bourgeois conditions of production, and of the bourgeoisie itself.

You are horrified at our intending to do away with private property. But in your existing society, private property is already done away with for nine-tenths of the population; its existence for the few is solely due to its non-existence in the hands of those nine-tenths. You reproach us, therefore, with intending to do away with a form of property, the necessary condition for whose existence is the non-existence of any property for the immense majority of society.

In one word, you reproach us with intending to do away with your property. Precisely so; that is just what we intend.

From the moment when labor can no longer be converted into capital, money, or rent, into a social power capable of being monopolized, i.e., from the moment when individual property can no longer be transformed into bourgeois property, into capital, from that moment, you say, individuality vanishes.

You must, therefore, confess that by "individual" you mean no other person than the bourgeois, than the middle-class owner of property. This person must, indeed, be swept out of the way, and made impossible.

Communism deprives no man of the power to appropriate the products of society; all that it does is to deprive him of the power to subjugate the labor of others by means of such appropriation.

It has been objected that upon the abolition of private property all work will cease, and universal laziness will overtake us.

According to this, bourgeois society ought long ago to have gone to the dogs through sheer idleness; for those of its members who work, acquire nothing, and those who acquire anything, do not work. The whole of this objection is but another expression of the tautology: that there can no longer be any wage labor when there is no longer any capital.

All objections urged against the communistic mode of producing and appropriating material products, have, in the same way, been urged against the communistic modes of producing and appropriating intellectual products. Just as, to the bourgeois, the disappearance of class property is the disappearance of production itself, so the disappearance of class culture is to him identical with the disappearance of all culture.

That culture, the loss of which he laments, is, for the enormous majority, a mere training to act as a machine.

But don't wrangle with us so long as you apply, to our intended abolition of bourgeois property, the standard of your bourgeois notions of freedom, culture, law, etc. Your very ideas are but the outgrowth of the conditions of your bourgeois production and bourgeois property, just as your jurisprudence is but the will of your class made into a law for all, a will whose essential character and direction are determined by the economical conditions of existence of your class.

The selfish misconception that induces you to transform into eternal laws of nature and of reason the social forms springing from your present mode of production and form of property—historical relations that rise and disappear in the progress of production—this misconception you share with every ruling class that has preceded you. What you see clearly in the case of ancient property, what you admit in the case of feudal property, you are of course forbidden to admit in the case of your own bourgeois form of property.

Abolition of the family! Even the most radical flare up at this infamous proposal of the Communists.

On what foundation is the present family, the bourgeois family, based? On capital, on private gain. In its completely developed form this family exists only among the bourgeoisie. But this state of things finds its complement in the practical absence of the family among the proletarians, and in public prostitution.

The bourgeois family will vanish as a matter of course when its complement vanishes, and both will vanish with the vanishing of capital.

Do you charge us with wanting to stop the exploitation of children by their parents? To this crime we plead guilty.

But, you will say, we destroy the most hallowed of relations, when we replace home education by social.

And your education! Is not that also social, and determined by the social conditions under which you educate, by the intervention, direct or indirect, of society, by means of schools, etc.? The Communists have not invented the intervention of society in education; they merely seek to alter the character of that intervention, and to rescue education from the influence of the ruling class.

The bourgeois clap-trap about the family and education, about the hallowed co-relation of parent and child, becomes all the more disgusting; the more, by the action of modern industry, all family ties among the proletarians are torn asunder, and their children transformed into simple articles of commerce and instruments of labor.

But you Communists would introduce free love [communal wives], screams the whole bourgeoisie in chorus.

The bourgeois sees in his wife a mere instrument of production. He hears that the instruments of production are to be exploited in common, and, naturally, can come to no other conclusion than that the lot of being common to all will likewise fall to the women.

He has not even a suspicion that the real point aimed at is to do away with the status of women as mere instruments of production.

For the rest, nothing is more ridiculous than the virtuous indignation of our bourgeois at free love which, they pretend, is to be openly and officially established by the Communists. The Communists have no need to introduce free love; it has existed almost from time immemorial.

Our bourgeoisie, not content with having the wives and daughters of their proletarians at their disposal, not to speak of common prostitutes, take supreme delight in seducing each others' wives.

Bourgeois marriage is in reality a system of wives in common and thus, at the most, what the Communists might possibly be reproached with, is that they desire to introduce, in substitution for a hypocritically concealed, an openly legalized system of free love. Moreover, it is self-evident that the abolition of the present system of production must bring with it the abolition of free love springing from that system, i.e., of prostitution both public and private.

The Communists are further reproached with desiring to abolish countries and nationality.

The workingmen have no country. We cannot take from them what they have not got. Since the proletariat must first of all acquire political supremacy, must rise to be the leading class of the nation, must constitute itself *the* nation, it is, so far, itself national, though not in the bourgeois sense of the word.

National differences and antagonisms between peoples are daily vanishing, owing to the development of the bourgeoisie, to freedom of commerce, to the world market, to uniformity in the mode of production and in the conditions of life corresponding thereto.

The supremacy of the proletariat will cause them to vanish still faster. United action, of the leading civilized countries at least, is one of the first conditions for the emancipation of the proletariat.

In proportion as the exploitation of one individual by another is put to an end, the exploitation of one nation by another will also be put to an end. In proportion as the antagonism between classes within the nation vanishes, the hostility of one nation to another will come to an end.

The charges against communism made from a religious,

a philosophical, and, generally, from an ideological standpoint are not deserving of serious examination.

Does it require deep intuition to comprehend that man's ideas, views and conceptions, in one word, man's consciousness, change with every change in the conditions of his material existence, in his social relations and in his social life?

What else does the history of ideas prove, than that intellectual production changes its character in proportion as material production is changed? The ruling ideas of each age have ever been the ideas of its ruling class.

When people speak of ideas that revolutionize society, they do but express the fact that within the old society the elements of a new one have been created, and that the dissolution of the old ideas keeps even pace with the dissolution of the old conditions of existence.

When the ancient world was in its last throes, the ancient religions were overcome by Christianity. When Christian ideas succumbed in the eighteenth century to rationalist ideas, feudal society fought its death battle with the then revolutionary bourgeoisie. The ideas of religious liberty and freedom of conscience merely gave expression to the sway of free competition within the domain of knowledge.

Undoubtedly, it will be said, religious, moral, philosophical, and juridical ideas have been modified in the course of historical development. But religion, morality, philosophy, political science, and law constantly survived this change.

There are, besides, eternal truths, such as Freedom, Justice, etc., that are common to all states of society. But communism abolishes eternal truths, it abolishes all religion, and all morality, instead of constituting them on a new basis; it therefore acts in contradiction to all past historical experience.

What does this accusation reduce itself to? The history of all past society has consisted in the development of class antagonisms, antagonisms that assumed different forms at different epochs.

But whatever form they may have taken, one fact is common to all past ages, viz., the exploitation of one part of society by the other. No wonder, then, that the social consciousness of past ages, despite all the multiplicity and variety it displays, moves within certain common forms, or general ideas, which cannot completely vanish except with the total disappearance of class antagonisms.

The communist revolution is the most radical rupture

with traditional property relations; no wonder that its development involves the most radical rupture with traditional ideas.

But let us have done with the bourgeois objections to communism.

We have seen above that the first step in the revolution by the working class is to raise the proletariat to the position of ruling class to win the battle of democracy.

The proletariat will use its political supremacy to wrest, by degrees, all capital from the bourgeoisie, to centralize all instruments of production in the hands of the state, i.e., of the proletariat organized as the ruling class; and to increase the total of productive forces as rapidly as possible.

Of course, in the beginning, this cannot be effected except by means of despotic inroads on the rights of property, and on the conditions of bourgeois production; by means of measures, therefore, which appear economically insufficient and untenable, but which, in the course of the movement, outstrip themselves, necessitate further inroads upon the old social order, and are unavoidable as a means of entirely revolutionizing the mode of production.

These measures will of course be different in different countries.

Nevertheless in the most advanced countries, the following will be pretty generally applicable.

1. Abolition of property in land and application of all rents of land to public purposes.

2. A heavy progressive or graduated income tax.

3. Abolition of all right of inheritance.

4. Confiscation of the property of all emigrants and rebels.

5. Centralization of credit in the hands of the state, by means of a national bank with state capital and an exclusive monopoly.

6. Centralization of the means of communication and transport in the hands of the state.

7. Extension of factories and instruments of production owned by the state; the bringing into cultivation of wastelands, and the improvement of the soil generally in accordance with a common plan.

8. Equal liability of all to labor. Establishment of industrial armies, especially for agriculture.

9. Combination of agriculture with manufacturing industries; gradual abolition of the distinction between town and country, by a more equable distribution of the population over the country.

10. Free education for all children in public schools. Abolition of children's factory labor in its present form. Combination of education with industrial production, etc., etc.

When, in the course of development, class distinctions have disappeared, and all production has been concentrated in the hands of a vast association of the whole nation, the public power will lose its political character. Political power, properly so called, is merely the organized power of one class for oppressing another. If the proletariat during its contest with the bourgeoisie is compelled, by the force of circumstances, to organize itself as a class, if, by means of a revolution, it makes itself the ruling class, and, as such, sweeps away by force the old conditions of production, then it will, along with these conditions, have swept away the conditions for the existence of class antagonisms and of classes generally, and will thereby have abolished its own supremacy as a class.

In place of the old bourgeois society, with its classes and class antagonisms, we shall have an association in which the free development of each is the condition for the free development of all.

CONCLUSION

. . . the Communists everywhere support every revolutionary movement against the existing social and political order of things.

In all these movements they bring to the front, as the leading question in each, the property question, no matter what its degree of development at the time.

Finally, they labor everywhere for the union and agreement of the democratic parties of all countries.

The Communists disdain to conceal their views and aims. They openly declare that their ends can be attained only by the forcible overthrow of all existing social conditions. Let the ruling classes tremble at a Communistic revolution. The proletarians have nothing to lose but their chains. They have a world to win.

WORKINGMEN OF ALL COUNTRIES, UNITE!

Friedrich Engels
(1820–1895)

Born in Bremen, Engels was the son of a wealthy textile manufacturer. In 1842 he went to Manchester where he took a position in a factory in which his father had an interest. In 1844, while traveling in France, Engels met Karl Marx.

He himself described how "our complete agreement in all theoretical fields" became evident from the moment of their first meeting, "and our joint work dates from that time. When, in the spring of 1845, we met again in Brussels, Marx had already fully developed his materialist theory of history in its main features . . . This discovery which revolutionised the science of history . . . is essentially the work of Marx— a discovery in which I can claim for myself only a very insignificant share." However, Engels subsequently assisted Marx financially, as well as collaborating with him on several works, the most important of which was The Communist Manifesto *(1848).*

Socialism: Utopian and Scientific

I

Modern Socialism is, in its essence, the direct product of the recognition, on the one hand, of the class antagonisms

Selected Writing, by Friedrich Engels, edited by W. O. Henderson, London, 1967.

existing in the society of to-day between proprietors and non-proprietors, between capitalists and wage-workers; on the other hand, of the anarchy existing in production. But, in its theoretical form, modern Socialism originally appears ostensibly as a more logical extension of the principles laid down by the great French philosophers of the eighteenth century. Like every new theory, modern Socialism had, at first, to connect itself with the intellectual stock-in-trade ready to its hand, however deeply its roots lay in material economic facts.

The great men, who in France prepared men's minds for the coming revolution, were themselves extreme revolutionists. They recognised no external authority of any kind whatever. Religion, natural science, society, political institutions—everything was subjected to the most unsparing criticism: everything must justify its existence before the judgment-seat of reason or give up existence. Reason became the sole measure of everything. It was the time when, as Hegel says, the world stood upon its head; first in the sense that the human head, and the principles arrived at by its thought, claimed to be the basis of all human action and association; but by and by, also, in the wider sense that the reality which was in contradiction to these principles had, in fact, to be turned upside down. Every form of society and government then existing, every old traditional notion was flung into the lumber-room as irrational; the world had hitherto allowed itself to be led solely by prejudices; everything in the past deserved only pity and contempt. Now, for the first time, appeared the light of day, the kingdom of reason; henceforth superstition, injustice, privilege, oppression, were to be superseded by eternal truth, eternal Right, equality based on Nature and the inalienable rights of man.

We know to-day that this kingdom of reason was nothing more than the idealised kingdom of the bourgeoisie; that this eternal Right found its realisation in bourgeois justice; that this equality reduced itself to bourgeois equality before the law; that bourgeois property was proclaimed as one of the essential rights of man; and that the government of reason, the *Contrat Social* of Rousseau, came into being, and only could come into being, as a democratic bourgeois republic. The great thinkers of the eighteenth century could, no more than their predecessors, go beyond the limits imposed upon them by their epoch.

But, side by side with the antagonism of the feudal nobility and the burghers, who claimed to represent all the rest of society, was the general antagonism of exploiters and exploited, of rich idlers and poor workers. It was this very circumstance that made it possible for the representatives of the bourgeoisie to put themselves forward as representing not one special class, but the whole of suffering humanity. Still further. From its origin the bourgeoisie was saddled with its antithesis: capitalists cannot exist without wage-workers, and, in the same proportion as the mediaeval burgher of the guild developed into the modern bourgeois, the guild journeyman and the day-labourer, outside the guilds, developed into the proletarian. And although, upon the whole, the bourgeoisie, in their struggle with the nobility, could claim to represent at the same time the interests of the different working classes of that period, yet in every great bourgeois movement there were independent outbursts of that class which was the forerunner, more or less developed, of the modern proletariat. For example, at the time of the German Reformation and the Peasants' War, the Anabaptists and Thomas Münzer; in the great English Revolution, the Levellers; in the great French Revolution, Babeuf.

There were theoretical enunciations corresponding with these revolutionary uprisings of a class not yet developed; in the sixteenth and seventeenth centuries, Utopian pictures of ideal social conditions; in the eighteenth, actual communistic theories (Morelly and Mably). The demand for equality was no longer limited to political rights; it was extended also to the social conditions of individuals. It was not simply class privileges that were to be abolished, but class distinctions themselves. A Communism, ascetic, denouncing all the pleasures of life, Spartan, was the first form of the new teaching. Then came the three great Utopians: Saint-Simon, to whom the middle-class movement, side by side with the proletarian, still had a certain significance; Fourier; and Owen, who in the country where capitalist production was most developed, and under the influence of the antagonisms begotten of this, worked out his proposals for the removal of class distinction systematically and in direct relation to French materialism.

One thing is common to all three. Not one of them appears as a representative of the interests of that proletariat which historical development had, in the meantime, produced. Like the French philosophers, they do not claim to emancipate a particular class to begin with, but all humanity at once. Like them, they wish to bring in the kingdom of reason and eternal justice, but this kingdom, as they see it, is as far as heaven from earth, from that of the French philosophers.

For, to our three social reformers, the bourgeois world, based upon the principles of these philosophers, is quite as irrational and unjust, and, therefore, finds its way to the dust-hole quite as readily as feudalism and all the earlier stages of society. If pure reason and justice have not, hitherto, ruled the world, this has been the case only because men have not rightly understood them. What was wanted was the individual man of genius, who has now arisen and who understands the truth. That he has now arisen, that the truth has now been clearly understood, is not an inevitable event, following of necessity in the chain of historical development, but a mere happy accident. He might just as well have been born 500 years earlier, and might then have spared humanity 500 years of error, strife, and suffering.

We saw how the French philosophers of the eighteenth century, the forerunners of the Revolution, appealed to reason as the sole judge of all that is. A rational government, rational society, were to be founded; everything that ran counter to eternal reason was to be remorselessly done away with. We saw also that this eternal reason was in reality nothing but the idealised understanding of the eighteenth-century citizen, just then evolving into the bourgeois. The French Revolution had realised this rational society and government.

But the new order of things, rational enough as compared with earlier conditions, turned out to be by no means absolutely rational. The state based upon reason completely collapsed. Rousseau's *Contrat Social* had found its realisation in the Reign of Terror, from which the bourgeoisie who had lost confidence in their own political capacity had taken refuge first in the corruption of the Directorate and, finally, under the wing of the Napoleonic despotism. The promised eternal peace was turned into an endless war of conquest. The society based upon reason had fared no better. The antagonism between rich and poor, instead of dissolving into general prosperity, had become intensified by the removal of the guild and other privileges, which had to some extent bridged it over, and by the removal of the charitable institutions of the Church. The "freedom of property" from feudal fetters, now veritably accomplished, turned out to be, for the small capitalists and small proprietors, the freedom to sell their small property, crushed under the overmastering competition of the large capitalists and landlords, to these great lords, and thus, as far as the small capitalists and peasant proprietors were concerned, become "freedom *from* property." The development of industry upon a capitalistic basis made poverty and misery of the working masses conditions of existence of society. Cash payment became more and more, in Carlyle's phrase, the sole nexus between man and man. The number of crimes increased from year to year. Formerly, the feudal vices had openly stalked about in broad daylight; though not eradicated, they were now at any rate thrust into the background. In their stead, the bourgeois vices, hitherto practised in secret, began to blossom all the more luxuriantly. Trade became to a greater and greater extent cheating. The "fraternity" of the revolutionary motto was realised in the chicanery and rivalries of the battle of competition. Oppression by force was replaced by corruption; the sword, as the first social level, by gold. The right of the first night was transferred from the feudal lords to the bourgeois manufacturers. Prostitution increased to an extent never heard of. Marriage itself remained, as before, the legally recognised form, the official cloak of prostitution, and, moreover, was supplemented by rich crops of adultery.

In a word, compared with the splendid promises of the philosophers, the social and political institutions born of the "triumph of reason" were bitterly disappointing caricatures. All that was wanting was the men to formulate this disappointment, and they came with the turn of the century. In 1802 Saint-Simon's Geneva letters appeared; in 1808 appeared Fourier's first work, although the groundwork of his theory dated from 1799; on January 1, 1800, Robert Owen undertook the direction of New Lanark. . . .

Already in his Geneva letters, Saint-Simon lays down the proposition that "all men ought to work." In the same work he recognises also that the Reign of Terror was the reign of the non-possessing masses. "See," says he to them, "what happened in France at the time when your comrades held sway there; they brought about a famine." But to recognise the French Revolution as a class war, and not simply one between nobility and bourgeoisie, but between nobility, bourgeoisie, and the non-possessors, was, in the year 1802, a most pregnant discovery. In 1816, he declares that politics is the science of production, and foretells the complete absorption of politics by economics. The knowledge that economic conditions are the basis of political institutions appears here only in embryo. Yet what is here already very plainly expressed is the idea of the future conversion of political rule over men into an administration of things and a direction of processes of production—that is to say, the "abolition of the state," about which recently there has been so much noise.

Saint-Simon shows the same superiority over his contemporaries, when in 1814, immediately after the entry of the allies into Paris, and again in 1815, during the Hundred Days' War, he proclaims the alliance of France with England, and then of both these countries with Germany, as the only guarantee for the prosperous development and peace of Europe. To preach to the French in 1815 an alliance with the victors of Waterloo required as much courage as historical foresight.

If in Saint-Simon we find a comprehensive breadth of view, by virtue of which almost all the ideas of later Socialists that are not strictly economic are found in him in embryo, we find in Fourier a criticism of the existing conditions of society, genuinely French and witty, but not upon that account any the less thorough. Fourier takes the bourgeoisie, their inspired prophets before the Revolution, and their interested eulogists after it, at their own word. He lays bare remorselessly the material and moral misery of the bourgeois world. He confronts it with the earlier philosophers' dazzling promises of a society in which reason alone should reign, of a civilisation in which happiness should be universal, of an illimitable human perfectibility, and with the rose-coloured phraseology of the bourgeois ideologists of his time. He points out how everywhere the most pitiful reality corresponds with the most high-sounding phrases, and he overwhelms this hopeless fiasco of phrases with his mordant sarcasm.

Fourier is not only a critic; his imperturbably serene nature makes him a satirist, and assuredly one of the greatest satirists of all time. He depicts, with equal power and charm, the swindling speculations that blossomed out upon the downfall of the Revolution, and the shopkeeping spirit prevalent in, and characteristic of, French commerce at that time. Still more masterly is his criticism of the bourgeois form of the relations between the sexes, and the position of woman in bourgeois society. He was the first to declare that in any given society the degree of woman's emancipation is the natural measure of the general emancipation.

But Fourier is at his greatest in his conception of the history of society. He divides its whole course, thus far, into four stages of evolution—savagery, barbarism, the patriarchate, civilisation. This last is identical with the so-called civil, or bourgeois, society of to-day—i.e., with the social order that came in with the sixteenth century. He proves "that the civilised stage raises every vice practised by barbarism in a simple fashion into a form of existence, complex, ambiguous, equivocal, hypocritical"—that civilisation moves in "a vicious circle," in contradictions which it constantly reproduces without being able to solve them; hence it constantly arrives at the very opposite to that which it wants to attain, or pretends to want to attain, so that, e.g., "under civilisation poverty is born of superabundance itself."

At this juncture there came forward as a reformer a manufacturer 29 years old—a man of almost sublime, childlike simplicity of character, and at the same time one of the few born leaders of men. Robert Owen had adopted the teaching of the materialistic philosophers: that man's character is the product, on the one hand, of heredity; on the other, of the environment of the individual during his lifetime, and especially during his period of development. In the industrial revolution most of his class saw only chaos and confusion, and the opportunity of fishing in these troubled waters and making large fortunes quickly. He saw in it the opportunity of putting into practice his favourite theory, and so of bringing order out of chaos. He had already tried it with success, as superintendent of more than five hundred men in a Manchester factory. From 1800 to 1829, he directed the great cotton mill at New Lanark, in Scotland, as managing partner, along the same lines, but with greater freedom of action and with a success that made him a European reputation. A population, originally consisting of the most diverse and, for the most part, very demoralised elements, a population that gradually grew to 2,500, he turned into a model colony, in which drunkenness, police, magistrates, lawsuits, poor laws, charity, were unknown. And all this simply by placing the people in conditions worthy of human beings, and especially by carefully bringing up the rising generation. He was the founder of infant schools, and introduced the first at New Lanark. At the age of two the children came to school, where they enjoyed themselves so much that they could scarcely be got home again. Whilst his competitors worked their people thirteen or fourteen hours a day, in New Lanark the working-day was only ten and a half hours. When a crisis in cotton stopped work for four months, his workers received their full wages all the time. And with all this the business more than doubled in value, and to the last yielded large profits to its proprietors.

In spite of all this, Owen was not content. The existence which he secured for his workers was, in his eyes, still far from being worthy of human beings. "The people were slaves at my mercy." The relatively favourable conditions in which he had placed them were still far from allowing a rational development of the character and of the intellect in all directions, much less of the free exercise of all their faculties. "And yet, the working part of this population of 2,500 persons was daily producing as much real wealth for society as, less than half a century before, it would have required the working part of a population of 600,000 to create. I asked myself, what became of the difference between the wealth consumed by 2,500 persons and that which would have been consumed by 600,000?"

The answer was clear. It had been used to pay the proprietors of the establishment 5 per cent on the capital they had laid out, in addition to over £300,000 clear profit. And that which held for New Lanark held to a still greater extent for all the factories in England. "If this new wealth had not been created by machinery, imperfectly as it has been applied, the wars of Europe, in opposition to Napoleon, and to support the aristocratic principles of society, could not have been maintained. And yet this new power was the creation of the working class." To them, therefore, the fruits of this new power belonged. The newly created gigantic productive forces, hitherto used only to enrich individuals and to enslave the masses, offered to Owen the foundations for a reconstruction of society; they were destined, as the common property of all, to be worked for the common good of all.

Owen's Communism was based upon this purely business foundation, the outcome, so to say, of commercial calculation. Throughout, it maintained this practical character. Thus, in 1823, Owen proposed the relief of the distress in Ireland by Communist colonies, and drew up complete estimates of costs of founding them, yearly expenditure, and probable revenue. And in his definite plan for the future, the technical working out of details is managed with such practical knowledge—ground plan, front and side and bird's eye views all included—that the Owen methods of social reform once accepted, there is from the practical point of view little to be said against the actual arrangement of details.

His advance in the direction of Communism was the

turning-point in Owen's life. As long as he was simply a philanthropist, he was rewarded with nothing but wealth, applause, honour, and glory. He was the most popular man in Europe. Not only men of his own class, but statesmen and princes listened to him approvingly. But when he came out with his Communist theories that was quite another thing. Three great obstacles seemed to him especially to block the path to social reform: private property, religion, the present form of marriage. He knew what confronted him if he attacked these—outlawry, excommunication from official society, the loss of his whole social position. But nothing of this prevented him from attacking them without fear of consequences, and what he had foreseen happened. Banished from official society, with a conspiracy of silence against him in the press, ruined by his unsuccessful Communist experiments in America, in which he sacrificed all his fortune, he turned directly to the working class and continued working in their midst for thirty years. Every social movement, every real advance in England on behalf of the workers links itself on to the name of Robert Owen. He forced through in 1819, after five years' fighting, the first law limiting the hours of labour of women and children in factories. He was president of the first Congress at which all the Trade Unions of England united in a single great trade association. He introduced as transition measures to the complete communistic organisation of society, on the one hand, co-operative societies for retail trade and production. ...

Nicolas Ivanovitch Bukharin (1888–1938)

Called by Lenin "the most valuable and greatest theoretician of the Party," Bukharin was born in Moscow and at eighteen joined the Social Democratic Labor Party. He was jailed in 1911 but escaped abroad. Bukharin met Lenin in Cracow in 1912 and in Vienna in 1913. In October, 1916, he arrived in New York with a false passport and edited a magazine called Novy Mir. *After the outbreak of the Revo-*

lution, he returned to Russia in 1917 via Japan. He opposed Lenin on the Brest–Litovsk pact and in 1920 published a book which Lenin criticized as "scholastic." In 1924 he became a member of the Politburo and supported Stalin against Kamenev, Trotsky, and Zinoviev. In 1928, however, he opposed Stalin's policies in his Notes of an Economist, *the only written criticism of Stalin to be published in the USSR during Stalin's lifetime. In 1929 Bukharin was expelled from the Politburo but drafted the Soviet Constitution in 1936. In 1937 he was arrested, in 1938 shot. Arthur Koestler is supposed to have taken Bukharin as his model hero Rubashov in* Darkness at Noon.

The ABC of Communism
OUR PROGRAMME

WHAT IS A PROGRAMME?

Every party pursues definite aims, whether it be a party of landowners or capitalists, on the one hand, or a party of workers or peasants, on the other. Every party must have definite aims, for otherwise it is not a party. If it be a party representing the interests of landowners, it will pursue the aims of landowners; it will endeavour to tighten the grasp of the owners upon the soil; to hold the peasants in bondage; to secure a high price for the produce of the landowners' estates; to hire labour cheaply; to rackrent the farms. If it be a party of capitalists and factory owners, it will likewise have its own aims: to procure cheap labour, to keep the workers well in hand, to find customers to whom the wares can be sold at the highest possible price, to obtain ever larger profits, for this purpose to compel the workers to toil harder—but, above all, so to arrange matters that the workers will have no tendency to allow their thoughts to turn towards ideas of a new social order; let the workers think that there always have been masters and always will be masters. Such are the aims of the factory owners. It is self-evident that the workers and peasants will have utterly different aims from these, seeing that their interests are utterly different from those of the capitalists and

From *The ABC of Communism*, by N. I. Bukharin, translated by Eden and Adar Paul, Harmondsworth, England, 1969.

landowners. People used to say: "What is wholesome for a Russian is death to a German." It would, in fact, be more accurate to say: "What is wholesome for a worker is death to a landowner or capitalist." That is to say, the worker has certain things to do, the capitalist other things, and the landowner yet others. Not every landowner, however, thinks out logically what is the best way of getting the last farthing out of the peasants; many landowners are drunk most of the time, and do not even trouble to consider their bailiff's reports. The same thing happens in the case of the peasants and of the workers. There are some who say: "Oh, well, we shall get along somehow; why bother? We shall go on living as our fathers have always lived." Such persons never achieve anything, and do not even understand their own interests. On the other hand, those who realize how they can best defend their own interests, organize themselves into a party. Of course the class as a whole does not enter the party, which is composed of the best and most energetic members of the class; thus those who enter the party lead the rest. To the Workers' Party (the Party of Communist Bolsheviks) adhere the best of the workers and poorer peasants; to the Party of Landowners and Capitalists (Cadets, the Party of Popular Freedom) adhere the most energetic among the landowners, the capitalists, and their hangers-on—lawyers, professors, military officers, etc. Consequently, every party is composed of the most intelligent elements in the class to which it corresponds. For this reason a landowner or capitalist who is a member of an organized party will combat the peasants and workers far more successfully than if he were not in such an organization. In like manner an organized worker will be better able than an unorganized worker to strive against the capitalists and landowners; for the organized worker has well pondered the aims and interests of the working class, knows how these interests are to be pursued, and has learned the shortest road.

ALL THE AIMS WHICH A PARTY REPRESENTING THE INTERESTS OF ITS CLASS VIGOROUSLY PURSUES, CONSTITUTE THE PARTY PROGRAMME. Thus in the programme is specified that for which any particular class has to strive. In the programme of the Communist Party is specified that for which the workers and the poorer peasants have to strive. The programme is for every party a matter of supreme importance. From the programme we can always learn what interests the party represents. . . .

THE CAPITALISTIC SOCIAL ORDER

COMMODITY ECONOMY

If we study how economic life is carried on under the capitalist régime, we see that its primary characteristic is the production of *commodities*. "Well, what is there remarkable about that?" the reader may ask. The remarkable point is that a commodity is not simply a product, but something produced for the *market*.

A product made for the producer himself, made for his own use, is not a commodity. When a peasant sows rye, gathers in the harvest, threshes it, mills the grain, and bakes bread for himself, this bread is certainly not a commodity; it is simply bread. It only becomes a commodity when it is bought and sold; when, that is to say, it is produced for a buyer, for the market. Whoever buys it, owns it.

Under the capitalist system, all products are produced for the market, they all become commodities. Every factory or workshop produces in ordinary circumstances one particular product only, and it is easy to understand that the producer is not producing for his own use. When an undertaker, in his workshop, has coffins made, it is perfectly clear that he does not produce these coffins for himself and his family, but for the market. Again, in the case of a castor oil manufacturer, it is equally clear that even if the man continually suffers from digestive disorder it will be impossible for him to use for his own purposes more than an infinitesimal proportion of all the castor oil which his factory turns out. The same considerations apply, under capitalism, to any products you like to consider.

In a button factory, buttons are made; but these millions of buttons are not produced in order that they may be sewn on to the manufacturer's waistcoat; they are for sale. Everything produced under the capitalist system is produced for the market. To this market come gloves and sausages; books and blacking; machines and whisky; bread, boots, and smallarms—in a word, everything that is made.

A commodity economy necessarily implies *private ownership*. The independent artisan who produces commodities owns his workshop and his tools; the factory owner or workshop owner owns the factory or the workshop, with all the buildings, machinery, etc. Now, wherever private ownership and commodity production exist, there is a struggle for buyers, or competition among sellers. Even in

the days before there were factory owners, workshop owners, and great capitalists, when there were only independent
artisans, these artisans struggled one with another for buyers. The strongest and most acquisitive among them, the one
who had the best tools and was the cleverest, especially the
one who put by money, was always the one who came to
the top, attracted custom, and ruined his rivals. Thus the
system of petty ownership and the commodity economy
that was based upon it, contained the germs of large-scale
ownership and implied the ruin of many.

WE SEE, THEREFORE, THAT THE PRIMARY CHARACTERISTIC
OF THE CAPITALIST SYSTEM IS A COMMODITY ECONOMY;
THAT IS, AN ECONOMY WHICH PRODUCES FOR THE MARKET.

MONOPOLIZATION OF THE MEANS OF PRODUCTION
BY THE CAPITALIST CLASS

The mere existence of a commodity economy does not
alone suffice to constitute capitalism. A commodity economy can exist although there are no capitalists; for instance,
the economy in which the only producers are independent
artisans. They produce for the market, they sell their products; thus these products are undoubtedly commodities, and
the whole production is commodity production. Nevertheless, this is not capitalist production; it is nothing more than
simple commodity production. In order that a simple commodity economy can be transformed into capitalist production, it is necessary, on the one hand, that the means of ·
production (tools, machinery, buildings, land, etc.) should
become the private property of a comparatively limited
class of wealthy capitalists; and, on the other, that there
should ensue the ruin of most of the independent artisans
and peasants and their conversion into wage workers.

We have already seen that a simple commodity economy
contains within itself the germs that will lead to the impoverishment of some and the enrichment of others. This is what
has actually occurred. In all countries alike, most of the
independent artisans and small masters have been ruined.
The poorest were forced in the end to sell their tools; from
"masters" they became "men" whose sole possession was
a pair of hands. Those on the other hand who were richer,
grew more wealthy still; they rebuilt their workshops on a
more extensive scale, installed new machinery, began to
employ more workpeople, became factory owners.

Little by little there passed into the hands of these wealthy persons all that was necessary for production: factory buildings, machinery, raw materials, warehouses and shops, dwelling houses, workshops, mines, railways, steamships, the land—in a word, all the means of production. All these means of production became the exclusive property of the capitalist class; they became, as the phrase runs, a "monopoly" of the capitalist class.

THE SMALL GROUP OF THE WEALTHY OWNS EVERYTHING; THE HUGE MASSES OF THE POOR OWN NOTHING BUT THE HANDS WITH WHICH THEY WORK. THIS MONOPOLY OF THE MEANS OF PRODUCTION BY THE CAPITALIST CLASS IS THE SECOND LEADING CHARACTERISTIC OF THE CAPITALIST SYSTEM.

WAGE LABOUR

The vast numbers who were left without any property were transformed into the wage labourers of capital. What indeed was left for the impoverished peasant or artisan to do? Either take service as agricultural labourer under the capitalist landowner, or else go to the town and there seek employment in factory or workshop. There was no other way out. Such was the origin of wage labour, the third characteristic of the capitalist system.

What is wage labour? In earlier days, when there were serfs or slaves, every serf or slave could be bought and sold. . . .

The wage labourer can be neither bought nor sold. What can be bought and sold is his *labour power;* not the man or woman, but the capacity for labour. The wage labourer is personally free; the factory owner cannot flog him in the stable, or sell him to a neighbour, or exchange him for a wolf-hound puppy, though all these things could be done when serfdom prevailed. The wage worker can merely be hired. To all appearance the capitalist and the wage worker are equals. "Don't work if you don't want to; there is no compulsion," says the factory owner. The employer actually declares that he feeds the worker, gives work to the employee.

In this manner, the essence of wage labour consists in the sale of labour power, or in the transformation of labour power into a commodity. In the simple commodity economy which was described in ["Commodity Economy"], there were to be found in the market: milk, bread, cloth, boots, etc.; but not labour power. Labour power was not for sale.

Its possessor, the independent artisan, had in addition his own little dwelling and his tools. He worked for himself, conducted his own enterprise, applied his own labour power to the carrying of it on.

Very different is it under capitalism. The worker no longer owns the means of production; he cannot make use of his labour power for the conduct of his own enterprise; if he would save himself from starvation, he must sell his labour power to the capitalist. Side by side with the markets where cotton, cheese, and machines are sold, there also comes into existence the *labour market* where proletarians, that is to say wage workers, sell their labour power.

WE SEE, THEN, THAT THE DIFFERENCE BETWEEN THE CAPITALIST ECONOMY AND THE SIMPLE COMMODITY ECONOMY CONSISTS IN THIS, THAT IN THE CAPITALIST ECONOMY LABOUR POWER ITSELF BECOMES A COMMODITY. THUS, THE THIRD CHARACTERISTIC OF THE CAPITALIST SYSTEM IS THE EXISTENCE OF WAGE LABOUR.

CONDITIONS OF PRODUCTION UNDER CAPITALISM

There are, therefore, three characteristics of the capitalist system, namely: production for the market (commodity production); the monopolization of the means of production by the capitalist class; wage labour, that is, labour founded upon the sale of labour power. . . .

THE EXPLOITATION OF LABOUR POWER

The question now arises, for what reason does the capitalist class hire workers? Everyone knows that the reason is by no means because the factory owners wish to feed the hungry workers, but because they wish *to extract profit from them*. For the sake of profit, the factory owner builds his factory; for the sake of profit, he engages workers; for the sake of profit, he is always nosing out where higher prices are paid. Profit is the motive of all his calculations. Herein, moreover, we discern a very interesting characteristic of capitalist society. For society does not itself produce the things which are necessary and useful to it; instead of this, the capitalist class compels the workers to produce those things for which more will be paid, those things from which the capitalists derive the largest profit. Whisky, for example, is a very harmful substance, and alcoholic liquors in general ought to be produced only for technical purposes and for their use in medicine. But throughout the world the capitalists produce alcohol with all their might. Why? Because to ply the people with drink is extremely profitable.

We must now make it perfectly clear, how profit is made. For this purpose we must examine the question in detail. The capitalist receives profit in the form of money when he sells commodities that have been produced in his factory. How much money does he get for his wares? That depends upon the price. The next question is, How is the price determined, or why does one commodity fetch a high price and another a low price? It is easy to understand that if, in any branch of production, new machinery is introduced and labour is advantageously applied (or, as the phrase goes, is very productive), then the price of the commodity falls. If, on the other hand, production is difficult, if the quantity of goods produced is small, if labour is unsuccessfully applied or is comparatively unproductive, then the price of the commodity rises.[1]

If society must expend on the average much labour in order to produce any article, the price of that article is high; if on the average little labour is required, the price of the article is low. Assuming average efficiency of manufacture (that is to say, when the machinery and tools employed are neither the very best nor the very worst), *the amount of social labour requisite for the production of a commodity is termed the value of that commodity*. We see that price depends upon value. In actual fact, price is sometimes higher than value and sometimes lower, but for simplicity we may here assume that they are one and the same.

We must now recall what we said concerning the hiring of wage workers. The hiring of a worker is the sale of a peculiar commodity, the name of which is "labour power." As soon as labour power has become a commodity, what applies to other commodities applies to labour power. When the capitalist hires the worker, the former pays the latter the price of his labour power (or, to speak simply, the value of his labour power). By what is this value deter-

[1] We are now speaking of a change of price without reference to money, without reference to the question whether there be much money or little, or whether the currency be gold or paper. Changes in price due to changes in the standard of value may be very large, but such changes affect all commodities simultaneously, and this does not explain the differences in price as between one commodity and another. For example, the great extension of paper currency has enormously inflated prices in all countries. But this universal dearness does not explain why one commodity should be dearer than another.

mined? We have seen that the value of all commodities is determined by the quantity of labour expended in producing them. The same thing applies to labour power.

What, however, do we mean by the production of labour power? Labour power is not indeed produced in a factory, like cloth, blacking, or machinery. How then are we to explain it? We have merely to look at contemporary life under capitalism in order to understand with what we are concerned. Let us suppose that the workers have just finished their day's work. They are tired out, all their vital energy has been used up, they cannot work any more. Their labour power is practically exhausted. What is needed to restore it? Food, rest, sleep, recuperation, and therewith strength will be restored. Then will reappear the capacity for work; then, once more, they will have labour power. This means that food, clothing, and shelter—in a word, the necessaries that the worker consumes—affect the production of his labour power. Additional elements have to be considered, such as expenditure upon training when skilled workers are needed, and so on.

Everything that the working class consumes in order to restore its labour power, has value. For this reason, the value of articles of consumption and also of expenditure upon training constitute the value of labour power. Different commodities possess different values. In like manner, each kind of labour power has its peculiar value. The labour power of the compositor has one value, the labour power of the unskilled labourer has another.

Let us now return to the factory. The capitalist buys raw materials, fuel, machinery, lubricants, and other necessaries; then he buys labour power, "engages hands." He pays cash for everything. The work of production begins. The workers work, the wheels turn, the fuel is burned, the lubricant is used, the factory buildings suffer wear and tear, the labour power is expended. As a result, there issues from the factory a new commodity. The commodity, like all commodities, has value. What is this value? First of all, the commodity has absorbed into itself the value of the means of production that have been used up; that which has passed into it—raw materials, fuel consumed, the worn parts of the machinery, and so on. All this has now been transformed into the value of the commodity. In the second place, there has passed into the commodity the labour of the workers. If the workers were 30 in number, and if in the production of the commodity each worked for 30 hours, then there will have been expended in all 900 working hours. The full value of the product will therefore consist of the value of the utilized materials (let us assume that the value of these is equivalent to 600 hours), together with the new value which the workers have added by their labour, namely 900 hours. The total is therefore 600+900 = 1,500 working hours.

But how much did the commodity cost the capitalist? For the raw materials he paid in full; that is to say, he paid a sum of money corresponding to the value of 600 working hours. But what did he pay for labour power? Did he pay for the whole 900 hours? Here lies the key to the riddle. By our hypothesis, he has paid the full value of the labour power for the working days. If 30 workers have worked 30 hours, three days for 10 hours a day, the factory owner will have paid them whatever sum was necessary for the recuperation of their labour power during these days. How much will this sum have been? The answer is plain; it will have been considerably less than 900. Why? Because the quantity of labour which is necessary to recuperate my labour power is one thing, whereas the quantity of labour which I am able to expend is another thing. I can work 10 hours a day. To provide a sufficiency of food, clothing, etc., my daily needs are a quantity of articles the total value of which is equal to 5 hours. That is to say, I can do more work than the work which is requisite to recuperate my labour power. In our example, the workers consume, let us say, in the form of food, clothing, etc., during the three days, articles to the value of 450 working hours; but they supply 900 hours of labour. There remain for the capitalist 450 hours; these form the source of his profit. In fact, the commodity has cost the capitalist, as we have seen, 600 + 450 = 1,050 hours; but he sells it for the value of 600 + 900 = 1,500 hours; 450 hours are *surplus value* created by labour power. It results that for half their working time (namely for 5 hours in a ten-hour working day) the workers are working to redintegrate what they have used up for themselves; but during the other half of the day they are working entirely for the capitalist.

Let us now consider society as a whole. What the individual factory owner or the individual worker does is of very little interest to us. What interests us is the structure of the huge machine which goes by the name of capitalist society. The capitalist class hires the working class, the latter being numerically of enormous size. In millions of factories, in mines and quarries, in forest and field, hundreds of millions of workers labour like ants. Capital pays them their wages, the value of their labour power, with which they unceasingly renew this labour power for the service of capital. By its labour, the working class does not merely pay its own wages, but it creates in addition the income of the upper classes, creates surplus value. Through a thousand runnels, this surplus value flows into the pockets of the master class. Part goes to the capitalist himself, in the form of entrepreneur's profit; part goes to the landowner; in the form of taxes, part enters the coffers of the capitalist State; other portions accrue to merchants, traders, and shopkeepers, are spent upon churches and in brothels, support actors, artists, bourgeois scribblers, and so on. Upon surplus value live all the parasites who are bred by the capitalist system.

Part of the surplus value is, however, used over again by the capitalists. They add it to their capital, and the capital grows. They extend their enterprises. They engage more workers. They install better machinery. The increased number of workers produces for them a still greater quantity of surplus value. The capitalist enterprises grow ever larger. Thus at each revolution of time, capital moves forward, heaping up surplus value. Squeezing surplus value out of the working class, *exploiting* the workers, capital continually increases in size.

As we have seen, capitalist society is based upon the exploitation of labour. A small minority owns everything; the working masses own nothing. The capitalists command. The workers obey. The capitalists exploit. The workers are exploited. The very essence of capitalist society is found in this merciless and ever-increasing exploitation.

Capitalist production is a practical instrument for the extraction of surplus value.

Why has this instrument been able to continue in operation so long? For what reason do the workers tolerate such a state of affairs?

This question is by no means easy to answer at first sight. Speaking generally there are two reasons for it: in the first place, because the capitalist class is well organized and powerful; secondly, because the bourgeoisie frequently controls the brains of the working class.

The most trustworthy means at the disposal of the bourgeoisie for this purpose is its organization as the State. In all capitalist countries the State is merely a union of the master class. Let us consider any country you like: Britain, the United States, France, or Japan. Everywhere we find that the ministers, high officials, members of parliament, are either capitalists, land-owners, factory owners, and financial magnates, or else the faithful and well-paid servants of these—lawyers, bank managers, professors, army officers, archbishops, and bishops, who serve the capitalists, not from fear but from conviction.

The union of all these individuals belonging to the bourgeoisie, a union which embraces the entire country and holds everything in its grasp, is known as the State. This organization of the bourgeoisie has two leading aims. The first and most important of these is to suppress disorders and insurrections on the part of the workers, to ensure the undisturbed extraction of surplus value from the working class, to increase the strength of the capitalist means of production. The second aim is to strive against other organizations of the same kind (that is to say, against other bourgeois States), to compete with them for a larger share in surplus value. Thus the capitalist State is a union of the master class, formed to safeguard exploitation. The interests of capital and nothing but the interests of capital—here we have the guiding star towards which are directed all the activities of this robber band. . . .

The capitalist State is not only the largest and most powerful among bourgeois organizations; it is at the same time the most complex of these organizations, for it has a very large number of subdivisions, and tentacles issue from these in every direction. The primary aim of all this is to protect, to consolidate, and to expand the exploitation of the working class. Against the working class, the State can employ measures of two different kinds, brute force and spiritual subjugation. These constitute the most important instruments of the capitalist State.

Among the organs of *brute force,* must first be enumerated the army and the police, the prisons and the law-courts. Next must be mentioned accessory organs, such as spies, provocative agents, organized strikebreakers, hired assassins, etc.

The *army* of the capitalist State is organized in a peculiar fashion. At the head is the officers' corps, the group of "epaulet wearers." They are drawn from the ranks of the landed gentry, from those of the wealthier bourgeoisie, and in part from those of the intelligentsia (professional classes). These are the bitterest enemies of the proletariat. From childhood they have been brought up in special schools (in Russia in cadet corps and in junker schools) where they have been taught how to knock the men about, and how "to maintain the honour of the uniform," this meaning to keep the rankers in absolute subjection and to make mere pawns of them. The most distinguished members of the nobility and the wealthier bourgeoisie, if they enter the military or naval profession, become generals or admirals, persons of high rank, wearing orders and ribbons. . . .

The *police* and the *gendarmerie*. In addition to the regular army, the capitalist State has an army of picked ruffians, and of specially trained troops, peculiarly adapted for the struggle with the workers. These institutions (the police, for instance) have, indeed, the function of combating theft and of "protecting the persons and property of citizens"; but at the same time the police are maintained for the arrest, prosecution, and punishment, of discontented workers. In Russia, the police have been the most trustworthy protectors of the landlords and the tsar. Especially brutal, in all capitalist countries, have been the members of the secret police and of the corps of gendarmes—in Russia the secret police force or "political police" was known as the *ohrana* (protection). Large numbers of detectives, provocative agents, spies, strikebreakers, etc., work in cooperation with the official police.

> Interesting, in this connexion, are the methods of the American secret police. They are in league with a vast number of private and semi-official "detective bureaux." The notorious adventures of Nat Pinkerton were really a campaign against the workers. The detectives palmed off bombs on the workers' leaders, incited them to kill the capitalists, and so forth. Such "detectives" likewise recruit vast numbers of strikebreakers (known in the United States as "scabs"), and troops of armed ruffians who murder strikers when opportunity arises. There is no villainy too black for these assassins, who are employed by the "democratic" State of the American capitalists!

The *administration of justice* in the bourgeois State is a means of self-defence for the bourgeois class. Above all, it is employed to settle with those who infringe the rights of capitalist property or interfere with the capitalist system. Bourgeois justice sent Liebknecht to prison, but acquitted Liebknecht's murderer. The *State prison service* settles accounts quite as effectively as does the executioner of the bourgeois State. Its shafts are directed, not against the rich, but against the poor.

Such are the institutions of the capitalist State, institutions which effect the direct and brutal oppression of the working class.

Among the means of *spiritual subjugation* at the disposal

of the capitalist State, three deserve especial mention: the State school; the State church; and the State, or State-supported, press.

The bourgeoisie is well aware that it cannot control the working masses by the use of force alone. It is necessary that the workers' brains should be completely enmeshed as if in a spider's web. The bourgeois State looks upon the workers as working cattle; these beasts must labour, but they must not bite. Consequently, they must not merely be whipped or shot when they attempt to bite, but they must be trained and tamed, just as wild beasts in a menagerie are trained by beast-tamers. Similarly, the capitalist State maintains specialists to stupefy and subdue the proletariat; it maintains bourgeois teachers and professors, the clergy, bourgeois authors and journalists. In the State schools these specialists teach children from their earliest years to obey capital and to despise and hate "rebels." The children's heads are stuffed with fables about the revolution and the revolutionary movement. Emperors, kings, and industrial magnates are glorified. In the churches, the priests, who are salaried by the State, preach that all authority comes from God. Day after day, the bourgeois newspapers trumpet these lies, whilst working-class papers are in most cases suppressed by the capitalist State. Under such conditions, is it easy for the workers to extract themselves from the quagmire? A German imperialist bandit wrote: "We do not only need the soldiers' legs, but also their brains and their hearts." The bourgeois State, in like manner, aims at educating the workers so that they may resemble domestic animals who will work like horses, and eat humble pie. . . .

FUNDAMENTAL CONTRADICTIONS OF THE CAPITALIST SYSTEM

We must now examine whether capitalist or bourgeois society is well or ill constructed. Anything is sound and good when the mutual adaptation of its parts is entirely satisfactory. Let us consider the mechanism of a clock. It works accurately and freely if all the cog-wheels are properly adjusted one to another.

Let us now look at capitalist society. We can perceive without difficulty that capitalist society is far less soundly constructed than it appears to be at the first glance. On the contrary, it exhibits grave contradictions and disastrous flaws. In the first place, under capitalism the production and distribution of goods is quite unorganized; "anarchy of production" prevails. What does this mean? It means that all the capitalist entrepreneurs (or capitalist companies) produce commodities independently of one another. Instead of society undertaking to reckon up what it needs and how much of each article, the factory owners simply produce upon the calculation of what will bring them most profit and will best enable them to defeat their rivals in the market. The consequence often is that commodities are produced in excessive quantities—we are talking, of course, of pre-war days. There is then no sale for them. The workers cannot buy them, for they have not enough money. Thereupon a crisis ensues. The factories are shut down, and the workers are turned out into the street. Furthermore, the anarchy of production entails a struggle for the market; each producer wants to entice away the others' customers, to corner the market. This struggle assumes various forms: it begins with the competition between two factory owners; it ends in the world war, wherein the capitalist States wrestle with one another for the world market. This signifies, not merely that the parts of capitalist society interfere with one another's working, but that there is a direct conflict between the constituent parts.

THE FIRST REASON, THEREFORE, FOR THE DISHARMONY OF CAPITALIST SOCIETY IS THE ANARCHY OF PRODUCTION, WHICH LEADS TO CRISES, INTERNECINE COMPETITION, AND WARS.

THE SECOND REASON FOR THE DISHARMONY OF CAPITALIST SOCIETY IS TO BE FOUND IN THE CLASS STRUCTURE OF THAT SOCIETY. Considered in its essence, capitalist society is not one society but two societies; it consists of capitalists, on the one hand, and of workers and poor peasants, on the other. Between these two classes there is continuous and irreconcilable enmity; this is what we speak of as the *class war*. Here, also, we see that the various parts of capitalist society are not merely ill-adapted to one another, but are actually in unceasing conflict.

Is capitalism going to collapse, or is it not? The answer to the question depends upon the following considerations. If we study the evolution of capitalism, if we examine the changes it has undergone in the course of time, and if we perceive that its disharmonies are diminishing, then we can confidently wish it a long life. If, on the other hand, we discover that in the course of time the various parts of the capitalist machine have come to clash with one another more and more violently, if we discern that the flaws in the structure are becoming positive chasms, then it is time to say, "Rest in peace." . . .

CAPITALISM LEADS TO REVOLUTION

Upon the initiative of the trickster Wilson, the leader of American capitalism, an attempt to form such an alliance of robber capitalists against the proletariat was made at the so-called peace conference of Versailles. The robber alliance was christened the League of Nations, this being intended to signify that is was a "league of peoples." In reality it is not a league of peoples, but a league of the capitalists of various countries and of their State authorities.

This league is in the nature of an attempt to form a worldwide trust of monstrous proportions which shall embrace the whole surface of the globe in a grasp of universal exploitation, and which, on the other hand, shall crush with the utmost ferocity the working class movement of revolt and revolution. It is pure fable to say that the League of Nations has been founded to promote the cause of peace. In actual fact it has a twofold aim: the ruthless exploitation of the proletariat throughout the world, of all colonies and of the colonial slaves; and the crushing of the incipient world revolution.

In the League of Nations, the USA, which became inordinately rich during the war, plays the first fiddle. All the bourgeois States of Europe are now heavily indebted to America. The United States is very powerful for the additional reason that she has vast quantities of raw materials and fuel, and is a great wheat-producing country. She wishes to use these advantages in such a way as to make all her fellow robbers dependent on her. Infallibly she will become the leader of the League of Nations.

Very interesting is the way in which the United States veils its preeminently predatory policy behind a cloud of fine phrases. When, in pursuit of plunder, she entered the war, her watchwords were "the salvation of mankind," "the rescue of the enslaved peoples," and so on. It suited the United States that Europe should be disintegrated, should consist of dozens of petty lands, formally "independent" but substantially dependent upon America. This predatory interest was masked by an exalted phrase concerning "the right of the nations to self-determination." The capitalist gendarmerie, the White Guards, and the White Police, which, according to Wilson's plan, were to be ready everywhere to crush the revolution, would exist to ensure punishment for "breaches of the peace." In the year 1919 all the imperialists suddenly became pacifically minded, and raised a clamour to the effect that the bolsheviks were the real imperialists, the true enemies of peace. Plans for the stifling of the revolution masqueraded as zeal for peace and democracy. . . .

THE ONLY ISSUE FOR HUMANITY IS COMMUNISM. AND SINCE COMMUNISM CAN BE REALIZED ONLY BY THE PROLETARIAT, THE PROLETARIAT IS TODAY THE TRUE SAVIOUR OF MANKIND FROM THE HORRORS OF CAPITALISM, FROM THE BARBARITIES OF EXPLOITATION, FROM COLONIAL POLICY, INCESSANT WARS, FAMINE, A LAPSE INTO SAVAGERY AND BRUTALIZATION, FROM ALL THE ABOMINATIONS THAT ARE ENTAILED BY FINANCIAL CAPITAL AND IMPERIALISM. HEREIN LIES THE SPLENDID HISTORIC SIGNIFICANCE OF THE PROLETARIAT. THE WORKERS MAY SUFFER DEFEAT IN INDIVIDUAL BATTLES, AND EVEN IN INDIVIDUAL COUNTRIES. BUT THE VICTORY OF THE PROLETARIAT IS NO LESS CERTAIN THAN THE RUIN OF THE BOURGEOISIE IS INEVITABLE. . . .

INTERNATIONALISM OF THE WORKERS' MOVEMENT ESSENTIAL TO THE VICTORY OF THE COMMUNIST REVOLUTION

The communist revolution can be victorious only as a world revolution. If a state of affairs arose in which one country was ruled by the working class, while in other countries the working class, not from fear but from conviction, remained submissive to capital, in the end the great robber States would crush the workers' State of the first country. THE WORKERS' COMMUNIST MOVEMENT CAN CONQUER ONLY AS AN INTERNATIONAL COMMUNIST MOVEMENT.

The need for an international struggle on the part of the proletariat has long been recognized. In the forties of the last century, on the eve of the revolution of 1848, there already existed an international secret organization known as the Communist Federation. Marx and Engels were its leaders. At the London conference of the organization they were instructed to write a manifesto in its name. Such was the origin of the Manifesto of the Communist Party, in which the great champions of the proletariat gave the first exposition of communist teaching.

In 1864 there was constituted under Marx's leadership the International Working Men's Association, now commonly spoken of as the *First International*. In the First International there were associated a number of working class leaders from various countries, but unity was lacking. Moreover, the organization was not yet based upon the broad masses of the workers, but rather took the form of an international society of revolutionary propagandists. In 1871 the members of the International took part in the rising of the Parisian workers (the Commune of Paris). There ensued everywhere a persecution of the branches of the International. It collapsed in 1874, having been greatly weakened by internal dissensions, by the struggles between the adherents of Marx and those of the anarchist, Bakunin. After the break-up of the First International, the growth of socialist parties began in various countries. The more rapid the development of industry, the more rapid was the growth of these parties. The need for mutual support was felt so strongly, that in 1889 there was held an international socialist congress attended by delegates of the socialist parties of numerous countries. Thus the *Second International* came into being. The Second International remained in existence till 1914, when the war gave it its death blow. . . .

The basic error of pacifism is that the bourgeoisie simply will not carry out any of these fine things like disarmament. It is absolutely absurd to preach disarmament in an era of imperialism and civil war. The bourgeoisie will take care to be well armed; and if the workers were to disarm or were to fail to arm themselves, they would be inviting destruction. We can thus realize how the pacifist watchwords cannot fail to lead the proletariat astray. PACIFISM TENDS TO PREVENT THE WORKERS FROM CONCENTRATING THEIR ATTENTION UPON THE ARMED STRUGGLE FOR COMMUNISM.

The best example of the fraudulent character of pacifism is furnished by the policy of Wilson, and by his fourteen points. Here, under a garnish of fine words, and in the name of the League of Nations, world-wide plunder and a civil war against the proletariat are promulgated. The following examples will show to what depths of baseness the pacifists can descend. Taft, sometime president of the USA, was one of the founders of the American Peace Society, and at the same time a rabid imperialist. Ford, the famous American motor-car manufacturer, financed entire expeditions to Europe in order to trumpet his pacifist views; but at the very same time he was netting millions of dollars from the work his factories were doing for the war. Fried, in his Handbook of the Peace Movement (*Handbuch der*

Friedensbewegung, vol. ii, pp. 149–50) assures his readers that the joint expedition of the imperialists against China in 1900 proved the "brotherhood of the nations." He writes as follows: "The expedition to China furnished another proof of the ascendancy of the idea of peace in contemporary affairs. An *international association of armies* was displayed. . . . The armies marched, as a pacific force, under the command of a European generalissimo. We, the friends of peace, regard this world generalissimo [he was writing about Count Waldersee, who was appointed generalissimo by William II] as merely the forerunner of that world statesman who will be in a position to realize our ideal of peaceful methods." Here we see open and universal robbery designated "the brotherhood of the nations." In like manner, the robber League of Capitalists is dished up with the League of Nations' sauce. . . .

In bourgeois democratic States, at the head of everything stands what is known as parliament. This is a representative institution, the electoral franchise varying in different countries. In some, only the rich have the vote; in some, a part of the poor are admitted to the franchise; in a third group, all the men of a certain age can vote; in a fourth country, all the women as well.

But even where parliament is elected by universal suffrage, the majority of the seats are invariably occupied by representatives of the bourgeoisie. Why does this always happen? The reason is obvious in view of what we have already learned. Let us suppose that the workers, who form the majority in the country, have the right to vote. But let us further suppose that all the wealth is in the hands of the capitalists, that they own all the newspapers and all the places where public meetings can be held, and that artists, printing presses, and millions of leaflets are at their service; that from all the pulpits the clergy advocate their cause; let us suppose, moreover, that the poor workers are engaged day after day in exhausting toil, that they have no meeting-places, that clever fellows circulate among them (agents of the bourgeoisie, lawyers, journalists, and other glib talkers) advocating what seem to be excellent watchwords, and thus confusing the workers' minds; let us remember the enormous financial resources of the trust magnates, which enable them to corrupt the workers' representatives—however honest these may have been at the outset—by offering comfortable jobs, by flattery in the daily press, and so on. Then we can understand why it is that even in such parliaments the majority always consists of the secret or declared agents of the bourgeoisie, of financial capital, of the bank kings.

It is, therefore, extraordinarily difficult for the working masses to elect any of their own folk as representatives.

Once a representative finds his way to parliament, the matter is finished; he can defy the electors; for three or four years his seat is secure. He is independent of them. He sells himself right and left. He cannot be recalled by the electors; the law makes no provision for anything of the kind.

Such is the state of affairs in a bourgeois democratic republic under parliamentarism. It is very different in the Soviet Republic. Here the parasites—the traders and the factory owners, the prelates and the landlords, the military officers and the rich peasants—have no right to the vote. They can neither elect nor be elected. On the other hand, the exercise of the franchise by the workers and the poor peasants is simple and easy. Moreover, every delegate to the soviet can be recalled by the electors, who can send another in his place. If the delegate fulfils his duties badly, if he turns his coat, etc., he can be recalled. This right of recall has nowhere been so extensively adopted as in the Soviet Republic. . . .

THE UNITY OF THE PROLETARIAT

First of all, however, we must propound and decide an extremely important and fundamental problem. Should the Russian worker and the Russian peasant look upon the Germans, the French, the British, the Jews, the Chinese, or the Tartars, as enemies, irrespective of the class to which these belong? Are the Russian workers and peasants entitled to hate or to regard with suspicion those who belong to another nation, for the sole reason that these latter speak a different tongue, that their skins are black or yellow, that they have different customs and laws? Obviously, this would be quite wrong. The German workers, the French workers, the Negro workers, are just as much proletarians as the Russians are. No matter what tongue the workers of other lands may speak, the essential feature of their condition lies in this, that they are all exploited by capital, that they are all comrades, that they all alike suffer from poverty, oppression, and injustice.

Is the Russian worker to love the Russian capitalist because his fellow-countryman abuses him in the familiar Russian terms, because his employer cuffs him with a Russian fist, or lashes him with a Russian whip? Of course not. Nor is the German workman likely to love the German capitalist any better because the latter taunts him in the German language and after the German fashion. The workers of all lands are brothers of one class, and they are the enemies of the capitalists of all lands.

The same considerations apply in the case of the poor peasants of every nation. To the Russian peasant (the poor peasant or the middle peasant), the semi-proletarian peasant of Hungary, or the poor peasant of Sicily or Belgium, is nearer and dearer than can possibly be the rich peasant of his own land who exploits him, or the skinflint landlord who happens to be born on Russian soil and to speak the Russian tongue.

But the workers of the whole world must not merely recognize themselves to be brothers by class, to be brothers in oppression and slavery. It would do no good if they were to rest content with railing against their capitalist compatriots in their respective tongues; if in each land the sufferers were to wipe one another's tears, and only within their own State were to carry on the struggle against the enemy. Brothers in oppression and slavery must be brothers in one world-wide league for the struggle with the capitalists. Forgetting all the national differences that tend to hinder union, they must unite in one great army to carry on a joint war against capitalism. Only by closing their ranks in such an international alliance, can they hope to conquer world capitalism. This is why, more than seventy years ago, the founders of communism, Marx and Engels, in their famous Communist Manifesto, fulminated the splendid slogan: "Proletarians of all lands, unite!"

It is essential that the working class should overcome all national prejudices and national enmities. This is requisite, not only for the world-wide attack upon capital and for the complete overthrow of the capitalist system, but also for the organization of a single world-wide economic system. Soviet Russia cannot exist without Donetz coal, Baku mineral oil, Turkestan cotton; but it is just as true that Central and Western Europe cannot do without Russian wood, hemp, flax, and platinum, or without American wheat; it is just as true that Italy finds British coal a vital necessity, and that Britain urgently needs Egyptian cotton, etc., etc. The bourgeoisie has found itself unable to organize a world economy, and the bourgeois system has been shipwrecked upon this difficulty. The proletariat is alone competent to organize such a system with success. To this end, however, it must proclaim the watchword, "All the world and all the wealth that it contains belong to the whole world of labour." This watchword implies that the German workers must completely renounce their national wealth, the British theirs, and so on. If national prejudice and national greed oppose the internationalization of industry and agriculture, away with them, wherever they may show themselves and under whatever colours they may sail! . . .

THE EQUAL RIGHTS OF THE NATIONS AND THE RIGHT TO SELF-DETERMINATION; FEDERATION

The Communist Party, declaring a relentless war upon all oppression of man by man, takes a decisive stand against that oppression of subject nationalities which is indispensable to the existence of the bourgeois system. Even more relentlessly do communists resist the slightest participation in this oppression on the part of the working class. It does not suffice, however, that the proletariat of a great and strong country should repudiate all attempts at the oppression of the other peoples which the bourgeoisie or the aristocracy of its own land has crushed. It is also essential that the proletarians of oppressed nations should not feel any mistrust of their comrades who belong to the lands of the oppressors. When the Czechs were oppressed by the German bourgeoisie of Austria, the Czech workers looked upon all Germans as their oppressors. Our tsarist government oppressed the Poles, and the population of Poland has continued to cherish mistrust of all Russians; not merely of the Russian tsar, the Russian landlord, and the Russian capitalist. If we are to eradicate the mistrust felt by the workers of oppressed nations for the workers of oppressor nations, we must not merely proclaim national equality, but must realize it in practice. This equality must find expression in the granting of equal rights in the matter of language, education, religion, etc. Nor is this all. The proletariat must be ready to grant complete national self-determination, must be ready, that is, to concede to the workers who form the majority in any nation the full right to decide the question whether that nation is to be completely integrated with the other, or is to be federated with it, or is to be entirely separated from it.

Is it possible, the reader will ask, that the communists

can advocate the severance of the nations? How then will come into existence that unified proletarian world-embracing State which the communists aspire to found? There seems to be a contradiction here.

There is no contradiction, however. In order to secure as speedily as possible the full union of all the workers of the world, it is sometimes necessary to countenance the temporary separation of one nation from another.

Let us consider the circumstances in which such a course may be requisite. We will suppose that in Bavaria, which now forms part of Germany, a Soviet republic has been declared, while at Berlin the bourgeois dictatorship of Noske and Scheidemann still prevails. Is it right for the Bavarian communists, in that case, to strive for the independence of Bavaria? Certainly! And not only the Bavarian communists, but also the communists of other parts of Germany, must welcome the separation of Soviet Bavaria, for this will not be a separation from the German proletariat, but will be a deliverance from the yoke of the German bourgeoisie.

Here is the obverse example. A Soviet republic has been proclaimed throughout Germany, Bavaria alone excepted. The Bavarian bourgeoisie desires separation from Soviet Germany, but the Bavarian proletariat desires union. What should the communists do? It is obvious that the communists of Germany should help the Bavarian workers, and should offer armed resistance to the separatist endeavours of the Bavarian bourgeoisie. This would not be the oppression of Bavaria, but the oppression of the Bavarian bourgeoisie.

Again, the Soviet Power has been proclaimed both in England and in Ireland, both in the land of the oppressors and in the land of the oppressed. Furthermore, the Irish workers will not trust the English workers, who belong to a country which has oppressed Ireland for centuries. From the economic point of view, the separation will be harmful. What course should the English communists pursue in these circumstances? Whatever happens, they must not use force, as the English bourgeoisie has done, to maintain the union with Ireland. They must grant the Irish absolute freedom to separate. Why must they do this?

First of all, because it is necessary to convince the Irish workers that the oppression of Ireland has been the work of the English bourgeoisie and not of the English proletariat. The English workers have to win the Irish workers' confidence.

Secondly, because the Irish workers will have to learn by

experience that it is disadvantageous for them to form a small independent State. They will have to learn by experience that production in Ireland cannot be properly organized unless Ireland is in close political and economic union with proletarian England and other proletarian lands.

Finally, take the case of a nation with a bourgeois government which wishes to separate from a nation with a proletarian régime, and let us suppose that, in the nation which desires to separate, the majority of the workers or a notable proportion of them are in favour of the separation. We may suppose that the workers of the separating country are distrustful, not only of the capitalists, but also of the workers belonging to the country whose bourgeoisie has oppressed them in the past. Even in this case it would be better to allow the proletariat of the separating land to come to terms in its own way with its own bourgeoisie, for otherwise the latter would retain the power of saying: "It is not I who oppress you, but the people of such and such a country." The working class will speedily realize that the bourgeoisie has desired independence that it may independently flay its own proletariat. The workers will speedily realize, moreover, that the proletariat of the neighbouring Soviet State desires the union, not for the sake of exploiting or oppressing the workers of the smaller land, but that all the workers may join in a common struggle for deliverance from exploitation and oppression.

The Communist Party recognizes that the nations have the right to self-determination even up to the point of secession; but it considers that the working majority of the nation and not the bourgeoisie embodies the will of the nation. It would, therefore, be more accurate to say that when we speak of recognizing the right of the nations to self-determination, we are referring to the right of the working majority in any nation. As far as the bourgeoisie is concerned, inasmuch as during the period of civil war and proletarian dictatorship we deprive it of civic freedoms, we deprive it of the right to any voice in the question of national affairs.

What have we to say concerning the right of self-determination and the right of secession in the case of nations at a comparatively low or extremely low level of cultural development? What is to happen to nations which not only have no proletariat, but have not even a bourgeoisie, or if they have it, have it only in an immature form? Consider, for example, the Tunguses, the Kalmucks, or the Buryats, who inhabit Russian territory. What is to be done if these nations demand complete separation from the great civilized nations? Still more, what is to be done if they wish to secede from nations which have realized socialism? Surely to permit such secessions would be to strengthen barbarism at the expense of civilization?

We are of opinion that when socialism has been realized in the more advanced countries of the world, the backward and semi-savage peoples will be perfectly willing to join the general alliance of the peoples. The imperialist bourgeoisie which has seized its colonial possessions and has annexed them by force has good reason to fear the secession of the colonies. The proletariat, having no desire to plunder the colonies, can procure from them by the exchange of goods such raw materials as are required, and can leave to the natives of backward lands the right to arrange their own internal affairs as they please. The Communist Party, therefore, wishing to put an end for ever to all forms of national oppression and national inequality, voices the demand for the national right of self-determination.

The proletariat of all lands will avail itself of this right, first of all in order to destroy nationalism, and secondly in order to form a voluntary federative league.

When this federative league proves incompetent to establish a world-wide economic system, and when the great majority has been convinced of its inadequacy by actual experience, the time will have come for the creation of one world-wide socialist republic. . . .

"Religion is the opium of the people," said Karl Marx. It is the task of the Communist Party to make this truth comprehensible to the widest possible circles of the labouring masses. It is the task of the party to impress firmly upon the minds of the workers, even upon the most backward, that religion has been in the past and still is today one of the most powerful means at the disposal of the oppressors for the maintenance of inequality, exploitation, and slavish obedience on the part of the toilers.

Many weak-kneed communists reason as follows: "Religion does not prevent my being a communist. I believe both in God and in communism. My faith in God does not hinder me from fighting for the cause of the proletarian revolution."

This train of thought is radically false. Religion and communism are incompatible, both theoretically and practically.

Every communist must regard social phenomena (the relationships between human beings, revolutions, wars, etc.) as processes which occur in accordance with definite laws. The laws of social development have been fully established by scientific communism on the basis of the theory of historical materialism which we owe to our great teachers Karl Marx and Friedrich Engels. This theory explains that social development is not brought about by any kind of supernatural forces. Nay more. The same theory has demonstrated that the very idea of God and of supernatural powers arises at a definite stage in human history, and at another definite stage begins to disappear as a childish notion which finds no confirmation in practical life and in the struggle between man and nature. But it is profitable to the predatory class to maintain the ignorance of the people and to maintain the people's childish belief in miracles (the key to the riddle really lies in the exploiters' pockets), and this is why religious prejudices are so tenacious, and why they confuse the minds even of persons who are in other respects able.

The general happenings throughout nature are, moreover, in no wise dependent upon supernatural causes. Man has been extremely successful in the struggle with nature. He influences nature in his own interests, and controls natural forces, achieving these conquests, not thanks to his faith in God and in divine assistance, but in spite of this faith. He achieves his conquests thanks to the fact that in practical life and in all serious matters he invariably conducts himself as an atheist. Scientific communism, in its judgements concerning natural phenomena, is guided by the data of the natural sciences, which are in irreconcilable conflict with all religious imaginings.

In practice, no less than in theory, communism is incompatible with religious faith. The tactic of the Communist Party prescribes for the members of the party definite lines of conduct. The moral code of every religion in like manner prescribes for the faithful some definite line of conduct. For example, the Christian code runs: "Whosoever shall smite thee on thy right cheek, turn to him the other also." In most cases there is an irreconcilable conflict between the principles of communist tactics and the commandments of religion. A communist who rejects the commandments of religion and acts in accordance with the directions of the party, ceases to be one of the faithful. On the other hand, one who, while calling himself a communist, continues to cling to his religious faith, one who in the name of religious commandments infringes the prescriptions of the party, ceases thereby to be a communist.

The struggle with religion has two sides, and every communist must distinguish clearly between them. On the one hand we have the struggle with the church, as a special organization existing for religious propaganda, materially interested in the maintenance of popular ignorance and religious enslavement. On the other hand we have the struggle with the widely diffused and deeply ingrained prejudices of the majority of the working population. . . .

The November revolution [25 October, old style; 7 November, new style, 1917] in Russia, realized the dictatorship of the proletariat, which began to build the foundations of communist society, with the aid of the poor peasants or the semi-proletariat. The development of the revolution in Germany and Austria-Hungary, the growth of the revolutionary movement of the proletariat in all advanced lands, the spread of the soviet form of that movement (the form which aimed directly at realizing the dictatorship of the proletariat)—these things combined to show that the era of the worldwide proletarian communist revolution had begun.

This revolution was the inevitable result of the development of capitalism, which had hitherto been dominant in the majority of civilized countries. If we ignore the misleading designation of the party as "social democratic," and use instead the word "communist," our old programme accurately characterized in the following theses the nature of capitalism and of bourgeois society:

"As the chief characteristic of this society, we have commodity production upon the foundation of capitalist productive relationships, in accordance with which the most important and significant part of the means of the production and distribution of commodities is owned by a comparatively small class of persons, whereas the great majority of the population consists of proletarians and semi-proletarians compelled by their economic position to sell their labour power permanently or from time to time, compelled, that is to say, to become wage workers in the service of the capitalists, and to create by their labour the income of the higher classes of society.

"The domain of capitalist productive relationships continually extends in proportion to the continued improvement of technique, which increases the economic importance of large-scale enterprises, and leads to the crushing out of petty independent producers, converting some of them into proletarians, restricting the role of the remainder in social and economic life, and in many places making them—more or less completely, more or less obviously, more or less miserably—the dependents of capital.

"Moreover, this technical progress enables the entrepreneurs, to an increasing extent, to apply the labour of women and children to the process of producing and distributing commodities. In like measure, on the other hand, it leads to a comparative restriction of the demand on the part of the entrepreneurs for the living labour of the workers, so that the demand for labour power is necessarily inferior to the supply. Hence arise, first, an increase in the dependence of wage labour upon capital, and, secondly, a rise in the rate of exploitation.

"This state of affairs in capitalist countries, and the continued intensification of their competition in the world market, give rise to more and more difficulty in disposing of the commodities which are produced in continually increasing quantities. Overproduction, manifesting itself in more or less acute crises of production which are followed by more or less prolonged periods of stagnation, is the inevitable outcome of the development of productive strength in bourgeois society. Crises, and periods in which production is stagnant, lead, in their turn, to the more and more widespread ruin of the small producers, increase the dependence of wage labour upon capital, and give rise all the more speedily to a comparative or absolute worsening of the position of the working class.

"In this manner, the improvement in technique, leading to an increase in the productivity of labour and to an increase in social wealth, entails in bourgeois society an increase in social inequality, a widening of the chasm between the haves and the have-nots, an increase in the insecurity of life, in unemployment, and in various kinds of deprivation for wider and wider circles among the labouring masses.

"In proportion as the contradictions peculiar to bourgeois society grow and develop, so also does there increase the discontent of the toiling and exploited masses with the existing order of things, and so also do there increase the number and the solidarity of the proletarians and the intensity of their struggle with the exploiters. At the same time the advance of technique, concentrating the means of production and distribution and socializing the labour process in capitalist undertakings, creates with greater and greater speed the material possibilities for the transformation of capitalist into communist productive relationships; it creates, that is to say, the social revolution, which takes as its final aim all the activities of the international communist parties, regarded as conscious expressions of the class movement.

"Transforming private ownership of the means of production and distribution into social ownership, and leading to the purposive organization of the social productive process for the safeguarding of the prosperity and the many-sided development of all the members of society, the social revolution of the proletariat puts an end to the division of society into classes, and thereby liberates the whole of oppressed mankind, thus abolishing all forms of exploitation of one section of society by another.

"A necessary condition for this social revolution is the dictatorship of the proletariat, this meaning the conquest by the proletariat of such a degree of political power as will enable it to crush the resistance of the exploiters. Determining to make the proletariat capable of fulfilling its great historic mission, the international Communist Party organizes the proletariat into an independent political party, opposed to all the bourgeois parties; leads the workers in all the manifestations of the class struggle; reveals to the exploited the irreconcilable conflict of interests between themselves and the exploiters; and explains to the proletariat the historical significance and the necessary conditions of the imminent social revolution. At the same time, the party reveals to the other sections of the toiling and exploited masses the hopelessness of their condition in capitalist society, and shows them that the social revolution is indispensable in order that they may secure their own deliverance from the yoke of capital. The party of the working class, the Communist Party, summons to its ranks all strata of the toiling and exploited population in so far as they have accepted the proletarian outlook."

The process of the concentration and centralization of capital, destroying free competition, led in the beginning of the twentieth century to the creation of powerful, monopolist, capitalist, combines—syndicates, cartels, and trusts —which acquired a decisive significance in economic life; it led also to the amalgamation of banking capital with highly concentrated industrial capital, and to the vigorous export of capital into foreign lands. Trusts comprising whole groups of capitalist Powers began the economic partition of the world which had already been partitioned territorially among the richer countries. This epoch of financial capital, inevitably intensifying the struggle between the capitalist States, is the epoch of imperialism.

Hence inevitably arise imperialist wars, wars for markets, for spheres for the investment of capital, for raw materials, and for labour power, that is to say, wars for world dominion and for power over small and weak nations. Such was the first great imperialist war of 1914 to 1918.

The vast development of world capitalism; the change from a system of free competition to a system in which monopolist capitalism was dominant; the creation by the banks, and also by the capitalist combines, of an apparatus for the joint regulation of the process of the production and distribution of commodities; the rise in the cost of living; the oppression of the workers by the employers' syndicates, the enslavement of the working class by the imperialist State, the colossal difficulties facing the proletariat in its economic and political struggle (phenomena inevitably associated with the growth of capitalist monopoly); the miseries, the poverty, and the ruin which issued from the imperalist war—all these things have inevitably contributed to the collapse of capitalism and to the transition to a higher type of social economy.

The imperialist war could not end in a just peace or even in any stable peace between the bourgeois governments. At the stage of development which capitalism has now reached this war must inevitably be transformed, and is being transformed under our very eyes, into a civil war between the exploited and toiling masses (led by the proletariat) and the bourgeoisie.

The vigorous onslaught made by the proletariat, and the victories secured by the workers in various lands, have intensified the resistance of the exploiters, and have led to the creation of new forms of international union among the capitalists (the League of Nations, etc.); these, organizing upon a world scale, by the systematic exploitation of all the peoples of the globe, and concentrating their forces, aim at the direct crushing of the proletarian movement in all lands.

All this inevitably leads to the conjuncture of civil wars within the individual States, with revolutionary wars, waged in part by the proletarian States that are defending themselves against capitalist attack, and in part by the oppressed peoples that are endeavouring to throw off the yoke of the imperialist Powers.

In these circumstances the watchwords of pacifism, international disarmament under capitalism, the founding of courts of arbitration, etc., are something worse than reactionary utopism; they are a direct fraud upon the workers, aiming at the disarmament of the proletariat and at diverting it from the task of disarming the exploiters.

Nothing but the proletarian, the communist revolution,

can lead humanity out of the blind alley in which it has been placed by imperialism and imperialist wars. However great the difficulties in the way of the revolution, whatever temporary defeats it may sustain, however high the waves of the counter-revolution, the ultimate victory of the proletariat is assured.

To bring about the victory of the world-wide proletarian revolution it is essential that there should be absolute and mutual trust, the most intimate brotherly alliance, and the highest possible cohesion of the revolutionary activities of the working class in the more advanced lands.

These conditions cannot be realized without making it a matter of principle to break off relations with and to wage a pitiless struggle against that bourgeois perversion of socialism which is dominant in the leading official social democratic and socialist parties.

In this perversion there is displayed, on the one hand, the trend of opportunism and jingo socialism, of that which calls itself socialism but is in fact jingoism, the mask of those who defend the predatory interests of their own national bourgeoisie under colour of the false watchword of the defence of the fatherland—a watchword applied both generally, and specifically to the imperialist war of 1914 to 1918. This trend originated because the seizure of colonies and the oppression of weak nations by the advanced capitalist States has enabled the bourgeoisies of these countries, out of the vast gains which have accrued from such plunderings, to offer a privileged position to the more highly skilled members of the proletariat, and thus in effect to buy them in peace time by giving them an advantageous petty-bourgeois status; at the same time the bourgeoisie takes into its service the leaders of this stratum. The opportunists and the jingo socialists, having become the servants of the bourgeoisie, are the direct class enemies of the proletariat, especially today, when in alliance with the capitalists they are endeavouring by force of arms to crush the revolutionary movement of the proletariat in their own and in other lands. . . .

Avoiding the mistakes made by the Commune of Paris, the Soviet Power in Russia first seized the State Bank, and then nationalized the private commercial banks, and formed a union of nationalized banks, and of their accumulated funds, merging them in the State Bank. In this way was created the framework of the People's Bank of the Soviet Republic. Thus, from being a centre for the economic dominion of financial capital and an instrument for the political rule of the exploiters, the bank became an instrument of the workers' power and a lever to promote economic transformation. In order to carry to its logical conclusion the work begun by the Soviet Power, the Russian Communist Party lays especial stress upon the following principles:

1. The monopolization of all banking business in the hands of the Soviet State.

2. The radical transformation and simplification of banking operations, so that the whole banking system shall become an apparatus for the unified book-keeping of the Soviet Republic. In proportion as the organization of a purposive social economy is achieved, this will lead to the disappearance of banks, and to their conversion into the central book-keeping establishment of communist society.

In the opening stages of the transition from capitalism to communism, and prior to the organization of a fully developed system for the communist production and distribution of goods, the abolition of money is impossible. In these circumstances, the bourgeois elements of the population continue to use for speculation, profit-making, and the plundering of the workers, the monetary tokens that still remain in private ownership. Upon this basis of the nationalization of banking, the Russian Communist Party endeavours to promote a series of measures favouring a moneyless system of account keeping, and paving the way for the abolition of money. These are: the compulsory deposit of money in the People's Bank; the introduction of budget-books; the replacement of money by written or printed tokens, by tickets giving the right to the receipt of goods but available for short periods only; etc. . . .

Vladimir Ilyich Ulyanov (Lenin) (1870–1924)

The founder of the Soviet Union, Lenin was born at Simbirsk (now Oulianovsk). He was one of the leaders of the 1905

From *Essential Works of Lenin,* edited by Henry M. Christman, New York, 1966.

revolution; exiled from Russia, he returned in 1917 in a sealed train from Zurich that crossed wartime Germany. He signed the peace treaty of Brest–Litovsk with the Germans in 1918 and until his death was the leading Marxist theoretician and head of State. His tomb in the Kremlin is visited by millions annually. His many books include: Materialism and Empiro-criticism *and* Imperialism, Final Stage of Capitalism.

What Is To Be Done

THE WORKING CLASS AS CHAMPION OF DEMOCRACY

We have seen that the carrying on of wide political agitation, and consequently the organization of all-sided political exposures, is an absolutely necessary and *paramount* task of activity, that is, if that activity is to be truly Social-Democratic. We arrived at this conclusion *solely* on the grounds of the pressing needs of the working class for political knowledge and political training. But this presentation of the question is too narrow, for it ignores the general democratic tasks of Social-Democracy in general, and of modern Russian Social-Democracy in particular. In order to explain the situation more concretely we shall approach the subject from an aspect that is "nearer" to the Economist, namely, from the practical aspect. "Everyone agrees" that it is necessary to develop the political consciousness of the working class. But the question arises, how is that to be done? What must be done to bring this about? The economic struggle merely brings the workers "up against" questions concerning the attitude of the government towards the working class. Consequently, *however much we may try* to give the "economic struggle itself a political character" *we shall never be able* to develop the political consciousness of the workers (to the degree of Social-Democratic consciousness) by confining ourselves to the economic struggle, for *the limits of this task are too narrow*. . . .

Class political consciousness can be brought to the workers *only from without,* that is, only outside of the economic struggle, outside of the sphere of relations between workers and employers. The sphere from which alone it is possible to obtain this knowledge is the sphere of relationships between *all* the various classes and strata and the state and the government—the sphere of the interrelations between *all* the various classes. For that reason, the reply to the question: what must be done in order to bring political knowledge to the workers? cannot be merely the one which, in the majority of cases, the practical workers, especially those who are inclined towards Economism, usually content themselves with, i.e., "go among the workers." To bring political knowledge to the *workers* the Social-Democrats must *go among all classes of the population,* must dispatch units of their army *in all directions.*

We deliberately select this awkward formula, we deliberately express ourselves in a simple, forcible way, not because we desire to indulge in paradoxes, but in order to "stimulate" the Economists to take up their tasks which they unpardonably ignore, to make them understand the difference between trade union and Social-Democratic politics, which they refuse to understand. Therefore, we beg the reader not to get excited, but to listen patiently to the end.

Take the type of Social-Democratic circle that has been most widespread during the past few years, and examine its work. It has "contacts with the workers," it issues leaflets —in which abuses in the factories, the government's partiality towards the capitalists and the tyranny of the police are strongly condemned—and it rests content with this. At meetings of workers the discussions never, or rarely, go beyond the limits of these subjects. Lectures and discussions on the history of the revolutionary movement, on questions of the home and foreign policy of our government, on questions of the economic evolution of Russia and of Europe, and the position of the various classes in modern society, etc., are extremely rare. Of systematically acquiring and extending contact with other classes of society, no one even dreams. The ideal leader, as the majority of the members of such circles picture him, is something in the nature of a trade union secretary rather than a Socialist political leader. Any trade union secretary, an English one for instance, helps the workers to conduct the economic struggle, helps to expose factory abuses, explains the injustice of the laws and of measures which hamper the freedom to strike and the freedom to picket (i.e., to warn all and sundry that a strike is proceeding at a certain factory), explains the partiality of arbitration court judges who belong to the bourgeois classes, etc., etc. In a word, every trade union secretary conducts and helps to conduct "the economic struggle against the employers and the government." It cannot be too strongly insisted that *this is not* enough to constitute Social-Democracy. The Social-Democrat's ideal should not be a trade union secretary, but *a tribune of the people*, able to react to every manifestation of tyranny and oppression, no matter where it takes place, no matter what stratum or class of the people it affects; he must be able to group all these manifestations into a single picture of police violence and capitalist exploitation; he must be able to take advantage of every petty event in order to explain his socialistic convictions and his Social-Democratic demands *to all*, in order to explain to *all* and everyone the world-historic significance of the struggle for the emancipation of the proletariat. Compare, for example, a leader like Robert Knight (the celebrated secretary and leader of the Boiler-Makers' Society, one of the most powerful trade unions in England) with Wilhelm Liebknecht, and then take the contrasts that Martynov draws in his controversy with *Iskra*. You will see—I am running through Martynov's article—that Robert Knight engaged more in "calling the masses to certain concrete actions," while Liebknecht engaged more in "the revolutionary explanation of the whole of modern society, or various manifestations of it"; that Robert Knight "formulated the immediate demands of the proletariat and pointed to the manner in which they can be achieved," whereas Wilhelm Liebknecht, while doing this, "simultaneously guided the activities of various opposition strata," "dictated to them a positive program of action"; that it was precisely Robert Knight who strove "as far as possible to give the economic struggle itself a political character" and was excellently able "to submit to the government concrete demands promising certain palpable results," while Liebknecht engaged more in "one-sided exposures"; that Robert Knight attached more significance to the "forward march of the drab, every-day struggle," while Liebknecht attached more significance to the "propaganda of brilliant and finished ideas"; that Liebknecht converted the paper he was directing into "an organ of revolutionary opposition exposing the present system and particularly the political conditions which came into conflict with the interests of the most varied strata of the population," whereas Robert

Knight "worked for the cause of labor in close organic contact with the proletarian struggle"—if by "close and organic contact" is meant the subservience to spontaneity which we studied above from the example of Krichevsky and Martynov—and "restricted the sphere of his influence," convinced, of course, as is Martynov, that "by that he intensified that influence." In a word, you will see that *de facto* Martynov reduces Social-Democracy to the level of trade unionism, and he does this, of course, not because he does not desire the good of Social-Democracy, but simply because he is a little too much in a hurry to make Plekhanov more profound, instead of taking the trouble to understand him.

Let us return, however, to the elucidation of our thesis. We said that a Social-Democrat, if he really believes it is necessary to develop the all-sided political consciousness of the proletariat, must "go among all classes of the people." This gives rise to the questions: How is this to be done? Have we enough forces to do this? Is there a base for such work among all the other classes? Will this not mean a retreat, or lead to a retreat, from the class point of view? We shall deal with these questions.

We must "go among all classes of the people" as theoreticians, as propagandists, as agitators and as organizers. No one doubts that the theoretical work of Social-Democrats should be directed towards studying all the features of the social and political position of the various classes. But extremely little is done in this direction as compared with the work that is done in studying the features of factory life. In the committees and circles, you will meet men who are immersed, say, in the study of some special branch of the metal industry, but you will hardly ever find members of organizations (obliged, as often happens, for some reason or other to give up practical work) especially engaged in the collection of material concerning some pressing question of social and political life which could serve as a means for conducting Social-Democratic work among other strata of the population. In speaking of the lack of training of the majority of present-day leaders of the labor movement, we cannot refrain from mentioning the point about training in this connection also, for it too is bound up with the "economic" conception of "close organic contact with the proletarian struggle." The principal thing, of course, is *propaganda and agitation* among all strata of the people. The West European Social-Democrats find their work in this field facilitated by the calling of public meetings, to which *all* are free to go, and by the parliament, in which they speak to the representatives of *all* classes. We have neither a parliament nor the freedom to call meetings, nevertheless we are able to arrange meetings of workers who desire to listen to *a Social-Democrat*. We must also find ways and means of calling meetings of representatives of all classes of the population that desire to listen to a *democrat;* for he who forgets that "the Communists support every revolutionary movement," that we are obliged for that reason to expound and emphasize *general democratic tasks before the whole people,* without for a moment concealing our socialistic convictions, is not a Social-Democrat. He who forgets his obligation to *be in advance of everybody* in bringing up, sharpening and solving *every* general democratic problem is not a Social-Democrat.

"But everybody agrees with this!"—the impatient reader will exclaim—and the new instructions given by the last Congress of the League to the editorial board of *Rabocheye Dyelo* say: "All events of social and political life that affect the proletariat either directly as a special class or *as the vanguard of all the revolutionary forces in the struggle for freedom* should serve as subjects for political propaganda and agitation." (*Two Congresses,* our italics.) Yes, these are very true and very good words and we would be satisfied if *Rabocheye Dyelo understood them and if it refrained from saying in the next breath things that are the very opposite of them.*

Ponder over the following piece of Martynov reasoning. On page 40 he says that *Iskra's* tactics of exposing abuses are one-sided, that "however much we may spread distrust and hatred towards the government, we shall not achieve our aim until we have succeeded in developing sufficiently active social energy for its overthrow."

This, it may be said in parentheses, is the concern, with which we are already familiar, for increasing the activity of the masses, while at the same time striving to restrict one's own activity. This is not the point we are now discussing, however. Martynov, therefore, speaks of *revolutionary* energy ("for overthrowing"). But what conclusion does he arrive at? As in ordinary times, various social strata inevitably march separately.

> In view of that, it is clear that we Social-Democrats cannot simultaneously guide the activities of various opposition strata, we cannot dictate to them a positive program of action, we cannot point out to them in what manner

they can fight for their daily interests. . . . The liberal strata
will themselves take care of the active struggle for their
immediate interests and this struggle will bring them up
against our political regime.

Thus, having commenced by speaking of revolutionary
energy, of the active struggle for the overthrow of the
autocracy, Martynov immediately turned towards trade
union energy and active struggle for immediate interests!
It goes without saying that we cannot guide the struggle of
the students, liberals, etc., for their "immediate interests,"
but this is not the point we are arguing about, most worthy
Economist! The point we are discussing is the possible and
necessary participation of various social strata in the overthrow of the autocracy; not only are we able, but it is our
duty, to guide *these* "activities of the various opposition
strata" if we desire to be the "vanguard." Not only will
the students and our liberals, etc., themselves take care of
"the struggle that will bring them up against our political
regime"; the police and the officials of the autocratic government will see to this more than anyone else. But if "we"
desire to be advanced democrats, we must make it our
business to *stimulate* in the minds of those who are dis-
satisfied only with university, or only with Zemstvo, etc.,
conditions the idea that the whole political system is worthless. We must take upon ourselves the task of organizing
a universal political struggle under the leadership of *our
Party* in such a manner as to obtain all the support possible
of all opposition strata for the struggle and for our Party.
We must train our Social-Democratic practical workers
to become political leaders, able to guide all the manifestations of this universal struggle, able at the right time to
"dictate a positive program of action" for the discontented
students, for the discontented Zemstvo Councillors, for the
discontented religious sects, for the offended elementary
school teachers, etc., etc. For that reason, Martynov's assertion—that "with regard to these we can come forward
merely in *the negative* role of exposers of abuses . . . we
can *only* [our italics] dissipate the hopes they have in various government commissions"—*is absolutely wrong*. By
saying this Martynov shows that *he absolutely fails to understand* the role the revolutionary "vanguard" must really
play. If the reader bears this in mind, the *real sense* of
the following concluding remarks by Martynov will be
clear to him:

Iskra is the organ of the revolutionary opposition which
exposes the abuses of our system, particularly political

abuses, in so far as they affect the interests of the most diverse classes of the population. We, however, are working and will continue to work for the cause of labor in close organic contact with the proletarian struggle. By restricting the sphere of our influence, we intensify that influence.

The true sense of this conclusion is as follows: *Iskra* desires to elevate working class trade union politics (to which, owing to misunderstanding, lack of training, or by conviction, our practical workers frequently confine themselves) to Social-Democratic politics, whereas *Rabocheye Dyelo* desires to *degrade* Social-Democratic politics to trade union politics. And while doing this, they assure the world that these two positions are "quite compatible in the common cause." *O! Sancta simplicitas!*

To proceed. Have we sufficient forces to be able to direct our propaganda and agitation among *all* classes of the population? Of course we have. Our Economists are frequently inclined to deny this. They lose sight of the gigantic progress our movement has made from (approximately) 1894 to 1901. Like real *"khvostists,"* they frequently live in the distant past, in the period of the beginning of the movement. At that time, indeed, we had astonishingly few forces, and it was perfectly natural and legitimate then to resolve to go exclusively among the workers, and severely condemn any deviation from this. The whole task then was to consolidate our position in the working class. At the present time, however, gigantic forces have been attracted to the movement; the best representatives of the young generation of the educated classes are coming over to us; all over the country there are people compelled to live in the provinces, who have taken part in the movement in the past and desire to do so now, who are gravitating towards Social-Democracy (in 1894 you could count the Social-Democrats on your fingers). One of the principal political and organizational shortcomings of our movement is that we are *unable* to utilize all these forces and give them appropriate work (we shall deal with this in detail in the next chapter). The overwhelming majority of these forces entirely lack the opportunity of "going among the workers," so there are no grounds for fearing that we shall deflect forces from our main cause. And in order to be able to provide the workers with real universal and live political knowledge, we must have "our own men," Social-Democrats, everywhere, among all social strata, and in all positions from which we can learn the inner springs of our state mechanism. Such men are required for propaganda and agitation, but in a still larger measure for organization.

Is there scope for activity among all classes of the population? Those who fail to see this also lag behind the spontaneous awakening of the masses as far as class consciousness is concerned. The labor movement has aroused and is continuing to arouse discontent in some, hopes for support for the opposition in others, and the consciousness of the intolerableness and inevitable downfall of autocracy in still others. We would be "politicians" and Social-Democrats only in name (as very often happens), if we failed to realize that our task is to utilize every manifestation of discontent, and to collect and utilize every grain of even rudimentary protest. This is quite apart from the fact that many millions of the peasantry, handicraftsmen, petty artisans, etc., always listen eagerly to the preachings of any Social-Democrat who is at all intelligent. Is there a single class of the population in which no individuals, groups or circles are to be found who are discontented with the state of tyranny and, therefore, accessible to the propaganda of Social-Democrats as the spokesmen of the most pressing general democratic needs? To those who desire to have a clear idea of what the political agitation of a Social-Democrat *among all* classes and strata of the population should be like, we would point to *political exposures* in the broad sense of the word as the principal (but of course not the sole) form of this agitation.

We must "arouse in every section of the population that is at all enlightened a passion for *political* exposure," I wrote in my article "Where to Begin?" (*Iskra*, No. 4, May 1901), with which I shall deal in greater detail later.

> We must not allow ourselves to be discouraged by the fact that the voice of political exposure is still feeble, rare and timid. This is not because of a general submission to political despotism, but because those who are able and ready to expose have no tribune from which to speak, because there is no audience to listen eagerly to and approve of what the orators say, and because the latter do not see anywhere among the people forces to whom it would be worth while directing their complaint against the "omnipotent" Russian government. . . . We are now in a position, and it is our duty, to set up a tribune for the national exposure of the tsarist government. That tribune must be a Social-Democratic paper.

The ideal audience for these political exposures is the working class, which is first and foremost in need of universal and live political knowledge, which is most capable of converting this knowledge into active struggle, even if it does not promise "palpable results." The only platform from which *public* exposures can be made is an all-Russian newspaper. "Without a political organ, a political movement deserving that name is inconceivable in modern Europe." In this connection Russia must undoubtedly be included in modern Europe. The press has long ago become a power in our country, otherwise the government would not spend tens of thousands of rubles to bribe it, and to subsidize the Katkovs and Meshcherskys. And it is no novelty in autocratic Russia for the underground press to break through the wall of censorship and *compel* the legal and conservative press to speak openly of it. This was the case in the 'seventies and even in the 'fifties. How much broader and deeper are now the strata of the people willing to read the illegal underground press, and to learn from it "how to live and how to die," to use the expression of the worker who sent a letter to *Iskra*. (No. 7.) Political exposures are as much a declaration of war against the *government* as economic exposures are a declaration of war against the employers. And the wider and more powerful this campaign of exposure is, the more numerous and determined the social *class*, which has *declared war in order to commence the war*, will be, the greater will be the moral significance of this declaration of war. Hence, political exposures in themselves serve as a powerful instrument for *disintegrating* the system we oppose, the means for diverting from the enemy his casual or temporary allies, the means for spreading enmity and distrust among those who permanently share power with the autocracy.

Only a party that will *organize* real, *public* exposures can become the vanguard of the revolutionary forces in our time. The word "public" has a very profound meaning. The overwhelming majority of the non-working class exposures (and in order to become the vanguard, we must attract other classes) are sober politicians and cool businessmen. They know perfectly well how dangerous it is to "complain" even against a minor official, let alone against the "omnipotent" Russian government. And they will come *to us* with their complaints only when they see that these complaints really have effect, and when they see that we represent a *political* force. In order to become this political force in the eyes of outsiders, much persistent and stubborn work is required to *raise* our own consciousness, initiative and energy. For this, it is not sufficient to stick the label "vanguard" on rearguard theory and practice.

But if we have to undertake the organization of the real, public exposure of the government, in what way will the class character of our movement be expressed?—the over-zealous advocates of "close organic contact with the proletarian struggle" will ask us. The reply is: in that we *Social-Democrats* will *organize* these public exposures; in that all the questions that are brought up by the agitation will be explained in the spirit of Social-Democracy, without any concessions to deliberate or unconscious distortions of Marxism: in the fact that *the Party* will carry on this universal political agitation, uniting into one inseparable whole the pressure upon the government in the name of the whole people, the revolutionary training of the proletariat—while preserving its political independence—the guidance of the economic struggle of the working class, the utilization of all its spontaneous conflicts with its exploiters, which rouse and bring into our camp increasing numbers of the proletariat. . . .

CONCLUSION

The history of Russian Social-Democracy can be divided into three distinct periods:

The first period covers about ten years, approximately the years 1884 to 1894. This was the period of the rise and consolidation of the theory and program of Social-Democracy. The number of adherents of the new tendency in Russia could be counted in units. Social-Democracy existed without a labor movement; it was, as it were, in its period of gestation.

The second period covers three or four years—1894–98. In this period Social-Democracy appeared in the world as a social movement, as the rising of the masses of the people, as a political party. This is the period of its childhood and adolescence. The fight against Narodism and going among the workers infected the intelligentsia wholesale like an epidemic, and the workers were equally infected by strikes. The movement made enormous strides. The majority of the leaders were very young people who had by no means reached the "age of thirty-five" which to N. Mikhailovsky appears to be a sort of natural borderline. Owing to their youth, they proved to be untrained for practical work and they left the scene with astonishing rapidity. But in the majority of cases the scope of their work was extremely wide. Many of them began their revolutionary thinking as Narodovolists. Nearly all of them in their early youth enthusiastically worshipped the terrorist heroes. It was a great wrench to abandon the captivating impressions of these heroic traditions and it was accompanied by the breaking off of personal relationships with people who were determined to remain loyal to *Narodnaya Volya* and for whom the young Social-Democrats had profound respect. The struggle compelled them to educate themselves, to read the illegal literature of all tendencies and to study closely the questions of legal Narodism. Trained in this struggle, Social-Democrats went into the labor movement without "for a moment" forgetting the theories of Marxism which illumined their path or the task of overthrowing the autocracy. The formation of the Party in the spring of 1898 was the most striking and at the same time the *last* act of the Social-Democrats in this period.

The third period, as we have seen, began in 1897 and definitely replaced the second period in 1898 (1898–?). This was the period of dispersion, dissolution and vacillation. In the period of adolescence the youth's voice breaks. And so, in this period, the voice of Russian Social-Democracy began to break, began to strike a false note—on the one hand, in the productions of Messrs. Struve and Prokopovich, Bulgarkov and Berdyaev, on the other hand, in the productions of V. I——n and R. M., B. Krichevsky and Martynov. But it was only the leaders who wandered about separately and went back; the movement itself continued to grow, and it advanced with enormous strides. The proletarian struggle spread to new strata of the workers over the whole of Russia and at the same time indirectly stimulated the revival of the democratic spirit among the students and among other strata of the population. The consciousness of the leaders, however, yielded to the breadth and power of the spontaneous rising; among Social-Democrats, a different streak predominated—a streak of Party workers who had been trained almost exclusively on "legal Marxian" literature, and the more the spontaneity of the masses called for consciousness, the more the inadequacy of this literature was felt. The leaders not only lagged behind in regard to theory ("freedom of criticism") and practice ("primitiveness"), but even tried to justify their backwardness by all sorts of high-flown arguments. Social-Democracy was degraded to the level of trade unionism in legal literature by the Brentano-ists and in illegal literature by the *khvostists*. The program of the *Credo* began to be put into operation, especially when the "primitiveness" of the Social-Democrats caused a revival of non-Social-Democratic revolutionary tendencies.

When this third period will come to an end and the fourth begin we do not know (at all events it is already heralded by many signs). We are passing from the sphere of history to the sphere of the present partly to the sphere of the future. But we firmly believe that the fourth period will see the consolidation of militant Marxism, that Russian Social-Democracy will emerge from the crisis in the full strength of manhood, that the place of the rearguard of opportunists will be taken by a genuine vanguard of the most revolutionary class.

In the sense of calling for such a "new guard" and summing up, as it were, all that has been expounded above, my reply to the question: "What is to be done?" can be put briefly: Liquidate the Third Period.

Imperialism, the Highest Stage of Capitalism

CHAPTER I
CONCENTRATION OF PRODUCTION AND MONOPOLIES

The enormous growth of industry and the remarkably rapid process of concentration of production in ever-larger enterprises represent one of the most characteristic features of capitalism. Modern censuses of production give complete and exact information on this process.

In Germany, for example, for every 1,000 industrial enterprises, large enterprises, i.e., those employing more than 50 workers, numbered three in 1882; six in 1895; nine in 1907; and out of every 100 workers employed, this group of enterprises, on the dates mentioned, employed 22, 30 and 37 respectively. Concentration of production, however, is much more intense than the concentration of workers, since labor in the large enterprises is much more productive. This is shown by the figures available on steam and electric motors. If we take what in Germany is called industry in the broad sense of the term, that is, including commerce, transport, etc., we get the following picture: Large-scale enterprises: 30,588 out of a total of 3,265,623, that is to say, 0.9 per cent. These large-scale enterprises employ 5,700,000 workers out of a total of 14,400,000, that is, 39.4 per cent; they use 6,600,000 steam horse power out of a total of 8,800,000, that is, 75.3 per cent, and 1,200,000 kilowatts of electricity out of a total of 1,500,000, that is, 77.2 per cent.

Less than one-hundredth of the total enterprises utilize *more than three-fourths* of the steam and electric power! Two million nine hundred and seventy thousand small enterprises (employing up to five workers), representing 91 per cent of the total, utilize only 7 per cent of the steam and electric power. Tens of thousands of large-scale enterprises are everything; millions of small ones are nothing.

In 1907, there were in Germany 586 establishments employing one thousand and more workers. They employed nearly one-tenth (1,380,000) of the total number of workers employed in industry and utilized *almost one-third* (32 per cent) of the total steam and electric power employed. As we shall see, money capital and the banks made this superiority of a handful of the largest enterprises still more overwhelming, in the most literal sense of the word, since millions of small, medium, and even some big "masters" are in fact in complete subjection to some hundreds of millionaire financiers.

In another advanced country of modern capitalism, the United States, the growth of the concentration of production is still greater. Here statistics single out industry in the narrow sense of the word, and group enterprises according to the value of their annual output. In 1904 in the United States, large-scale enterprises with an annual output of one million dollars and over numbered 1,900 (out of 216,180, that is, 0.9 per cent). These employed 1,400,000 workers (out of 5,500,000, i.e., 25.6 per cent) and their combined annual output was valued at $5,600,000,000 (out of $14,800,000,000, i.e., 38 per cent). Five years later, in

1909, the corresponding figures were: Large-scale enterprises: 3,060 (out of 268,491, i.e., 1.1 per cent); employing: 2,000,000 workers (out of 6,600,000, i.e., 30.5 per cent); producing: $9,000,000,000 (out of $20,700,000,000, i.e., 43.8 per cent).

Almost half the total production of all the enterprises of the country was carried on by a *hundredth* part of those enterprises! These 3,000 giant enterprises embrace 268 branches of industry. From this it can be seen that, at a certain stage of its development, concentration itself, as it were, leads right to monopoly; for a score or so of giant enterprises can easily arrive at an agreement, while on the other hand the difficulty of competition and the tendency towards monopoly arise from the very dimensions of the enterprises. This transformation of competition into monopoly is one of the most important—if not the most important—phenomena of modern capitalist economy, and we must deal with it in greater detail. But first we must clear up one possible misunderstanding.

American statistics say: 3,000 giant enterprises in 250 branches of industry, as if there were only a dozen large-scale enterprises for each branch of industry.

But this is not the case. Not in every branch of industry are there large-scale enterprises; and, moreover, a very important feature of capitalism in its highest stage of development is the so-called *combine,* that is to say, the grouping in a single enterprise of different branches of industry, which either represent the consecutive stages in the working up of raw materials (for example, the smelting of iron ore into pig iron, the conversion of pig iron into steel, and then, perhaps, the manufacture of steel goods)—or are auxiliary to one another (for example, the utilization of waste or of by-products, the manufacture of packing materials, etc.).

> . . . Combination, [writes Hilferding,] levels out the fluctuations of trade and therefore assures to the combined enterprises a more stable rate of profit. Secondly, combination has the effect of eliminating trading. Thirdly, it has the effect of rendering possible technical improvements and, consequently, the acquisition of super-profits over and above those obtained by the "pure," [i.e., non-combined,] enterprises. Fourthly, it strengthens the position of the combined enterprises compared with that of "pure" enterprises, it increases their competitive power in periods of serious depression when the fall in prices of raw materials does not keep pace with the fall in prices of manufactured articles.

The German bourgeois economist, Heymann, who has written a book especially on "mixed," that is, combined, enterprises in the German iron industry, says: "Non-combined enterprises perish, crushed by the high price of raw material and the low price of the finished product." Thus we get the following picture:

> There remain, on the one hand, the great coal companies, producing millions of tons yearly, strongly organized in their coal syndicate, and closely connected with them the big steel plants and their steel syndicate; and these great enterprises, producing 400,000 tons of steel per annum, with correspondingly extensive coal, ore and blast furnace operations, as well as the manufacturing of finished goods, employing 10,000 workers quartered in company houses, sometimes owning their own wharves and railways, are today the standard type of German iron and steel plant. And concentration continues. Individual enterprises are becoming larger and larger. An ever increasing number of enterprises in one given industry, or in several different industries, join together in giant combined enterprises. In the German mining industry, the truth of the teachings of Karl Marx on the concentration of capital is definitely proved, at any rate in a country where it is protected by tariffs and freight rates. The German mining industry is ripe for expropriation.

Such is the conclusion which a conscientious bourgeois economist, and such are exceptional, had to arrive at. It must be noted that he seems to place Germany in a special category because her industries are protected by high tariffs. But the concentration of industry and the formation of monopolist, manufacturers' combines, cartels, syndicates, etc., could only be accelerated by these circumstances. It is extremely important to note that in free trade England, concentration *also* leads to monopoly, although somewhat later and perhaps in another form. Professor Hermann Levy, in his special investigation entitled *Monopolies, Cartels and Trusts,* based on data on British economic development, writes as follows:

> In Great Britain it is the size of the enterprise and its capacity which harbor a monopolist tendency. This, for one thing, is due to the fact that the great investment of capital per enterprise, once the concentration movement has commenced, gives rise to increasing demands for new capital for the new enterprises and thereby renders their launching more difficult. Moreover (and this seems to us to be the more important point), every new enterprise that wants to keep pace with the gigantic enterprises that have

arisen on the basis of the process of concentration produces such an enormous quantity of surplus goods that it can only dispose of them either by being able to sell them profitably as a result of an enormous increase in demand or by immediately forcing down prices to a level that would be unprofitable both for itself and for the monopoly combines.

In England, unlike other countries where the protective tariffs facilitate the formation of cartels, monopolist alliances of *entrepreneurs,* cartels and trusts, arise in the majority of cases only when the number of competing enterprises is reduced to a "couple of dozen or so." "Here the influence of the concentration movement on the formation of large industrial monopolies in a whole sphere of industry stands out with crystal clarity."

Fifty years ago, when Marx was writing *Capital,* free competition appeared to most economists to be a "natural law." The official scientists tried, by a conspiracy of silence, to kill the works of Marx, which by a theoretical and historical analysis of capitalism showed that free competition gives rise to the concentration of production, which, in turn, at a certain stage of development, leads to monopoly. Today, monopoly has become a fact. The economists are writing mountains of books in which they describe the diverse manifestations of monopoly, and continue to declare in chorus that "Marxism is refuted." But facts are stubborn things, as the English proverb says, and they have to be reckoned with, whether we like it or not. The facts show that differences between capitalist countries, e.g., in the matter of protection or free trade, only give rise to insignificant variations in the form of monopolies or in the moment of their appearance, and that the rise of monopolies, as the result of the concentration of production, is a general and fundamental law of the present stage of development of capitalism.

For Europe, the time when the new capitalism was *definitely* substituted for the old can be established fairly precisely: it was the beginning of the twentieth century. In one of the latest compilations on the history of the "formation of monopolies," we read:

A few isolated examples of capitalist monopoly could be cited from the period preceding 1860; in these could be discerned the embryo of the forms that are common today; but all undoubtedly represent pre-history. The real beginning of modern monopoly goes back, at the earliest, to the 'sixties. The first important period of development of monopoly commenced with the international industrial depression of the 'seventies and lasted until the beginning of the 'nineties. . . . If we examine the question on a European scale, we will find that the development of free competition reached its apex in the 'sixties and 'seventies. Then it was that England completed the construction of its old style capitalist organization. In Germany, this organization had entered into a decisive struggle with handicraft and domestic industry, and had begun to create for itself its own forms of existence. . . .

The great revolutionization commenced with the crash of 1873, or rather, the depression which followed it and which, with hardly discernible interruptions in the early 'eighties and the unusually violent, but short-lived boom about 1889, marks twenty-two years of European economic history. During the short boom of 1889–90, the system of cartels was widely resorted to in order to take advantage of the favorable business conditions. An ill-considered policy drove prices still higher than would have been the case otherwise and nearly all these cartels perished ingloriously in the smash. Another five-year period of bad trade and low prices followed, but a new spirit reigned in industry; the depression was no longer regarded as something to be taken for granted: it was regarded as nothing more than a pause before another boom.

The cartel movement entered its second epoch. Instead of being a transitory phenomenon, the cartels became one of the foundations of economic life. They are winning one field after another, primarily, the raw materials industry. At the beginning of the 'nineties the cartel system had already acquired—in the organization of the coke syndicate on the model of which the coal syndicate was later formed—a cartel technique which could hardly be improved. For the first time the great boom at the close of the nineteenth century and the crisis of 1900–03 occurred entirely—in the mining and iron industries at least—under the aegis of the cartels. And while at that time it appeared to be something novel, now the general public takes it for granted that large spheres of economy have been, as a general rule, systematically removed from the realm of free competition.

Thus, the principal stages in the history of monopolies are the following: (1) 1860–70, the highest stage, the apex of development of free competition; monopoly is in the barely discernible, embryonic stage. (2) After the crisis of 1873, a wide zone of development of cartels; but they are still the exception. They are not yet durable. They are still a transitory phenomenon. (3) The boom at the end of the nineteenth century and the crisis of 1900–03. Cartels become one of the foundations of the whole of economic life. Capitalism has been transformed into imperialism.

CHAPTER VI
THE DIVISION OF THE WORLD AMONG THE GREAT POWERS

In his book, *The Territorial Development of the European Colonies,* A. Supan, the geographer, briefly sums up this development at the end of the nineteenth century, as follows:

PERCENTAGE OF TERRITORIES BELONGING TO THE EUROPEAN COLONIAL POWERS (INCLUDING UNITED STATES)

	1876	1900	Increase or Decrease
Africa	10.8	90.4	+79.6
Polynesia	56.8	98.9	+42.1
Asia	51.5	56.6	+ 5.1
Australia	100.0	100.0	—
America	27.5	27.2	— 0.3

"The characteristic feature of this period," he concludes. "is, therefore, the division of Africa and Polynesia."

As there are no unoccupied territories—that is, territories that do not belong to any state—in Asia and America, Mr. Supan's conclusion must be carried further and we must say that the characteristic feature of this period is the final partition of the globe—not in the sense that a *new partition* is impossible—on the contrary, new partitions are possible and inevitable—but in the sense that the colonial policy of the capitalist countries has *completed* the seizure of the unoccupied territories on our planet. For the first time the world is completely shared out, so that in the future *only re-division* is possible; territories can only pass from one "owner" to another, instead of passing as un-owned territory to an "owner."

Hence, we are passing through a peculiar period of world colonial policy, which is closely associated with the "latest phase of capitalist development," with finance capital. For this reason, it is essential to deal in detail with the facts, in order to ascertain exactly what distinguishes this period from those preceding it, and what the present situation is. In the first place, two questions of fact arise here. Is an intensification of colonial policy, an intensification of the struggle for colonies, observed in this period of finance capital? And how, in this respect, is the world divided at the present time?

The American writer, Morris, in his book *The History of Colonization,* has made an attempt to compile data on the colonial possessions of Great Britain, France and Germany during different periods of the nineteenth century. The following is a brief summary of the results he has obtained:

COLONIAL POSSESSIONS

	Great Britain		France		Germany	
	Area *(million sq. miles)*	Popula- tion *(millions)*	Area *(million sq. miles)*	Popula- tion *(millions)*	Area *(million sq. miles)*	Popula- tion *(millions)*
1815–30..	?	126.4	0.02	0.5	—	—
1860.....	2.5	145.1	0.2	3.4	—	—
1880.....	7.7	267.9	0.7	7.5	—	—
1899.....	9.3	309.0	3.7	56.4	1.0	14.7

For Great Britain, the period of the enormous expansion of colonial conquests is that between 1860 and 1880, and it was also very considerable in the last twenty years of the nineteenth century. For France and Germany this period falls precisely in these last twenty years. We saw above that the apex of pre-monopoly capitalist development, of capitalism in which free competition was predominant, was reached in the sixties and seventies of the last century. We now see that it is *precisely following that period* that the "boom" in colonial annexations begins, and that the struggle for a territorial division of the world becomes extraordinarily keen. It is beyond doubt, therefore, that the transition of capitalism to monopoly capitalism, to finance capitalism, is *connected* with the intensification of the struggle for the partition of the world.

Hobson, in his work on imperialism, marks the years 1884–1900 as the period of the intensification of the colonial "expansion" of the chief European states. According to his estimate, Great Britain during these years acquired 3,700,000 square miles of territory with a population of 57,000,000 inhabitants; France acquired 3,600,000 square miles with a population of 36,500,000 inhabitants; Germany, 1,000,000 square miles with a population of

16,700,000 inhabitants; Belgium, 900,000 square miles with 30,000,000 inhabitants; Portugal, 800,000 square miles with 9,000,000 inhabitants. The quest for colonies by all the capitalist states at the end of the nineteenth century, and particularly since the 1880's, is a commonly known fact in the history of diplomacy and of foreign affairs.

When free competition in Great Britain was at its height, i.e., between 1840 and 1860, the leading British bourgeois politicians were opposed to colonial policy and were of the opinion that the liberation of the colonies and their complete separation from Great Britain was inevitable and desirable. M. Beer, in an article, "Modern British Imperialism," published in 1898, shows that in 1852, Disraeli, a statesman generally inclined towards imperialism, declared: "The colonies are millstones round our necks." But at the end of the nineteenth century the heroes of the hour were Cecil Rhodes and Joseph Chamberlain, open advocates of imperialism, who applied the imperialist policy in the most cynical manner.

It is not without interest to observe that even at that time these leading British bourgeois politicians fully appreciated the connection between what might be called the purely economic and the politico-social roots of modern imperialism. Chamberlain advocated imperialism by calling it a "true, wise and economical policy," and he pointed particularly to the German, American and Belgian competition which Great Britain was encountering in the world market. Salvation lies in monopolies, said the capitalists as they formed cartels, syndicates and trusts. Salvation lies in monopolies, echoed the political leaders of the bourgeoisie, hastening to appropriate the parts of the world not yet shared out. The journalist, Stead, relates the following remarks uttered by his close friend Cecil Rhodes in 1895 regarding his imperialist ideas:

> I was in the East End of London yesterday and attended a meeting of the unemployed. I listened to the wild speeches, which were just a cry for "bread," "bread," "bread," and on my way home I pondered over the scene and I became more than ever convinced of the importance of imperialism. . . . My cherished idea is a solution for the social problem, i.e., in order to save the 40,000,000 inhabitants of the United Kingdom from a bloody civil war, we colonial statesmen must acquire new lands for settling the surplus population, to provide new markets for the goods produced in the factories and mines. The Empire, as I have always said, is a bread and butter question. If you want to avoid civil war, you must become imperialists.

This is what Cecil Rhodes, millionaire, king of finance, the man who was mainly responsible for the Boer War, said in 1895. His defense of imperialism is just crude and cynical, but in substance it does not differ from the "theory" advocated by Messrs. Maslov, Südekum, Potresov, David, the founder of Russian Marxism and others. Cecil Rhodes was a somewhat more honest social-chauvinist.

To tabulate as exactly as possible the territorial division of the world, and the changes which have occurred during the last decades, we will take the data furnished by Supan in the work already quoted on the colonial possessions of all the powers of the world. Supan examines the years 1876 and 1900; we will take the year 1876—a year aptly selected, for it is precisely at that time that the pre-monopolist stage of development of West European capitalism can be said to have been completed, in the main, and we will take the year 1914, and in place of Supan's figures we will quote the more recent statistics of Hübner (*Geographical and Statistical Tables*). Supan gives figures for colonies only: we think it useful, in order to present a complete picture of the division of the world, to add brief figures on non-colonial and semi-colonial countries like Persia, China and Turkey. Persia is already almost completely a colony; China and Turkey are on the way to becoming colonies. We thus get the following summary:

COLONIAL POSSESSIONS OF THE GREAT POWERS

(*In millions of square kilometers and in millions of inhabitants*)

| | Colonies | | | | Home Countries | | Total | |
| | 1876 | | 1914 | | 1914 | | 1914 | |
	Area	Pop.	Area	Pop.	Area	Pop.	Area	Pop.
Great Britain ..	22.5	251.9	33.5	393.5	0.3	46.5	33.8	440.0
Russia	17.0	15.9	17.4	33.2	5.4	136.2	22.8	169.4
France	0.9	6.0	10.6	55.5	0.5	39.6	11.1	95.1
Germany	—	—	2.9	12.3	0.5	64.9	3.4	77.2
U. S. A.	—	—	0.3	9.7	9.4	97.0	9.7	106.7
Japan	—	—	0.3	19.2	0.4	53.0	0.7	72.2
Total	40.4	273.8	65.0	523.4	16.5	437.2	81.5	960.6

	Area	Pop.
Colonies of other Powers (Belgium, Holland, etc.) ..	9.9	45.3
Semi-colonial countries (Persia, China, Turkey)	14.5	361.2
Other countries	28.0	289.9
Total area and population of the world	133.9	1,657.0

We see from these figures how "complete" was the partition of the world at the end of the nineteenth and beginning of the twentieth centuries. After 1876 colonial possessions increased to an enormous degree, more than one and a half times, from 40,000,000 to 65,000,000 square kilometers in area for the six biggest powers, an increase of 25,000,000 square kilometers, that is, one and a half times greater than the area of the "home" countries, which have a total of 16,500,000 square kilometers. In 1876 three powers had no colonies, and a fourth, France, had scarcely any. In 1914 these four powers had 14,100,000 square kilometers of colonies, or an area one and a half times greater than that of Europe, with a population of nearly 100,000,000. The unevenness in the rate of expansion of colonial possessions is very marked. If, for instance, we compare France, Germany and Japan which do not differ very much in area and population, we will see that the first (France) has annexed almost three times as much colonial territory as the other two combined. . . .

CHAPTER IX
THE CRITIQUE OF IMPERIALISM

By the critique of imperialism, in the broad sense of the term, we mean the attitude towards imperialist policy of the different classes of society as part of their general ideology.

The enormous dimensions of finance capital concentrated in a few hands and creating an extremely extensive and close network of ties and relationships which subordinate not only the small and medium, but also even the very small capitalists and small masters, on the one hand, and the intense struggle waged against other national state groups of financiers for the partition of the world and the power to rule over other countries, on the other hand, cause the whole transition of the possessing classes to the side of imperialism. The signs of the times are a "general" enthusiasm regarding its prospects, a passionate defense of imperialism, and every possible embellishment of its real nature. The imperialist ideology also permeates the working class. There is no Chinese Wall between it and the other classes. The leaders of the so-called "Social-Democratic" Party of Germany are today justly called social-imperialists, that is, socialists in words and imperialists in deeds; but as early as 1902, Hobson noted the existence of "Fabian imperialists" who belonged to the opportunist Fabian Society in England.

The bourgeois scholars and publicists usually come out in defense of imperialism in a somewhat veiled form and obscure its complete domination and its profound roots; they strive to concentrate attention on details and secondary characteristics and do their very best to distract attention from the main issue by means of ridiculous schemes for "reform," such as police supervision of the trusts and banks, etc. Less frequently, cynical and frank imperialists speak out and are bold enough to admit the absurdity of the idea of "reforming" the fundamental features of imperialism. . . .

Since the reform of the basis of imperialism is a deception, a pious "wish," since the bourgeois representatives of oppressed nations go no "further" forward, the bourgeois representatives of the oppressing nation go "further" *backward,* to servility towards imperialism, concealed by the cloak of "science." "Logic," indeed!

The question as to whether it is possible to reform the basis of imperialism, whether to go forward to the aggravation of the antagonisms which it engenders, or backwards, towards allaying these antagonisms, is a fundamental question in the critique of imperialism. As a consequence of the fact that the political features of imperialism are reaction all along the line, and increased national oppression, resulting from the oppression of the financial oligarchy and the elimination of free competition, a democratic petty-bourgeois opposition has been rising against imperialism in almost all imperialist countries since the beginning of the twentieth century. And the desertion of Kautsky and of the broad international Kautskyan trend from Marxism is displayed in the very fact that Kautsky not only did not trouble to oppose, not only was not able to oppose this petty-bourgeois reformist opposition, which is really reactionary in its economic basis, but in practice actually became merged with it.

In the United States, the imperialist war waged against Spain in 1898 stirred up the opposition of the "anti-imperialists," the last of the Mohicans of bourgeois democracy. They declared this war to be "criminal," denounced the annexation of foreign territories as being a violation of the constitution, and denounced the "Jingo treachery" by means of which Aguinaldo, leader of the native Filipinos, was deceived (the Americans promised him the independence of his country, but later they landed troops and annexed it). They quoted the words of Lincoln:

> When the white man governs himself, that is self-government, but when he governs himself and also governs others, it is no longer self-government; it is despotism. . . .

CHAPTER X
THE PLACE OF IMPERIALISM
IN HISTORY

We have seen that the economic quintessence of imperialism is monopoly capitalism. This very fact determines its place in history, for monopoly that grew up on the basis of free competition, and out of free competition, is the transition from the capitalist system to a higher social economic order. We must take special note of the four principal forms of monopoly, or the four principal manifestations of monopoly capitalism, which are characteristic of the period under review.

(1) Monopoly arose out of the concentration of production at a very advanced stage of development. This refers to the monopolist capitalist combines: cartels, syndicates and trusts. We have seen the important role these play in modern economic life. At the beginning of the twentieth century, monopolies acquired complete supremacy in the advanced countries. And although the first steps toward the formation of the combines were first taken by countries enjoying the protection of high tariffs (Germany, America), England, with her system of free trade, was not far behind in revealing the same phenomenon, namely, the birth of monopoly out of the concentration of production.

(2) Monopolies have accelerated the capture of the most important sources of raw materials, especially for the coal and iron industry, which is the basic and most highly trustified industry in capitalist society. The monopoly of the most important sources of raw materials has enormously increased the power of big capital, and has sharpened the antagonism between trustified and non-trustified industry.

(3) Monopoly has sprung from the banks. The banks have developed from modest intermediary enterprises into the monopolists of finance capital. Some three or five of the biggest banks in each of the foremost capitalist countries have achieved the "personal union" of industrial and bank capital, and have concentrated in their hands the power to dispose of thousands upon thousands of millions which form the greater part of the capital and revenue of entire countries. A financial oligarchy, which throws a close net of relations of dependence over all the economic and political institutions of contemporary bourgeois society

without exception—such is the most striking manifestation of this monopoly.

(4) Monopoly has grown out of colonial policy. To the numerous "old" motives of colonial policy, finance capital has added the struggle for the sources of raw materials, for the export of capital, for "spheres of influence," i.e., for spheres of good business, concessions, monopolist profits, and so on; in fine, for economic territory in general. When the colonies of the European powers in Africa comprised only one-tenth of that territory (as was the case in 1876), colonial policy was able to develop by methods other than those of monopoly—by the "free grabbing" of territories, so to speak. But when nine-tenths of Africa had been seized (approximately in 1900), when the whole world had been shared out, there was inevitably ushered in a period of colonial monopoly and, consequently, a period of intense struggle for the partition and the reparation of the world.

The extent to which monopolist capital has intensified all the contradictions of capitalism is generally known. It is sufficient to mention the high cost of living and the power of the trusts. This intensification of contradictions constitutes the most powerful driving force of the transitional period of history, which began at the time of the definite victory of world finance capital.

Monopolies, oligarchy, the striving for domination instead of the striving for liberty, the exploitation of an increasing number of small or weak nations by an extremely small group of the richest or most powerful nations —all these have given birth to those distinctive features of imperialism which compel us to define it as parasitic of decaying capitalism. More and more there emerges, as one of the tendencies of imperialism, the creation of the "bondholding" (*rentier*) state, the usurer state, in which the bourgeoisie lives on the proceeds of capital exports and by "clipping coupons." It would be a mistake to believe that this tendency to decay precludes the possibility of the rapid growth of capitalism. It does not. In the epoch of imperialism, certain branches of industry, certain strata of the bourgeoisie and certain countries betray, to a greater or less degree, one or other of these tendencies. On the whole capitalism is growing far more rapidly than before, but it is not only that this growth is becoming more and more uneven; this unevenness manifests itself also, in particular, in the decay of the countries which are richest in capital. . . .

Joseph Vissarionovitch Dzhugashvili (Stalin) (1879–1953)

Stalin was born at Gori in (now) Soviet Georgia, the son of a shoemaker. He first became a seminarian, then joined the revolutionary underground in 1898 and was frequently deported. Editor-in-chief of Pravda from 1917, he became secretary-general of the Communist Party in 1922, and Lenin's successor by eliminating Trotsky, Bukharin, and many others. Author of the purges of 1936–1938, he negotiated the Hitler–Stalin pact of 1939, then became commander-in-chief (1942) and marshal (1943) leading the war against Germany. His writings established him as one of the great Marxist theoreticians.

Foundations of Leninism

I. THE HISTORICAL ROOTS OF LENINISM

Leninism grew up and took shape under the conditions of imperialism, when the contradictions of capitalism had reached their extreme, when the proletarian revolution had become an immediate practical question, when the old period of preparation of the working class for the revolution had culminated in a new period, the period of the direct onslaught upon capitalism.

From *Foundations of Leninism*, by Joseph Stalin, New York, 1939.

Lenin called imperialism "moribund capitalism." Why? Because imperialism carries the contradictions of capitalism to their last bounds, to the extreme limit, beyond which revolution begins. Of these contradictions, there are three which must be regarded as the most important.

The *first contradiction* is the contradiction between labour and capital. Imperialism is the omnipotence of the monopolist trusts and syndicates, of the banks and the financial oligarchy, in the industrial countries. In the fight against this omnipotence, the customary methods of the working class—trade unions and co-operative organizations, parliamentary parties and the parliamentary struggle—have proved to be totally inadequate. Either place yourself at the mercy of capital, linger in misery as of old and sink lower and lower, or adopt a new weapon—this is the alternative imperialism puts before the vast masses of the proletariat. Imperialism brings the working class to revolution.

The *second contradiction* is the contradiction among the various financial groups and imperialist powers in their struggle for sources of raw materials, for foreign territory. Imperialism is the export of capital to the sources of raw materials, the frenzied struggle for monopolist possession of these sources, the struggle for a redivision of the already divided world, a struggle waged with particular fury by new financial groups and powers seeking a "place in the sun" against the old groups and powers which cling tightly to what they have grabbed. This frenzied struggle among the various groups of capitalists is notable in that it includes as an inevitable element imperialist wars, wars for the annexation of foreign territories. This circumstance, in its turn, is notable in that it leads to the mutual weakening of the imperialists, to the weakening of the position of capitalism in general, to the acceleration of the advent of the proletarian revolution and to the practical inevitability of this revolution.

The *third contradiction* is the contradiction between the handful of ruling "civilised" nations and the hundreds of millions of the colonial and dependent peoples of the world. Imperialism is the most barefaced exploitation and the most inhuman oppression of hundreds of millions of people inhabiting vast colonies and dependent countries. The purpose of this exploitation and of this oppression is to squeeze out super-profits. But in exploiting these countries imperialism is compelled to build railroads, factories and mills there, to create industrial and commercial centres. The appearance of a class of proletarians, the emergence of a native intelligentsia, the awakening of national consciousness, the growth of the movement for emancipation—such are the inevitable results of this "policy." The growth of the revolutionary movement in all colonies and dependent countries without exception clearly testifies to this fact. This circumstance is of importance for the proletariat in that it radically undermines the position of capitalism by converting the colonies and dependent countries from reserves of imperialism into reserves of the proletarian revolution.

. . . Such is the international situation which gave birth to Leninism.

Some may say: this is all very well, but what has it to do with Russia, which was not and could not be a classical land of imperialism? What has it to do with Lenin, who worked primarily in Russia and for Russia? Why did Russia, of all countries, become the home of Leninism, the birthplace of the theory and tactics of the proletarian revolution?

Because Russia represented the focus of all these contradictions of imperialism.

Because Russia, more than any other country, was pregnant with revolution, and she alone was therefore in a position to solve these contradictions in a revolutionary way.

To begin with, tsarist Russia was the home of every kind of oppression—capitalist, colonial and militarist—in its most inhuman and barbarous form. Who does not know that in Russia the omnipotence of capital coalesced with the despotism of tsarism, the aggressiveness of Russian nationalism with tsarism's role of executioner in regard to the non-Russian peoples, the exploitation of entire regions—Turkey, Persia, China—with the seizure of these regions by tsarism, with wars of conquest? Lenin was right in saying that tsarism was "militarist-feudal imperialism." Tsarism was the concentration of the worst features of imperialism, raised to the second power.

To proceed. Tsarist Russia was an immense reserve of Western imperialism, not only in that it gave free entry to foreign capital, which controlled such basic branches of Russia's national economy as the fuel and metal industries, but also in that it could supply the Western imperialists with millions of soldiers. Remember the Russian army, twelve million strong, which shed its blood on the imperialist fronts to safeguard the staggering profits of the British and French capitalists.

Further, Tsarism was not only the watchdog of imperialism in the east of Europe, but, in addition, it was the agent of Western imperialism for squeezing out of the population hundreds of millions by way of interest on loans floated in Paris and London, Berlin and Brussels.

Finally, tsarism was the most faithful ally of Western imperialism in the partition of Turkey, Persia, China, etc. Who does not know that the imperialist war was waged by tsarism in alliance with the imperialists of the Entente, and that Russia was an essential element in that war?

That is why the interests of tsarism and of Western imperialism were interwoven and ultimately became merged in a single skein of imperialist interests. Could Western imperialism resign itself to the loss of such a powerful support in the East and of such a rich reservoir of power and resources as old, tsarist, bourgeois Russia was without exerting all its strength to wage a life and death struggle against the Russian revolution, with the object of defending and preserving tsarism? Of course not.

But from this it follows that whoever wanted to strike at tsarism necessarily raised his hand against imperialism, whoever rose against tsarism had to rise against imperialism as well; for whoever was bent on overthrowing tsarism had to overthrow imperialism too, if he really intended not merely to defeat tsarism, but to make a clean sweep of it. . . .

The same thing, approximately, "happened" in the case of Russia and Lenin as had happened in the case of Germany and Marx and Engels in the 'forties of the last century. Like Russia at the beginning of the twentieth century, Germany was then pregnant with the bourgeois revolution. Marx wrote at that time in *The Communist Manifesto*:

> The Communists turn their attention chiefly to Germany, because that country is on the eve of a bourgeois revolution that is bound to be carried out under more advanced conditions of European civilisation and with a much more developed proletariat than that of England was in the seventeenth, and of France in the eighteenth century, and because the bourgeois revolution in Germany will be but the prelude to an immediately following proletarian revolution. (Karl Marx, *Selected Works*, Vol. I, p. 241.)

In other words, the centre of the revolutionary movement was shifting to Germany.

There can hardly be any doubt that it was this very circumstance, noted by Marx in the above-quoted passage, that served as the probable reason why it was precisely Germany that became the birthplace of Scientific Socialism and why the leaders of the German proletariat, Marx and Engels, became its creators. . . .

II. METHOD

I have already said that between Marx and Engels, on the one hand, and Lenin, on the other, there lies a whole period of domination of the opportunism of the Second International. For the sake of exactitude I must add that it is not formal domination of opportunism I have in mind, but only its actual domination. Formally, the Second International was headed by "faithful" Marxists, by the "orthodox"—Kautsky and others. Actually, however, the main work of the Second International followed the line of opportunism. The opportunists adapted themselves to the bourgeoisie, because of their adaptive, petty-bourgeois nature; the "orthodox," in their turn, adapted themselves to the opportunists in order to "preserve unity" with them, to preserve "peace within the party." As a result, opportunism dominated; for there always proved to be a link between the policy of the bourgeoisie and the policy of the "orthodox."

This was the period of the relatively peaceful development of capitalism, the pre-war period, so to speak, when the catastrophic contradictions of imperialism had not yet become so glaringly evident, when workers' economic strikes and trade unions were developing more or less "normally," when election campaigns and parliamentary parties yielded "dizzying" successes, when legal forms of struggle were lauded to the skies, and when it was thought that capitalism would be "killed" by legal means—in short, when the parties of the Second International were vegetating and there was no inclination to think seriously about revolution, about the dictatorship of the proletariat, or about the revolutionary education of the masses.

Instead of an integral revolutionary theory there were contradictory theoretical postulates and fragments of theory, which were divorced from the actual revolutionary struggle of the masses and had degenerated into threadbare dogmas. For the sake of appearances, Marx's theory was mentioned, of course, but only to rob it of its living, revolutionary spirit.

Instead of a revolutionary policy there was flabby philistinism and sober political bargaining, parliamentary diplomacy and parliamentary scheming. For the sake of appearances, of course, "revolutionary" resolutions and slogans were adopted, but only to be pigeonholed.

Instead of training the party and teaching it correct

revolutionary tactics by helping it learn from its own mistakes, there was a studied evasion of acute questions, which they glossed over and veiled. For the sake of appearances, of course, they were not averse to talking about the acute questions, but only to wind up with some sort of "elastic" resolution.

Such was the physiognomy of the Second International, its method of work, its arsenal. . . .

As to the political slogans and the political resolutions of the parties of the Second International, it is sufficient to recall the history of the slogan "war against war" to realize how utterly false and utterly putrid are the political practices of these parties, which use pompous revolutionary slogans and resolutions to cloak their anti-revolutionary deeds. We all remember the pompous demonstration of the Second International at the Basle Congress, at which it threatened the imperialists with all the horrors of insurrection if they should dare to start war, and proclaimed the menacing slogan "war against war." But who does not remember that some time after, on the very eve of the war, the Basle resolution was pigeonholed and the workers were given a new slogan—to exterminate each other for the glory of their capitalist fatherlands? Is it not clear that revolutionary slogans and resolutions are not worth a farthing if they are not backed by deeds? One need only contrast the Leninist policy of transforming the imperialist war into civil war with the treacherous policy of the Second International during the war to understand the utter vulgarity of the opportunist politicians and the full grandeur of the method of Leninism. . . .

III. THEORY

THE THEORY OF THE PROLETARIAN REVOLUTION

The Leninist theory of the proletarian revolution proceeds from three fundamental theses.

First Thesis: The domination of finance capital in the advanced capitalist countries; the issue of stocks and bonds as the principal operation of finance capital; the export of capital to the sources of raw materials, which is one of the foundations of imperialism; the omnipotence of a financial oligarchy, which is the result of the domination of finance capital—all this reveals the grossly parasitic character of monopolist capitalism, makes the yoke of the capitalist trusts and syndicates a hundred times more burdensome, quickens the revolt of the working class against the foundations of capitalism, and brings the masses to the proletarian revolution as their only salvation. (Cf. Lenin, *Imperialism, the Highest Stage of Capitalism.*)

Hence the first conclusion: intensification of the revolutionary crisis within the capitalist countries and growth of the elements of an explosion on the internal, proletarian front in the "mother countries."

Second Thesis: The increase in the export of capital to the colonies and dependent countries; the extension of "spheres of influence" and colonial possessions until they cover the whole globe; the transformation of capitalism into a *world system* of financial enslavement and colonial oppression of the vast majority of the population of the earth by a handful of "advanced" countries—all this has, on the one hand, converted the separate national economies and national territories into links in a single chain called world economy and, on the other hand, split the population of the globe into two camps: a handful of "advanced" capitalist countries which exploit and oppress vast colonies and dependencies, and the vast majority of colonial and dependent countries which are compelled to fight for their liberation from the imperialist yoke. (Cf. *Imperialism.*)

Hence the second conclusion: intensification of the revolutionary crisis in the colonial countries and growth of the elements of revolt against imperialism on the external, colonial front.

Third Thesis: The monopolistic possession of "spheres of influence" and colonies; the uneven development of the different capitalist countries, leading to a frenzied struggle for the redivision of the world between the countries which have already seized territories and those claiming their "share"; imperialist wars as the only method of restoring the disturbed "equilibrium"—all this leads to the aggravation of the third front, the intercapitalist front, which weakens imperialism and facilitates the amalgamation of the first two fronts against imperialism: the front of the revolutionary proletariat and the front of colonial emancipation. (Cf. *Imperialism.*)

Hence the third conclusion: that under imperialism wars cannot be averted, and that a coalition between the proletarian revolution in Europe and the colonial revolution in the East in a united world front of revolution against the world front of imperialism is inevitable.

Lenin combines all these conclusions into one general conclusion that *"imperialism is the eve of the socialist revolution."* (*Selected Works,* Vol. V, p. 5.)

The very approach to the question of the proletarian revolution, of the character of the revolution, of its scope, of its depth, the scheme of the revolution in general, changes accordingly.

Formerly, the analysis of the conditions for the proletarian revolution was usually approached from the point of view of the economic state of individual countries. Now, this approach is no longer adequate. Now the matter must be approached from the point of view of the economic state of all or the majority of countries, from the point of view of the state of world economy; for individual countries and individual national economies have ceased to be self-sufficient units, have become links in a single chain called world economy; for the old "cultured" capitalism has evolved into imperialism, and imperialism is a world system of financial enslavement and colonial oppression of the vast majority of the population of the earth by a handful of "advanced" countries.

Formerly, it was the accepted thing to speak of the existence or absence of objective conditions for the proletarian revolution in individual countries, or, to be more precise, in one or another developed country. Now this point of view is no longer adequate. Now we must speak of the existence of objective conditions for the revolution in the entire system of world imperialist economy as an integral unit; the existence within this system of some countries that are not sufficiently developed industrially cannot serve as an insurmountable obstacle to the revolution, *if* the system as a whole, or, more correctly, *because* the system as a whole is already ripe for revolution.

Formerly it was the accepted thing to speak of the proletarian revolution in one or another developed country as of something separate and self-sufficient, facing a separate national front of capital as its opposite. Now this point of view is no longer adequate. Now we must speak of the world proletarian revolution; for the separate national fronts of capital have become links in a single chain called the world front of imperialism, which must be opposed by a common front of the revolutionary movement in all countries.

Formerly, the proletarian revolution was regarded exclusively as the result of the internal development of a given country. Now this point of view is no longer adequate. Now the proletarian revolution must be regarded primarily as the result of the development of the contradictions within the world system of imperialism, as the result of the snapping of the chain of the imperialist world front in one country or another.

Where will the revolution begin? Where, in what country can the front of capital be pierced first?

Where industry is more developed, where the proletariat constitutes the majority, where there is more culture, where there is more democracy—that was the reply usually given formerly.

No, objects the Leninist theory of revolution; *not necessarily where industry is more developed,* and so forth. The front of capital will be pierced where the chain of imperialism is weakest, for the proletarian revolution is the result of the breaking of the chain of the world imperialist front at its weakest link, and it may turn out that the country which has started the revolution, which has made a breach in the front of capital is less developed in a capitalist sense than other, more developed countries, which have, however, remained within the framework of capitalism.

In 1917 the chain of the imperialist world front proved to be weaker in Russia than in the other countries. It was there that the chain gave way and provided an outlet for the proletarian revolution. Why? Because in Russia a great popular revolution was unfolding, and at its head marched the revolutionary proletariat, which had such an important ally as the vast mass of the peasantry who were oppressed and exploited by the landlords. Because the revolution there was opposed by such a hideous representative of imperialism as tsarism, which lacked all moral prestige and was deservedly hated by the whole population. The chain proved to be weaker in Russia, although that country was less developed in a capitalist sense than, say, France or Germany, England or America.

Where will the chain break in the near future? Again, where it is weakest. It is not precluded that the chain may break, say, in India. Why? Because that country has a young, militant, revolutionary proletariat, which has such an ally as the national liberation movement—an undoubtedly powerful and undoubtedly important ally. Because there the revolution is opposed by such a well-known foe as foreign imperialism, which lacks all moral credit and is deservedly hated by the oppressed and exploited masses of India. . . .

"The fundamental question of revolution is the question of power." (*Lenin.*) Does this mean that all that is required is to assume power, to seize it? No, it does not mean that. The seizure of power is only the beginning. For many reasons the bourgeoisie that is overthrown in one country remains for a long time stronger than the proletariat which has overthrown it. Therefore, the whole point is to retain power, to consolidate it, to make it invincible. What is needed to attain this? To attain this it is necessary to carry out at least the three main tasks that confront the dictatorship of the proletariat "on the morrow" of victory:

(a) to break the resistance of the landlords and capitalists who have been overthrown and expropriated by the revolution, to liquidate every attempt on their part to restore the power of capital;

(b) to organize construction in such a way as to rally all the labouring people around the proletariat, and to carry on this work along the lines of preparing for the liquidation, the abolition of classes;

(c) to arm the revolution, to organize the army of the revolution for the struggle against foreign enemies, for the struggle against imperialism.

The dictatorship of the proletariat is needed to carry out, to fulfil these tasks.

> The transition from capitalism to communism, [says Lenin] represents an entire historical epoch. Until this epoch has terminated, the exploiters will inevitably cherish the hope of restoration, and this *hope* will be converted into *attempts* at restoration. And after their first serious defeat, the overthrown exploiters—who had not expected their overthrow, never believed it possible, never conceded the thought of it—will throw themselves with tenfold energy, with furious passion and hatred grown a hundredfold, into the battle for the recovery of their lost "paradise," on behalf of their families, who had been leading such a sweet and easy life and whom now the "common herd" is condemning to ruin and destitution or to "common" work. . . . In the train of the capitalist exploiters will be found the broad masses of the petty bourgeoisie, with regard to whom the historical experience of every country for decades testifies that they vacillate and hesitate, one day marching behind the proletariat and the next day taking fright at the difficulties of the revolution; that they become panic-stricken at the first defeat or semi-defeat of

the workers, grow nervous, run about aimlessly, snivel, and rush from one camp to the other. [*Selected Works*, Vol. VII, pp. 140–41.]

And the bourgeoisie has its grounds for making attempts at restoration, because for a long time after its overthrow it remains stronger than the proletariat which has overthrown it.

If the exploiters are defeated in one country only, [says Lenin,] and this, of course, is typical, since a simultaneous revolution in a number of countries is a rare exception, they *still* remain *stronger* than the exploited. [*Ibid.*, p. 140.]

Wherein lies the strength of the overthrown bourgeoisie? Firstly, "in the strength of international capital, in the strength and durability of the international connections of the bourgeoisie." [Lenin, *Selected Works*, Vol. X, p. 60.]
Secondly, in the fact that:

for a long time after the revolution the exploiters inevitably continue to enjoy a number of great practical advantages: they still have money (since it is impossible to abolish money all at once), some movable property—often fairly considerable; they still have various connections, habits of organization and management, knowledge of all the "secrets" (customs, methods, means and possibilities) of management, superior education, close connections with the higher technical personnel (who live and think like the bourgeoisie), incomparably greater experience in the art of war (this is very important) and so on, and so forth. [Lenin, *Selected Works*, Vol. VII, p. 140.]

Thirdly,

in the *force of habit*, in the strength of *small-scale production*. For unfortunately, there is still very, very much of small-scale production left in the world, and small-scale production *engenders* capitalism and the bourgeoisie continuously, daily, hourly, spontaneously and on a mass scale; . . . [for] the abolition of classes means not only driving out the landlords and capitalists—that we accomplished with comparative ease; it means also *getting rid of the small commodity producers,* and they *cannot be driven out,* they cannot be crushed, we must live *in harmony* with them; they can (and must) be remoulded and re-educated only by very prolonged, slow, cautious organizational work. [Lenin, *Selected Works*, Vol. X, pp. 60, 83.]

That is why Lenin says:

The dictatorship of the proletariat is a most determined and most ruthless war waged by the new class against a *more powerful* enemy, the bourgeoisie, whose resistance is increased *tenfold* by its overthrow; [that] the dictatorship of the proletariat is a persistent struggle—sanguinary and bloodless, violent and peaceful, military and economic, educational and administrative—against the forces and traditions of the old society. [*Selected Works,* Vol. X, pp. 60, 84.]

It need hardly be proved that there is not the slightest possibility of carrying out these tasks in a short period, of doing all this in a few years. Therefore, the dictatorship of the proletariat, the transition from capitalism to communism, must not be regarded as a fleeting period of "superrevolutionary" acts and decrees, but as an entire historical era, replete with civil wars and external conflicts, with persistent organizational work and economic construction, with advances and retreats, victories and defeats. This historical era is needed not only to create the economic and cultural prerequisites for the complete victory of socialism, but also to enable the proletariat, first, to educate itself and become steeled as a force capable of governing the country, and, secondly, to re-educate and remould the petty-bourgeois strata along such lines as will assure the organization of socialist production.

Marx said to the workers:

> You will have to go through fifteen, twenty or fifty years of civil wars and international conflicts, not only to change existing conditions, but also to change yourselves and to make yourselves capable of wielding political power.

Continuing and developing Marx's idea still further, Lenin wrote that: It will be necessary under the dictatorship of the proletariat to re-educate:

> millions of peasants and small proprietors and hundreds of thousands of office employees, officials and bourgeois intellectuals, [to subordinate] all these to the proletarian state and to proletarian leadership, [to overcome] their bourgeois habits and traditions . . . [just as it will be necessary] to re-educate—in a protracted struggle, on the basis of the dictatorship of the proletariat—the proletarians themselves, who do not abandon their petty-bourgeois prejudices at one stroke, by a miracle, at the behest of the Virgin Mary, at the behest of a slogan, resolution or decree, but only in the course of a long and difficult mass struggle against mass petty-bourgeois influences. [*Selected Works,* Vol. X, pp. 157, 156.] . . .

But the Party cannot be only a *vanguard* detachment. It must at the same time be a detachment of the *class,* part of the class, closely bound up with it by all the fibres of its being. The distinction between the vanguard and the main body of the working class, between Party members and non-Party people, cannot disappear until classes disappear; it will exist as long as the ranks of the proletariat continue to be replenished with newcomers from other classes, as long as the working class as a whole lacks the possibility of rising to the level of the vanguard. But the Party would cease to be a party if this distinction were widened into a gap, if it shut itself up in its own shell and became divorced from the non-Party masses. The party cannot lead the class if it is not connected with the non-Party masses, if there is no bond between the Party and the non-Party masses, if these masses do not accept its leadership, if the Party enjoys no moral and political credit among the masses. . . .

THE PARTY

1. THE PARTY AS THE VANGUARD OF THE WORKING CLASS

. . . The Party must be, first of all, the *vanguard* of the working class. The Party must absorb all the best elements of the working class, their experience, their revolutionary spirit, their selfless devotion to the cause of the proletariat. But in order that it may really be the vanguard, the Party must be armed with revolutionary theory, with a knowledge of the laws of the movement, with a knowledge of the laws of revolution. Without this it will be incapable of directing the struggle of the proletariat, of leading the proletariat. The Party cannot be a real party if it limits itself to registering what the masses of the working class feel and think, if it follows in the tail of the spontaneous movement, if it is unable to overcome the inertness and the political indifference of the spontaneous movement, if it is unable to rise above the momentary interest of the proletariat, if it is unable to elevate the masses to the level of the class interests of the proletariat. The Party must stand at the head of the working class; it must see farther than the working class; it must lead the proletariat, and not follow in the tail of the spontaneous movement. The parties of the Second International, which preach "khvostism," are vehicles of bourgeois policy, which condemns the proletariat to the role of a tool in the hands of the bourgeoisie. Only a party which takes the standpoint of the vanguard of the proletariat and is able to elevate the masses to the level of the class interests of the proletariat—only such a party can divert the working class from the path of trade unionism and convert it into an independent political force. The Party is the political leader of the working class.

The Withering Away
of the State

It is sometimes asked: "We have abolished the exploiting classes; there are no longer any hostile classes in the country; there is nobody to suppress; hence there is no more need for the state; it must die away. Why, then, do we not help our socialist state to die away? Why do we not strive to put an end to it? Is it not time to throw out all this rubbish of a state?"

Or further: "The exploiting classes have already been abolished in our country; socialism has been built in the main; we are advancing towards communism. Now, the Marxist doctrine of the state says that there is to be no state under communism. Why, then, do we not help our socialist state to die away? Is it not time we relegated the state to the museum of antiquities?"

These questions show that those who ask them have conscientiously memorised certain propositions contained in the doctrine of Marx and Engels about the state. But they also show that these comrades have failed to understand the essential meaning of this doctrine; that they have failed to realise in what historical conditions the various propositions of this doctrine were elaborated; and, what is more, that they do not understand present-day international conditions, have overlooked the capitalist encirclement and the dangers it entails for the socialist country. These questions not only betray an underestimation of the capitalist encirclement, but also an underestimation of the rôle and significance of the bourgeois states and their organs, which send spies, assassins and wreckers into our country and are waiting for a favourable opportunity to attack it by armed force. They likewise betray an underestimation of the rôle and significance of our socialist state and of its military, punitive and intelligence organs, which are essential for the defence of the socialist land from foreign attack. It must be confessed that the comrades mentioned are not the only ones to sin in this underestimation. All the Bolsheviks, all of us without exception, sin to a certain extent in this respect. Is it not surprising that we learnt about the espionage and conspiratorial activities of the Trotskyite and Bukharinite leaders only quite recently, in 1937 and 1938, although, as the evidence shows, these gentry were in the service of foreign espionage organisations and carried on conspiratorial activities from the very first days of the October Revolution? How could we have failed to notice so grave a matter? How are we to explain this blunder? The usual answer to this question is that we could not possibly have assumed that these people could have fallen so low. But that is no explanation, still less is it a justification; for the blunder was a blunder. How is this blunder to be explained? It is to be explained by an underestimation of the strength and consequence of the mechanism of the bourgeois states surrounding us and of their espionage organs, which endeavour to take advantage of people's weaknesses, their vanity, their slackness of will, to enmesh them in their espionage nets and use them to surround the organs of the Soviet state. It is to be explained by an underestimation of the rôle and significance of the mechanism of our socialist state and of its intelligence service, by an underestimation of this intelligence service, by the twaddle that an intelligence service in a Soviet state is an unimportant trifle, and the Soviet intelligence service and the Soviet state itself will soon have to be relegated to the museum of antiquities.

What could have given rise to this underestimation?

It arose owing to the fact that certain of the general propositions in the Marxist doctrine of the state were incompletely worked out and inadequate. It received currency owing to our unpardonable heedless attitude to matters pertaining to the theory of the state, in spite of the fact that we have twenty years of practical experience in matters of state which provide rich material for theoretical generalisations, and in spite of the fact that, given the desire, we have every opportunity of successfully filling this gap in theory. We have forgotten Lenin's highly important injunction about the theoretical duties of Russian Marxists, that it is their mission to further develop the Marxist theory. This is what Lenin said in this connection:

> We do not regard Marxist theory as something completed and inviolable; on the contrary, we are convinced that it has only laid the corner-stone of the science which socialists *must* further advance in all directions if they wish to keep pace with life. We think that an *independent* elaboration of the Marxist theory is especially essential for Russian socialists, for this theory provides only general *guiding* principles, which, *in particular,* are applied in England differently from France, in France differently from Germany, and in Germany differently from Russia. [Lenin, *Collected Works,* Russian Edition, Vol. II, p. 492.]

Consider, for example, the classical formulation of the theory of the development of the socialist state given by Engels:

> As soon as there is no longer any class of society to be held in subjection; as soon as, along with class domination and the struggle for individual existence based on the former anarchy of production, the collisions and excesses arising from these have also been abolished, there is nothing more to be repressed which would make a special repressive force, a state, necessary. The first act in which the state really comes forward as the representative of society as a whole—the taking possession of the means of production in the name of society—is at the same time its last independent act as a state. The interference of the state power in social relations becomes superfluous in one sphere after another, and then ceases of itself. The government of persons is replaced by the administration of things and the direction of the process of production. The state is not "abolished," *it withers away.* [*Herr Eugen Dühring's Revolution in Science (Anti-Dühring),* English Edition, p. 315.]

Is this proposition of Engels' correct?

Yes, it is correct, but only on one of two conditions: (1) *if* we study the socialist state only from the angle of the internal development of the country, abstracting ourselves in advance from the international factor, isolating, for the convenience of investigation, the country and the state from the international situation; or (2) *if* we assume that socialism is already victorious in all countries, or in the majority of countries, that a socialist encirclement exists instead of a capitalist encirclement, that there is no more danger of foreign attack, and that there is no more need to strengthen the army and the state.

Well, but what if socialism has been victorious only in one country, and if, in view of this, it is quite impossible to abstract oneself from international conditions—what then? Engels' formula does not furnish an answer to this question. As a matter of fact, Engels did not set himself this question, and therefore could not have given an answer to it. Engels proceeds from the assumption that socialism has already been victorious in all countries, or in a majority of countries, more or less simultaneously. Consequently, Engels is not here investigating any specific socialist state of any particular country, but the development of the socialist state in general, on the assumption that socialism has been victorious in a majority of countries—according to the formula: "Assuming that socialism is victorious in a majority of countries, what changes must the proletarian, socialist state undergo?" Only this general and abstract character of the problem can explain why in his investigation of the question of the socialist state Engels completely abstracted himself from such a factor as international conditions, the international situation.

But it follows from this that Engels' general formula about the destiny of the socialist state in general cannot be extended to the partial and specific case of the victory of socialism in one country only, a country which is surrounded by a capitalist world, is subject to the menace of foreign military attack, cannot therefore abstract itself from the international situation, and must have at its disposal a well-trained army, well organised punitive organs, and a strong intelligence service—consequently, must have its own state, strong enough to defend the conquests of socialism from foreign attack.

We have no right to expect of the classical Marxist writers, separated as they were from our day by a period of forty-five or fifty-five years, that they should have foreseen each and every zigzag of history in the distant future in every separate country. It would be ridiculous to expect that the classical Marxist writers should have elaborated for our benefit ready-made solutions for each and every theoretical problem that might arise in any particular country fifty or one hundred years afterwards, so that we, the descendants of the classical Marxist writers, might calmly doze at the fireside and munch ready-made solutions. But we can and should expect of the Marxists-Leninists of our day that they do not confine themselves to learning by rote a few general tenets of Marxism; that they delve deeply into the essence of Marxism; that they learn to take account of the experience gained in the twenty years of existence of the socialist state in our country; that, lastly, they learn, with the use of this experience and with knowledge of the essence of Marxism, to apply the various general theses of Marxism concretely, to lend them greater precision and improve them. Lenin wrote his famous book, *The State and Revolution,* in August 1917, that is, a few months before the October Revolution and the establishment of the Soviet state. Lenin considered it the main task of this book to defend Marx's and Engels' doctrine of the state from the distortions and vulgarisations of the opportunists. Lenin was preparing to write a second volume of *The State and Revolution,* in which he intended to sum up the principal lessons of the experience of the Russian revolutions of 1905 and 1917. There can be no doubt that Lenin intended the second volume of his book to elaborate and develop the theory of the state on the basis of the experience gained during the existence of Soviet power in our country. Death, however, prevented him from carrying this task into execution. But what Lenin did not manage to do should be done by his disciples.

The state arose because society split up into antagonistic classes; it arose in order to keep in restraint the exploited majority in the interests of the exploiting minority. The instruments of state authority have been mainly concentrated in the army, the punitive organs, the espionage service, the prisons. Two basic functions characterise the activity of the state: at home (the main function), to keep in restraint the exploited majority; abroad (not the main function), to extend the territory of its class, the ruling class, at the expense of the territory of other states, or to defend the territory of its own state from attack by other states. Such was the case in slave society and under feudalism. Such is the case under capitalism.

In order to overthrow capitalism it was not only necessary to remove the bourgeoisie from power, it was not only necessary to expropriate the capitalists, but also to smash entirely the bourgeois state machine and its old army, its bureaucratic officialdom and its police force, and to substitute for it a new, proletarian form of state, a new, socialist state. And that, as we know, is exactly what the Bolsheviks did. But it does not follow that the new proletarian state may not preserve certain functions of the old state, changed to suit the requirements of the proletarian state. Still less does it follow that the forms of our socialist state must remain unchanged, that all the original functions of our state must be fully preserved in future. As a matter of fact, the forms of our state are changing and will continue to change in line with the development of our country and with the changes in the international situation.

Lenin was absolutely right when he said:

> The forms of bourgeois states are extremely varied, but in essence they are all the same: in one way or another, in the final analysis, all these states are inevitably the *dictatorship of the bourgeoisie*. The transition from capitalism to communism will certainly create a great variety and abundance of political forms, but in essence there will inevitably be only one: *the dictatorship of the proletariat*. [Lenin, *The State and Revolution*.]

Since the October Revolution, our socialist state has passed through two main phases in its development.

The first phase was the period from the October Revolution to the elimination of the exploiting classes. The principal task in that period was to suppress the resistance of the overthrown classes, to organise the defence of the country against the attack of the interventionists, to restore industry and agriculture, and to prepare the conditions for the elimination of the capitalist elements. Accordingly, in this period our state performed two main functions. The first function was to suppress the overthrown classes inside the country. In this respect our state bore a superficial resemblance to previous states whose functions had also been to suppress recalcitrants, with the fundamental difference, however, that our state suppressed the exploiting minority in the interests of the labouring majority, while previous states had suppressed the exploited majority in the interests of the exploiting minority. The second function was to defend the country from foreign attack. In this respect it likewise bore a superficial resemblance to previous states, which also undertook the armed defence of their countries, with the fundamental difference, however, that our state defended from foreign attack the gains of the labouring majority, while previous states in such cases defended the wealth and privileges of the exploiting minority. Our state had yet a third function: this was the work of economic organisation and cultural education performed by our state bodies with the purpose of developing the infant shoots of the new, socialist economic system and re-educating the people in the spirit of socialism. But this new function did not attain to any considerable development in that period.

The second phase was the period from the elimination of the capitalist elements in town and country to the complete victory of the socialist economic system and the adoption of the new Constitution. The principal task in this period was to establish the socialist economic system all over the country and to eliminate the last remnants of the capitalist elements, to bring about a cultural revolution, and to form a thoroughly modern army for the defence of the country. And the functions of our socialist state changed accordingly. The function of military suppression inside the country ceased, died away; for exploitation had been abolished, there were no more exploiters left, and so there was no one to suppress. In place of this function of suppression, the state acquired the function of protecting socialist property from thieves and pilferers of the people's property. The function of defending the country from foreign attack remained; consequently, the Red Army and the Navy also fully remained, as did the punitive organs and the intelligence service, which are indispensable for the detection and punishment of the spies, assassins and wreckers sent into our country by foreign espionage services. The function of economic organisation and cultural education by the state organs also remained, and was developed to the full. Now the main task of our state inside the country is the work of peaceful economic organisation and cultural education. As for our army, punitive organs, and intelligence service, their edge is no longer turned to the inside of the country but to the outside, against external enemies.

As you see, we now have an entirely new, socialist state, without precedent in history and differing considerably in form and functions from the socialist state of the first phase. . . .

Marx and Social Democracy

The Gotha Congress of 1876 united the two German Socialist parties, that of Ferdinand Lassalle (1825–1864) who had been a disciple of Karl Marx from 1848 but parted from

From *Basic Writings on Politics and Philosophy*, by Karl Marx and Friedrich Engels, edited by Lewis S. Feuer, New York and London, 1959.

him to become the founder of the German Social Democratic Party and that of Marx and William Liebknecht (1826–1900). The two men together founded the German Democratic Labor Party. The Gotha program was violently attacked by Marx.

Lassalle was killed in a duel over a Rumanian woman. William Liebknecht was the father of Karl Liebknecht (1871–1919), Communist leader in the German Reichstag (1912) who, after World War I, became a leader of the Spartacus group and was arrested and murdered (with Rosa Luxemburg [1870–1919]) in 1919.

Critique of the Gotha Programme

(Karl Marx)

1. "Labour is the source of all wealth and all culture, *and since* useful labour is possible only in society and through society, the proceeds of labour belong undiminished, with equal right, to all members of society."

First part of the paragraph: "Labour is the source of all wealth and all culture."

Labour is *not the source* of all wealth. *Nature* is just as much the source of use values (and it is surely of such that material wealth consists!) as labour, which itself is only the manifestation of a force of nature, human labour power. The above phrase is to be found in all children's primers and is correct in so far as it is *implied* that labour is performed with appurtenant subjects and instruments. But a socialist programme cannot allow such bourgeois phrases to pass over in silence the *conditions* that alone give them meaning. And in so far as man from the beginning behaves towards nature, the primary source of all instruments and subjects of labour, as an owner, treats her as belonging to him, his labour becomes the source of use values, therefore also of wealth. The bourgeois have very poor grounds for falsely ascribing *supernatural creative power* to labour, since precisely from the fact that labour depends on nature it follows that the man who possesses no other property than his labour power must, in all conditions of society and culture, be the slave of other men, who have made themselves the owners of the material conditions of labour. He can work only with their permission, hence live only with their permission.

Let us now leave the sentence as it stands, or rather limps. What would one have expected in conclusion? Obviously this:

"Since labour is the source of all wealth, no one in society can appropriate wealth except as the product of labour. Therefore if he himself does not work he lives by the labour of others and also acquires his culture at the expense of the labour of others."

Instead of this, by means of the verbal rivet *"and since"* a second proposition is added in order to draw a conclusion from this and not from the first one.

Second part of the paragraph: "Useful labour is possible only in society and through society."

According to the first proposition, labour was the source of all wealth and all culture; therefore no society is possible without labour. Now we learn, conversely, that no "useful" labour is possible without society.

One could just as well have said that only in society can useless and even socially harmful labour become a branch of gainful occupation, that only in society can one live by being idle, etc.,—in short, one could just as well have copied the whole of Rousseau.

And what is "useful" labour? Surely only labour which produces the intended useful result. A savage—and man was a savage after he had ceased to be an ape—who kills an animal with a stone, who collects fruits, etc., performs "useful" labour.

Third, the conclusion: "And since useful labour is possible only in society and through society, the proceeds of labour belong undiminished, with equal right, to all members of society."

A fine conclusion! If useful labour is possible only in society and through society, the proceeds of labour belong to society—and only so much therefrom accrues to the individual worker as is not required to maintain the "condition" of labour, society.

In fact, this proposition has at all times been made use of by the champions of the *state of society prevailing at any given time.* First come the claims of the government and everything that sticks to it, since it is the social organ for the maintenance of the social order; then come the claims of the various kinds of private property, for the various kinds of private property are the foundations of society, etc. One sees that such hollow phrases can be twisted and turned as desired.

The first and second parts of the paragraph have some intelligible connection only in the following wording:

"Labour becomes the source of wealth and culture only as social labour," or, what is the same thing, "in and through society."

This proposition is incontestably correct, for although isolated labour (its material conditions presupposed) can create use values it can create neither wealth or culture.

But equally incontestable is this other proposition:

"In proportion as labour develops socially, and becomes thereby a source of wealth and culture, poverty and destitution develop among the workers, and wealth and culture among the non-workers."

This is the law of all history hitherto. What, therefore, had to be done here, instead of setting down general phrases about "labour" and "society," was to prove concretely how in present capitalist society the material, etc., conditions have at last been created which enable and compel the workers to lift this social curse.

In fact, however, the whole paragraph, bungled in style and content, is there only in order to inscribe the Lassallean catchword of the "undiminished proceeds of labour" as a slogan at the top of the party banner. I shall return later to the "proceeds of labour," "equal right," etc., since the same thing recurs in a somewhat different form further on.

2. "In present-day society the instruments of labour are the monopoly of the capitalist class; the resulting dependence of the working class is the cause of misery and servitude in all its forms."

This sentence, borrowed from the Rules of the International, is incorrect in this "improved" edition.

In present-day society the instruments of labour are the monopoly of the landowners (the monopoly of property in land is even the basis of the monopoly of capital) *and* the capitalists. In the passage in question the Rules of the International do not mention either the one or the other class of monopolists. They speak of the *"monopoliser of the means of labour,* that is, *the sources of life."* The addition, *"sources of life,"* makes it sufficiently clear that land is included in the instruments of labour.

The correction was introduced because Lassalle, for reasons now generally known, attacked *only* the capitalist class and not the landowners. In England the capitalist is usually not even the owner of the land on which his factory stands.

> 3. "The emancipation of labour demands the promotion of the instruments of labour to the common property of society and the co-operative regulation of the total labour with a fair distribution of the proceeds of labour."

"Promotion of the instruments of labour to the common property" ought obviously to read their "conversion into the common property," but this only in passing.

What are "proceeds of labour"? The product of labour or its value? And in the latter case is it the total value of the product or only that part of the value which labour has newly added to the value of the means of production consumed?

"Proceeds of labour" is a loose notion which Lassalle has put in the place of definite economic conceptions.

What is "a fair distribution"?

Do not the bourgeois assert that the present-day distribution is "fair"? And is it not, in fact, the only "fair" distribution on the basis of the present-day mode of production? Are economic relations regulated by legal conceptions or do not, on the contrary, legal relations arise from economic ones? Have not also the socialist sectarians the most varied notions about "fair" distribution?

To understand what is implied in this connection by the phrase "fair distribution," we must take the first paragraph and this one together. The latter presupposes a society wherein "the instruments of labour" are "common property" and the "total labour" is co-operatively regulated, and from the first paragraph we learn that "the proceeds of labour belong undiminished, with equal right, to all members of society."

"To all members of society"? To those who do not work as well? What remains then of the "undiminished proceeds of labour"? Only to those members of society who work? What remains then of the "equal right" of all members of society?

But "all members of society" and "equal right" are obviously mere phrases. The kernel consists in this, that in this communist society every worker must receive the "undiminished" Lassallean "proceeds of labour."

Let us take first of all the words "proceeds of labour" in the sense of the product of labour; then the co-operative proceeds of labour are the *total social product*.

From this must now be deducted:

First, provision for replacement of the means of production used up.

Second, additional portion for expansion of production.

Third, reserve or insurance funds to provide against accidents, dislocations caused by natural calamities, etc.

These deductions from the "undiminished proceeds of labour" are an economic necessity, and their magnitude is to be determined according to available means and forces, and partly by computation of probabilities, but they are in no way calculable by equity.

There remains the other part of the total product, intended to serve as means of consumption.

Before this is divided among the individuals, there has to be deducted again from it:

First, the general costs of administration not belonging to production.

This part will, from the outset, be very considerably restricted in comparison with present-day society, and it diminishes in proportion as the new society develops.

Second, that which is intended for the common satisfaction of needs, such as schools, health services, etc.

From the outset this part grows considerably in comparison with present-day society, and it grows in proportion as the new society develops.

Third, funds for those unable to work, etc., in short, for what is included under so-called official poor relief today.

Only now do we come to the "distribution" which the programme, under Lassallean influence, alone has in view in its narrow fashion, namely, to that part of the means of consumption which is divided among the individual producers of the co-operative society.

The "undiminished proceeds of labour" have already unnoticeably become converted into the "diminished" proceeds, although what the producer is deprived of in his capacity as a private individual benefits him directly or indirectly in his capacity as a member of society.

Just as the phrase of the "undiminished proceeds of labour" has disappeared, so now does the phrase of the "proceeds of labour" disappear altogether.

Within the co-operative society based on common ownership of the means of production, the producers do not exchange their products; just as little does the labour employed on the products appear here *at the value* of these products, as a material quality possessed by them, since now, in contrast to capitalist society, individual labour no longer exists in an indirect fashion, but directly as a component part of the total labour. The phrase "proceeds of labour," objectionable also today on account of its ambiguity, thus loses all meaning.

What we have to deal with here is communist society, not as it has *developed* on its own foundations, but, on the contrary, just as it *emerges* from capitalist society, which is thus in every respect, economically, morally, and intellectually, still stamped with the birthmarks of the old society from whose womb it emerges. Accordingly, the individual producer receives back from society—after the deductions have been made—exactly what he gives to it. What he has given to it is his individual quantum of labour. For example, the social working day consists of the sum of the individual hours of work; the individual labour time of the individual producer is the part of the social working day contributed by him, his share in it. He receives a certificate from society that he has furnished such and such an amount of labour (after deducting his labour for the common funds), and with this certificate he draws from the social stock of means of consumption as much as costs the same amount of labour. The same amount of labour which he has given to society in one form he receives back in another.

Here obviously the same principle prevails as that which regulates the exchange of commodities, as far as this is exchange of equal values. Content and form are changed because under the altered circumstances no one can give anything except his labour, and because, on the other hand, nothing can pass to the ownership of individuals except individual means of consumption. But, as far as the distribution of the latter among the individual producers is concerned, the same principle prevails as in the exchange of commodity equivalents: a given amount of labour in one form is exchanged for an equal amount of labour in another form.

Hence *equal right* here is still in principle—*bourgeois right*, although principle and practice are no longer at loggerheads, while the exchange of equivalents in commodity exchange exists only *on the average* and not in the individual case.

In spite of this advance this *equal right* is still constantly stigmatised by a bourgeois limitation. The right of the producers is *proportional* to the labour they supply; the equality consists in the fact that measurement is made with an *equal standard*, labour.

But one man is superior to another physically or mentally, and so supplies more labour in the same time, or can labour for a longer time; and labour, to serve as a measure, must be defined by its duration or intensity, otherwise it ceases to be a standard of measurement. This *equal* right is an unequal right for unequal labour. It recognises no class differences because everyone is only a worker like everyone else, but it tacitly recognises unequal individual endowment and thus productive capacity as natural privileges. *It is, therefore, a right of inequality, in its content, like every right.* Right by its very nature can consist only in the application of an equal standard; but unequal individuals (and they would not be different individuals if they were not unequal) are measurable only by an equal standard in so far as they are brought under an equal point of view, are taken from one *definite* side only, for instance, in the present case, are regarded *only as workers*, and nothing more is seen in them, everything else being ignored. Further, one worker is married, another not; one has more children than another, and so on and so forth. Thus, with an equal performance of labour, and hence an equal share in the social consumption fund, one will in fact receive more than another, one will be richer than another, and so on. To avoid all these defects, right instead of being equal would have to be unequal.

But these defects are inevitable in the first phase of communist society as it is when it has just emerged after prolonged birth pangs from capitalist society. Right can never be higher than the economic structure of society and the cultural development conditioned by it.

In a higher phase of communist society, after the enslaving subordination of the individual to the division of labour, and therewith also the antithesis between mental and physical labour, has vanished; after labour has become not only a means of life but life's prime want; after the productive forces have also increased with the all-round development of the individual, and all the springs of co-operative wealth flow more abundantly—only then can the narrow horizon of bourgeois right be crossed in its entirety and society inscribe on its banners: "From each according to his ability, to each according to his needs!"

I have dealt more at length with the "undiminished proceeds of labour" on the one hand, and with "equal right" and "fair distribution," on the other, in order to show what a crime it is to attempt, on the one hand, to force on our party again, as dogmas, ideas which in a certain period had some meaning but have now become obsolete verbal rubbish, while again perverting, on the other, the realistic outlook, which it cost so much effort to instill into the party, but which has now taken root in it, by means of ideological nonsense about right and other trash so common among the democrats and French socialists.

Quite apart from the analysis so far given, it was in general a mistake to make a fuss about so-called *distribution* and put the principal stress on it.

Any distribution whatever of the means of consumption is only a consequence of the distribution of the conditions of production themselves. The latter distribution, however, is a feature of the mode of production itself. The capitalist mode of production, for example, rests on the fact that the material conditions of production are in the hands of non-workers in the form of property in capital and land, while the masses are only owners of the personal condition of production, of labour power. If the elements of production are so distributed, then the present-day distribution of the means of consumption results automatically. If the material conditions of production are the co-operative property of the workers themselves, then there likewise results a distribution of the means of consumption different from the present one. Vulgar socialism (and from it in turn a section of the democracy) has taken over from the bourgeois economists the consideration and treatment of distribution as independent of the mode of production and hence the presentation of socialism as turning principally on distribution. After the real relation has long been made clear, why retrogress again?

4. "The emancipation of labour must be the work of the working class, relative to which all other classes are *only one reactionary mass.*"

The first strophe is taken from the introductory words of the Rules of the International, but "improved." There it is said: "The emancipation of the working class must be the act of the workers themselves"; here, on the contrary, the "working class" has to emancipate—what? "Labour." Let him understand who can.

In compensation, the antistrophe, on the other hand, is a Lassallean quotation of the first water: "relative to which [the working class] all other classes are *only one reactionary mass.*"

In the *Communist Manifesto* it is said: "Of all the classes that stand face to face with the bourgeoisie today, the proletariat alone is a *really revolutionary class.* The other classes decay and finally disappear in the face of modern industry; the proletariat is its special and essential product."

The bourgeoisie is here conceived as a revolutionary class —as the bearer of large-scale industry—relative to the feudal lords and the lower-middle class, who desire to maintain all social positions that are the creation of obsolete modes of production. Thus they do not form *together* with the *bourgeoisie* only one reactionary mass.

On the other hand, the proletariat is revolutionary relatively to the bourgeoisie because, having itself grown up on the basis of large-scale industry, it strives to strip off from production the capitalist character that the bourgeoisie seeks to perpetuate. But the *Manifesto* adds that the "lower-middle class" is becoming revolutionary "in view of [its] impending transfer into the proletariat."

From this point of view, therefore, it is again nonsense to say that it, together with the bourgeoisie, and with the feudal lords into the bargain, form "only one reactionary mass" relative to the working class.

Has one proclaimed to the artisans, small manufacturers, etc., and *peasants* during the last elections: "Relative to us you, together with the bourgeoisie and feudal lords, form only one reactionary mass"?

Lassalle knew the *Communist Manifesto* by heart, as his faithful followers know the gospels written by him. If, therefore, he has falsified it so grossly, this has occurred only to put a good colour on his alliance with absolutist and feudal opponents against the bourgeoisie.

In the above paragraph, moreover, his oracular saying is dragged in by main force without any connection with the botched quotation from the Rules of the International. Thus it is here simply an impertinence, and indeed not at all displeasing to Herr Bismarck, one of these cheap pieces of insolence in which the Marat of Berlin deals.

5. "The working class strives for its emancipation first of all *within the framework of the present-day national state,* conscious that the necessary result of its

efforts, which are common to the workers of all
civilised countries, will be the international brotherhood of peoples."

Lassalle, in opposition to the *Communist Manifesto* and
to all earlier socialism, conceived the workers' movement
from the narrowest national standpoint. He is being followed in this—and that after the work of the International!

It is altogether self-evident that, to be able to fight at all,
the working class must organise itself at home *as a class*
and that its own country is the immediate arena of its
struggle. In so far its class struggle is national, not in substance, but, as the *Communist Manifesto* says, "in form."
But the "framework of the present-day national state," for
instance, the German Empire, is itself in its turn economically "within the framework" of the world market, politically "within the framework" of the system of states. Every
businessman knows that German trade is at the same time
foreign trade, and the greatness of Herr Bismarck consists,
to be sure, precisely in his pursuing a kind of *international*
policy.

And to what does the German workers' party reduce its
internationalism? To the consciousness that the result of its
efforts will be *"the international brotherhood of peoples"*—
a phrase borrowed from the bourgeois League of Peace and
Freedom, which is intended to pass as equivalent to the
international brotherhood of the working classes in the
joint struggle against the ruling classes and their governments. Not a word, therefore, *about the international
functions* of the German working class! And it is thus that
it is to challenge its own bourgeoisie—which is already
linked up in brotherhood against it with the bourgeois of
all other countries—and Herr Bismarck's international
policy of conspiracy!

In fact, the internationalism of the programme stands
even infinitely below that of the Free Trade party. The
latter also asserts that the result of its efforts will be "the
international brotherhood of peoples." But it also *does*
something to make trade international, and by no means
contents itself with the consciousness that all peoples are
carrying on trade at home.

The international activity of the working classes does
not in any way depend on the existence of the International
Workingmen's Association. This was only the first attempt
to create a central organ for that activity, an attempt which
was a lasting success on account of the impulse which it

gave, but which was no longer realisable in its *first histori-cal form* after the fall of the Paris Commune.

Marx and Economics

For the communist, since man is the measure of history, so man's labor is the measure of value. Man, like every plant and every animal, is defined by his needs and is distinguished from them by his production. For work is man's essential vocation. The purpose of man's work is "the objectivization of man's generic life" (Marx). For, as the creation of man "is the final aim of human history," the true being of man is work. History is "the process of man's practical development" (Marx). But man never ex-ists in the abstract, he exists as a member of a family, of a society, of a State. In primitive society man's work ex-pressed "the active relatedness of man to nature." Before tools man had a purely "gregarious-animal" consciousness of himself, and the only division of labor was one result-ing from the physical differences between male and female. With increasing productivity—leading to private property and a division of labor based more and more on affirmation of the individual against the collectivity, on differences be-tween one collectivity and the next, on distinctions between town and country, between classes, between physical and mental work—labor and its projects now became objects outside of man, alienated from him, and man's power func-tion (work), became a hostile and foreign force, which dominated him instead of being dominated by him.

"The object produced by labor, its product, now stands opposed to it as an alien being, as a power independent of the producer. The product of labor is labor which has been embodied in an object . . . this product is an objectification of labor," therefore man "does not fulfill himself in his work but denies himself, has a feeling of misery rather than well-being, does not freely develop his mental and

From *Selected Writings in Sociology and Social Philosophy*, by Karl Marx, New York, 1964.

physical energies but is physically exhausted and mentally debased. The worker therefore feels himself at home only during his leisure time."[1]

Not only does private property and the division of labor alienate man from his essential activity, but the price of labor (wages) is increasingly less than its value. On this "surplus value" Marx declared the capitalist system to be based, and by it the worker is transformed into a thing. *"All human servitude is involved in the relation of the worker to production, and all types of servitude are only modifications or consequences of this relation . . . It cannot be otherwise in a mode of production in which the laborer exists to satisfy the need of self-expansion of existing values, instead of, on the contrary, material wealth existing to satisfy the needs of development on the part of the laborer."*[2]

Excerpts from classic Marxist text follow.

The Social System of Capitalism

Capital consists of raw materials, instruments of labour, and means of subsistence of all kinds, which are employed in producing new raw materials, new instruments of labour, and new means of subsistence. All these components of capital are created by labour, products of labour, *accumulated labour*. Accumulated labour that serves as a means to new production is capital. So say the economists.

What is a negro slave? A man of the black race. The one explanation is worthy of the other.

A negro is a negro. Only under certain conditions does he become a *slave*. A cotton-spinning machine is a machine for spinning cotton. Only under certain conditions does it become *capital*. Torn away from these conditions, it is as little capital as *gold* by itself is *money*, or as sugar is the *price* of sugar.

In the process of production, human beings do not only enter into a relation with Nature. They produce only by

[1] Karl Marx, *Economic and Philosophical Manuscripts*, translated by T. B. Bottomore, New York, 1961, p. 98.
[2] *Ibid.*, p. 143.

working together in a specific manner and by reciprocally exchanging their activities. In order to produce, they enter into definite connections and relations with one another, and only within these social connections and relations does their connection with Nature, i.e. production, take place.

These social relations between the producers, and the conditions under which they exchange their activities and share in the total act of production, will naturally vary according to the character of the means of production. With the discovery of a new instrument of warfare, the fire-arm, the whole internal organization of the army was necessarily altered, the relations within which individuals compose an army and can act as an army were transformed, and the relation of different armies to one another was likewise changed.

The social relations within which individuals produce, *the social relations of production, are altered, transformed, with the change and development of the material means of production, of the forces of production. The relations of production in their totality constitute what is called the social relations, society,* and, moreover, a society at a definite stage of historical development, a society with a unique and distinctive character. Ancient society, feudal society, bourgeois (or capitalist) society, are such totalities of relations of production, each of which denotes a particular stage of development in the history of mankind.

Capital also is a social relation of production. It is a *bourgeois relation of production,* a relation of production of bourgeois society. The means of subsistence, the instruments of labour, the raw materials, of which capital consists —have they not been produced and accumulated under given social conditions, within definite social relations? Are they not employed for new production, under given social conditions, within definite social relations? And does not just this definite social character stamp the products which serve for new production *as capital?*

Capital consists not only of means of subsistence, instruments of labour, and raw materials, not only of material products: it consists just as much of *exchange values.* All products of which it consists are *commodities.* Capital, consequently, is not only a sum of material products, it is a sum of commodities, of exchange values, of social magnitudes.

Wage-Labor and Capital
(1849)
Marx-Engels Gesamtausgabe I/6, pp. 482–3

Capital therefore presupposes wage-labour; wage-labour presupposes capital. They condition each other; each brings the other into existence.

MEGA I/6, p. 485

Capitalism and Human Alienation

Political economy begins with the fact of private property; it does not explain it. It conceives the processes of private property, as these occur in reality, in general and abstract formulas which then serve it as laws. It does not understand these laws; that is, it does not show how they arise out of the nature of private property. Political economy provides no explanation of the basis of the distinction of labour from capital, of capital from land. When, for example, the relation of wages to profit is defined, this is explained in terms of the interests of capitalists; in other words, what should be explained is assumed. Similarly, competition is referred to at every point, and is explained in terms of external conditions. Political economy tells us nothing about the extent to which these external and apparently accidental conditions are simply the expression of a necessary development. We have seen how exchange itself seems an accidental fact. The only moving forces which political economy recognizes are the *lust for gain* and the *war between seekers after gain,* competition.

Just because political economy fails to understand the interconnections within this movement, it was possible to oppose the doctrine of competition to that of monopoly, the doctrine of freedom of the crafts to that of the guilds, the doctrine of the division of landed property to that of great estates, for competition, freedom of the crafts, and the division of landed property were conceived only as accidental consequences brought about by will and force, rather than as necessary, inevitable, and natural consequences of monopoly, the guild system, and feudal property.

Economic & Philosophical MSS (1844)
MEGA I/3, pp. 81–2

Every alienation of man from himself and from Nature appears in the relation which he postulates between other men and himself and Nature. Thus religious alienation is necessarily exemplified in the relation between laity and priest, or, since it is here a question of the spiritual world, between the laity and a mediator. In the real world of practice, this self-alienation can only be expressed in the real, practical relation of man to his fellow men. The medium through which alienation occurs is itself a practical one. Through alienated labour, therefore, man not only produces his relation to the object, and to the process of production as alien and hostile men; he also produces the relation of other men to his production and his product, and the relation between himself and other men.

EPM (1844)
MEGA I/3, p. 91

However, alienation shows itself not merely in the result, but also in the *process, of production,* within *productive activity* itself. . . .

In what does this alienation of labour consist? First, that the work is *external* to the worker, that it is not a part of his nature, that consequently he does not fulfil himself in his work but denies himself, has a feeling of misery, not of well-being, does not develop freely a physical and mental energy, but is physically exhausted and mentally debased. The worker therefore feels himself at home only during his leisure, whereas at work he feels homeless. His work is not voluntary but imposed, *forced labour.* It is not the satisfaction of a need, but only a *means* for satisfying other needs.

The more the worker expends himself in work, the more powerful becomes the world of objects which he creates in face of himself, and the poorer he himself becomes in his inner life, the less he belongs to himself. It is just the same as in religion. The more of himself man attributes to God the less he has left in himself. The worker puts his life into the object and his life then belongs no longer to him but to the object. The greater his activity, therefore, the less he possesses. What is embodied in the product of his labor is no longer his. The greater this product is, therefore, the more he himself is diminished. The *alienation* of the worker in his product means not only that his labour becomes an object, takes on its own existence, but that it exists outside him, independently, and alien to him, and that it stands opposed to him as an autonomous power. The life which he has given to the object sets itself against him as an alien and hostile force.

EPM (1844)
MEGA I/3, pp. 83–34

Communism, on the contrary, requires the positive abolition of private property, and thus of human self-alienation. It is the real appropriation of human nature through and for man. It is, therefore, the return of man to himself as a social, i.e. really human being. This is a complete and conscious return which assimilates all the wealth of previous development. Communism as a fully developed naturalism is humanism, and as a fully developed humanism is naturalism. It is the definitive resolution of the antagonism between man and nature, and between man and man.

EPM, p. 127

Marx and Religion

"Do you then consider socialism as a religion?"
"How could you have me do otherwise?"

Alexander Herzen (1869)

"Religious suffering is at the same time an expression of real suffering and a protest against real suffering. Religion is the sigh of the oppressed creature, the sentiment of a heartless world, and the soul of soulless conditions. It is the opium of the people. The abolition of religion as the illusory happiness of men, is a demand for their real happiness. The call to abandon their illusions is a call to abandon a condition which requires illusions." [Contribution to the Critique of Hegel's Philosophy of Right.]

Karl Marx, says Antonio Gramsci (1891–1957), got this— one of his most famous definitions— from Honoré de Balzac, who wrote of lotteries as the "opium of misery."

Religion also, Marx declared (in his introduction to the Critique of Hegel's Philosophy of Law), *"is only an illusory*

From *Marx and Engels: Basic Writings on Politics and Philosophy*, by Karl Marx and Friedrich Engels, edited by Lewis S. Feuer, London, 1969.

sun which moves around man as long as he does not move around himself."

Marx found his idea of religious alienation in Ludwig Feuerbach, who declared that man's representation of God is his alienation "for what ever he affirms in God he denies in himself. Man is bereft of everything he gives to God. For God to become rich man must become poor."

Marx (as Mircea Eliade among others has emphasized) was a Christian heretic, and it is even possible to speak of a "Christology" of Marx. Marx's doctoral thesis was on the difference of the philosophy of nature in Democritus and Epicurus, two pre-Christian philosophers, but he never lost his basic Judeo-Christian concern with man's fall (into alienation) and man's redemption (by communism). Hegel had found the three modes of dialectic in the Trinity; Marx declared that "the State is the mediator between man and the liberty of man, just as Christ is the mediator to whom man imputes all his divinity, all his religious perplexity." (Karl Marx: The Jewish Question, 1/11/583.)

In practice, communism has historically been antireligious. A person is as much forbidden in a communist country to to be a communicant Christian if he wishes to be a Communist Party member, as he is in a noncommunist country forbidden by the church to be a Communist Party member if he wishes to be a communicant Christian. As early as 1905 Lenin declared, "We consider religion to be a private matter with regard to the State, but not with regard to our Party."

The following remarks by Engels on early Christianity are followed by excerpts from the Soviet Encyclopedia *and by an appeal to Catholics made in 1938 by Maurice Thorez (president of the French Communist Party until his death in 1964).*

On the History of Early Christianity

[This essay is noteworthy for Engels' explicit recognition of the religious character of the communist movement, and his endorsement of Renan's words: "If I wanted to give you an idea of the early Christian communities I would tell you to look at a local section of the International Workingmen's Association." It was first published in *Die Neue Zeit,* Volume XIII, Band 1, 1894–95, pages 4–13, 36–43. —ED.]

I

The history of early Christianity has notable points of resemblance with the modern working-class movement. Like the latter, Christianity was originally a movement of oppressed people: it first appeared as the religion of slaves and emancipated slaves, of poor people deprived of all rights, of peoples subjugated or dispersed by Rome. Both Christianity and the workers' socialism preach forthcoming salvation from bondage and misery; Christianity places this salvation in a life beyond, after death, in heaven; socialism places it in this world, in a transformation of society. Both are persecuted and baited, their adherents are despised and made the objects of exclusive laws, the former as enemies of the human race, the latter as enemies of the state, enemies of religion, the family, social order. And in spite of all persecution, nay, even spurred on by it, they forge victoriously, irresistibly ahead. Three hundred years after its appearance Christianity was the recognised state religion in the Roman world empire, and in barely sixty years socialism has won itself a position which makes its victory absolutely certain.

We therefore see that the Christianity of that time, which was still unaware of itself, was as different as heaven from earth from the later dogmatically fixed universal religion of the Nicene Council; one cannot be recognised in the other. Here we have neither the dogma nor the morals of later Christianity, but instead a feeling that one is struggling against the whole world and that the struggle will be a victorious one, an eagerness for the struggle and a certainty of victory which are totally lacking in Christians of today and which are to be found in our time only at the other pole of society, among the socialists.

In fact, the struggle against a world that at the beginning was superior in force, and at the same time against the innovators themselves, is common to the early Christians and the socialists. Neither of these two great movements was made by leaders or prophets—although there are prophets enough among both of them—they are mass movements. And mass movements are bound to be confused at the beginning, confused because the thinking of the masses at first moves among contradictions, lack of clarity, and lack of cohesion, and also because of the role that prophets still play in them at the beginning. This confusion is to be seen in the formation of numerous sects which fight against one another with at least the same zeal as against the common external enemy. So it was with early Christianity, so it was in the beginning of the socialist movement, no matter how much that worried the well-meaning worthies who preached unity where no unity was possible.

Was the International held together by a uniform dogma? On the contrary. There were communists of the French pre-1848 tradition, among whom again were various shades: communists of Weitling's school and others of the regenerated Communist League, Proudhonists dominating in France and Belgium, Blanquists, the German workers' party, and finally the Bakuninist anarchists, who for a while had the upper hand in Spain and Italy, to mention only the principal groups. It took a whole quarter of a century from the foundation of the International before the separation from the anarchists was final and complete everywhere and unity could be established, at least in respect of most general economic viewpoints. And that with our means of communication—railways, telegraph, giant industrial cities, the press, organised people's assemblies.

There was among the early Christians the same division into countless sects, which was the very means by which discussion and thereby later unity were achieved.

Religion

Religion (from the Latin *religio*) is a form of social conscience; a deformed, fantastic reflex within the conscience of men to the natural and social forces to which man is

From *The Great Soviet Encyclopedia (Bolsaja Sovetskaya Encyclopediya)*, Wisconsin, 1961.

subjected. Religion is faith in the existence of supernatural forces: gods, spirits, souls and similar things; it is anti-scientific by definition. Its product is impotence and ignorance; it is, according to the statement of Marx which Lenin used to define the basic Marxist doctrine of matter, the "opium of the masses."

Religion's ideology diverts the workers from the earthly struggle by lulling them into a hope of freedom in heaven. "The helplessness of the exploited in the struggle against their overseers generates a faith in a better life in the next world, as inevitably as the helplessness of the savage in his struggle with nature generates a faith in demons, gods, miracles, etc." (Lenin, Op., 4 ed., V.10, p. 65). In the history of society, the substitution of certain religious conceptions with other ones, within specific conditions of social being, can be a factor of progress in the life of a people, as is the case, for example, with primitive Christianity, with the conversion of Russia, and with similar instances, but that does not deny either the causal factors or the essential of the religious phenomenon.

Religious conceptions, and the corresponding institutions, are a superstructure related to an economic base, and they change according to the conditions of life in a society and its particular economic structure; they are historical phenomena, and exist only within determined historical conditions. Marxism-Leninism has done away with the idealistic daydreams about the "eternity" of religion, the indelibility of "religious feeling," the "coessentiality" of religion and man, almost as though religion were an intimate part of the very nature of man, or could express the bonds which exist between men, or could constitute the link between the individual and society. Marxism-Leninism has shown how bourgeois idealistic philosophy, in its various forms and schools, tries to justify religion, to reconcile it with science, and to show eternity as the most important "manifestation of the spirit."

The determining causes of religion in a class society. At the time of the dissolution of the primitive communal structure, religious ideology underwent modifications. Religion was no longer only a reflection of impotence in the struggle against nature, but also of the weakness of the exploited against the exploiters, and of the situation of social subjection of the masses. Bourgeois science tries to ignore this duplicity in the characters of the gods of nature, although the history of religion amply confirms it. (In Egypt Osiris is pharaoh and god of vegetation, Amon is god of the sun and of regal sovereignty.) The cult of the dead is centered more and more on the defunct representatives of the social aristocracy, who come to be buried with great pomp in sepulchral barrows, prototypes of the Egyptian pyramids. Myths appear, legends, dogmas of a particular link between dominant classes, gods and spirits, of the procreation of kings by gods, of sovereigns who are half-gods (divination of pharaoh, Child of the Sun in Egypt, divination of imperial sovereignty in Rome). The preceding confused representation of the life of the soul after death begins to change. Inequality becomes important, and with it the image of two supernatural worlds, the one for ordinary members of society, the other for the privileged. Also, with the growing diversification of society, appears the doctrine of holiness after death as compensation for forbearance and resignation on earth.

With the development of the ancient states, one can begin to distinguish among the various gods the principal divinities, to whom the others are subject. Slowly to the supreme god are transferred the attributes of the other divinities. ". . . A single god," writes Engels, "would never have appeared without a single king, and the idea of a single god is only a copy of the eastern idea of a supreme despot" (Marx and Engels, Op. V. 21, p. 45). With the evolution of the enslaving structures of society, the gods of vegetation and of the sun appear more and more as saviours, and from them the masses expect not just natural gifts, but also liberation from the distress of social life. At the same time, the religions of the ancient world conserved the cult of animals (particularly developed in Egypt) and of ancestors, which hallowed the patriarchal family of the slave society, as well as that of various spirits and devils, and fetishism. A rich mythology grew up, which told the histories of the gods and half-gods.

At the moment of crisis in the slave society, *Christianity* was born, as the religion of the humiliated and oppressed masses of the Roman Empire, a religion which keeps, while re-elaborating them, elements of the cult and mythology of the ancient world. Christianity was originally formed as a distinct movement within the orbit of the dispersion (Diaspora) of the Jews, characterized by the idea of the Messiah-Saviour, by philosophical-religious elements, with their ideas of the sinfulness of the world, of the soul and the divine intermediary, of the cult of gods which die and rise again, and of the image, which develops itself into the idea of the Roman emperor, of man-god. On this base is formed the mythical figure of Christ. During the course of its subsequent development, Christianity with its preaching of resignation and of renunciation was exploited for its own interest by the governing classes and in the 4th Century became the predominant religion of the Roman Empire. After the division of the Empire into East and West, between the 9th and 11th Centuries, Christianity divided itself into the two churches existing to this day: Catholic in the West and Orthodox in the East.

God, a mythical imaginary being, is a fundamental concept to every vision of the religious world. Faith in God is the principal dogma of religion. According to religious affirmation, god is an omnipotent being, supernatural, a supreme incorporeal force, which created the world, gave to it a certain order, governs it and determines the destinies both of individuals and of all humanity.

Religious ideas already existed among primitive men, a result of natural man's impotence before the happenings of nature. External natural forces which controlled primitive man are reflected in his conscience, in the fantastic form of supernatural beings capable of controlling natural phenomena, causing now good and joy, now damage and mishap. With the birth of class-society and exploitation, religion began to reflect the forces of social oppression. The gods "now represent social attributes and become symbols of historical forces." (Engels, F., *Anti-Dühring,* 1950, page 299). In this way God is not an immaterial omnipotent being, as the propagandists of religion claim, but "a group of ideas born from the blind projection of man; either of natural phenomena, or of the yoke of class, a group of ideas which reinforce that projection and feed the class-struggle" (Lenin, Op., 3 ed., V. 17, p. 85). The primitive side of faith in god was *soul-ism,* faith in spirits, especially those of dead ancestors, and in general, the spiritualism of natural forces and phenomena. An aspect of soul-ism is *fetish-ism,* a deification of inanimate objects; a residuary of fetishism is the representation of God under the form of icons, of statues and the like, a practice still carried on in our own times. The worship of ancestors led to the formation of images of racial and tribal gods: it was thus that polytheism originated. Later, together with the formation of the large state units, particularly of the monarchical type, was born the idea of a single all-possessing god, as the "king of the heavens"; ". . . the single God," wrote Engels, "would never have been thought of without a single king. The unit of god, which controls the numerous phenomena of nature, which unifies the contrasting forces of nature, is only a copy of the single oriental despot who visibly and actively unifies men pulled by differing interests" (Marx, K. & Engels, F., Op., V. 21, p. 45).

The idea of god, together with faith in the punishment and reward dispensed by him, is meant to make the exploited accept the class-yoke; in the real struggle for a better life, it produces an illusory consolation of a divine bestowal in the next world. Thus also the affirmation of priests about "divine-rights" is inspired by the principle of resignation: you must accept the power of the exploiters, because you aren't capable of changing the order laid down by God.

Faith in God, or religion, is sister of philosophical idealism, which the classicists of Marxism-Leninism define as perfectionism and a purification of the clerical idea. Thus just as religion considers the world a creation of god, so philosophical idealism, as I. V. Stalin points out, "considers the world as an incarnation of the absolute idea, of the universal soul, of conscience" (Stalin, I., *Questions of Leninism,* 11 ed., p. 54). Idealistic philosophy attempts to beautify in whatever way possible, the idea of God, to reconcile it with common sense and with science, delineating God as a powerful and supernatural personality, creator and mover of the universe, or delineating him as a rational principle not exactly defined, who communicates to the universe "the first impulse," setting it thus into motion, or as a personification of nature as a whole. Idealistic philosophers have always striven, and continue to strive, to veil the concept of god, to make it more abstract and more nebulous. "The idea of the absolute, of universal spirit, of universal will, of 'total submission' of the physical to the psychical; all of this is the same idea, put in different terms" (Lenin, Op., 4 ed., V. 14, p. 216). *Theology,* and thus idealistic philosophy, exerted themselves for many centuries to demonstrate by any and every means the existence of God.

The scientific, materialistic conception of the world is irreconcilable with faith in God; it is born and develops in acute and constant antagonism with religion. "Religion is the opium of the people; this statement of Marx is the basic conception of the Marxist world regarding the problem of religion" (Lenin, Op., 4 ed., V. 15, p. 371). "The idea of god has always lulled and blunted the 'social senses,' substituting for that which is alive that which is dead, always identifying itself with the idea of slavery (the worst sort of slavery, without escape). The idea of God has never "reconciled the individual with the social, rather it has clogged the exploited classes with faith in the divinity of the oppressors" (Lenin, Op., 3 ed., V. 17, p. 85). Dialectical materialism, taking advantage of the gains made by modern knowledge of natural things, will eliminate at the root the idea of God in all its forms. The liquidation of the religious wreckage and of the most important of this, faith in God, constitutes one of the objectives of the Communist education of the Soviet people. *Atheism* (from the Greek a = negation, *theos* = god), negation of god, is a conception of the world, which denies religion, faith in supernatural forces, in god or gods, in the next-world; atheism explains all the phenomena which appear in nature and in society by means of natural laws; it struggles against religious ideas. The appearance and development of atheism are bound to the development of the class struggle and the development of scientific knowledge of the laws of nature and of society.

In this history of the class struggle, atheism has been an ideological weapon of the progressive classes of society, who used it to eliminate the old, out-used social structures, of economics and societies which slowed down the evolution of the powers of productivity, of science and of culture. Because religion so strongly justified the existing social order, it was necessary with equal force for each new class, aiming at power, to fight religion, since it sanctioned the ideology of the old order. This battle usually took place under the banner of purification and reform of the old religion, but in the more radically revolutionary phenomena it became authentic, battling atheism; a total negation of religion. Although the history of peoples gives not a few luminous examples of struggle against the religious narcotic, an atheism scientifically reasonable only became possible with the evolution of the proletariat, with the appearance of Marxist-Leninist scientific theory, i.e., of dialectic materialism.

The enslaving merchant and industrial classes in power always did everything possible to reinforce and safeguard exploitation and oppression. Materialism and atheism then became dangerous for this class. Onto the stage then came to the defense of religion the idealistic philosophers. This last, renewed and reformed into new forms, became, in the hands of the enslaving-classes, an instrument to induce lethargy into the exploited masses. During the whole course of the Middle Ages the Catholic Church was a mighty feudal organisation, an international center of the feudal system. It had at its disposition not only vast properties and serfs but also schools and universities. All branches of culture were ruled over by theology. Any gleam of atheism and of free thought was persecuted and smothered. The Inquisition put to the flames thinkers and scholars who had dared pronounce against the "sacred" books and in defence of science. The criticism of religion was able to show itself only stealthily, in guarded and veiled terms. But even under these painful conditions, atheistic thought cleared the way. A medieval form of criticism of religion was expressed in the 12th Century by Averroës in his doctrine of the *double truth.* Under the conditions of medieval society this doctrine had a progressive importance, because, although timidly, it admitted a truth which contradicted the ecclesiastical dogmas, and by this unblocked the way to free thought. This was also true of *nominalism,* which was, in the words of Marx, the first appearance of materialism in that epoch (Marx-Engels, Op., V. 3, p. 157). The nominalists didn't dare to criticize religion openly, but with their struggle against the medieval realists, who claimed that concepts exist in themselves independently of concrete things, they contributed towards the liberation of scientific thought from the ecclesiastical yoke.

Not a small contribution to the development of atheism was made by the Peasant's War in Germany (1525). "The clergy suffered most from the consequences of this War . . . it was above all upon them that popular anger turned its violence" (Marx-Engels, V. 8, p. 194). The peasants called the Catholic Church "the instrument of the devil." The head of the rebels, Thomas Münzer, attacked not just Catholicism, but the whole of Christianity. He refused to recognize the Bible and condemned as fairy tales of the priests the idea of the "kingdom of God."

Atheism reached its major development in France, at the time of the preparation of the bourgeois revolution. In France in the 17th Century, the struggle of the revolutionary bourgeoisie against feudalism, was closely connected with the struggle against religion and the church, seal and highest sanction of feudal structures (Engels, *ibidem,* V. 8, p. 128) since, in order to overthrow these latter, it was necessary to deveil them of their priestliness. Already on the threshold of the 18th Century Pierre *Bayle* "predicted the appearance of an atheistic society" (Marx, *ibidem,* V. 3, p. 156). The country priest Jean Melier, in his "testament," protested in an uncompromisingly decided manner against religion, the clergy and feudal structures. He writes: "Natural phenomena were always caused, and are still always caused, only by blind natural laws of movement, inherent in the particles of matter by which these phenomena manifest themselves; because of this, there is nothing in nature which could demonstrate the existence of an omnipotent and supreme god." The French materialists of the 18th Century, Diderot and Holbach, fought openly in their works against religion and the church. The proletarian atheism of Marx and Engels is a logically complete atheism from beginning to end. While pre-Marxist bourgeois atheism was based upon a metaphysical materialism, proletariat atheism is based upon the granite foundations of historical dialectical materialism, the mighty instrument of the scientific knowledge of truth and of the revolutionary transformation of truth itself. Bourgeois atheism, due to its classical and scientific limitations, was not able to destroy completely the antiscientific characteristics of religion and its reactionary function: no bourgeois atheism definitely unmasked religion, without leaving to priests the slightest pretext. Bourgeois atheism was afraid of the masses and was an ideology of the "privileged," proletarian atheism is an ideology of millions of persons, an ideological weapon of the working class in its battle for a new world, for communism. Proletarian atheism is a materialistic ideology which has triumphed in the country of socialism, the Soviet Union, and which unites all over the world unlimited masses of workers.

Marx and Engels paid attention in their great work to the questions of religion. From 1844, the year of Marx's work, *Towards a Criticism of Hegel's Philosophy of Law,* we find the fundamental propositions of Marxist theory, which considers religion as a degenerate fantastic reflex of reality. "Religion," wrote Marx, "is the sigh of an overtaxed creature; the soul of a heartless world, the breath of life of an eternity without any soul, it is the opium of the people" (Marx and Engels, Op. V. I, 1938, p. 385).

Under new historical conditions, Lenin and Stalin further developed the theory of Marxist atheism, enriching it with the weight of new experiences of class struggle and of the construction of socialism. Marxism-Leninism showed beyond doubt that the roots of religion lie in the material life of society and that the religious-ness and the consequent religious instruction of a society pertain to the superstructure. "All religions are nothing but the fantastic reflex, in the mind of men, of those external forces which dominate them and their lives, a reflex in which earthly forces assume the aspect of supernatural ones" (Engels, *Anti-Dühring*).

Maurice Thorez
(1900–1964)

Thorez was the son of a coal miner. In 1930, he became secretary of the French Communist Party and, in 1936, leader of the party in the chamber of deputies. The party successes in the elections of 1945 and 1946 resulted in Thorez' becoming vice premier (1946–1947), a post he soon left and returned to the opposition. He served as president of the French Communist Party from 1964 until his death later that year.

Profession of Materialistic Faith

First of all let us recall the declaration made over the air last year:

> "We stretch out our hand to you, Catholics—workers, black-coated[1] workers, artisans, peasants—we who are a secular party, because you are our brothers and because you like ourselves are oppressed by the same cares."

From *Catholics and Communists,* speech of October 1938.

[1] "Black-coated" is the French expression corresponding to the American "white collar." [*Ed.*]

This proposal contains two affirmations:

1. The Communists are secularists, materialists.
2. There exists a factual solidarity—material, economic and social—between Catholic and Communist workers.

We are indeed, we Communists, the disciples of Marx and Engels, of Lenin and Stalin. We are Marxists-Leninists, convinced partisans of dialectical materialism, leading theory of the revolutionary proletariat. We are by virtue of this fact the authentic heirs and the continuers of the revolutionary thought of the French materialists of the eighteenth century, of the great Encyclopedists, themselves spiritual sons of that other French philosopher, Descartes, to whose memory we have recently paid tribute. Marx himself underlined this direct doctrinal relationship in his book *The Holy Family:*

> In the same way as Cartesian Materialism has its conclusion in physical and natural science properly speaking, the other tendency of French materialism ends directly in socialism and communism. When one studies the theories of materialism on the original goodness and the equal intelligence of men, on omnipotence, experience, upbringing, the influence of external conditions on men, the great importance of industry, the basis of enjoyment, etc., . . . it doesn't take a great penetration to discover what necessarily links them up with communism and socialism.

The Communists give a rational, scientific explanation of the world and its evolution. Since we are confident of the value of our doctrine, we only wish to employ in the spreading of our ideas exclusively ideological weapons.

Particularly in what concerns religion we intend to follow the counsels of Engels, of Lenin and of Guesde, who warned against "the slightest affront to the workers' religious convictions." (*Lenin on Religion,* p. 17.) Engels in an article on the program of the Blanquist refugees from the Commune criticized in 1874 those who want "to proclaim atheism as an obligatory article of faith." Lenin wrote that "proclaiming war on religion as a political objective of the workers' party is a mere Anarchist pose." (*Ibid,* p. 12.) More, Lenin admitted the possibility of accepting the entry into the Party not only of "all workers who still retain faith in God," but even of priests, on the one obvious condition that "he comes to cooperate with us in our work, conscientiously performs Party work and does not oppose the Party program."

The French Workers' Party, at its Twentieth National Congress in 1902, adopted a resolution that:

In the anti-clericalism which our rulers have been ostentatiously professing for some time past and which is only aimed at a certain number of orders in rebellion against their laws, the French Workers' Party can only see a new maneuver of the capitalist class to divert the workers from their struggle against economic slavery, the progenitor of all other forms of political and religious slavery.

The first Socialist Mayor of Roubaix, the Guesdist Henri Carrette, instituted a meatless meal on Fridays, when in 1892 he founded the school canteens. And he did this so as not to offend the religious convictions of the Catholic workers of Roubaix.

The philosophical materialism of the Communists is far from the religious faith of the Catholics. Yet, however far opposed their doctrinal conceptions may be, it is impossible not to see in both the same burning desire to answer the profound aspirations of men towards a better life. "The promise of a redeemer illumines the first page of human history," says the Catholic. The hope of a universal society united in labor and in love sustains the endeavor of the proletarians who are fighting for the happiness of all men, affirms the Communist. . . .

Engels, in his contribution to the *History of Christianity*, published in 1885, wrote:

> The history of Primitive Christianity offers some remarkable parallels with the modern working class movement. Like the latter Christianity in its beginnings was the movement of the oppressed, it appeared first of all as the religion of the slaves and freed slaves, of the poor and the men without rights, of the peoples subjugated or scattered by Rome. Both of them, Christianity like working class socialism, preach the coming deliverance from slavery and misery; Christianity transfers this deliverance to the next world, to a life after death, in heaven; socialism places it in this world, in a transformation of society. Both are pursued and hunted, their adherents are proscribed and put under exceptional laws in one case as enemies of the human race, in the other as enemies of government, of religion, of the family, of social order. And in spite of all persecutions and even assisted by them, both movements force their way on victoriously and irresistibly.

The progressive role of Christianity appears again later in its endeavor towards the organization of charity, of solidarity, in the attempt to make the relations between men in the feudal epoch more just and more peaceful, in the solicitude of the religious communities—Communist groups in aim, fact and action—which took upon themselves the mission of preserving, developing and handing down to future ages the sum of human knowledge and the artistic treasures of the past. Who can call to mind without a throb of emotion the centuries which saw the spires of our wonderful cathedrals rise towards the sky, these pure jewels of a people's art, which proclaim with every one of their ancient stones—which live for those who can understand them—against the legend of the gloomy Middle Ages?

I often start comparing with the cathedral builders, men animated by that burning faith which "moveth mountains" and makes the realization of great schemes possible, the constructors of the new socialist city, the Stakhanovites, the heroes of toil, who are raising on the free soil of the Soviet Union the giant factories, the entire towns and at the same time the imposing monuments in which today the inspired upward drive of communism is affirmed.

To approach still nearer to our own times, in 1789, is it not true to say that the poor village priests, won over to the cause of the French people, accelerated the progress of the Revolution by joining the delegates of the Third Estate, by thus determining the adoption, instead of the vote by order, of the numerical vote—favorable to the people's representatives—by allowing the proclamation of the National Constituent Assembly? It is a fact that the French clergy had been able to remain closer to the people, and that from this contact it drew a certain taste for independence, a more pronounced national sense.

Idealism of the Communists

Nothing is more foreign to Communism than that vulgar materialism with which certain people still affect to reproach us.

> By the word materialism the Philistine understands gluttony, drunkenness, lust of the eye, lust of the flesh, arrogance, cupidity, avarice, miserliness, profit-hunting and stock-exchange swindling—in short, all the filthy vices in which he himself indulges in private. (Engels, *Ludwig Feuerbach*, p. 41.)

Communism is on the contrary a noble and pure ideal, an inexhaustible source of generous impulses, which exalts in its adherents devotion and the spirit of sacrifice. Besides, let us hear what a Catholic priest says:

> That Communism can even offer splendid examples of such an asceticism is beyond doubt. Starting with its great masters: Marx, Engels, Lenin. What these men endured in suffering, privation and ill-treatment certainly oversteps the common mark and reaches an amazing greatness: exile, prison, concentration camp, Siberia, often the threat of death! How many militant Communists have not been fired by such men with a similar spirit of sacrifice! . . . It is undeniable that the materialism of the Communists is sometimes actually accompanied by a very keen sense of the ideal, of grandeur, of beauty, even by an inspiration towards saintliness, pursued confusedly in a false path, but with vehemence, with that intensity, of which Christ said that it was highly pleasing to Heaven. (Father Ducatillon, *Le Communisme et les Chrétiens,* p. 29.)

Communism is the struggle for a free and happy humanity. Far from wanting to destroy human greatness, Communism, attached to life above all, wishes to put it on true, on real, foundations. It wishes to create the conditions necessary to the full flowering of all human faculties; *Communism is indeed humanism.* Communism wants to save the family, which is threatened socially and morally by economic slavery, by the inhuman conditions forced on the father of a family, by the situation created for the mother who has been forced to abandon her home, to neglect her children in order to work at the factory and in the store. Communism wants to assure order in society through the brotherly collaboration of free producers. Communism wants to create the conditions for a boundless progress of knowledge and the arts.

Thus Communists obey a higher morality for "the true morality, like the true political policy, is the one which seeks to draw men closer to one another to make them work by united efforts for their mutual happiness. . . ." (Holbach, *Système Social,* p. 116.)

What at the present time is the essential obstacle to the drawing together of men, to their mutual happiness? It is the economic oppression which a small number of wealthy and opulent people, of greedy, inhuman masters inflicts on the infinite multitude of proletarians, whose status is practically that of slaves.

The Encyclical *Rerum Novarum* of Pope Leo XIII denounced this evil in 1891 in almost the same terms as *The Communist Manifesto* of Marx and Engels half a century before; and for some decades now the situation has become even more terrible for the laboring masses. But listen:

> What in our day springs first to the eye is not merely the concentration of wealth, but also the accumulation of an enormous power, a discretionary economic power, in the hands of a small number of men, who are not as a rule the proprietors, but simply the depositaries and managers of the capital, which they administer as they please. This power is important above all when it is in the hands of those who, being the holders and absolute masters of money, govern credit and dispense it at their pleasure. By virtue of this they distribute as it were the blood to the economic organism, whose life they hold in their hands, so that without their consent none can continue to live. This concentration of power and resources, which is as it were the distinguishing feature of contemporary economy, is the national fruit of a competition, the freedom of which knows no bounds; only the strongest can survive, which often amounts to saying those who fight with the most violence, who are the least hindered by scruples of conscience.

Who is the author of this page in which we find the tendencies of modern capitalism to fascism and war justly emphasized? Is it Lenin who analyzed in so brilliant a way the decomposition of capitalism when it has reached its last phase, imperialism? No, the page is taken from the Encyclical *Quadragesimo Anno* promulgated in 1931 by Pope Pius XI. It is a simple confirmation of facts, which alas are too true. To refuse in the face of this to envisage the consequences of such a state of affairs, in particular the aggravation of the class struggle, is to try to deny evidence. The class struggle was not proclaimed or called into being by wicked Communists; it exists independent of our good or ill will; we propose to end it by abolishing the exploitation of man by man, by proceeding to the destruction of classes themselves.

Does not the last Encyclical, dated September 29, 1937, say:

> Thus we see on the one hand the classes of citizens fighting a struggle to the death because some possess great riches, whilst the others have to earn their and their family's bread by hard, daily toil.

The class struggle is a fact; it is even—Father Ducatillon recognizes this—"*a factor in historical evolution.*" (*Le Communisme et les Chrétiens*, p. 78.)

Where then does the remedy to this evil, which all recognize, lie, except in the completion of an economic transformation, which is taking place before our eyes and which the privileged classes would like to retard, because they want to preserve a regime, in which the collective and social labor of the immense mass of non-possessing producers brings profit only to the parasitical minority which has usurped the wealth of the nation? Where does the remedy lie except in the conclusion of that progressive evolution of the forms of production, which has led from the primitive communities to the slavery of antiquity, from slavery to feudalism, from feudalism to capitalism, and which leads inevitably to socialism, to communism?

II.

MARX AND HISTORY

"Theoretical Communism sees history as a dialogue between collectivism and individualism" declares Shlomo Avineri,[1] and Sir Isaiah Berlin declares that *"when Hegel, and after him Marx, describe historical processes, they too assume that human beings and their societies are part and parcel of a wider nature, which Hegel regards as spiritual, and Marx as material, in character . . . from time to time the real forces —impersonal and irresistible—which truly govern the world develop to a point where a new historical advance is due. Then the crucial moments of advance are reached: these take the form of violent cataclysmic leaps, destructive revolutions which, often with fire and sword, establish a new order upon the ruins of the old"?*

Marx himself acknowledged his debt to Giambattista Vico (1668–1744), an Italian philosopher and historian, who declared all peoples went through the same sequence: *"first crude, then severe, then benign, then delicate, finally dissolute"* and that there were three ages of a people: the divine, the heroic and the human. But Marx, while deciding to devote most of his life to an historical study of capitalism (Leo Labedz suggests that Marx was never really interested in economics), was careful to say that though in Western Europe, the capitalist order emerged from the womb of the feudal order one will never find the clue to the phenomena by using as one's master key a general historico-philosophical

[1] *Karl Marx on Colonialism and Modernization*, edited by Shlomo Avineri, London, 1969, p. 95.

[2] Sir Isaiah Berlin, *Four Essays on Liberty*, London, 1969, pp. 60-61.

171

theory, the supreme virtue of which consists in being super-historical.

The ensuing definitions of the materialist conception of history are followed by articles on historical moments claimed by Marxists as illustrative.

The Materialist Conception of History

Let us admit, with M. Proudhon, that real history, history as temporal order, is the historical succession in which ideas, categories and principles have manifested themselves.

Each principle had its own century in which to reveal itself: the principle of authority, for instance, had the eleventh century just as the principle of individualism had the eighteenth century. Accordingly, it was the century which belonged to the principle, and not the principle which belonged to the century. In other words, it was the principle which made history, and not history which made the principle. When further, in order to save the principles as well as history, we ask ourselves why a particular principle appeared in the eleventh or the eighteenth century rather than in any other, we are bound to study closely the men of the eleventh century and those of the eighteenth, to examine their respective needs, their productive forces, their mode of production, the raw materials of their production, and finally the relations of man to man which resulted from all these conditions of life. In making a thorough study of these questions, are we not presenting the real, profane history of men in every century, showing men to be at the same time the authors and the actors of their own drama? But from the moment that men are represented as the authors and actors of their own history, we arrive, by a roundabout route, at the real point of departure, for we have now abandoned the eternal principles from which at first we began.

. . . men, who every day remake their own life, begin to make other men, to propagate their kind: the relation between man and wife, parents and children, *the family*. The family, which is at first the only social relationship, becomes later, when increased needs create new social relations and increased population needs, a subordinate one. . . . The production of life, both of one's own by labor and

From *Gesamtausgabe*, by Karl Marx & Friedrich Engels, New York, 1949.

of fresh life by procreation, appears at once as a double relationship, on the one hand as a natural, on the other as a social relationship. By social is meant the co-operation of several individuals, no matter under what conditions, in what manner or to what end. It follows from this, that a determinate mode of production, or industrial stage, is always bound up with a determinate mode of co-operation or social stage, and this mode of co-operation is itself a "production force." It also follows, that the mass of productive forces accessible to men determines the condition of society, and that the "history of humanity" must therefore always be studied and treated in relation to the history of industry and exchange.

George Lukacs
(1885–   )

Born in Budapest, Lukacs joined the Communist Party in 1918 and became a member of Bela Kun's revolutionary government (1919). After Kun's defeat, Lukacs fled to Berlin, where he lived in exile for twelve years until Hitler's rise when he escaped to Moscow. He returned to Hungary after World World War II. It was Lukacs who rediscovered Marx's debt to Hegel.

Lukacs is currently professor of aesthetics in Lorand Eotvos University, Budapest.

History and
Class Consciousness

The Marxist philosophy of history is a comprehensive doctrine dealing with the necessary progress made by hu-

From *History and Class Consciousness*, by George Lukacs, Berlin, 1923.

manity from primitive communism to our own time and the perspectives of our further advance along the same road. As such it also gives us indications for the historical future. But such indications—born of the recognition of certain laws governing development—are not a cookery book providing recipes for each phenomenon or period; Marxism is not a Baedeker of history, but a signpost pointing the direction in which history moves forward. The final certainty it affords consists in the assurance that the development of mankind does not and cannot finally lead to nothing and nowhere.

Of course, such generalizations do not do full justice to the guidance given by Marxism, a guidance extending to every topical problem of life. Marxism combines a consistent following of an unchanging direction with incessant theoretical and practical allowances for the deviousness of the path of evolution. Its well-defined philosophy of history is based on a flexible and adaptable acceptance and analysis of historical development. This apparent duality—which is in reality the dialectic unity of the materialist world-view —is also the guiding principle of Marxist aesthetics and literary theory.

Those who do not know Marxism at all or know it only superficially or at second-hand, may be surprised by the respect for the classical heritage of mankind which one finds in the really great representatives of this doctrine and by their incessant references to that classical heritage. Without wishing to enter into too much detail, we mention as an instance, in philosophy, the heritage of Hegelian dialectics, as opposed to the various trends in the latest philosophies. "But all this is long out of date," the modernists cry. "All this is the undesirable, outworn legacy of the nineteenth century," say those who—intentionally or unintentionally, consciously or unconsciously—support the Fascist ideology and its pseudo-revolutionary rejection of the past, which is in reality a rejection of culture and humanism. Let us look without prejudice at the bankruptcy of the very latest philosophies; let us consider how most philosophers of our day are compelled to pick up the broken and scattered fragments of dialectic (falsified and distorted in this decomposition) whenever they want to say something even remotely touching its essence about present-day life; let us look at the modern attempts at a philosophical synthesis and we shall find them miserable, pitiful caricatures of the old genuine dialectic, now consigned to oblivion.

It is not by chance that the great Marxists were jealous

guardians of our classical heritage in their aesthetics as well as in other spheres. But they do not regard this classical heritage as a reversion to the past; it is a necessary outcome of their philosophy of history that they should regard the past as irretrievably gone and not susceptible of renewal. Respect for the classical heritage of humanity in aesthetics means that the great Marxists look for the true highroad of history, the true direction of its development, the true course of the historical curve, the formula of which they know; and because they know the formula they do not fly off at a tangent at every hump in the graph, as modern thinkers often do because of their theoretical rejection of the idea that there is any such thing as an unchanged general line of development.

For the sphere of aesthetics this classical heritage consists in the great arts which depict man as a whole in the whole of society. Again it is the general philosophy (here: proletarian humanism) which determines the central problems posed in aesthetics. The Marxist philosophy of history analyses man as a whole, and contemplates the history of human evolution as a whole, together with the partial achievement, or non-achievement of completeness in its various periods of development. It strives to unearth the hidden laws governing all human relationships. Thus the object of proletarian humanism is to reconstruct the complete human personality and free it from the distortion and dismemberment to which it has been subjected in class society. These theoretical and practical perspectives determine the criteria by means of which Marxist aesthetics establish a bridge back to the classics and at the same time discover new classics in the thick of the literary struggles of our own time. The ancient Greeks, Dante, Shakespeare, Goethe, Balzac, Tolstoy all give adequate pictures of great periods of human development and at the same time serve as signposts in the ideological battle fought for the restoration of the unbroken human personality.

Friedrich Engels
(1820–1895)

The Rise of the Middle Class

When Europe emerged from the Middle Ages, the rising middle-class of the towns constituted its revolutionary element. It had conquered a recognised position within mediaeval feudal organisation, but this position, also, had become too narrow for its expansive power. The development of the middle-class, the *bourgeoisie*, became incompatible with the maintenance of the feudal system; the feudal system, therefore, had to fall.

But the great international centre of feudalism was the Roman Catholic Church. It united the whole of feudalised Western Europe, in spite of all internal wars, into one grand political system, opposed as much to the schismatic Greeks as to the Mohammedan countries. It surrounded feudal institutions with the halo of divine consecration. It had organised its own hierarchy on the feudal model, and, lastly, it was itself by far the most powerful feudal lord, holding, as it did, fully one-third of the soil of the Catholic world. Before profane feudalism could be successfully attacked in each country and in detail, this, its sacred central organisation, had to be destroyed.

Moreover, parallel with the rise of the middle-class went on the great revival of science; astronomy, mechanics, physics, anatomy, physiology, were again cultivated. And the bourgeoisie, for the development of its industrial production, required a science which ascertained the physical

From *Socialism: Utopian and Scientific,* by Friedrich Engels, Moscow, 1968.

properties of natural objects and the modes of action of the forces of Nature. Now up to then science had but been the humble handmaid of the Church, had not been allowed to overstep the limits set by faith, and for that reason had been no science at all. Science rebelled against the Church; the bourgeoisie could not do without science, and, therefore, had to join in the rebellion.

The above, though touching but two of the points where the rising middle-class was bound to come into collision with the established religion, will be sufficient to show, first, that the class most directly interested in the struggle against the pretensions of the Roman Church was the bourgeoisie; and second, that every struggle against feudalism, at that time, had to take on a religious disguise, had to be directed against the Church in the first instance. But if the universities and the traders of the cities started the cry, it was sure to find, and did find, a strong echo in the masses of the country people, the peasants, who everywhere had to struggle for their very existence with their feudal lords, spiritual and temporal.

The long fight of the bourgeoisie against feudalism culminated in three great, decisive battles.

The first was what is called the Protestant Reformation in Germany. The war cry raised against the Church by Luther was responded to by two insurrections of a political nature: first that of the lower nobility under Franz von Sickingen (1523), then the great Peasants' War, 1525. Both were defeated, chiefly in consequence of the indecision of the parties most interested, the burghers of the towns—an indecision into the causes of which we cannot here enter. From that moment the struggle degenerated into a fight between the local princes and the central power, and ended by blotting out Germany for two hundred years, from the politically active nations of Europe. The Lutheran Reformation produced a new creed indeed, a religion adapted to absolute monarchy. No sooner were the peasants of North-East Germany converted to Lutheranism than they were from free-men reduced to serfs.

But where Luther failed, Calvin won the day. Calvin's creed was one fit for the boldest of the bourgeoisie of his time. His predestination doctrine was the religious expression of the fact that in the commercial world of competition success or failure does not depend upon a man's activity or cleverness, but upon circumstances uncontrollable by him. It is not of him that willeth or of him that runneth, but of the mercy of unknown superior economic powers; and this was especially true at a period of economic revolution, when all old commercial routes and centres were replaced by new ones, when India and America were opened to the world, and when even most sacred economic articles of faith—the value of gold and silver—began to totter and to break down. Calvin's church constitution was thoroughly democratic and republican; and where the kingdom of God was republicanised, could the kingdoms of this world remain subject to monarchs, bishops and lords? While German Lutheranism became a willing tool in the hands of princes, Calvinism founded a republic in Holland, and active republican parties in England, and, above all, Scotland.

In Calvinism, the second great bourgeois upheaval found its doctrine ready cut and dried. This upheaval took place in England. The middle-class of the towns brought it on, and the yeomanry of the country districts fought it out. Curiously enough, in all the three great bourgeois risings, the peasantry furnishes the army that has to do the fighting; and the peasantry is just the class that, the victory once gained, is most surely ruined by the economic consequences of that victory. A hundred years after Cromwell, the yeomanry of England had almost disappeared. Anyhow, had it not been for that yeomanry and for the *plebeian* element in the towns, the bourgeoisie alone would never have fought the matter out to the bitter end, and would never have brought Charles I to the scaffold. In order to secure even those conquests of the bourgeoisie that were ripe for gathering at the time, the revolution had to be carried considerably further—exactly as in 1793 in France and 1848 in Germany. This seems, in fact, to be one of the laws of evolution of bourgeois society.

Well, upon this excess of revolutionary activity there necessarily followed the inevitable reaction which in its turn went beyond the point where it might have maintained itself. After a series of oscillations, the new centre of gravity was at last attained and became a new starting-point. The grand period of English history, known to respectability under the name of "the Great Rebellion," and the struggles succeeding it, were brought to a close by the comparatively puny event entitled by Liberal historians "the Glorious Revolution."

The new starting-point was a compromise between the rising middle-class and the exfeudal landowners. The latter, though called, as now, the aristocracy, had been long since on the way which led them to become what Louis Philippe in France became at a much later period, "the first bourgeois of the kingdom." Fortunately for England, the old feudal barons had killed one another during the Wars of the Roses. Their successors, though mostly scions of the old families, had been so much out of the direct line of descent that they constituted quite a new body, with habits and tendencies far more bourgeois than feudal. They fully understood the value of money, and at once began to increase their rents by turning hundreds of small farmers out and replacing them by sheep. Henry VIII, while squandering the Church lands, created fresh bourgeois landlords by wholesale; the innumerable confiscations of estates, regranted to absolute or relative upstarts, and continued during the whole of the seventeenth century, had the same result. Consequently, ever since Henry VII, the English "aristocracy," far from counteracting the development of industrial production, had, on the contrary, sought to indirectly profit thereby; and there had always been a section of the great landowners willing, for economical or political reasons, to co-operate with the leading men of the financial and industrial bourgeoisie. The compromise of 1689 was, therefore, easily accomplished. The political spoils of "pelf and place" were left to the great landowning families, provided the economic interests of the financial, manufacturing and commercial middle-class were sufficiently attended to. And these economic interests were at that time powerful enough to determine the general policy of the nation. There might be squabbles about matters of detail, but, on the whole, the aristocratic oligarchy knew too well that its own economic prosperity was irretrievably bound up with that of the industrial and commercial middle-class.

From that time, the bourgeoisie was a humble, but still a recognised component of the ruling classes of England.

Ernst Bloch
(1885–   )

Born in Germany, Bloch fled to Switzerland during the Nazi regime. He taught philosophy at the University of Leipzig after World War II until his dismissal as a revisionist in 1956. He now teaches at Tübingin in West Germany.

Thomas Münzer

V

... Let us concentrate only on this principle, to leave the dead behind. Nothing detains us any more where the party is over. We go forward, we project ourselves in dream towards our future. The vital thrust of our times, gathering vast weight, already is being fed from new sources; its incontrovertible evidence initiates a secret, still hidden faith.

If strong forces are able to lean upon that faith, man at last will leave the ground and will vigorously launch out toward the heights. We will no longer feel the weight of our life, we will escape from it, this life that is increasingly a slave to the machine and to that domination of the inessential which finally sets us free. This same force which created the machine and which, transforming the will, drives us towards socialism, this force it is which also sets in motion that other mysterious reality, hitherto only latent in socialism, which Marx misunderstood, which he could not have failed to misunderstand, since he wanted to do away once for all with misery and hazard, but which necessarily haunts a memory inherited from religious revolutionism in Münzer's Germany and in Russia. Of course at the same time the enemy remains in sight, safely entrenched behind our solid military industrial complex, but his ideology has crumbled into dust. Above all, it will now be easier, more reasonable, to pry him out from this last bastion than from the badly put together, corporative, lower middle-class and feudal, antique fortress on which the revolutionary impetus of the Baptists broke. The world of economic and political powers which surrounds us, so false, such a stranger to real values, so long haloed by the lying glamour of a "culture" which was nothing but the inconsistent atmosphere of luxury reserved to the dominant class— is at present broken down, and is deprived of any fixed point, stripped of any teological value for those who depended on it and who up until now had provided it with its ideology. An *internal* dynamism propels it towards the

From *Thomas Münzer*, by Ernst Bloch, London, 1948.

loss of its own force, and towards a constructive horizon, open to all the oppressed, to the victims of all the lies accumulated since the Peasants' War and the Later Middle Ages, to all the imperatives of absolute will.

So the course of events can no longer be an obstacle to virtue, to justice, to everything that is the object of a real premonition. But the centrifugal force of this same liberating movement draws effervescent humanity all the way to its real realm, and now the immensity of the higher worlds is spread before it, those worlds of premonition, of conscience, and of that which constitutes one-half of the Kingdom.

Time returns, reborn of the proletarian shock of the West. In Germany and in Russia it will come to its full flowering; there the peoples feel the presence of a light which banishes the thickest darkness, which suddenly brings back to the center of things the forgotten subterranean celestial realities which finally erect, as powerful effective public evidence, heresy's secret, now become the pole and directive principle of society. This underground history of the revolution whose movement has already started in the right direction, waits for its voice to be heard by us. But already the Brothers of the Valley, the Cathars, the Vaudois, the Albigenses, Abbot Joachim of Flora, the Brothers of Good Will, the Brothers of the Free Spirit, Eckhardt, the Hussites, Münzer and the Baptists, Sebastian Franck, the Illuminati, Rousseau, and the rational mysticism of Kant, Weitling, Baader, Tolstoi, all join forces and the moral conscience of this immense tradition is knocking on the door to put an end to fear, to the State, to every inhuman power. Now the bright spark is shining that will delay no longer, obeying the most certain of biblical exigencies: that here we have no abiding habitation, we seek an habitation that is to come. A new messianism is in preparation, at last familiar with our wandering and with our nostalgia's real strength; not at all an aspiration towards the quiet of the solid earth, of stiff work, of false cathedrals, whose cooked-up transcendance is cut off now from all its sources—but an aspiration to the light of the very moment in which we live, to the rendering adequate of our astonishment, of our apprehension, of our deep and sustained dream of happiness, of truth, of disenchantment with ourselves, of deification and of interior glory. The sky would never be so somber *above us*, were it not for the presence of an absolute storm and of a central light, the most immediate of all. Yet even so, our further shore has already been given a name and we have heard it, albeit still from behind a thin, cracked wall. Here is its most intimate name: Princess Sabbath, a name superior to the names of all the gods who have abandoned us here below with the simple palliative of a tearful and choleric miracle. Lifted high above the rubble of a ruined civilization, behold the spirit of the ineradicable utopia arises, for the first time assured of its true North: the most intimate of Ophirs, of Atlantises, of Orplids, in the dwelling of its true absolute communal manifestation. Thus, at last, Marxism and the dream of the unconditioned are finally united, walking in step, incorporated in the same plan of campaign—a power for progress and an end to all this ambiant universe where man was nothing but an oppressed, despised, exhausted being; a reconstruction of the planet Earth, vocation, creation, violent seizure of the Kingdom. With the Millenarists, Münzer remains the one who called men to this stormy pilgrimage. There can be no question of a new simple life infused into an old reality: there is room for every excess. This world and eternity, the new world of fervor and of penetration, of the light widely and tumultuously diffused from that which is most intimate in a man, these are opening to us. Now it is impossible that the time of the Kingdom will not come: in us a spirit radiates toward that time, refusing to give up, ignoring every disappointment. We have sufficiently lived the world's history, we have known enough, we have known too many, forms, cities, work, fantasies, obstacles, born of culture; here another life beckons, an irresistible life; here the thin background of the historical scene, of the political scene, of the cultural scene, fades; here the soul, the depths are manifest, those depths above all the sky spaces, where our dreams are, starry from ground to zenith; here the true firmaments unfold and the way of our destiny tirelessly mounts, up to that mysterious symbol towards which moves, since the beginning of time, the dark, the restless, the ponderous earth. . . .

Denis Diderot
(1713–1784)

A French encyclopedist and philosopher of materialism, Diderot was also a novelist and dramatist. The following extracts indicate the intellectual debt of modern communism to the French Enlightenment and the French Revolution.

The Fall of Natural Man

He was the father of a large family. At the arrival of the Europeans, he looked disdainfully at them, showing neither astonishment, fear nor curiosity. They accosted him. He turned his back on them, and withdrew into his hut. His silence and his anxiety revealed his thoughts only too well: he lamented within himself for the great days of his country now eclipsed. At the departure of Bougainville, when the inhabitants ran in a crowd to the shore, clinging to his garments, embracing his companions and weeping, the old man came forward with a stern air and said:

"Weep, poor folk of Tahiti, weep! Would that this were the arrival and not the departure of these ambitious and wicked men. One day you will know them better. One day they will return, in one hand the piece of wood you now see attached to the belt of this one, and the other grasping the blade you now see hanging from the belt of another. And with these they will enslave you, murder you or subject you to their extravagances and vices. One day you will

From *Supplement on Voyage de Bougainville*, translated by Jonathan Kemp in *Diderot: Interpreter of Nature*, edited by Jonathan Kemp, New York, 1963.

serve under them, as corrupted, as vile, as loathsome as themselves.

"But I console myself; I am reaching the end of my journey; I shall not live to see the calamity I foretell. Oh people of Tahiti! Oh my friends! You have a means to escape this tragic future; but I would rather die than counsel it. Let them go their ways, let them live."

Then, addressing himself to Bougainville, he continued:

"And you, chief of these brigands who obey you, quickly take your vessel from our shores. We are innocent, we are happy; and you can only spoil our happiness. We follow the pure instincts of nature; and you have tried to wipe its impress from our souls. Here everything belongs to everybody. You have preached to us I know not what distinctions between mine and thine. Our daughters and our wives are common to us all. You have shared this privilege with us; and you have lighted passions in them before unknown. They have become maddened in your arms; you have become ferocious in theirs. They have begun to hate each other; you have slain each other for them, and they have returned to us stained with your blood.

"We are a free people; and now you have planted in our country the title deeds of our future slavery. You are neither god nor demon; who are you, then, to make slaves? Orou! You understand the language of these men, tell us all, as you have told me, what they have written on this sheet of metal: 'This country is ours.' This country yours? And why? Because you have walked thereon? If a Tahitian landed one day on your shores, and scratched on one of your rocks or on the bark of your trees: 'This country belongs to the people of Tahiti'—what would you think?

"You are the strongest! And what of that? When someone took one of the contemptible trifles with which your vessel is filled, you cried out and you were revenged. Yet at the same time in the depths of your heart you plotted the theft of a whole country! You are not a slave; you would suffer death rather than be one; yet you want to enslave us. Do you think the Tahitian does not know how to defend his liberty and to die? The Tahitian you want to seize like a wild animal is your brother. You are both children of nature; what right have you over him that he has not over you? When you came, did we rush upon you, did we pillage your ship? Did we seize you and expose you to the arrows of our enemies? Did we yoke you with the animals for toil in our fields? No. We respected our own likeness in you. Leave us to our ways; they are wiser and more honest than yours. We do not want to barter what you call our ignorance for your useless civilization. Everything that is necessary and good for us we possess. Do we deserve contempt, because we have not known how to develop superfluous wants? When we hunger, we have enough to eat; when we are cold we have wherewith to clothe us. You have been in our huts; what is lacking there, in your opinion? You may pursue as far as you like what you call the comforts of life; but allow sensible people to stop, when they would only have obtained imaginary good from the continuation of their painful efforts. If you persuade us to exceed the narrow limits of our wants, when shall we ever finish toiling? When shall we enjoy ourselves? We have reduced the sum of our annual and daily labors to the least possible, because nothing seems to us preferable to repose. Go to your own country to agitate and torment yourself as much as you like; leave us in peace. Do not worry us with your artificial needs nor with your imaginary virtues. Look on these men; see how upright, healthy, and robust they are. Look on these women; see how upright, healthy, fresh, and beautiful they are. Take this bow; it is my own. Call one, two, three, or four of your friends to help you and try to bend it. I can bend it myself, alone. I till the soil. I climb mountains. I pierce the forest. I can run a league on the plains in less than an hour. Your young companions would be hard put to follow me, yet I am more than ninety years old.

"Woe unto this island! Woe to these people of Tahiti and to all who will come after them, woe from the day you first visited us! We should know only one disease; that to which all men, animals, and plants are subject—old age; but you have brought us another; you have infected our blood.

"It will perhaps be necessary to exterminate our daughters, wives, children, with our own hands; all those who have approached your women; those who have approached your men.

"Our fields shall be soaked with the foul blood which has passed from your veins into ours; or else our children, condemned to nourish and perpetuate the evil which you have given to the fathers and mothers, will transmit it for ever to their descendants. Villains! You will be the guilty ones; guilty either of the ravages of disease that will follow the fatal embraces of your people, or of the murders which we shall commit to stop the spread of the poison.

"You speak of crimes! Do you know any more enormous than your own? What is your punishment for him who kills his neighbor?—death by the sword; what is your punishment for the coward who poisons?—death by fire. Compare your crime to his; tell us then, poisoner of whole peoples, what should be the torment you deserve? But a short while ago, the young Tahitian girl yielded herself to the transports and embraces of the Tahitian youth; waited impatiently until her mother, authorized by her having reached the age of marriage, should remove her veil and make naked her breast. She was proud to excite the desire and to attract the amorous glances of unknown men, of relatives, of her brother. Without dread and without shame, in our presence, in the midst of a circle of innocent Tahitians, to the sound of flutes, between the dances, she accepted the caresses of the one to whom her young heart and the secret voice of her senses urged her. The idea of crime and the peril of disease came with you. Our enjoyments, once so sweet, are now accompanied by remorse and terror. That man in black who stands near you listening to me, has spoken to our lads. I do not know what he has said to our girls. But our lads are hesitant; our girls blush. Plunge if you will into the dark depths of the forest with the perverse companion of your pleasure; but let the good and simple Tahitians reproduce themselves without shame, under the open sky, in the full light of day. What finer and more noble feeling could you put in place of that with which we have inspired them, and which animates them now? They think that the moment to enrich the nation and the family with a new citizen is come, and they glory in it. They eat to live and to grow; they grow in order to multiply and they find in it nothing vicious nor shameful.

"Listen to the continuation of your crimes. You had hardly come among our people than they became thieves. You had scarcely landed on our soil, than it reeked with blood. That Tahitian who ran to meet you, to receive you crying 'Taio! friend, friend,' you slew. And why did you slay him—because he had been taken by the glitter of your little serpents' eggs. He gave you of his fruits; he offered you his wife and daughter, he ceded you his hut; yet you killed him for a handful of beads which he had taken without having asked. And the people? At the noise of your murderous shot, terror seized them, and they fled to the mountains. But be assured that they would not have waited long to descend again. Then you would all have perished, but for me. Ah! why did I pacify them, why did I hold them back, why do I still restrain them, even now? I do not know; for you deserve no pity; for you have a ferocious soul which will never feel it. You have wandered, you and yours, everywhere in our island. You have been respected; you have enjoyed all things; you have found neither barrier nor refusal in your ways; you have been invited within, you have sat, and all the abundance of our country has been spread before you. When you desired young girls, only excepting those who had not yet the privilege of unveiling their faces and breasts, their mothers have presented to you all the others, quite naked. You have possessed the tender victim of the duties of hospitality; flowers and leaves were heaped up for you and her; musicians sounded their instruments; nothing has spoiled the sweetness, nor hindered the freedom of your caresses nor of hers. They have sung the anthem exhorting you to be a man, and our child to be a woman, yielding and voluptuous. They danced around your couch. And it was when you came from the arms of this woman, after experiencing on her breast the sweetest of all intoxications, that you slew her brother, friend, or father.

"You have done still worse. Look over there, see that enclosure bristling with weapons. These arms which have menaced only your enemies are now turned against our own children. See these unhappy companions of our pleasures. See their sadness, the grief of their fathers and the despair of their mothers. They are those condemned to die, either by our hands or by the diseases you have given them.

"Away now, unless your cruel eyes revel in the spectacle of death. Go now, go; and may the guilty seas which spared you on your voyage hither, absolve themselves and avenge us, by engulfing you before you return.

"And you, oh people of Tahiti! Go into your huts, go, all of you; and let these strangers as they leave hear only the roar of the tide and see only the foam of its fury whitening a deserted shore."

He had scarcely finished before the crowd of people had disappeared. A vast silence reigned over the whole island, and only the keen whistling of the wind and the dull sound of the breakers along the shore could be heard. One might have said that the air and the sea, conscious of the voice of the aged man, were moved to obey him.

François-Noël Babeuf
(1760–1797)

Babeuf became a land surveyor and, in 1777, a domestic servant; married a housemaid four years older than himself; and went to Paris in 1789 during the revolution. He wrote against Mirabeau and founded a journal; he attacked Robespierre and was jailed. He was released in 1795, but was persistently antigovernment; he prepared in the crypt of a convent a conspiracy which was a "hybrid of a secret society and a political party"; it boasted 2,000 members. In April, 1796, Babeuf composed the Manifesto of the Equals *which was to arrive at a Republic of Equals. He was tried and guillotined in September 1797.*

The following is from Philippe Buonarroti's History of Babeuf's Conspiracy. *Buonarroti (1761–1837) (a direct descendent of Michelangelo, 1475–1564) was an Italian revolutionary, a nobleman from Pisa who was converted by reading Rousseau. He became a French citizen and met Gracchus Babeuf in prison in Paris in March, 1795, when he became Babeuf's most devoted follower. After Babeuf's execution he became involved in plots to overthrow Napoleon. His book,* La Conspiration des Egaux *(translated as* The History of Babeuf's Conspiracy), *was a "text book almost a breviary" for the revolutionaries of 1848 and for the French "Communards" of 1870.*

The History of Babeuf's Conspiracy

MANIFESTO OF THE EQUALS

"REAL EQUALITY—THE LAST END OF THE SO-
CIAL ART."—CONDORCET, *Picture of the Human Mind,
page 329.*

PEOPLE OF FRANCE!—During fifteen ages you have lived
slaves, and consequently unhappy. During six years you
breathe with difficulty in the expectation of independance,
of prosperity, and of equality.

EQUALITY!—first vow of nature, first want of man, and
chief bond of all legitimate association! People of France!
you have not been more favoured than the other nations
which vegetate on this ill-fated globe! Always and everywhere does the unfortunate human species, delivered over
to cannibals more or less artful, serve for a plaything to all
ambitions—for pasture to all tyrannies. Always and everywhere have men been fooled by fine words; never and
nowhere have they obtained the *thing* with the word. From
time immemorial we have been hypocritically told—*men
are equal;* and from time immemorial does the most de-
grading and monstrous inequality insolently oppress the
human race. Ever since the first existence of civil societies
has the finest apanage of man been uncontradictedly
acknowledged; but never, up to this moment, has it been
once *realized.* Equality has never been other than a beautiful and barren fiction of law. Even now, when it is claimed
with a stronger voice, we are answered, "Be silent, miser-
ables!—absolute equality is but a chimaera; be content with
conditional equality; you are all equal before the law.
Rabble! what more do you want?" What more do we want?
Legislators, governors, rich proprietors—listen in your turn.

From *The History of Babeuf's Conspiracy*, by Philippe Buonarroti, London, 1836.

We are all equal, are we not? This principle remains uncontested, because, without being self-convicted of folly, one cannot seriously say that it is night when it is day.

Well! we pretend henceforward to live and die equal, as we are born so. We desire real equality or death; behold what we want. And we shall have this real equality, no matter at what price. Woe to them who will interpose themselves between it and us! Woe to him who will offer resistance to so determined a resolve!

The French Revolution is but the forerunner of another revolution far more grand, far more solemn, and which will be the last. The people has marched over dead bodies against the kings and priests coalesced against it; it will do the same against the new tyrants—against the new political Tartuffes who have usurped the places of the old.

"What do we want," you ask, "more than equality of rights?" We want that equality not merely written in the "Declaration of the Rights of Man and of the Citizen"; we want it in the midst of us—under the roofs of our houses. We consent to everything for it—to become as *pliable wax, in order to have its characters engraven upon us.* Perish, if needs be, all the arts, provided real equality abides with us!

Legislators and governors, who are as destitute of genius as of honesty—you rich proprietors, without bowels of pity —in vain do you essay to neutralize our holy enterprise, by saying, "They are only re-producing the old Agrarian law, so often demanded already before them."

Calumniators! be silent in your turn; and in the silence of confusion hearken to our pretensions, dictated by nature herself, and based upon eternal justice. The Agrarian law, or partition of lands, was only the instantaneous wish of certain soldiers without principles—of certain small tribes, moved by instinct rather than by reason. We aim at something more sublime, and more equitable; we look to *common property*, or the *community of goods!* No more individual property in lands. *The earth belongs to no one.* We claim—we demand—we *will* the communal enjoyment of the fruits of the earth; *the fruits belong to all.*

We declare that we can no longer suffer that the great majority of men shall labour and sweat to serve and pamper the extreme minority. Long enough, and too long, have less than a million of individuals disposed of what belongs to more than twenty millions of men like themselves—of men in every respect their equals. Let there be at length an end to this enormous scandal, which posterity will scarcely credit. Away for ever with the revolting distinctions of rich and poor, of great and little, of masters and servants, of *governors* and *governed*.

Let there be no longer any other differences in mankind than those of age and sex. Since all have the same wants, and the same faculties, let all have accordingly the same education—the same nourishment. They are content with one sun, and the same air for all; why should not the like portion, and the same quality of food, suffice for each according to his wants?

But already do the enemies of an order of things, the most natural that can be imagined, declaim against us, —"Disorganizers, and seditionists," they exclaim, "you want but massacres and plunder."

PEOPLE OF FRANCE! We will not waste our time to answer them; but we will tell you,—"the holy enterprise we are organizing has no other object in view than to put an end to civil dissensions and to public disorder. Never was a more vast design conceived and put in execution. At distant intervals in the history of the world it has been talked of by some men of genius—by a few philosophers—but they spoke it with a low and trembling voice. Not one of them has had the courage to speak the entire truth."

The moment for great measures has arrived. Evil is at its height; it has reached its *maximum,* and covers the face of the earth. Chaos, under the name of politics, has too long reigned over it. Let everything revert to order, and resume its proper place. At the voice of equality, let the elements of justice and felicity be organized. The moment is come to found the REPUBLIC OF EQUALS—that grand asylum open to all human kind. The days of general restitution are come. Weeping families, come and seat yourselves at the common table provided by nature for all her children.

PEOPLE OF FRANCE! The purest of all earthly glories has been reserved for you—yes, 'tis you who are first destined to present the world with this touching spectacle.

Old habits, old prejudices, will again seek to oppose obstacles to the establishment of the REPUBLIC OF EQUALS. The organization of real equality—the only one which satisfies all wants, without making victims, without costing sacrifices—will not, perhaps, at first please everybody. The egotist, the ambitious, will yell with rage. Those who possess unjustly, will raise the cry of injustice. Exclusive enjoyments, solitary pleasures, personal ease and privileges, will cause poignant regrets to some few individuals who are dead or callous to the pangs of others. The lovers of absolute power, the vile instruments of arbitrary authority, will feel it hard that their haughty chiefs should bend to the level of equality. Their short-sightedness will, with difficulty, penetrate into the future of public happiness, however near; but what can avail a few thousand malcontents against such a mass of human beings, all happy, and astonished at having been so long in quest of a felicity which they had within hands' reach. On the day that follows this real revolution, they will say to one another in amazement—"What—universal happiness depended on so little! We had but to will it. Ah, why had we not willed it sooner? Was it then necessary to have it told to us so often?" Yes, no doubt, a single man on the earth, more rich, more powerful, than his fellow men, than his equals, destroys the equilibrium, and crime and misfortune come on the world.

PEOPLE OF FRANCE! By what sign then ought you henceforward to recognise the excellence of a constitution? . . . That which altogether reposes on actual, absolute equality, is the only one that can be suitable to you, and satisfy all your desires.

The aristocratic charters of 1791 and 1795 riveted your chains, instead of breaking them. That of 1793 was a great practical step towards real equality; never before was equality so nearly approached; but that Constitution did not yet touch the end, nor was it fully competent to attain general happiness, of which, however, it has solemnly consecrated the great principle.

PEOPLE OF FRANCE! Open your eyes and hearts to the fulness of felicity; recognize and proclaim with us the

REPUBLIC OF EQUALS!

ANALYSIS OF BABEUF'S DOCTRINE

1. Nature has given every man an equal right to the enjoyment of all wealth.
2. The aim of society is to defend this equality, often attacked by the strong and the wicked in the state of nature, and to increase, by the co-operation of all, this enjoyment.

3. Nature has imposed on each man the duty to work; no one can, without committing a crime, abstain from working.
4. Labour and enjoyment ought to be in common.
5. Oppression exists when one man exhausts himself working and wants for everything, while another wallows in abundance without doing anything.
6. No one can, without committing a crime, appropriate to himself alone the wealth of the earth or of industry.
7. In a true society there should be neither rich nor poor.
8. The rich who will not give up their superfluity to help the needy are enemies of the people.
9. No one should be able, by monopolizing the means, to deprive another of the education necessary for his happiness; education ought to be in common.
10. The aim of the Revolution is to destroy inequality and establish the common happiness.
11. The Revolution is not finished, because the rich absorb all wealth and rule exclusively while the poor work like veritable slaves, languishing in poverty and counting for nothing in the state.
12. The Constitution of 1793 is the true law of the French nation because the People have solemnly accepted it.

Man's condition ought not to have deteriorated in passing from a state of nature to a state of social organization. In the beginning the soil belonged to none, its fruits to all. The introduction of private property was a piece of trickery put over on the simple and unsuspecting masses. The laws that buttressed property operated inevitably to create social classes—privileged and oppressed, masters and slaves.

The law of inheritance is a sovereign wrong. It breeds misery even from the second generation. Two sons of a rich man receive equal shares of their father's fortune. One son has but one child, the other, twelve. Of these twelve each receives only a twelfth part of the fortune of his uncle and the twenty-fourth part of the fortune of his grandfather. This portion is not enough to live on; and so twelve poor men must work for one rich one. Hence we find masters and servants among the grandchildren of a single man.

The law of alienability is no less unjust. This one man, already master over all the other grandchildren in the same line, pays what he will for the work that they must do for him. Their wages are insufficient to maintain life and they are obliged to sell their meager inheritance to their master.

They become landless men; and if they have children of their own, these inherit nothing.

The gulf between rich and poor, rulers and ruled, proceeds from yet another cause, the difference in value and in price that arbitrary opinion attaches to the diverse products of toil and manufacture. Thus a watchmaker's working day has been valued twenty times higher than a ploughman's or laborer's. The wages of the watchmaker enable him to get possession of the inheritance of twenty ploughmen whom he is thus in a position to expropriate, and enhance his own condition.

These three roots of our public woes—heredity, alienability, and the differing values which arbitrary opinion assigns to different types of social product—proceed from the institution of private property. All the evils of society flow from them. They isolate the people from each other; they convert every family into a private commonwealth, pit it against society at large, and dedicate it with an ever growing emphasis to inequality in all its vicious, suicidal forms.

I formulated these observations and came to think of them as self-evident truths. It did not take me very long to draw the following conclusions:

If the earth belongs to none and its fruits to all; if private ownership of public wealth is only the result of certain institutions that violate fundamental human rights; then it follows that this private ownership is a usurpation; and it further follows that all that a man takes of the land and its fruits beyond what is necessary for sustenance is theft from society.

And being drawn from one conclusion to another, believing as I did that no truth must be permitted to remain hidden from the minds of men, I became convinced of the truth of the following ideas, which I caused to be published:

All that a citizen lacks for the satisfaction of his various daily needs, he lacks because he has been deprived of a natural property right by the engrossers of the public domain. All that a citizen enjoys beyond what is necessary for the satisfaction of his daily needs he enjoys as a result of a theft from the other members of society. In this way a more or less numerous group of people is deprived of its rightful share in the public domain.

Inheritance and alienability are institutions destructive of basic human rights.

The plea of superior ability and industry is an empty rationalization to mask the machinations of those who conspire against human equality and happiness. It is ridiculous and unfair to lay claim to a higher wage for the man whose work requires more concentrated thought and more mental effort. Such effort in no way expands the capacity of the stomach. No wage can be defended over and above what is necessary for the satisfaction of a person's needs.

The worth of intelligence is only a matter of opinion, and it still remains to be determined if natural, physical strength is not of equal worth. Clever people have set a high value upon the creations of their minds; if the toilers had also had a hand in the ordering of things, they would doubtless have insisted that brawn is entitled to equal consideration with brain and that physical fatigue is no less real than mental fatigue.

If wages are not equalized, the clever and persevering are given a licence to rob and despoil with impunity those less fortunately endowed with natural gifts. In this way the economic equilibrium of society is upset, for nothing has been more conclusively proven than the maxim: a man only succeeds in becoming rich through the spoliation of others.

All our civic institutions, our social relationships, are nothing else but the expression of legalized barbarism and piracy, in which every man cheats and robs his neighbor. In its festering swamp our swindling society generates vice, crime, and misery of every kind. A handful of well-intentioned people band together and wage war on these evils, but their efforts are futile. They can make no headway because they do not tackle the problem at its roots, but apply palliatives based upon the distorted thinking of a sick society.

It is clear from the foregoing that whatever a man possesses over and above his rightful share of the social product has been stolen. It is therefore right and proper to take this wealth back again from those who have wrongfully appropriated it.

Pierre Joseph Proudhon
(1809–1865)

The son of a Besançon barrelmaker, Proudhon's first book,
What Is Property?, had as its thesis the concept of property
as theft. In 1848, during the revolutionary outbreaks, Proud-
hon attempted to found a people's bank but was jailed. He
escaped to Brussels and later returned to Paris, where he ex-
erted a strong influence on the French workers during the
First International. Proudhon commented on one of Marx's
frequent personal attacks on him: "Marx regrets that I
thought like him and said it first."

What Is Property?

If I were asked to answer the following question: "What is
slavery?" and I should answer in one word, "It is murder,"
my meaning would be understood at once. No extended
argument would be required to show that the power to take
from a man his thought, his will, his personality, is a power
of life and death; and that to enslave him is to kill him.
Why, then, to this other question: "What is property?" may
I not likewise answer, "It is robbery," without the certainty
of being misunderstood, the second proposition being no
other than a transformation of the first?

I undertake to discuss the vital principle of our government and our institutions, property: I am in my right. I
may be mistaken in the conclusion that shall result from my

From *What Is Property? An Inquiry into the Principle of Right
and Government,* by Pierre Joseph Proudhon, translated by Ben-
jamin R. Tucker, W. Reeves, London, 1890.

investigations: I am in my right. I think best to place the last thought of my book first: still I am in my right.

Such an author teaches that property is a civil right, born of occupation and sanctioned by law; another maintains that it is a natural right, originating in labor—and both of these doctrines, totally opposed as they may seem, are encouraged and applauded. I contend that neither labor, nor occupation, nor law, can create property; that it is an effect without a cause: am I censurable?

But murmurs arise! *Property is robbery!* This is the war cry of '93! That is the signal of revolutions!

Reader, calm yourself. I am no agent of discord, no firebrand of sedition. I anticipate history by a few days. I disclose a truth whose development we may try in vain to arrest. I write the preamble of our future constitution. This proposition which seems to you blasphemous—property is robbery—would, if our prejudices allowed us to consider it, be recognized as the lightning rod to shield us from the coming thunderbolt: but too many interests stand in the way. . . .

Property is robbery: What a revolution in human ideas! "Proprietor" and "robber" have been at all times expressions as contradictory as the beings whom they designate are hostile: all languages have perpetuated this opposition. On what authority, then, do you venture to attack universal consent and give the lie to the human race? Who are you, that you should question the judgment of the nations and the ages?

Of what consequence to you, reader, is my obscure individuality? I live like you in a century in which reason submits only to fact and to evidence. My name like yours is truth seeker. . . .

Nevertheless, I build no system. I ask an end to privilege, the abolition of slavery, equality of rights, and the reign of law. Justice, nothing else; that is the alpha and omega of my argument. To others I leave the business of governing the world.

One day I asked myself: Why is there so much sorrow and misery in society? Must man always be wretched? And not satisfied with the explanations given by the reformers— these attributing the general distress to governmental cowardice and incapacity, those to conspirators and *émeutes*, still others to ignorance and general corruption—and weary of the interminable quarrels of the tribune and the press, I sought to fathom the matter myself. I have consulted the masters of science. I have read a hundred volumes of

philosophy, law, political economy, and history. Would to
God that I had lived in a century in which so much reading
had been useless! I have made every effort to obtain exact
information, comparing doctrines, replying to objections,
continually constructing equations and reductions from
arguments, and weighing thousands of syllogisms in the
scales of the most rigorous logic. In this laborious work, I
have collected many interesting facts, which I shall share
with my friends and the public as soon as I have leisure.
But I must say that I recognized at once that we had never
understood the meaning of these words, so common and
yet so sacred: "justice," "equity," "liberty"; that concerning each of these principles our ideas have been utterly
obscure. And in fact, that this ignorance was the sole cause,
both of the poverty that devours us and of all the calamities
that have ever afflicted the human race.

My mind was frightened by this strange result. I doubted
my reason. What! said I, that which eye has not seen, nor
ear heard, nor insight penetrated, you have discovered!
Wretch, mistake not the visions of your diseased brain for
the truths of science! Do you not know (great philosophers
have said so) that in points of practical morality universal
error is a contradiction?

I resolved then to test my arguments, and in entering
upon this new labor I sought an answer to the following
questions: Is it possible that humanity can have so long and
so universally been mistaken in the application of moral
principles? How and why could it be mistaken? How can its
error, being universal, be capable of correction? Yes, all
men believe and repeat that equality of condition is identical
with equality of rights; that "property" and "robbery" are
synonomous terms: that every social advantage accorded, or
rather usurped in the name of superior talent or service,
is iniquity and extortion. All men in their hearts, I say, bear
witness to these truths. They need only be made to understand. . . .

Finally a book appeared, summing up the whole matter
in these two propositions: "What is the third estate?—
Nothing. What ought it to be?—Everything." Someone
added by way of comment: "What is the king?—The servant of the people."

This was a sudden revelation. The veil was torn aside,
a thick bondage fell from all eyes. The people commenced
to reason thus:

If the king is our servant, he ought to report to us.

If he ought to report to us, he is subject to control.

If he can be controlled, he is responsible.

If he is responsible, he is punishable.

If he is punishable, he ought to be punished according to his merits.

If he can be punished according to his merits, he can be punished with death.

Five years after the publication of the brochure of Sieyès, the third estate was everything. The king, the nobility, the clergy, were no more. In 1793, the nation, without stopping at the constitutional fiction of the inviolability of the sovereign, conducted Louis XVI to the scaffold. In 1830, it accompanied Charles X to Cherbourg. In each case, it may have erred, in fact, in its judgment of the offense. But, in right, the logic that led to its action was irreproachable. The people, in punishing their sovereign, did precisely that which the government of July was so severely censured for failing to do when it refused to execute Louis Bonaparte after the affair of Strassburg. They struck the true culprit. It was an application of the common law, a solemn decree of justice enforcing the penal laws.

The spirit that gave rise to the movement of '89 was a spirit of negation; that, of itself, proves that the order of things that was substituted for the old system was not methodical or well considered; that, born of anger and hatred, it could not have the effect of a science based on observation and study; that its foundations, in a word, were not derived from a profound knowledge of the laws of Nature and society. Thus the people found that the republic, among the so-called new institutions, was acting on the very principles that they had intended to destroy. We congratulate ourselves . . . on the glorious French Revolution, the regeneration of 1789, the great changes that have been effected . . . a delusion! . . . a delusion!

The nation, so long a victim of monarchical selfishness, thought to deliver itself forever by declaring that it alone was sovereign. But what was monarchy? The sovereignty of one man. What is democracy? The sovereignty of the nation, or, rather, of the national majority. But it is, in both cases, the sovereignty of many instead of the sovereignty of the law, the sovereignty of the will instead of the sovereignty of reason; in one word, the passions instead of justice. Undoubtedly, when a nation passes from the monarchical to the democratic state, there is progress, because in multiplying the sovereigns we increase the opportunities of reason to substitute itself for the will. But in reality there is no revolution in the government, since the principle remains the same. Now we have the proof today that, with the most perfect democracy, we cannot be free.

Nor is that all. The nation-king cannot exercise its sovereignty itself. It is obliged to delegate it to agents. This is constantly reiterated by those who seek to win its favor. Be these agents five, ten, one hundred, or a thousand, of what consequence is the number and what matters the name? It is always the government of man, the rule of will and caprice. I ask what this pretended revolution has revolutionized?

We know, too, how this sovereignty was exercised; first by the Convention, then by the Directory, afterwards confiscated by the Consul. As for the Emperor, the strong man so much adored and mourned by the nation, he never wanted to be dependent on it. But, as if intending to set its sovereignty at defiance, he dared to demand its suffrage; that is, its abdication, the abdication of this inalienable sovereignty, and he obtained it.

But what is sovereignty? It is, they say, the "power to make laws." Another absurdity, a relic of despotism. The nation had long seen kings issuing their commands in this form: "for such is our pleasure." It wished to taste in its turn the pleasure of making laws. For fifty years it has brought them forth by myriads; always, be it understood, through the agency of representatives. The play is far from ended. . . . The definition of sovereignty was derived from the definition of the law. The law, they said, is "the expression of the will of the sovereign": then, under a monarchy, the law is the expression of the will of the king. In a republic, the law is the expression of the will of the people. Aside from the difference in the number of wills, the two systems are exactly identical. Both share the same error, namely that the law is the expression of a will. It ought to be the expression of a fact.

. . . Bias and prejudice are apparent in all the phrases of the new legislators. The nation had suffered from a multitude of exclusions and privileges. Its representatives issued the following declaration: "All men are equal by nature and before the law"—an ambiguous and redundant declaration, "Men are equal by nature": Does this mean that they are equal in size, beauty, talents and virtue? No. They meant, then, political and civil equality. Then it would have been sufficient to have said: Men are equal before the law.

But what is equality before the law? Neither the constitution of 1790, nor that of '93, nor the granted charter, nor the accepted charter, have defined it accurately. All imply an inequality in fortune and station incompatible with even a shadow of equality in rights. In this respect it may be said that all our constitutions have been faithful expressions of the popular will. I am going to prove it. Formerly the people were excluded from civil and military offices. It was considered a wonder when the following high-sounding article was inserted in the Declaration of Rights: "All citizens are equally eligible to office; free nations know no qualification in their choice of officers save virtues and talents."

They certainly ought to have admired so beautiful an idea. They admired a piece of nonsense. Why, the sovereign people, legislators, and reformers see in public offices, to speak plainly, only opportunities for pecuniary advancement. And, because it regards them as a source of profit, it decrees the eligibility of citizens. For of what use would this precaution be, if there were nothing to gain by it? No one would think of ordaining that none but astronomers and geographers should be pilots, nor of prohibiting stutterers from acting at the theater and the opera. The nation was still aping the kings. Like them it wished to award the lucrative positions to its friends and flatterers. Unfortunately, and this last feature completes the resemblance, the nation did not control the list of livings. That was in the hands of its agents and representatives. They, on the other hand, took care not to thwart the will of their gracious sovereign.

This edifying article of the Declaration of Rights, retained in the charters of 1814 and 1830, implies several kinds of civil inequality; that is, of inequality before the law: inequality of station, since the public functions are sought only for the consideration and emoluments that they bring; inequality of wealth, since, if it had been desired to equalize fortunes, public service would have been regarded as a duty, not as a reward; inequality of privilege, the law not stating what it means by "talents" and "virtues." Under the empire, virtue and talent consisted simply in military bravery and devotion to the emperor. That was shown when Napoleon created his nobility and attempted to connect it with the ancients. Today, the man who pays taxes to the amount of two hundred francs is virtuous. The talented man is the honest pickpocket. Such truths as these are accounted trivial.

The people finally legalized property. God forgive them, for they know not what they did! For fifty years they have suffered for their miserable folly. But how came the people, whose voice, they tell us, is the voice of God and whose conscience is infallible—how came the people to err? How happens it that, when seeking liberty and equality, they fell back into privilege and slavery? Always through copying the ancient regime.

Formerly, the nobility and the clergy contributed towards the expenses of the State only by voluntary aid and gratuitous gift. Their property could not be seized even for debt—while the plebeian, overwhelmed by taxes and statute labor, was continually tormented. . . . The people wanted conditions of ownership to be alike for all. They thought that everyone should enjoy and freely dispose of his possessions, his income, and the fruit of his labor and industry. The people did not invent property. But . . . the principle still remains the same. . . . There has been no revolution.

III.

REVISIONIST COMMUNISM

During his lifetime, Karl Marx fought with many of his original disciples, such as Ferdinand Lassalle and Michael Bakunin (1814–1876). Bakunin, son of a Russian nobleman, translated Das Kapital into Russian (1869). He had met Marx and Proudhon in Berlin between 1843 and 1846. He hailed the 1848 risings with enthusiasm, and attended the Slav Congress in Prague that year. He was captured in an abortive rising in Dresden in 1849, turned over to the Russians, who incarcerated him in the fortress of SS Peter and Paul in St. Petersburg. Later exiled to Siberia, he escaped to London where he squabbled with Marx and helped the disintegration of the First International by preparing the secession of the anarchists.

Later defections from pure Marxism were Karl Kautsky (1854–1938) who, born in Prague, became minister of foreign affairs in Germany in 1918, and G. V. Plekhanov (1856–1918), who brought Marx's theories to Russia and translated Marx into Russian but opposed the Bolshevists from 1903 on. Marxism, as a vehicle of secular salvation, was further impoverished by the defection of P. B. Struve (1870–1944), S. N. Bulgakov (1871–1944) and N. A. Berdyaev (1874–1948). In fact, revisionism triumphed in the West; Marxist orthodoxy (until Mao Tse-tung) in the East. "Revisionism," American historian Arthur Schlesinger has written, "is an essential element in the process by which history, in posing new problems and exploring new possibilities, widens its perspectives and enriches its interpretations."[1]

The most famous of all revisionists from the Russian point of view of course, is Mao Tse-tung (1893–   ), founder-member of the Chinese Communist Party and the most successful communist leader the world has so far known. Mao refused to leave China when he could have gone to study as a young man in Russia (as did for example, Chou

[1] In French magazine *Preuves*, 1969.

*En-lai) or in France (as did Ho Chi Minh, who was a found-
ing member of the French Communist Party); and Mao insisted, in the face of Marxist orthodoxy, that the Chinese
peasant, rather than the proletariat or the industrial workers,
was the "vehicle of secular salvation" for China.*

Michael Bakunin
(1814–1876)

A Russian-born aristocrat, Bakunin took part in the German revolution of 1848. On returning to Russia, he was exiled, yet he managed to escape. A critic of Marx, with whom he frequently quarreled, Bakunin wrote A Revolutionary Catechism *(1869) and* God and the State *(1862). An avowed anarchist, Bakunin promoted the cause of nihilism in Russia. He visited the United States in 1861.*

Marxism, Freedom and the State

By the *flower of the proletariat*, I mean above all, that great mass, those millions of non-civilized, disinherited, wretched and illiterates whom Messrs. Engels and Marx mean to subject to the paternal regime of *a very strong government*, to employ an expression used by Engels in a letter to our friend Cafiero. Without doubt, this will be for their own salvation, as of course all governments, as is well-known, have been established solely in the interests of the masses themselves. By the flower of the proletariat I mean precisely that eternal "meat" for governments, that great *rabble of the people* ordinarily designated by Messrs. Marx and Engels by the phrase at once picturesque and contemptuous of *"lumpenproletariat,"* the "riff-raff," that rabble which, being very nearly unpolluted by all bourgeois civilization, carries in its heart, in its aspirations, in

From *Marxism, Freedom and the State*, edited and translated by K. J. Kenafick, London, 1950.

all the necessities and the miseries of its collectivist position, all the germs of the Socialism of the future, and which alone is powerful enough today to inaugurate the Social Revolution and bring it to triumph.

Karl Kautsky
(1854–1938)

Born in Prague, Kautsky was the creator of the Erfurt Program, a major figure in the Second International, and, along with Hugo Haase, a founder of the German Independent Social Democratic party. Kautsky also was opposed to Lenin and Bolshevism. In 1918 he became German secretary of state for foreign affairs.

The Dictatorship
of the Proletariat

CHAPTER I
THE PROBLEM

The present Russian Revolution has, for the first time in the history of the world, made a Socialist Party the rulers of a great Empire. A far more powerful event than the seizing of control of the town of Paris by the proletariat in 1871. Yet, in one important aspect, the Paris Commune was superior to the Soviet Republic. The former was the work of the entire proletariat. All shades of the Socialist

From *The Dictatorship of the Proletariat*, by Karl Kautsky, translated by H. J. Stenning, Ann Arbor, Michigan, 1964.

movement took part in it, none drew back from it, none was excluded.

On the other hand, the Socialist Party which governs Russia to-day gained power in fighting against other Socialist Parties, and exercises its authority while excluding other Socialist Parties from the executive.

The antagonism of the two Socialist movements is not based on small personal jealousies: it is the clashing of two fundamentally distinct methods, that of democracy and that of dictatorship. Both movements have the same end in view: to free the proletariat, and with it humanity, through Socialism. But the view taken by the one is held by the other to be erroneous and likely to lead to destruction.

It is impossible to regard so gigantic an event as the proletarian struggle in Russia without taking sides. Each of us feels impelled to violent partisanship. And the more so because the problem which to-day occupies our Russian comrades will to-morrow assume practical significance for Western Europe, and does already decisively influence the character of our propaganda and tactics.

It is, however, our party duty not to decide for one or the other side in the Russian internal quarrel before we have thoroughly tested the arguments of both. In this many comrades would hinder us. They declare it to be our duty blindly to pronounce in favour of the section now at the helm. Any other attitude would endanger the Revolution, and Socialism itself. This is nothing less than to ask us to accept as already proved that which is still to be examined, viz., that one of the sections has struck out in the right path, and we must encourage it by following.

We place ourselves, of course, by asking for the fullest discussion, already on the ground of democracy. Dictatorship does not ask for the refutation of contrary views, but the forcible suppression of their utterance. Thus, the two methods of democracy and dictatorship are already irreconcilably opposed before the discussion has started. The one demands, the other forbids it.

In the meantime, dictatorship does not yet reign in our Party; discussion amongst us is still free. And we consider it not only as our right, but as our duty to express our opinions freely, because an appropriate and fruitful decision is only possible after hearing all the arguments. One man's speech is notoriously no man's speech. Both sides must be listened to.

We will, therefore, examine the significance which democracy has for the proletariat—what we understand by the dictatorship of the proletariat—and what conditions dictatorship, as a form of government, creates in the struggle for freedom of the proletariat.

CHAPTER II
DEMOCRACY AND THE CONQUEST OF POLITICAL POWER

The distinction is sometimes drawn between democracy and Socialism, that is, the socialisation of the means of production and of production, by saying that the latter is our goal, the object of our movement, while democracy is merely the means to this end, which occasionally might become unsuitable, or even a hindrance.

To be exact, however, Socialism as such is not our goal, which is the abolition of every kind of exploitation and oppression, be it directed against a class, a party, a sex, or a race.

We seek to achieve this object by supporting the proletarian class struggle, because the proletariat, being the undermost class, cannot free itself without abolishing all causes of exploitation and oppression, and because the industrial proletariat, of all the oppressed and exploited classes, is the one which constantly grows in strength, fighting capacity and inclination to carry on the struggle, its ultimate victory being inevitable. Therefore, to-day every genuine opponent of exploitation and oppression must take part in the class struggle, from whatever class he may come.

If in this struggle we place the Socialist way of production as the goal, it is because in the technical and economic conditions which prevail to-day Socialistic production appears to be the sole means of attaining our object. Should it be proved to us that we are wrong in so doing, and that somehow the emancipation of the proletariat and of mankind could be achieved solely on the basis of private property, or could be most easily realised in the manner indicated by Proudhon, then we would throw Socialism overboard, without in the least giving up our object, and even in the interests of this object. Socialism and democracy are therefore not distinguished by the one being the means and the other the end. Both are means to the same end. The distinction between them must be sought elsewhere.

Socialism as a means to the emancipation of the proletariat, without democracy, is unthinkable.

Social production, it is true, is also possible in a system other than a democratic one. In primitive conditions communistic methods became the basis of despotism, as Engels noted in 1875, when dealing with the village communism which has existed in India and Russia down to our own day.

For modern men, however, such a patriarchal regime would be intolerable. It is only possible under circumstances where the rulers are vastly superior to the ruled in knowledge, and where the latter are absolutely unable to raise themselves to an equal standard. A section or class which is engaged in a struggle for freedom cannot regard such a system of tutelage as its goal, but must decisively reject it.

For us, therefore, Socialism without democracy is unthinkable. We understand by Modern Socialism not merely social organisation of production, but democratic organisation of society as well. Accordingly, Socialism is for us inseparably connected with democracy. No Socialism without democracy. But this proposition is not equally true if reversed. Democracy is quite possible without Socialism. A pure democracy is even conceivable apart from Socialism, for example, in small peasant communities, where complete equality of economic conditions for everybody exists on the basis of participating in privately owned means of production.

In any case, it may be said that democracy is possible without Socialism, and precedes it. It is this pre-Socialist democracy which is apparently in the minds of those who consider that democracy and Socialism are related to each other as the means to an end, although they mostly hasten to add that, strictly speaking, it is really no means to an end. This interpretation must be most emphatically repudiated, because, should it win general acceptance, it would lead our movement into most dangerous tracks.

Why would democracy be an unsuitable means for the achievement of Socialism?

It is a question of conquest of political power.

It is said that if in a hitherto middle-class democratic State the possibility exists of the Social Democrats becoming the majority at an election, the ruling classes would make use of all the forces at their command in order to prevent democracy from asserting itself. Therefore, it is not by democracy, but only by a political revolution that the proletariat can conquer the political power.

Doubtless, in cases where the proletariat of a democratic State attains to power, one must reckon with attempts of the ruling classes to nullify by violence the realisation of democracy by the rising class. This, however, does not prove the worthlessness of democracy for the proletariat. Should a ruling class, under the suppositions here discussed, resort to force, it would do so precisely because it feared the consequences of democracy. And its violence would be nothing but the subversion of democracy. Therefore, not the uselessness of democracy for the proletariat is demonstrated by anticipated attempts of the ruling classes to destroy democracy, but rather the necessity for the proletariat to defend democracy with tooth and nail. Of course, if the proletariat is told that democracy is a useless ornament, the needful strength for its defence will not be created. The mass of the people are everywhere too attached to their political rights willingly to abandon them. On the contrary, it is rather to be expected that they would defend their rights with such vigour that if the other side endeavored to destroy the people's privileges, a political overthrow would be the result. The higher the proletariat values democracy, and the closer is its attachment to its rights, the more may one anticipate this course of events.

On the other hand, it must not be thought that the forebodings above mentioned will everywhere be realised. We need not be so fainthearted. The more democratic the State is, the more dependent are the forces exerted by the Executive, even the military ones, on public opinion. These forces may become, even in a democracy, a means of holding down the proletarian movement, if the proletariat is still weak in numbers, as in an agrarian State, or if it is politically weak, because unorganised, and lacking self-consciousness. But if the proletariat in a democratic State grows until it is numerous and strong enough to conquer political power by making use of the liberties which exist, then it would be a task of great difficulty for the capitalist dictatorship to manipulate the force necessary for the suppression of democracy.

As a matter of fact, Marx thought it possible, and even probable, that in England and America the proletariat might peacefully conquer political power. On the conclusion of the Congress of the International at the Hague in 1872, Marx spoke at a meeting, and among other things said:

"The worker must one day capture political power in order to found the new organisation of labour. He must reverse the old policy, which the old institutions maintain, if he will not, like the Christians of old who despised and neglected such things, renounce the things of this world.

"But we do not assert that the way to reach this goal is the same everywhere.

"We know that the institutions, the manners and the customs of the various countries must be considered, and we do not deny that there are countries like England and America, and, if I understood your arrangements better, I might even add Holland, where the worker may attain his object by peaceful means. But not in all countries is this the case."

It remains to be seen whether Marx's expectations will be realised. . . .

The working classes of the whole of Europe, in numerous—often bloody—struggles, have conquered one instalment of democracy after the other, and by their endeavours to win, maintain and extend democracy, and by constantly making use of each instalment for organisation, for propaganda, and for wresting social reforms, have they grown in maturity from year to year, and from the lowest have become the highest placed section of the masses of the people.

Has the proletariat already attained the maturity which Socialism postulates? And are the other conditions now in existence? These questions are to-day much disputed, the answers given being by some as decisively in the affirmative as by others in the negative. Both answers seem to me rather over hasty. Ripeness for Socialism is not a condition which lends itself to statistical calculation before the proof can be put to the test. In any case, it is wrong, as so often happens in discussing this question, to put the material pre-requisites of Socialism too much in the foreground. No doubt, without a certain development of the large industry no Socialism is possible, but when it is asserted that Socialism would only become practicable when capitalism is no more in a position to expand, all proof of this is lacking. It is correct to say that Socialism would be the more easily realisable the more developed the large industry is, and therefore the more compact the productive forces are which must be socially organised.

Yet this is only relevant to the problem, when it is considered from the standpoint of a particular State. The simplification of the problem in this form is, however, counteracted by the fact that the growth of the large industry is accompanied by an expansion of its markets, the progress of the division of labour and of international communications, and therewith the constant widening and increasing complication of the problem of the social organisation of production. There is, indeed, no reason for believing that the organisation of the largest part of production for social ends, by the State, Municipalities, and Co-operative Societies, is not already possible in modern industrial States, with their banking facilities and their machinery for the conduct of businesses.

The decisive factor is no longer the material, but the personal one. Is the proletariat strong and intelligent enough to take in hand the regulation of society, that is, does it possess the power and the capacity to transfer democracy from politics to economics? This cannot be foretold with certainty. The factor in question is one which is in different stages of development in different countries, and it fluctuates considerably at various times in the same country. Adequate strength and capacity are relative conceptions. The same measure of strength may be insufficient to-day, when the opponents are strong, but to-morrow quite adequate, when they have suffered a moral, economic or military collapse.

The modern State is a rigidly centralised organism, an organisation comprising the greatest power within modern society, and influencing in the most effective way the fate of each individual, as is especially obvious in time of war. . . .

Before the united pressure of the other classes, which may include the landed gentry, the lower clergy, the industrial capitalists, the absolute regime must give way. In a greater or lesser degree it must concede freedom of the Press, of public meeting, of organisation, and a Parliament. All the States of Europe have successfully passed through this development.

Every class will, however, endeavour to shape the new form of the State in a manner corresponding to its particular interests. This attempt is especially manifested in the struggle over the character of the Parliament, that is in the fight for the franchise. The watchword of the lower classes, of the people, is Universal Suffrage. Not only the wage-earner, but the small peasant and the lower middle classes have an interest in the franchise.

Everywhere and under all circumstances these classes form the great majority of the population. Whether the proletariat is the predominant class amongst these depends on the extent of the economic development, although this factor does not determine whether the proletariat comprises the majority of the population. The exploiters are always a small minority of the population.

In the long run no modern State can withstand the pressure of these classes, and anything short of general suffrage in our society to-day would be an absurdity. In capitalist society, with its constantly changing conditions, the classes cannot be stereotyped in fixed grooves. All social conditions are in a state of flux. A franchise based on status is consequently excluded. A class which is not organised as such is a formless fluctuating mass, whose exact boundaries it is quite impossible to mark. A class is an economic entity, not a legal one. Class-membership is always changing. Many handworkers who, under the regime of small industry, think they are possessors, feel like proletarians under large industry, and are really proletarians even when for purposes of statistics they are included with the possessing classes and independent producers. There is also no franchise based on the census which would secure to the possessing classes a lasting monopoly of Parliament. It would be upset by every depreciation in money values. Finally, a franchise based on education would be even more futile, in view of the progress of culture amongst the masses. Thus various factors combine to render general suffrage the only solution in the society of to-day, and bring the question more and more to the front. Above all, it is the only rational solution from the standpoint of the proletariat as the lowest class of the population. The most effective weapon of the proletariat is its numerical strength. It cannot emancipate itself until it has become the largest class of the population, and until capitalist society is so far developed that the small peasants and the lower middle classes no longer overweight the proletariat.

The proletariat has also an interest in the fact that the suffrage should not only be universal and equal, but also non-discriminatory, so that men and women, or wage earners and capitalists, do not vote in separate sections. . . .

Parties and classes are therefore not necessarily coterminous. A class can split up into various parties, and a party may consist of members of various classes. A class may still remain the rulers, while changes occur in the governing party, if the majority of the ruling class considers the methods of the existing governing party unsuitable, and that of its opponents to be more appropriate.

Government by parties in a democracy changes more rapidly than the rule of classes. Under these circumstances, no party is certain of retaining power, and must always count on the possibility of being in the minority, but by virtue of the nature of the State no party need remain in a minority for ever.

These conditions account for the growing practice of protecting minorities in a democracy. The deeper the roots which a democracy has struck, and the longer it has lasted and influenced political customs, the more effective is the minority, and the more successfully it can oppose the pretensions of any party which seeks to remain in power at all costs.

What significance the protection of minorities has for the early stages of the Socialist Party, which everywhere started as a small minority, and how much it has helped the proletariat to mature, is clear. In the ranks of the Socialist Party the protection of minorities is very important. Every new doctrine, be it of a theoretical or a tactical nature, is represented in the first place by minorities. If these are forcibly suppressed, instead of being discussed, the majority is spared much trouble and inconvenience. Much unnecessary labour might be saved—a doctrine does not mean progress because it is new and championed by a minority. Most of what arises as new thought has already been discussed long before, and recognised as untenable, either by practice or by refutation.

Ignorance is always bringing out old wares as if they were something new. Other new ideas may be original, but put in a perverted shape. Although only a few of the new ideas and doctrines may spell real progress, yet progress is only possible through new ideas, which at the outset are put forward by minorities. The suppression of the new ideas of minorities in the Party would only cause harm to the proletarian class struggle, and an obstacle to the development of the proletariat. The world is always bringing us against new problems, which are not to be solved by the existing methods.

Tedious as it may be to sift the wheat from the chaff, this is an unavoidable task if our movement is not to stagnate, and is to rise to the height of the tasks before it. And what is needful for a party is also needful for the State. Protection of minorities is an indispensable condition for democratic development, and no less important than the rule of the majority. . . .

The social revolution, the political revolution, and civil war must be distinguished from each other.

The social revolution is a profound transformation of the entire social structure brought about by the establishment of a new method of production. It is a protracted process, which may be spread over decades, and no definite boundaries can be drawn for its conclusion. It will be the more successful, according to the peaceful nature of the forms under which it is consummated. Civil and foreign wars are its deadly foes. As a rule a social revolution is brought about by a political revolution, through a sudden alteration in the relative strength of classes in the State, whereby a class hitherto excluded from the political power possesses itself of the machinery of government. The political revolution is a sudden act, which is rapidly concluded. Its forms depend on the constitution of the State in which it is accomplished. The more democracy rules, not merely formally, but actually anchored in the strength of the working classes, the greater is the likelihood that the political revolution will be a peaceful one. Contrariwise, the more the system which has hitherto prevailed has been without the support of a majority of the people, and has represented a minority which kept control by military force, the greater is the likelihood that the political revolution will take the form of a civil war.

Yet, even in the last case, the supporters of the social revolution have a pressing interest in seeing that the civil war is only a transitory episode which quickly terminates, that it is made to serve the sole end of introducing and setting up democracy, to whose pace the social revolution should be adapted. In other words, the social revolution must not, for the time being, be carried out farther than the majority of the people are inclined to go, because beyond this the Social Revolution, desirable as it may seem to far-seeing individuals, would not find the necessary conditions for establishing itself permanently.

But did not the Reign of Terror of the proletariat and lower middle-class of Paris, that is the dictatorship of a Minority, in the great French Revolution, bring with it enormous consequences of the highest historical significance?

Of course. But of what kind were they? That dictatorship was a child of the war which the allied Monarchs of

Europe had waged against Revolutionary France. To have victoriously beaten off this attack was the historical achievement of the Reign of Terror. Thereby is again proved distinctly the old truth, that dictatorship is better able to wage war than democracy. It proves in no way that dictatorship is the method of the proletariat to carry through social transformations to its own liking, and to keep control of political power.

In energy the Reign of Terror of 1793 cannot be surpassed. Yet the proletariat of Paris did not succeed, by this means, in retaining power. The dictatorship was a method by means of which the various factions belonging to proletarian and small middle-class politics fought amongst themselves, and, finally, it was the means of making an end of all proletarian and lower middle-class politics. . . .

The dictatorship of the lower classes opens the way for dictatorship of the sword.

Should it be said, after the example of the middle-class revolutions, that the Revolution is synonymous with civil war and dictatorship, then the consequences must also be recognized, and it must be added the Revolution would necessarily end in the rule of a Cromwell or a Napoleon.

This is, however, by no means the necessary upshot of a proletarian revolution where the proletariat forms the majority of the nation, which is democratically organised, and only in such cases do the conditions for Socialist production exist.

By the dictatorship of the proletariat we are unable to understand anything else than its rule on the basis of democracy.

We may popularly express the essentials of Socialism in the words: Freedom and bread for all. This is what the masses expect from it, and why they rally to it. Freedom is not less important than bread. Even well-to-do and rich classes have fought for their freedom, and not seldom have made the biggest sacrifices for their convictions in blood and treasure. The need for freedom, for self-determination, is as natural as the need for food.

Hitherto Social Democracy did represent to the masses of the people the object lesson of being the most tireless champion of the freedom of all who were oppressed, not merely the wage-earner, but also of women, persecuted religions and races, the Jews, Negroes and Chinese. By this object lesson it has won adherents quite outside the circle of wage-earners.

Now, so soon as Social Democracy attains to power, this object lesson is to be replaced by one of an opposite character. The first step consists in the suspension of universal suffrage and of liberty of the Press, the disfranchisement of large masses of the people, for this must always take place if dictatorship is substituted for democracy. In order to break the political influence of the upper ten thousand, it is not necessary to exclude them from the franchise. They exercise this influence not by their personal votes. As regards small shopkeepers, home workers, peasants who are well off and in moderate condition, the greater part of the intellectuals, so soon as the dictatorship deprives them of their rights, they are changed at once into enemies of Socialism by this kind of object lesson, so far as they are not inimical from the beginning. Thus all those who adhere to Socialism on the ground that it fights for the freedom of all would become enemies of the proletarian dictatorship.

This method will win nobody who is not already a Socialist. It can only increase the enemies of Socialism.

But we saw that Socialism not only promised freedom, but also bread. This ought to reconcile those whom the Communist dictatorship robbed of freedom.

They are not the best of the masses who are consoled in their loss of freedom with bread and pleasure. But without doubt material well-being will lead many to Communism who regard it sceptically, or who are by it deprived of their rights. Only this prosperity must really come, and that quickly, not as a promise for the future, if the object lesson is to be effective.

How is this prosperity to be attained? The necessity for dictatorship pre-supposes that a minority of the population have possessed themselves of the power of the State. A minority composed of those who possess nothing. The greatest weapon of the proletariat is, however, its numbers, and in normal times it can only progress on these lines, conquering the political power only when it forms the majority. As a minority it can only achieve power by the combination of extraordinary circumstances, by a catastrophe which causes the collapse of a regime, and leaves the State helpless and impoverished.

Under such circumstances, Socialism, that is general well-being within modern civilisation, would only be possible through a powerful development of the productive forces which capitalism brings into existence, and with the aid of the enormous riches which it creates and concentrates in the hands of the capitalist class. A State which by a foolish policy or by unsuccessful war has dissipated these riches, is by its nature condemned to be an unfavourable starting point for the rapid diffusion of prosperity in all classes.

If, as the heir of the bankrupt State, not a democratic but a dictatorial regime enters into power, it even renders the position worse, as civil war is its necessary consequence. What might still be left in the shape of material resources is wasted by anarchy.

In fine, the uninterrupted progress of production is essential for the prosperity of all. The destruction of capitalism is not Socialism. Where capitalist production cannot be transformed at once into Socialist production, it must go on as before, otherwise the process of production will be interrupted, and that hardship for the masses will ensue which the modern proletariat so much fears in the shape of general unemployment.

In those places where, under the new conditions, capitalist production has been rendered impossible, Socialist production will only be able to replace it if the proletariat has acquired experience in self-government, in trade unions, and on town councils, and has participated in the making of laws and the control of government, and if numerous intellectuals are prepared to assist with their services the new methods.

In a country which is so little developed economically that the proletariat only forms a minority, such maturity of the proletariat is not to be expected.

It may therefore be taken for granted that in all places where the proletariat can only maintain itself in power by a dictatorship, instead of by democracy, the difficulties with which Socialism is confronted are so great that it would seem to be out of the question that dictatorship could rapidly bring about prosperity for all, and in this manner reconcile to the reign of force the masses of the people who are thereby deprived of political rights.

Georgii Valentinovich
Plekhanov
(1857–1918)

Russian philosopher, born at Goudalovka, Plekhanov was a theoretical socialist who opposed the Bolshevists from 1903 on. Sir Isaiah Berlin called him "the most brilliant and many-sided of all later writers on Marxism." Plekhanov translated Marx into Russian. He violently disapproved of the Russian workers' 1905 uprising.

Fundamental Problems
of Marxism

The main point with which we are now concerned is that Marx showed how property relations, when the forces of production have attained a certain degree of development, favour for a time an increase in these forces, and subsequently begin to hinder their development.[1] Although a given condition of the forces of production is the exciting

From *Fundamental Problems of Marxism*, by Georgii V. Plekhanov, edited by D. Ryazanov, London, 1929.

[1] Consider slavery, for instance. At a certain level of development, it favours the growth of the forces of production, but subsequently it begins to hinder their growth. The disappearance of slavery in the civilised nations of the West is due to their economic evolution.— Concerning slavery in classical times, consult Professor E. Cicotti's interesting work, *Il tramonto della schiavitù*, Turin, 1899.—J. H. Speke, in his book, *Journal of the Discovery of the Sources of the*

cause of particular relations of production and, in especial, of particular property relations, these latter, when they have once come into being as the outcome of the before-mentioned cause, begin, in their turn, to affect this same cause. Thus there arises a system of action and reaction, of reciprocal interaction, between the forces of production and the economic system. On the other hand, there builds itself up upon the economic foundation an entire super-structure of social relations and of appropriate feelings and ideas. Now, inasmuch as this superstructure, likewise, be-gins by favouring economic development, but comes in due course to hinder that development, here also there is estab-lished a system of mutual interaction between the super-structure and the foundation. This dispels the enigma which at first sight surrounds these phenomena and seems to conflict with the fundamental thesis of historical mate-rialism.

All that has hitherto been said by the critics of Marx as regards the supposed one-sidedness of Marxism and its alleged disdain for any but the economic factors of social evolution is simply due to a misunderstanding of the part assigned by Marx and Engels to the reciprocal interactions between the foundation and the superstructure. Those who wish to convince themselves how little Marx and Engels were inclined to underestimate the importance of the politi-cal factor will find it enough to read the pages of the *Communist Manifesto* referring to the movement for the emancipation of the bourgeoisie. There we are told: "Each step in the development of the bourgeoisie was accom-panied by a corresponding political advance. An oppressed class under the dominion of the feudal lords, it became an armed and self-governing association in the commune; here an independent republic, there the taxable 'third estate' under the monarchy; in the days of manufacture, the bourgeoisie was the counterpoise of the nobility in the semi-feudal or in the absolute monarchy, and was the corner-stone of great monarchies in general—to fight its way upwards in the end, after the rise of large-scale indus-try and the establishment of the world market, to exclusive political hegemony in the modern representative State. The

---

Nile, 1863, says that, among the negroes, slaves consider that to run away is to behave in a disgraceful way towards the master who has paid money for them. It should be added that these slaves regard their situation as a more honourable one than that of a wage-earner. Such outlooks correspond to a phase of social evolution in which slavery is still a progressive phenomenon.

modern State authority is nothing more than a committee for the administration of the consolidated affairs of the bourgeois class as a whole."

The importance of the political factor is here plainly disclosed, so plainly that some critics consider that it is unduly stressed. But the origin and the influence of this factor, together with the way in which it exerts its influence in any given period of the development of bourgeois society, are explained in the *Manifesto* by the course of economic development, and, consequently, though the factors vary in their nature, the initial determinant is always the same.

Indisputably, political relations influence economic development; but it is no less indisputable that, before influencing this movement, they are created thereby.

We have to say the same thing about the psychological conditions of man as a social being; to say the same thing of what Stammler called, somewhat one-sidedly, social concepts. The *Manifesto* shows beyond question that its authors were well aware of the importance of the ideological factor; but the same document shows that, even though the ideological factor plays an important part in the development of society, it is itself first of all created by this development.

"When the classical world was in its decline, the old religions were conquered by Christianity. When Christian ideas were put to flight by eighteenth-century rationalism, it was at the time when feudal society was fighting for very existence against the bourgeoisie, which was then the revolutionary class." But in the matter with which we are now concerned, the closing section of the *Manifesto* is even more convincing. Here we are told that the communists want to do all they can to impress upon the minds of the workers that there is an essential antagonism between the bourgeoisie and the proletariat. Assuredly one who has attached no importance whatever to the ideological factor would have no reason for trying to impress anything upon the minds of the members of any social group whatever.

X

I have quoted the *Manifesto* in preference to other works by Marx and Engels because it was composed during that early period of their activity when, according to some of their critics, they had an especially "one-sided" view of the relations between the various factors of social evolution. We see clearly, however, that, at this period no less than later, Marx and Engels were not characterized by a "one-sided way" of looking at things, but only by an inclination towards monism, by a strong hostility towards the eclecticism which is so obvious in their critics.

Reference has often been made to two letters written by Engels, one in 1890, and the other in 1894, published in the "Sozialistischer Akademiker." Bernstein makes much of these two letters, regarding them as plain proof of a change of views in Marx's friend and collaborator. He gives two extracts which seem to him of especial importance in this connection, and I shall myself quote them likewise, as proving the exact opposite of what Bernstein wants to prove.

Here is the first of these passages: "Consequently there exist innumerable forces which interlace, an infinite number of parallelograms of forces giving a resultant, the historical happening. This, in its turn, can be regarded as the outcome of a force acting as a whole, without consciousness or will. For that which each individual wishes separately, is hindered by all the others, and the general upshot is something which no one in particular has willed." (Letter of 1890.)

Here is the other extract: "Political, legal, philosophical, religious, literary, artistic, etc., development, is grounded upon economic development. But all of them react, conjointly and separately, one upon another, and upon the economic foundation." (Letter of 1894.)

According to Bernstein, "this sounds a very different note" from the preface to *Zur Kritik der politischen Oekonomie,* where we read about the link between the economic foundation and the superstructure which is erected thereon. I cannot see the difference. The passage quoted above merely repeats what Marx said in the preface. Political development and other kinds of development are based upon economic development. Bernstein blunts the significance of the words "all of them react, conjointly and separately, one upon another, and upon the economic foundation." He put a different interpretation upon the preface to *Zur Kritik der politischen Oekonomie,* and thinks that when Marx speaks there of the social and ideological superstructure erected upon the economic foundation, he means to imply that the superstructure exerts no influence upon the foundation. We know perfectly well that there could not be a more erroneous way of interpreting Marx's thought. Those who have taken the trouble to watch Bernstein's "critical" exploits cannot but shrug their shoulders when they see how the man who undertook, at one time, to popularise Marxian doctrine has not taken the trouble to understand (or, to put the matter more accurately, is incapable of understanding) Marxian doctrines.

In the second of the two letters which Bernstein quotes, there are other passages, besides the one already given (the one which Bernstein understands so little), still more important, perhaps, in the light they throw upon the causal significance of Marx's and Engels' historical theory. One of these passages runs as follows: "There is, therefore, no automatic outcome of the economic situation as some find it convenient to fancy. Men make their own history, but in a given environment in which they live, upon the foundation of extant relations. Among these relations, economic relations, however great may be the influence exercised on them by other relations of a political and ideological order, are those whose action is ultimately decisive, forming a red thread which runs through all the other relations and enables us to understand them."

Among those who interpret the historical doctrine of Marx and Engels as signifying that the economic situation works itself out automatically in the historical process, Bernstein, as we know, was numbered in the days when he was still "orthodox." Among them, too, we must class a great number of modern critics of Marx who have backslid "from Marxism to idealism." These profound thinkers are extremely pleased with themselves when they show, in opposition to the "one-sided" doctrine of Marx and Engels, that history is made by men and not by an automatic economic movement. They thus sacrifice to Marx his own goods, and never even suspect (so simple-minded are they) that the Marx whom they are criticising has nothing in common save the name with the true Marx. The Marx they are criticising is the creation of their own ignorance, which is indeed "many-sided." It is natural that critics of this order should be utterly incapable of supplementing or amending a jot or tittle of historical materialism. We need not trouble ourselves about them any more, and can return to the study of those who laid the foundations of the theory.

It is extremely important to note that when Engels, shortly before his death, repudiated the "automatic" way of looking upon the historical activity of economic influences, he was only repeating (almost in the same words) what Marx had written half a century before, in the third of the *Theses on Feuerbach,* in the passage I have reproduced above. There Marx complained of the earlier materialists because they had failed to take into account the fact that, if on the one hand, men are the products of environment, environment itself, on the other hand, is modified by men. . . . In Marx's view, therefore, the task of materialism in the domain of history was to explain exactly how environment can be modified by men who are themselves a product of this environment. He solved this problem by pointing to the relations of production which come into being under the working of conditions independent of the human will. The relations of production are relations established among human beings in the social process of production. To say that the relations of production are transformed, is to say that the relations between men engaged in the process of production are transformed. A change in these relations cannot occur "automatically," that is to say independently of human activity, because these relations are among those which come into being between men in the course of their activity.

But these relations can undergo transformation, and very often do undergo transformation, in a direction very different from that in which men would like to transform them. The character of the "economic structure" and the direction in which this character undergoes transformation do not depend upon the human will, but upon the condition of the forces of production, and upon the nature of the changes which occur in the relations of production and which become necessary to society owing to the development of these forces. Engels explains this as follows: "Men make their own history; but, hitherto, even within isolated societies, they have not done so as the outcome of a general will, or in accordance with a general plan. Their aspirations conflict one with another; and that is why, in all such societies, necessity rules—necessity, of which chance is the complement and the form under which it manifests itself." Here human activity exhibits itself, not as free activity, but as necessary activity, that is to say in conformity with law and able to be subjected to scientific study. Thus historical materialism, while continually pointing out that the environment is modified by human beings, enables us for the first time to regard the course of this modification from a scientific standpoint. That is why we are entitled to say that the materialist conception of history is the essential preliminary to any sociological doctrine which can claim the title of science.

So true is this that, henceforward, no study of social life can have any scientific value except in proportion to the degree in which it inclines towards a materialist explanation of its topic. Despite the widely-trumpeted "revival of idealism" in sociology, materialist explanations are more and more in vogue wherever men of science, instead of giving themselves up to edifying meditations and grandiloquent discourses concerning the "ideal," devote themselves to the task of discovering the causal ties between phenomena. In actual fact, persons who, far from being open advocates of the materialist conception of history, have never even heard of it, none the less act as materialists in their historical researches. Thereupon, their ignorance of the materialist conception, or their prejudice against it, making it impossible for them to understand it in all its aspects, misleads them into the adoption of what we are entitled to call one-sided and narrow views. . . .

Anarchist Doctrine

Religion, conscience, morality, right, law, family, state, are but so many fetters forced upon me in the name of an abstraction, but so many despotic lords whom "I," the individual conscious of my own "concerns," combat by every means in my power. Your *"morality,"* not merely the morality of the bourgeois philistines, but the most elevated, the most humanitarian morality is only religion which has changed its supreme beings. Your *"right,"* that you believe born with man, is but a ghost, and if you respect it, you are no farther advanced than the heroes of Homer who were afraid when they beheld a god fighting in the ranks of their enemies. Right is might. "Whoever has might, he has right; if you have not the former you have not the latter. Is this wisdom so difficult of attain-

From *Anarchism and Socialism,* by Georgii V. Plekhanov, translated by Eleanor Marx Aveling, Chicago, 1906.

ment?"[1] You would persuade me to sacrifice my interests to those of the State. I, on the contrary, declare war to the knife to all States, even the most democratic. "Every State is a despotism, whether it is the despotism of one or many, or whether, as one might suppose would be the case in a Republic, all are masters, i.e., one tyrannises over the rest. For this is the case whenever a given law, the expressed will perhaps of some assemblage of the people, is immediately to become a law to the individual, which he must obey, and which it is his *duty* to obey. Even if one were to suppose a case in which every individual among the people had expressed the same will, and thus a perfect 'will of all' had easily been arrived at, the thing would still be the same. Should I not to-day and in the future be bound by my will of yesterday? In this event my will would be paralysed. Fatal stagnation! My creation, i.e., a certain expression of will would have become my master. But I, in my will should be constrained, I, the creator should be constrained in my development, my working out. Because I was a fool yesterday, I must remain one all my life. So that in my life in relation to the State I am at best—I might as well say at worst—a slave to my own self. Because yesterday I had a will, I am to-day without one; yesterday free, today bound."[2]

Here a partisan of the "People's State" might observe to Stirner, that his "I" goes a little too far in his desire to reduce democratic liberty to absurdity; further, that a bad law may be abrogated as soon as a majority of citizens desire it, and that one is not forced to submit to it "all one's life." But this is only an insignificant detail, to which, moreover, Stirner would reply that the very necessity for appealing to a majority proves that "I" am no longer the master of my own conduct. The conclusions of our author are irrefutable, for the simple reason that to say, I recognise nothing above myself, is to say, I feel oppressed by every institution that imposes any duty upon me. It is simply tautology.

It is evident that no "Ego" can exist quite alone. Stirner knows this perfectly, and this is why he advocates "Leagues of Egoists," that is to say, free associations into which every "Ego" enters, and in which he remains when and so long as it suits his interests.

Here let us pause. We are now face to face with an

[1] *Der Einzige und sein Eigenthum*, 2nd ed., Leipzig, 1882, pp. 196–197.
[2] *Ibid*, p. 200.

"egoist" system *par excellence*. It is, perhaps, the only one that the history of human thought has to chronicle. The French Materialists of the last century have been accused of preaching egoism. The accusation was quite wrong. The French Materialists always preached "Virtue," and preached it with such unlimited zeal that Grimm could, not without reason, make fun of their *capucinades* on the subject. The question of egoism presented to them a double problem. (1) Man is all sensation (this was the basis of all their speculations upon man); by his very nature he is forced to shun suffering and to seek pleasure; how comes it then that we find men capable of enduring the greatest sufferings for the sake of some idea, that is to say, in its final analysis, in order to provide agreeable sensations for their fellow-men. (2) Since man is all sensation he will harm his fellow-man if he is placed in a social environment where the interests of an individual conflict with those of others. What form of legislation therefore can harmonise public good and that of individuals? Here, in this double problem, lies the whole significance of what is called the materialist ethics of the 18th century. Max Stirner pursues an end entirely opposed to this. He laughs at "Virtue," and, far from desiring its triumph, he sees reasonable men only in egoists, for whom there is nothing above their own "Ego." Once again, he is the theorist *par excellence* of egoism.

The good bourgeois whose ears are as chaste and virtuous as their hearts are hard; they who, "drinking wine, publicly preach water," were scandalised to the last degree by the "immorality" of Stirner. "It is the complete ruin of the moral world," they cried. But as usual the virtue of the philistines showed itself very weak in argument. "The real merit of Stirner is that he has spoken the last word of the young atheist school" (i.e., the left wing of the Hegelian school), wrote the Frenchman, St. Réné Taillandier. The philistines of other lands shared this view of the "merits" of the daring publicist. From the point of view of modern Socialism this "merit" appears in a very different light.

To begin with, the incontestable merit of Stirner consists in his having openly and energetically combatted the sickly sentimentalism of the bourgeois reformers and of many of the Utopian Socialists, according to which the emancipation of the proletariat would be brought about by the virtuous activity of "devoted" persons of all classes, and especially of those of the possessing-class. Stirner knew perfectly what to expect from the "devotion" of the exploiters. The "rich" are harsh, hard-hearted, but the "poor" (the terminology is that of our author) are wrong to complain of it, since it is not the rich who create the poverty of the poor, but the poor who create the wealth of the rich. They ought to blame themselves then if their condition is a hard one. In order to change it they have only to revolt against the rich; as soon as they seriously wish it, they will be the strongest and the reign of wealth will be at an end. Salvation lies in struggle, and not in fruitless appeals to the generosity of the oppressors. Stirner, therefore, preaches the class war. It is true that he represents it in the abstract form of the struggle of a certain number of egoist "Egos" against another smaller number of "Egos" not less egoist. But here we come to another merit of Stirner's.

According to Taillandier, he has spoken the last word of the young atheist school of German philosophers. As a matter of fact he has only spoken the last word of idealist speculation. But that word he has incontestably the merit of having spoken.

In his criticism of religion Feuerbach is but half a Materialist. In worshipping God, man only worships his own Being idealised. This is true. But religions spring up and die out, like everything else upon earth. Does this not prove that the human Being is not immutable, but changes in the process of the historical evolution of societies? Clearly, yes. But, then, what is the cause of the historical transformation of the "human Being"? Feuerbach does not know. For him the human Being is only an abstract notion, as human Nature was for the French Materialists. This is the fundamental fault of his criticism of religion. Stirner said that it had no very robust constitution. He wished to strengthen it by making it breathe the fresh air of reality. He turns his back upon all phantoms, upon all things of the imagination. In reality, he said to himself, these are only individuals. Let us take the individual for our starting-point. But *what* individual does he take for his starting-point? Tom, Dick, or Harry? Neither. He takes the *individual in general*—he takes a new abstraction, the thinnest of them all—he takes the "Ego."

Stirner naïvely imagined that he was finally solving an old philosophical question, which had already divided the Nominalists and the Realists of the Middle Ages. "No Idea has an existence," he says, "for none is capable of becoming corporeal. The scholastic controversy of Realism and Nominalism had the same content." Alas! The first Nominalist he came across could have demonstrated to our author by the completest evidence, that his "Ego" is as much an "Idea" as any other, and that it is as little real as a mathematical unit.

Tom, Dick and Harry have relations with one another that do not depend upon the will of their "Ego," but are imposed upon them by the structure of the society in which they live. To criticise social institutions in the name of the "Ego," is therefore to abandon the only profitable point of view in the case, i.e., that of society, of the laws of its existence and evolution, and to lose oneself in the mists of abstraction. But it is just in these mists that the "Nominalist" Stirner delights. I am I—that is his starting-point; not I is not I—that is his result. I + I + I + etc.— is his social Utopia. It is subjective Idealism, pure and simple, applied to social and political criticism. It is the suicide of idealist speculation.

But in the same year (1845) in which "Der Einzige" of Stirner appeared, there appeared also, at Frankfort-on-Maine, the work of Marx and Engels, "Die heilige Familie, oder Kritik der Kritischen Kritik, gegen Bruno Bauer und Consorten."[3] In it Idealist speculation was attacked and beaten by Materialist dialectic, the theoretical basis of modern Socialism. "Der Einzige" came too late.

We have just said that I + I + I + etc. represents the social Utopia of Stirner. His League of Egoists is, in fact, nothing but a mass of abstract quantities. What are, what can be the basis of their union? Their interests, answers Stirner. But what will, what can be the true basis of any given combination of their interests? Stirner says nothing about it, and he can say nothing definite since from the abstract heights on which he stands, one cannot see clearly economic reality, the mother and nurse of all the "Egos," egoistic or altruistic. Nor is it surprising that he is not able to explain clearly even this idea of the class struggle, of which he nevertheless had a happy inkling. The "poor" must combat the "rich." And after, when they have conquered these? Then every one of the former "poor," like every one of the former "rich," will combat everyone of the former poor, and against every one of the former rich. There will be the war of all against all. (These are Stirner's own words.) And the rules of the "Leagues of Egoists" will be so many partial truces in this colossal and universal warfare. There is plenty of fight in this idea, but of the "realism" Max Stirner dreamed of, nothing.

[3] "The Holy Family, or Criticism of Critical Criticism, against Bruno Bauer and Company."

But enough of the "Leagues of Egoists." A Utopian may shut his eyes to economic reality, but it forces itself upon him in spite of himself; it pursues him everywhere with the brutality of a natural force not controlled by force. The elevated regions of the abstract "I" do not save Stirner from the attacks of economic reality. He does not speak to us only of the "Individual"; his theme is "the Individual *and his property*." Now, what sort of a figure does the property of the "Individual" cut?

It goes without saying, that Stirner is little inclined to respect property as an "acquired right." "Only that property will be legally and lawfully another's which it suits *you* should be his property. When it ceases to suit you, it has lost its legality for you, and any absolute right in it you will laugh at." [4] It is always the same tune: "For me there is nothing above myself." But his scant respect for the property of others does not prevent the "Ego" of Stirner from having the tendencies of a property-owner. The strongest argument against Communism, is, in his opinion, the consideration that Communism by abolishing individual property transforms all members of society into mere beggars. Stirner is indignant at such an iniquity.

"Communists think that the Commune should be the property-owner. On the contrary, *I* am a property-owner, and can only agree with others as to my property. If the Commune does not do as I wish I rebel against it, and defend my property, I am the owner of property, but property *is not sacred*. Should I only be the holder of property [an allusion to Proudhon]? No, hitherto one was only a holder of property, assured of possession of a piece of land, because one left others also in possession of a piece of land; but now *everything* belongs to me, I am the owner of *everything* I need, and can get hold of. If the Socialist says, society gives me what I need, the Egoist says, I take what I want. If the Communists behave like beggars, the Egoist behaves like an owner of property." The property of the egoist seems pretty shaky. An "Egoist," retains his property only as long as the other "Egoists" do not care to take it from him, thus transforming him into a "beggar." But the devil is not so black as he is painted. Stirner pictures the mutual relations of the "Egoist" proprietors rather as relations of exchange than of pillage. And force, to which he constantly appeals, is rather the economic force of a producer of commodities freed from the trammels

[4] *Der Einzige und sein Eigenthum.*

which the State and "Society" in general impose, or seem
to impose, upon him.

It is the soul of a producer of commodities that speaks
through the mouth of Stirner. If he falls foul of the State,
it is because the State does not seem to respect the "property" of the producers of commodities sufficiently. He
wants *his* property, his *whole* property. The State makes
him pay taxes; it ventures to expropriate him for the public
good. He wants a *jus utendi et abutendi;* the State says
"agreed"—but adds that there are abuses and abuses. Then
Stirner cries "stop thief!" "I am the enemy of the State,"
says he, "which is always fluctuating between the alternative: He or I. . . . With the State there is no property, i.e.,
no individual property, only State property. Only through
the State have I what I have, as it is only through the State
that I am what I am. My private property is only what the
State leaves me of its own, while it deprives other citizens
of it: that is State property." So down with the State and
long live full and complete individual property! . . .

Rosa Luxemburg
(1870–1919)

*A German-Jewish Socialist, born in Ruthenia, she took part
in the 1905 Russian uprisings, later was a leader of the radical wing of the German Social Democrats. She helped Karl
Liebknecht organize the Spartacus Party and was assassinated with him during the 1919 Spartacist uprising.*

Reform or Revolution

The production relations of capitalist society approach
more and more the production relations of socialist society.

From *Reform or Revolution*, by Rosa Luxemburg, New York,
1937.

But on the other hand, its political and juridical relations establish between capitalist society and socialist society a steadily rising wall. This wall is not overthrown, but is on the contrary strengthened and consolidated by the development of social reforms and the course of democracy. Only the hammer blow of revolution, that is to say, the conquest of political power by the proletariat can break down this wall. . . . It is not true that socialism will arise automatically from the daily struggle of the working class. Socialism will be the consequence of (1), the growing contradictions of capitalist economy and (2), of the comprehension by the working class of the unavoidability of the suppression of these contradictions through a social transformation. When, in the manner of revisionism, the first condition is denied and the second rejected, the labor movement finds itself reduced to a simple corporative and reformist movement. We move here in a straight line toward the total abandonment of the class viewpoint.

This consequence also becomes evident when we investigate the general character of revisionism. It is obvious that revisionism does not wish to concede that its standpoint is that of the capitalist apologist. It does not join the bourgeois economists in denying the existence of the contradictions of capitalism. But, on the other hand, what precisely constitutes the fundamental point of revisionism and distinguishes it from the attitude taken by the Social-Democracy up to now, is that it does not base its theory on the belief that the contradictions of capitalism will be suppressed as a result of the logical inner development of the present economic system.

We may say that the theory of revisionism occupies an intermediate place between two extremes. Revisionism does not expect to see the contradictions of capitalism mature. It does not propose to suppress these contradictions through a revolutionary transformation. It wants to lessen, to attenuate, the capitalist contradictions. So that the antagonism existing between production and exchange is to be mollified by the cessation of crises and the formation of capitalist combines. The antagonism between Capital and Labor is to be adjusted by bettering the situation of the workers and by the conservation of the middle classes. And the contradiction between the class State and society is to be liquidated through increased State control and the progress of democracy.

It is true that the present procedure of the Social-Democracy does not consist in waiting for the antagonisms of capitalism to develop and in passing on, only then, to the task of suppressing them. On the contrary, the essence of revolutionary procedure is to be guided by the direction of this development, once it is ascertained, and inferring from this direction what consequences are necessary for the political struggle. Thus the Social-Democracy has combated tariff wars and militarism without waiting for their reactionary character to become fully evident. Bernstein's procedure is not guided by a consideration of the development of capitalism, by the prospect of the aggravation of its contradictions. It is guided by the prospect of the attenuation of these contradictions. He shows this when he speaks of the "adaptation" of capitalist economy. . . .

The Social-Democratic movement must logically grope on its road of development between the following two rocks: abandoning the mass character of the party or abandoning its final aim, falling into bourgeois reformism or into sectarianism, anarchism or opportunism.

In its theoretic arsenal, Marxist doctrine furnished, more than half a century ago, arms that are effective against both of these two extremes. But because our movement is a mass movement and because the dangers menacing it are not derived from the human brain but from social conditions, Marxist doctrine could not assure us, in advance and once for always, against the anarchist and opportunist tendencies. The latter can be overcome only as we pass from the domain of theory to the domain of practice, but only with the help of the arms furnished us by Marx.

"Bourgeois revolutions," wrote Marx a half century ago, "like those of the eighteenth century, rush onward rapidly from success to success, their stage effects outbid one another, men and things seem to be set in flaming brilliants, ecstasy is the prevailing spirit; but they are shortlived, they reach their climax speedily, and then society relapses into a long fit of nervous reaction before it learns how to appropriate the fruits of its period of feverish excitement. Proletarian revolutions on the contrary, such as those of the nineteenth century, criticize themselves constantly; constantly interrupt themselves in their own course; come back to what seems to have been accomplished, in order to start anew; scorn with cruel thoroughness the half-measures, weaknesses and meanness of their first attempts; seem to throw down their adversary only to enable him to draw fresh strength from the earth and again to rise up against them in more gigantic stature; constantly recoil in fear before the undefined monster magnitude of their own objects

—until finally that situation is created which renders all retreat impossible, and conditions themselves cry out: '*Hic Rhodus, hic salta!*' Here is the rose. And here we must dance!"

This has remained true even after the elaboration of the doctrine of scientific socialism. The proletarian movement has not yet, all at once, become social-democratic, even in Germany. But it is becoming more social-democratic, surmounting continuously the extreme deviations of anarchism and opportunism, both of which are only determining phases of the development of social democracy, considered as a process.

Peter B. Struve
(1870–1944)

Until the late eighteen-nineties Struve, a Russian politician and writer, was a theorist of "legal Marxism" and author of the Manifesto of the Russian Social Democratic Labour Party. *He later joined the Constitutional Democratic Party. In 1906 he was elected to the second Duma (Russian Parliament). From 1907 to 1917 he was professor at the St. Petersburg Polytechnic. After 1917 Struve was a member of the anti-Bolshevist Government of the South.*

Manifesto of the Russian Social Democratic Labour Party

Fifty years ago the revolutionary wave of 1848 brought new life and vigour to Europe.

From *Manifesto of the Russian Social Democratic Labour Party*, by P. B. Struve, translated by Nina Taylor, Geneva, 1903.

The working class as it is today appeared on the scenes for the first time as a forceful historical power in its own right. The bourgeoisie exploited the resources it offered to make a clean sweep of many outdated feudal and monarchical institutions. It was not however long before the same bourgeoisie saw in its newly-found ally its bitterest enemy; and hence betrayed not only itself but the working class and the very cause of freedom into the hands of reaction. Yet it was by now too late to retreat; momentarily appeased, the working class appeared again on the scene some ten or fifteen years later; endowed with twice its former strength and greatly increased self-awareness, it was ready to fight in a mature way for its final liberation.

For the whole of this period Russia appeared to stand aside from the high road of historical movement. No class struggle was apparent on the surface, though it persisted in a quiet way beneath and, more important still, it was growing and maturing there. With a zeal that is greatly to their credit, the Russian government itself sowed the seeds of class conflict: by depriving the peasants of their rightful share, by patronizing and protecting the landowners, by fostering and fattening up the well-to-do capitalists to the detriment of the working population. But we can only speak of the bourgeois-capitalist set-up in terms of a proletariat or working class, for the latter derives its existence from capitalism, grows and develops in its midst, and as it grows and develops, enters into progressively sharper conflict with the bourgeoisie.

The Russian factory worker, whether free or enslaved, has been constantly involved in secret and in overt conflict with his exploiters. The scale of his struggle has increased, together with the spread of capitalism, involving successively more layers of the working population. The awakening of class consciousness amongst the Russian Proletariat and the growth of a spontaneous labour movement coincided with the definitive development of international social democracy, which stands for class struggle and the class ideal of articulate and aware workers all over the world. All the newest Russian organisations have acted consciously or unconsciously in the spirit of social democratic ideals. The significance and impact of the labour movement and of social democracy, which is based on the labour movement, is emphasized by the series of strikes that have taken place of late in Russia and Poland, especially the well-known strikes of the Petersburg spinners and weavers in 1896 and 1897, which induced the government to promulge the law of 2nd June 1897 on the length of working hours. For all its failings, this law remains a permanent testimony to the power of pressure that united workers can exert on legislative and other governmental activities. The government is wrong in thinking that concessions will appease the workers. The more the working class achieves, and this is true all over the world, the more it will demand. The same applies to the Russian proletariat. It has succeeded only when it has voiced its needs, and in future it will achieve only its own articulate demands.

The Russian working class would appear to be totally lacking in everything that its opposite number in Europe enjoys in peace and freedom: participation in government, freedom of speech and of press, freedom of union and association; in short, it lacks all the means and conditions which improve the lot of the West European and American proletariat and help it in its struggle against private property for the sake of socialism and of its eventual liberation. The Russian proletariat urgently needs political freedom, for this is the basic condition and requirement for its uncramped development and successful struggle for partial improvements and eventual liberation.

The Russian proletariat must however fight for the requisite political freedom by dint of its own efforts.

Politically speaking, the bourgeoisie increases in cowardice, feebleness, and despicability the further East we go in Europe; and the great cultural and political issues fall increasingly to the lot of the proletariat. The Russian working class bears the whole burden in the struggle for political freedom; and it shall continue to do so till the end. Though only a first step, it is an essential stage towards fulfilling the great historical mission of the proletariat and creating a social structure where the exploitation of one man by another will be quite unthinkable.

The Russian proletariat will shake off the yoke of autocracy and with increased energy will carry on the struggle with capitalism and the bourgeois order until it establishes the final victory of socialism. . . .

As a socialist-inspired movement and tendency, the Russian social democratic party pursues the tasks and traditions of the earlier revolutionary movements in Russia; by setting itself the first and foremost task of securing total political freedom, Social Democracy sets itself the aim that inspired the great men of the "Will of the People." But Social Democracy has chosen different ways and means. The choice is defined by the fact that Social Democracy wants to become and to remain a class movement of the organized working masses. It is firmly convinced that "the liberation of the working class concerns none but the working class" and will unswervingly weigh all its actions against this basic principle of international social democracy.

Long live Russian and International Social Democracy!

Leon Trotsky
(Lev Davidovitch Bronstein)
(1879–1940)

Born in the Ukraine, Trotsky early joined the Bolshevists and was associated with Lenin during the 1917 Revolution. He became people's commissar for foreign affairs (1917) and was minister of war of the Soviet Union (1918–1925). After Lenin's death (1924), Stalin secured control over the Communist Party and expelled Trotsky from the party (1927). He was exiled from the USSR in 1929. Stalin had Trotsky murdered in Mexico in 1940.

Terrorism and Communism

INTRODUCTION

The slow development of the revolution in the West brought about a far-reaching change in the economic methods of the Soviets. The period of the New Economic Policy started. It led on the one hand to a general quickening of the economic life, and on the other to a new birth of the

From *Terrorism and Communism*, by Leon Trotsky, Ann Arbor, Michigan, 1961.

small bourgeoisie, especially of the kulaks. The Soviet bureaucracy for the first time felt itself less dependent on the proletariat. It was now standing "between the classes," regulating their relations to one another. At the same time as this it was losing piece by piece its trust and interest in the Western proletariat. It is from the autumn of 1924 that Stalin, in utter contradiction with the party traditions and with what he wrote himself as late as the spring of the same year, puts forward for the first time the theory of "Socialism in one country." Bukharin supplements it by a theory of the "gradual growth of the kulak into Socialism." Stalin and Bukharin go along arm in arm.

The difficulties of the revolution, the deprivations, the sacrifices, the death of the best workers during the civil war, the slow coming of economic successes led in those days to an inevitable reaction among the masses of the population. The loss of hope in the European workers made greater the dependence of the Russian workers on their own bureaucracy. On the other hand the reaction arising out of weariness among the masses favoured a further growth of independence in the machinery of government. Taking its stand on the conservative forces among the small bourgeoisie, and making every use of the defeat of the world proletariat and of the fallen spirit among the Soviet masses, Stalin's section, that staff of the bureaucracy, comes down with a heavy hand on the so-called left opposition ("the Trotskyites"). The October revolution enters on the stage of bureaucratic degeneration.

But the kulak is not at all allured by the vision of a "peaceful growth into Socialism." What he wishes is the restoration of freedom to trade. He accumulates in his hands the wheat supplies and refuses them to the Government. He demands payment against the notes he was given by the bureaucracy during the struggle with the opposition of the left. From an ally he becomes a foe.

The bureaucracy is driven to defend itself. It starts a campaign against the kulak, whose existence it had yesterday denied, and against the right wing of the party, its ally in the struggle with the opposition of the left. The new political course which was set in 1928 threw a strong light on the dependence of the Soviet bureaucracy upon the economic foundations laid by the October revolution. Unwillingly and always struggling, it was forced to take the road of industrialisation and collectivisation. Here for the first time it brings to light those unbounded productive possibilities that are the necessary results of the concentration of the means of production in the hands of the State.

The wonderful, though very uneven, successes of the five-year plan naturally raised the self-confidence of the bureaucracy. The collectivisation of millions of small peasant holdings gave it at the same time a new social basis. The defeats suffered by the world proletariat, the growth of Fascist and Bonapartist dictatorships in Europe all helped towards the success of the doctrine of "Socialism in one country." The bureaucracy succeeded, indeed, in breaking up the Bolshevist Party and the Soviets, too, which were left only in name. The power passed from the masses, from the party, to a centralised bureaucracy; from this to a close supreme authority; and in the end to one man as the embodiment of an unchecked bureaucracy.

Many onlookers are astounded and repelled by the worship of the "leader," which so humiliatingly brings the Soviet system of today not far away from Hitler's system. The "party" in Russia and Germany alike has one, and only one, right: the right to agree with the leader. The party meetings become nothing else than demonstrations of a unanimity that is assured beforehand. In what way is the Soviet order of things better than the Fascist? is the question put by the democrats, the pacifists, the idealists, who are none of them capable of looking below the political superstructure. Without in the slightest wishing to defend the bureaucratic caricature of the Soviet system, we will answer this one-sided criticism of it by pointing to its social basis. Hitler's system is seen to be the last and truly desperate form of self-defence taken by a capitalism rotting to destruction. Stalin's system is seen to be the misshapen bureaucratic form of self-defence taken by a Socialism that is rising. These two are not the same.

In so far as the Soviet bureaucracy is forced in its own interest to preserve the frontiers and the institutions of the Russian Soviet republic against foes without and within, and to give heed to the development of the nationalised productive forces, this bureaucracy is still fulfilling a progressive historical task, and has so far a right to the support of the workers of the world. But the root of the matter is this: that the farther ahead the tasks of economic and cultural construction lie, the less capable are they of being carried through by bureaucratic methods. The distribution of productive forces and materials is now carried out by the authorities under orders from above, without any share by the workers in deciding those questions on which their labor and their life depend. Cases where there is a lack of proportion or ill-adjustment in management grow more and more. The raising of the standard of life among the masses goes on exceedingly slowly and unevenly, and lags far behind technical achievements and the output of energy by the workers. Thus, economic successes, while for a time they strengthen the bureaucratic autocracy, in their further development turn more and more against it.

The Socialistic economy must be directed to ensuring the satisfaction of every possible human need. Such a problem it is impossible to solve by way of commands only. The greater the scale of the productive forces, the more involved the technique; the more complex the needs, then the more indispensable is a wide and free creative initiative of the organized producers and consumers. The Socialist culture implies the utmost development of the human personality. Progress along this path is made possible not through a standardised cringing before irresponsible "leaders," but only through a fully conscious and critical participation by all in a Socialistic creative activity. The youthful generations stand in need of independence, which is wholly consistent with a firm leadership but rules out any police regimentation. Thus the bureaucratic system in crushing the Soviets and the party is coming ever more clearly into opposition with the basic needs of economic and cultural development.

The workers' state has come into existence for the first time in history. Neither its forms and methods, nor the stages it must go through could be, and they cannot now be, laid down beforehand. Bourgeois society developed itself in the course of centuries and came into power by stepping into the place of scores of political systems. There are good grounds for believing that the Socialist society will reach its full development by an incomparably shorter and more economical road. But it would, anyhow, be a poor kind of illusion to imagine that an "enlightened bureaucracy" is capable of leading mankind by the bridle in a straight line to Socialism. The workers' state will more than once again reform its methods before it becomes dissolved in a Communist society. The great historical reform whose turn has now come demands that the Soviet state be set free from bureaucratic absolutism; in other words: the restoration of the creative character of the Soviets on new and deeper economic and cultural foundations. This task cannot be carried through unless the working masses take up the fight against the usurping bureaucracy.

The historical part played by government violence naturally changes along with changes in the character of the workers' state. So far as bureaucratic violence, however grim it may sometimes be, is defending the social foundations of the new system, it is historically justified. But to defend the Soviet state and to defend the positions of bureaucracy within the Soviet state is not one and the same thing. As time goes on the bureaucracy has recourse more and more cynically to terror against the party and the working class, so as to defend its economic and political privileges. Its object, of course, is to make its caste defence look like the defence of the highest interests of Socialism. Hence comes the ever-growing falseness of the official ideology, the repulsive worship of the leaders, and the downright deception of the working masses through political and legal forgeries.

I

THE BALANCE OF POWER: A REPLY TO KARL KAUTSKY

The balance of political power at any given moment is determined under the influence of fundamental and secondary factors of differing degrees of effectiveness, and only in its most fundamental quality is it determined by the stage of the development of production. The social structure of a people is extraordinarily behind the development of its productive forces. The lower middle classes, and particularly the peasantry, retain their existence long after their economic methods have been made obsolete, and have been condemned, by the technical development of the productive powers of society. The consciousness of the masses, in its turn, is extraordinarily behind the development of their social relations, the consciousness of the old Socialist parties is a whole epoch behind the state of mind of the masses, and the consciousness of the old parliamentary and trade union leaders, more reactionary than the consciousness of their party, represents a petrified mass which history has been unable hitherto either to digest or reject. In the parliamentary epoch, during the period of stability of social relations, the psychological factor—without great error—was the foundation upon which all current calculations were based. It was considered that parliamentary elections reflected the balance of power with sufficient exactness. The imperialist war, which upset all bourgeois society, displayed the complete uselessness of the old criteria. The latter completely ignored those profound historical factors which had gradually been accumulating in the preceding period, and have now, all at once, appeared on the surface, and have begun to determine the course of history.

The political worshippers of routine, incapable of surveying the historical process in its complexity, in its internal clashes and contradictions, imagined to themselves that history was preparing the way for the Socialist order simultaneously and systematically on all sides, so that concentration of production and the development of a Communist morality in the producer and the consumer mature simultaneously with the electric plough and a parliamentary majority. Hence the purely mechanical attitude towards parliamentarism, which in the eyes of the majority of the statesmen of the Second International, indicated the degree to which society was prepared for Socialism as accurately as the manometer indicates the pressure of steam. Yet there is nothing more senseless than this mechanized representation of the development of social relations.

If, beginning with the productive bases of society, we ascend the stages of the superstructure—classes, the State, laws, parties, and so on—it may be established that the weight of each additional part of the superstructure is not simply to be added to, but in many cases to be multiplied by, the weight of all the preceding stages. As a result, the political consciousness of groups which long imagined themselves to be among the most advanced, displays itself, at a moment of change, as a colossal obstacle in the path of historical development. To-day it is quite beyond doubt that the parties of the Second International, standing at the head of the proletariat, which dared not, could not, and would not, take power into their hands at the most critical moment of human history, and which led the proletariat along the road of mutual destruction in the interests of imperialism, proved a *decisive factor* of the counter-revolution.

The great forces of production—that shock factor in historical development—were choked in those obsolete institutions of the superstructure (private property and the national State) in which they found themselves locked by all preceding development. Engendered by capitalism, the forces of production were knocking at all the walls of the bourgeois national State, demanding their emancipation by means of the Socialist organization of economic life on a world scale. The stagnation of social groupings, the stagnation of political forces, which proved themselves incapable of destroying the old class groupings, the stagnation, stupidity and treachery of the directing Socialist parties, which had assumed to themselves in reality the defense of bourgeois society—all these factors led to an elemental revolt of the forces of production, in the shape of the imperialist war. Human technical skill, the most revolutionary factor in history, arose with the might accumulated during scores of years against the disgusting conservatism and criminal stupidity of the Scheidemanns, Kautskies, Renaudels, Vanderveldes and Longuets, and by means of its howitzers, machine-guns, dreadnoughts and aeroplanes, it began a furious pogrom of human culture.

In this way the cause of the misfortunes at present experienced by humanity is precisely that the development of the technical command of men over nature has *long ago* grown ripe for the socialization of economic life. The proletariat has occupied a place in production which completely guarantees its dictatorship, while the most intelligent forces in history—the parties and their leaders—have been discovered to be still wholly under the yoke of the old prejudices, and only fostered a lack of faith among the masses in their own power. In quite recent years Kautsky used to understand this. "The proletariat at the present time has grown so strong," wrote Kautsky in his pamphlet, *The Path to Power,* "that it can calmly await the coming war. There can be no more talk of a *premature revolution,* now that the proletariat has drawn from the present structure of the State such strength as could be drawn therefrom, and now that its reconstruction has become a condition of the proletariat's further progress." From the moment that the development of productive forces, outgrowing the framework of the bourgeois national State, drew mankind into an epoch of crises and convulsions, the consciousness of the masses was shaken by dread shocks out of the comparative equilibrium of the preceding epoch. The routine and stagnation of its mode of living, the hypnotic suggestion of peaceful legality, had already ceased to dominate the proletariat. But it had not yet stepped, consciously and courageously, on to the path of open revolutionary struggle. It wavered, passing through the last moment of unstable equilibrium. At such a moment of psychological change, the part played by the summit—the State, on the one hand, and the revolutionary Party on the other—acquires a colossal importance. A determined push from left or right is sufficient to move the proletariat, for a certain period, to one or the other side. We saw this in 1914, when, under the united pressure of imperialist governments and Socialist patriotic parties, the working class was all at once thrown out of its equilibrium and hurled on to the path of imperialism. We have since seen how the experience of the war, the contrasts between its results and its first objects, is shaking the masses in a revolutionary sense, making them more and more capable of an open revolt against capitalism. In such conditions, the presence of a revolutionary party, which renders to itself a clear account of the motive forces of the present epoch, and understands the exceptional role amongst them of a revolutionary class; which knows its inexhaustible, but unrevealed, powers; which believes in that class and believes in itself; which knows the power of revolutionary method in an epoch of instability of all social relations; which is ready to employ that method and carry it through to the end—the presence of such a party represents a factor of incalculable historical importance.

And, on the other hand, the Socialist party, enjoying traditional influence, which does *not* render itself an account of what is going on around it, which does *not* understand the revolutionary situation, and, therefore, finds no key to it, which does *not* believe in either the proletariat or itself—such a party in our time is the most mischievous stumbling block in history, and a source of confusion and inevitable chaos.

Such is now the role of Kautsky and his sympathizers. They teach the proletariat not to believe in itself, but to believe its reflection in the crooked mirror of democracy which has been shattered by the jack-boot of militarism into a thousand fragments. The decisive factor in the revolutionary policy of the working class must be, in their view, not the international situation, not the actual collapse of capitalism, not that social collapse which is generated thereby, not that concrete necessity of the supremacy of the working class for which the cry arises from the smoking ruins of capitalist civilization—not all this must determine the policy of the revolutionary party of the proletariat —but that counting of votes which is carried out by the capitalist tellers of parliamentarism. Only a few years ago, we repeat, Kautsky seemed to understand the real inner meaning of the problem of revolution. "Yes, the proletariat represents the sole revolutionary class of the nation," wrote Kautsky in his pamphlet, *The Path to Power*. It follows that every collapse of the capitalist order, whether it be of a moral, financial, or military character, implies the bankruptcy of all the bourgeois parties responsible for it, and signifies that the sole way out of the blind alley is the establishment of the power of the *proletariat*. And to-day the party of prostration and cowardice, the party of Kautsky, says to the working class: "The question is not whether you to-day are the sole creative force in history; whether you are capable of throwing aside that ruling band of robbers into which the propertied classes have developed; the question is not whether anyone else can accomplish this task on your behalf; the question is not whether history allows you any postponement (for the present condition of bloody chaos threatens to bury you yourself, in the near future, under the last ruins of capitalism). The problem is for the ruling imperialist bandits to succeed—yesterday or to-day— to deceive, violate, and swindle public opinion, by collecting 51 per cent. of the votes against your 49. Perish the world, but long live the parliamentary majority!"

II
THE DICTATORSHIP OF THE PROLETARIAT

"Marx and Engels hammered out the idea of the dictatorship of the proletariat, which Engels stubbornly defended in 1891, shortly before his death—the idea that the political autocracy of the proletariat is the sole form in which it can realize its control of the State."

That is what Kautsky wrote about ten years ago. The sole form of power for the proletariat he considered to be not a Socialist majority in a democratic parliament, but the political autocracy of the proletariat, its dictatorship. And it is quite clear that, if our problem is the abolition of private property in the means of production, the only road to its solution lies through the concentration of State power in its entirety in the hands of the proletariat, and the setting up for the transitional period of an exceptional regime—a regime in which the ruling class is guided, not by general principles calculated for a prolonged period, but by considerations of revolutionary policy.

The dictatorship is necessary because it is a case, not of partial changes, but of the very existence of the bourgeoisie. No agreement is possible on this ground. Only force can be the deciding factor. The dictatorship of the proletariat does not exclude, of course, either separate agreements, or considerable concessions, especially in connection with the lower middle class and the peasantry. But the proletariat can only conclude these agreements after having gained possession of the apparatus of power, and having guaranteed to itself the possibility of independently deciding on which points to yield and on which to stand firm, in the interests of the general Socialist task.

Kautsky now repudiates the dictatorship of the proletariat at the very outset, as the "tyranny of the minority over the majority." That is, he discerns in the revolutionary regime of the proletariat those very features by which the honest Socialists of all countries invariably describe the dictatorship of the exploiters, albeit masked by the forms of democracy.

Abandoning the idea of a revolutionary dictatorship, Kautsky transforms the question of the conquest of power by the proletariat into a question of the conquest of a majority of votes by the Social-Democratic Party in one of the electoral campaigns of the future. Universal suffrage, according to the legal fiction of parliamentarism, expresses the will of the citizens of all classes in the nation, and, consequently, gives a possibility of attracting a majority to the side of Socialism. While the theoretical possibility has not been realized. the Socialist minority must submit to the bourgeois majority. This fetishism of the parliamentary majority represents a brutal repudiation, not only of the dictatorship of the proletariat, but of Marxism and of the revolution altogether. If, in principle, we are to subordinate Socialist policy to the parliamentary mystery of majority and minority, it follows that, in countries where formal democracy prevails, there is no place at all for the revolutionary struggle. If the majority elected on the basis of universal suffrage in Switzerland pass draconian legislation against strikers, or if the executive elected by the will of a formal majority in Northern America shoots workers, have the Swiss and American workers the "right" of protest by organizing a general strike? Obviously, no. The political strike is a form of extra-parliamentary pressure on the "national will," as it has expressed itself through universal suffrage. True, Kautsky himself, apparently, is ashamed to go as far as the logic of his new position demands. Bound by some sort of remnant of the past, he is obliged to acknowledge the possibility of correcting universal suffrage by action. Parliamentary elections, at all events in principle, never took the place, in the eyes of the Social-Democrats, of the real class struggle, of its conflicts, repulses, attacks, revolts; they were considered merely as a contributory fact in this struggle, playing a greater part at one period, a smaller at another, and no part at all in the period of dictatorship. . . .

Who aims at the end cannot reject the means. The struggle must be carried on with such intensity as actually to guarantee the supremacy of the proletariat. If the Socialist revolution requires a dictatorship—"the sole form in which the proletariat can achieve control of the State"—it follows that the dictatorship must be guaranteed at all cost.

To write a pamphlet about dictatorship one needs an ink-pot and a pile of paper, and possibly, in addition, a certain number of ideas in one's head. But in order to establish and consolidate the dictatorship, one has to prevent the bourgeoisie from undermining the State power of the proletariat. Kautsky apparently thinks that this can be achieved by tearful pamphlets. But his own experience ought to have shown him that it is not sufficient to have lost all influence with the proletariat, to acquire influence with the bourgeoisie.

It is only possible to safeguard the supremacy of the working class by forcing the bourgeoisie accustomed to rule, to realize that it is too dangerous an undertaking for it to revolt against the dictatorship of the proletariat, to undermine it by conspiracies, sabotage, insurrections, or the calling in of foreign troops. The bourgeoisie, hurled from power, must be forced to obey. In what way? The priests used to terrify the people with future penalties. We have no such resources at our disposal. But even the priests' hell never stood alone, but was always bracketed with the material fire of the Holy Inquisition, and with the scorpions of the democratic State. Is it possible that Kautsky is leaning to the idea that the bourgeoisie can be held down with the help of the categorical imperative, which in his last writings plays the part of the Holy Ghost? . . .

The man who repudiates terrorism in principle—i.e., repudiates measures of suppression and intimidation towards determined and armed counter-revolution, must reject all idea of the political supremacy of the working class and its revolutionary dictatorship. The man who repudiates the dictatorship of the proletariat repudiates the Socialist revolution, and digs the grave of Socialism.

No one, of course, attempted to reckon up beforehand the number of victims that will be called for by the revolutionary insurrection of the proletariat, and by the regime of its dictatorship. But it was clear to all that the number of victims will vary with the strength of resistance of the propertied classes. If Kautsky desires to say in his book that a democratic upbringing has not weakened the class egoism of the bourgeoisie, this can be admitted without further parley.

If he wishes to add that the imperialist war, which broke out and continued for four years, *in spite of* democracy, brought about a degradation of morals and accustomed men to violent methods and action, and completely stripped the bourgeoisie of the last vestige of awkwardness in ordering the destruction of masses of humanity—here also he will be right.

All this is true on the face of it. But one has to struggle in real conditions. The contending forces are not proletarian and bourgeois manikins produced in the retort of Wagner-Kautsky, but a real proletariat against a real bourgeoisie, as they have emerged from the last imperialist slaughter.

In this fact of merciless civil war that is spreading over the whole world, Kautsky sees only the result of a fatal lapse from the "experienced tactics" of the Second International.

"In reality, since the time," he writes, "that Marxism has dominated the Socialist movement, the latter, up to the world war, was, in spite of its great activities, preserved from great defeats. And the idea of insuring victory by means of terrorist domination had completely disappeared from its ranks.

"Much was contributed in this connection by the fact that, at the time when Marxism was the dominating Socialist teaching, democracy threw out firm roots in Western Europe, and began there to change from an end of the struggle to a trustworthy basis of political life." . . .

In this "formula of progress" there is not one atom of Marxism. The real process of the struggle of classes and their material conflicts has been lost in Marxist propaganda, which, thanks to the conditions of democracy, guarantees, forsooth, a painless transition to a new and "wiser" order. This is the most vulgar liberalism, a belated piece of rationalism in the spirit of the eighteenth century—with the difference that the ideas of Condorcet are replaced by a vulgarisation of the Communist Manifesto. All history resolves itself into an endless sheet of printed paper, and the centre of this "humane" process proves to be the well-worn writing table of Kautsky.

We are given as an example the working-class movement in the period of the Second International, which, going forward under the banner of Marxism, never sustained great defeats whenever it deliberately challenged them. But did not the whole working-class movement, the proletariat of the whole world, and with it the whole of human culture, sustain an incalculable defeat in August, 1914, when history cast up the accounts of all the forces and possibilities of the Socialist parties, amongst whom, we are told, the guiding role belonged to Marxism, "on the firm footing of democracy"? *Those parties proved bankrupt.* Those features of their previous work which Kautsky now wishes to render permanent—self-adaptation, repudiation of "illegal" activity, repudiation of the open fight, hopes placed in democracy as the road to a painless revolution—all these fell into dust. In their fear of defeat, holding back the masses from open conflict, dissolving the general strike discussions, the parties of the Second International were preparing their own terrifying defeat; for they were not able to move one finger to avert the greatest catastrophe in world history, the four years' imperialist slaughter, which foreshadowed the violent character of the civil war. Truly, one has to put a wadded nightcap not only over one's eyes, but over one's nose and ears, to be able to-day, after the inglorious collapse of the Second International, after the disgraceful bankruptcy of its leading party—the German Social Democracy—after the bloody lunacy of the world slaughter and the gigantic sweep of the civil war, to set up in contrast to us, the profundity, the loyalty, the peacefulness and the sobriety of the Second International, the heritage of which we are still liquidating. . . .

The chief theme of Kautsky's book is terrorism. The view that terrorism is of the essence of revolution Kautsky proclaims to be a widespread delusion. It is untrue that he who desires revolution must put up with terrorism. As far as he, Kautsky, is concerned, he is, generally speaking, for revolution, but decidedly against terrorism. From there, however, complications begin.

The Revolution, "logically," does not demand terrorism, just as "logically" it does not demand an armed insurrection. What a profound commonplace! But the revolution does require of the revolutionary class that it should attain its end by all methods at its disposal—if necessary, by an armed rising: if required, by terrorism. A revolutionary class which has conquered power with arms in its hands is bound to, and will, suppress, rifle in hand, all attempts to tear the power out of its hands. Where it has against it a hostile army, it will oppose to it its own army. Where it is confronted with armed conspiracy, attempt at murder, or rising, it will hurl at the heads of its enemies an unsparing penality. Perhaps Kautsky has invented other methods? Or does he reduce the whole question to the *degree* of repression, and recommend in all circumstances imprisonment instead of execution?

The question of the form of repression, or of its degree, of course, is not one of "principle." It is a question of expediency. In a revolutionary period, the party which has been thrown from power, which does not reconcile itself with the stability of the ruling class, and which proves this by its desperate struggle against the latter, cannot be terrorized by the threat of imprisonment, as it does not believe in its duration. It is just this simple but decisive fact that explains the widespread recourse to shooting in a civil war.

Or, perhaps, Kautsky wishes to say that execution is not expedient, that "classes cannot be cowed." This is untrue. Terror is helpless—and then only "in the long run"—if it is employed by reaction against a historically rising class. But terror can be very efficient against a reactionary class which does not want to leave the scene of operations. *Intimidation* is a powerful weapon of policy, both internationally and internally. War, like revolution, is founded upon intimidation. A victorious war, generally speaking, destroys only an insignificant part of the conquered army, intimidating the remainder and breaking their will. The revolution works in the same way: it kills individuals, and intimidates thousands. In this sense, the Red Terror is not distinguishable from the armed insurrection, the direct continuation of which it represents. The State terror of a revolutionary class can be condemned "morally" only by a man who, as a principle, rejects (in words) every form of violence whatsoever—consequently, every war and every rising. . . .

FREEDOM OF THE PRESS

One point particularly worries Kautsky, the author of a great many books and articles—the freedom of the Press. Is it permissible to suppress newspapers?

During war all institutions and organs of the State and of public opinion become, directly or indirectly, weapons of warfare. This is particularly true of the Press. No government carrying on a serious war will allow publications to exist on its territory which, openly or indirectly, support the enemy. Still more so in a civil war. The nature of the latter is such that each of the struggling sides has in the rear of its armies considerable circles of the population on the side of the enemy. In war, where both success and failure are repaid by death, hostile agents who penetrate into the rear are subject to execution. This is inhumane, but no one ever considered war a school of humanity— still less civil war. . . .

We are fighting. We are fighting a life-and-death struggle. The Press is a weapon not of an abstract society, but of two irreconcilable, armed and contending sides. We are destroying the Press of the counter-revolution, just as we destroyed its fortified positions, its stores, its communications, and its intelligence system. Are we depriving ourselves of Cadet and Menshevik criticisms of the corruption of the working class? In return we are victoriously destroying the very foundations of capitalist corruption. . . .

What is the meaning of the principle of the sacredness of human life in practice, and in what does it differ from the commandment, "Thou shalt not kill," Kautsky does not explain. When a murderer raises his knife over a child, may one kill the murderer to save the child? Will not thereby the principle of the "sacredness of human life" be infringed? May one kill the murderer to save oneself? Is an insurrection of oppressed slaves against their masters permissible? Is it permissible to purchase one's freedom at the cost of the life of one's jailers? If human life in general is sacred and inviolable, we must deny ourselves not only the use of terror, not only war, but also revolution itself. Kautsky simply does not realize the counter-revolutionary meaning of the "principle" which he attempts to force upon

us. Elsewhere we shall see that Kautsky accuses us of concluding the Brest–Litovsk peace: in his opinion we ought
to have continued war. But what then becomes of the
sacredness of human life? Does life cease to be sacred
when it is a question of people talking another language,
or does Kautsky consider that mass murders organized on
principles of strategy and tactics are not murders at all?
Truly it is difficult to put forward in our age a principle
more hypocritical and more stupid. As long as human labor
power, and, consequently, life itself, remain articles of sale
and purchase, of exploitation and robbery, the principle of
the "sacredness of human life" remains a shameful lie,
uttered with the object of keeping the oppressed slaves in
their chains.

We used to fight against the death penalty introduced by
Kerensky, because that penalty was inflicted by the courts-
martial of the old army on soldiers who refused to continue
the imperialist war. We tore this weapon out of the hands
the old courts-martial, destroyed the courts-martial themselves, and demobilized the old army which had brought
them forth. Destroying in the Red Army, and generally
throughout the country, counter-revolutionary conspirators
who strive by means of insurrections, murders, and dis-
organization, to restore the old regime, we are acting in
accordance with the iron laws of a war in which we desire
to guarantee our victory.

If it is a question of seeking formal contradictions, then
obviously we must do so on the side of the White Terror,
which is the weapon of classes which consider themselves
"Christian," patronize idealist philosophy, and are firmly
convinced that the individuality (their own) is an end-
in-itself. As for us, we were never concerned with the
Kantian-priestly and vegetarian-Quaker prattle about the
"sacredness of human life." We were revolutionaries in
opposition, and have remained revolutionaries in power.
To make the individual sacred we must destroy the social
order which crucifies him. And this problem can only be
solved by blood and iron. . . .

We have more than once been accused of having substituted for the dictatorship of the Soviets the dictatorship
of our party. Yet it can be said with complete justice that
the dictatorship of the Soviets became possible only by
means of the dictatorship of the party. It is thanks to the
clarity of its theoretical vision and its strong revolutionary
organization that the party has afforded to the Soviets the
possibility of becoming transformed from shapeless parlia-

ments of labor into the apparatus of the supremacy of labor. In this "substitution" of the power of the party for the power of the working class there is nothing accidental, and in reality there is no substitution at all. The Communists express the fundamental interests of the working class. It is quite natural that, in the period in which history brings up those interests, in all their magnitude, on to the order of the day, the Communists have become the recognized representatives of the working class as a whole.

But where is your guarantee, certain wise men ask us, that it is just your party that expresses the interests of historical development? Destroying or driving underground the other parties, you have thereby prevented their political competition with you, and consequently you have deprived yourselves of the possibility of testing your line of action.

This idea is dictated by a purely liberal conception of the course of the revolution. In a period in which all antagonisms assume an open character, and the political struggle swiftly passes into a civil war, the ruling party has sufficient material standard by which to test its line of action, without the possible circulation of Menshevik papers. Noske crushes the Communists, but they grow. We have suppressed the Mensheviks and the S.R.s—and they have disappeared. This criterion is sufficient for us. At all events, our problem is not at every given moment statistically to measure the grouping of tendencies; but to render victory for our tendency secure. For that tendency is the tendency of the revolutionary dictatorship; and in the course of the latter, in its internal friction, we must find a sufficient criterion for self-examination.

The continuous "independence" of the trade union movement, in the period of the proletarian revolution, is just as much an impossibility as the policy of coalition. The trade unions become the most important economic organs of the proletariat in power. Thereby they fall under the leadership of the Communist Party. Not only questions of principle in the trade union movement, but serious conflicts of organization within it, are decided by the Central Committee of our party.

The Kautskians attack the Soviet Government as the dictatorship of a "section" of the working class. "If only," they say, "the dictatorship was carried out by the *whole* class!" It is not easy to understand what actually they imagine when they say this. The dictatorship of the proletariat, in its very essence, signifies the immediate supremacy of the revolutionary vanguard, which relies upon the heavy masses, and, where necessary, obliges the backward tail to dress by the head. This refers also to the trade unions. After the conquest of power by the proletariat, they acquire a compulsory character. They must include all industrial workers. The party, on other hand, as before, includes in its ranks only the most class-conscious and devoted; and only in a process of careful selection does it widen its ranks. Hence follows the guiding role of the Communist minority in the trade unions, which answers to the supremacy of the Communist Party in the Soviets, and represents the political expression of the dictatorship of the proletariat.

The trade unions become the direct organizers of social production. They express not only the interests of the industrial workers, but the interests of industry itself. During the first period, the old currents in trade unionism more than once raised their head, urging the unions to haggle with the Soviet State, lay down conditions for it, and demand from it guarantees. The further we go, however, the more do the unions recognize that they are organs of production of the Soviet State, and assume responsibility for its fortunes—not opposing themselves to it, but identifying themselves with it. The unions become the organizers of labor discipline. They demand from the workers intensive labor under the most difficult conditions, to the extent that the Labor State is not yet able to alter those conditions.

The unions become the apparatus of revolutionary repression against undisciplined, anarchical, parasitic elements in the working class. From the old policy of trade unionism, which at a certain stage is inseparable from the industrial movement within the framework of capitalist society, the unions pass along the whole line on to the new path of the policy of revolutionary Communism. . . .

"To-day, when the power of the Soviets has been set on a firm footing," Lenin said at the Moscow City Conference on March 28, 1918, "the struggle with sabotage must express itself in the form of transforming the saboteurs of yesterday into the servants, executive officials, technical guides, of the new regime, wherever it requires them. If we do not grapple with this, if we do not attract all the forces necessary to us and enlist them in the Soviet service, our struggle of yesterday with sabotage would thereby be condemned as an absolutely vain and fruitless struggle.

"Just as in dead machines, so into those technical experts, engineers, doctors, teachers, former officers, there is sunk a certain portion of our national capital, which we are obliged to exploit and utilize if we want to solve the root problems standing before us.

"Democratization does not at all consist—as every Marxist learns in his A B C—in abolishing the meaning of skilled forces, the meaning of persons possessing special knowledge, and in replacing them everywhere and anywhere by elective boards.

"Elective boards, consisting of the best representatives of the working class, but not equipped with the necessary technical knowledge, cannot replace one expert who has passed through the technical school, and who knows how to carry out the given technical work. That flood-tide of the collegiate principle which is at present to be observed in all spheres is the quite natural reaction of a young, revolutionary, only yesterday oppressed class, which is throwing out the one-man principle of its rulers of yesterday—the landlords and the generals—and everywhere is appointing its elected representatives. This, I say, is quite a natural and, in its origin, quite a healthy revolutionary reaction; but it is not the last word in the economic constructive work of the proletarian class.

"The next step must consist in the self-limitation of the collegiate principle, in a healthy and necessary act of self-limitation by the working class, which knows where the decisive word can be spoken by the elected representatives of the workers themselves, and where it is necessary to give way to a technical specialist, who is equipped with certain knowledge, on whom a great measure of responsibility must be laid, and who must be kept under careful political control. But it is necessary to allow the expert freedom to act, freedom to create; because no expert, be he ever so little gifted or capable, can work in his department when subordinate in his own technical work to a board of men who do not know that department. Political, collegiate and Soviet control everywhere and anywhere; but for the executive functions, we must appoint technical experts, put them in responsible positions, and impose responsibility upon them.

"Those who fear this are quite unconsciously adopting an attitude of profound internal distrust towards the Soviet regime. Those who think that the enlisting of the saboteurs of yesterday in the administration of technically expert posts threatens the very foundations of the Soviet regime, do not realize that it is not through the work of some engineer or of some general of yesterday that the Soviet regime may stumble—in the political, in the revolutionary, in the military sense, the Soviet regime is unconquerable. But it *may* stumble through its own incapacity to grapple with the problems of creative organization. The Soviet regime is bound to draw from the old institutions all that was vital and valuable in them, and harness it on to the new work. If, comrades, we do not accomplish this, we shall not deal successfully with our principal problems: for it would be absolutely impossible for us to bring forth from our masses, in the shortest possible time, all the necessary experts, and throw aside all that was accumulated in the past.

"As a matter of fact, it would be just the same as if we said that all the machines which hitherto had served to exploit the workers were now to be thrown aside. It would be madness. The enlisting of scientific experts is for us just as essential as the administration of resources of production and transport, and all the wealth of the country generally. We must, and in addition we must immediately, bring under our control all the technical experts we possess, and introduce in practice for them compulsory labor; at the same time leaving them a wide margin of activity and maintaining over them careful political control." . . .

Compulsory labor, we are told, is always unproductive. We ask what does compulsory labor mean here, that is, to what kind of labor is it opposed? Obviously, to free labor. What are we to understand, in that case, by free labor? That phrase was formulated by the progressive philosophers of the bourgeoisie, in the struggle against unfree, i.e., against serf labor of peasants, and against the standardized and regulated labor of the craft guilds. Free labor meant labor which might be "freely" bought in the market; freedom was reduced to a legal fiction, on the basis of freely-hired slavery. We know of no other form of free labor in history. Let the very few representatives of the Mensheviks at this Congress explain to us what they mean by free, non-compulsory labor, if not the market of labor-power.

History has known slave labor. History has known serf labor. History has known the regulated labor of the mediaeval craft guilds. Throughout the world there now prevails hired labor, which the yellow journalists of all countries oppose, as the highest possible form of liberty, to Soviet "slavery." We, on the other hand, oppose capitalist slavery by socially regulated labor on the basis of an economic plan, obligatory for the whole people and consequently compulsory for each worker in the country. Without this we cannot even dream of a transition to Socialism. The element of material, physical compulsion may be greater or less; that depends on many conditions—on the degree of wealth or poverty of the country, on the heritage of the past, on the general level of culture, on the condition of transport, on the administrative apparatus, etc., etc. But obligation, and, consequently, compulsion, are essential conditions in order to bind down the bourgeois anarchy, to secure socialization of the means of production and labor, and to reconstruct economic life on the basis of a single plan.

For the Liberal, freedom in the long run means the market. Can or cannot the capitalist buy labor-power at a moderate price—that is for him the sole measure of the freedom of labor. That measure is false, not only in relation to the future but also in connection with the past. . . .

It would be absurd to imagine that, during the time of bondage-right, work was carried entirely under the stick of physical compulsion, as if an overseer stood with a whip behind the back of every peasant. Mediaeval forms of economic life grew up out of definite conditions of production, and created definite forms of social life, with which the peasant grew accustomed, and which he at certain periods considered just, or at any rate unalterable. Whenever, he, under the influence of a change in material conditions, displayed hostility, the State descended upon him with its material force, thereby displaying the compulsory character of the organization of labor.

The foundations of the militarization of labor are those forms of State compulsion without which the replacement of capitalist economy by the Socialist will for ever remain an empty sound. Why do we speak of *militarization?* Of course, this is only an analogy—but an analogy very rich in content. No social organization except the army has ever considered itself justified in subordinating citizens to itself in such a measure, and to control them by its will on all sides to such a degree, as the State of the proletarian dictatorship considers itself justified in doing, and does. Only the army—just because in its way it used to decide questions of the life or death of nations, States, and ruling classes—was endowed with powers of demanding from each and all complete submission to its problems, aims, regulations, and orders. And it achieved this to the greater degree, the more the problems of military organization coincided with the requirements of social development.

The question of the life or death of Soviet Russia is at present being settled on the labor front; our economic, and together with them our professional and productive organizations, have the right to demand from their members all that devotion, discipline, and executive thoroughness, which hitherto only the army required.

On the other hand, the relation of the capitalist to the worker is not at all founded merely on the "free" contract, but includes the very powerful elements of State regulation and material compulsion.

The competition of capitalist with capitalist imparted a certain very limited reality to the fiction of freedom of labor; but this competition, reduced to a minimum by trusts and syndicates, we have finally eliminated by destroying private property in the means of production. The transition to Socialism, verbally acknowledged by the Mensheviks, means the transition from anarchical distribution of labor-power—by means of the game of buying and selling, the movement of market prices and wages—to systematic distribution of the workers by the economic organizations of the county, the province, and the whole country. Such a form of planned distribution pre-supposes the subordination of those distributed to the economic plan of the State. And this is the essence of *compulsory labor service,* which inevitably enters into the programme of the Socialist organization of labor, as its fundamental element.

If organized economic life is unthinkable without compulsory labor service, the latter is not to be realized without the abolition of fiction of the freedom of labor, and without the substitution for it of the obligatory principle, which is supplemented by real compulsion.

Antonio Gramsci
(1891–1937)

Gramsci was a Sardinian-born Italian writer and politician. One of the founders of the Italian Communist Party, he was jailed by Mussolini in 1926 and died in prison.

The Modern Prince

THE STUDY OF PHILOSOPHY AND OF HISTORICAL MATERIALISM

The widespread prejudice that philosophy is something which is very difficult because it is the intellectual activity of a specific category of specialist scholars or of professional and systematic philosophers must be destroyed. To do this we must first show that all men are "philosophers," defining the limitations of this "spontaneous philosophy" possessed by "everyone," that is, of the philosophy which is contained in:

1. language itself, which is a totality of determined notions and concepts and not simply and solely of words grammatically void of content;

2. common sense and good sense;

3. popular religion and therefore also in the entire system of beliefs, superstitions, opinions, ways of perceiving and acting which make up what is generally called "folklore."

Having shown that everyone is a philosopher, even if in his own way, unconsciously (because even in the smallest manifestation of any intellectual activity—"language"—is contained a definite conception of the world), we pass to the second stage, the stage of criticism and awareness. We pass to the question: is it preferable to "think" without having critical awareness, in a disjointed and irregular way, in other words to "participate" in a conception of the world "imposed" mechanically by external environment, that is, by one of the many social groups in which everyone is automatically involved from the time he enters the conscious world (this might be one's own village or province, might have its origin in the parish and the "intellectual activity" of the curate or the patriarchal old man whose "wisdom" is law, of the crone who has inherited the knowledge of the

From *The Modern Prince*, by Antonio Gramsci, New York, 1968.

witches, or of the puny intellectual soured by his own stupidities and impotence); or is it preferable to work out one's own conception of the world consciously and critically, and so out of this work of one's own brain to choose one's own sphere of activity, to participate actively in making the history of the world, and not simply to accept passively and without care the imprint of one's own personality from outside?

Note 1. For his own conception of the world a man always belongs to a certain grouping, and precisely to that of all the social elements who share the same ways of thinking and working. He is a conformist to some conformity, he is always man-mass or man-collective. The question is this: of what historical type is the conformity, the man-mass, of which he is a part? When his conception of the world is not critical and coherent but haphazard and disconnected he belongs simultaneously to a multiplicity of men-masses, his own personality is made up in a queer way. It contains elements of the cave-man and principles of the most modern and advanced learning, shabby, local prejudices of all past historical phases and intuitions of a future philosophy of the human race united all over the world. Criticising one's own conception of the world means, therefore, to make it coherent and unified and to raise it to the point reached by the most advanced modern thought. It also means criticising all hitherto existing philosophy in so far as it has left layers incorporated into the popular philosophy. The beginning of the critical elaboration is the consciousness of what one really is, that is, a "know thyself" as the product of the historical process which has left you an infinity of traces gathered together without the advantage of an inventory. First of all it is necessary to compile such an inventory.

Note 2. Philosophy cannot be separated from the history of philosophy nor culture from the history of culture. In the most immediate and pertinent sense one cannot be a philosopher, that is, have a critically coherent conception of the world, without being aware of its history, of the phases of development it represents and of the fact that it stands in contradiction to other conceptions or elements of them. The correct conception of the world answers certain problems posed by reality which are very much determined and "original" in their actuality. How is it possible to think about the present, and a very much determined present, with a thought elaborated from problems of a past which is often remote and superseded? If this happens it means that one is an "anachronism" in one's own time, a fossil and not a modern living being. Or at least one is "made up" strangely. And in fact it happens that social groups which in certain ways express the most developed modernity, are retarded in others by their social position and so are incapable of complete historical independence. . . .

With regard to the historical rôle played by the fatalist interpretation of Marxism, one could pronounce a funeral eulogy of it, vindicating its usefulness for a certain historical period but precisely because of this urging the necessity of burying it with all honours. Its rôle could be likened to that of the theory of grace and predestination for the beginnings of the modern world, which, however, culminated in the classical German philosophy with its conception of freedom as the awareness of necessity. It has been a popular substitute of the cry "God wills it," although even on this primitive and elementary plane it was the beginning of a more modern and fertile conception than that contained in the cry "God wills it" or in the theory of grace. Is it possible that "formally" a new conception should present itself in other garb than the rough unadorned dress of the plebeian? Nevertheless the historian, with all the necessary perspective, succeeds in establishing and understanding that the beginnings of a new world, always hard and stony, are superior to the agonies of a declining world and to the swan-song which it brings forth. . . .

In history, real "equality," that is the degree of "spirituality" achieved through the historical development of "human nature," is identified in the system of "public and private," "explicit and implicit" associations that are linked in the "State" and in the world political system; the "equality" here meant is that which is felt as such between the members of an association and the "inequality" felt between different associations; equality and inequality which are of value because there is both individual and group understanding of them. Thus one arrives at the equality or equation between "philosophy and politics," between thought and action, Marxism. All is politics, philosophy as well as the philosophies, and the only "philosophy" is history in action, life itself. . . .

Marxism was confronted with two tasks: to combat modern ideologies in their most refined form in order to create its own core of independent intellectuals; and to educate the masses of the people whose level of culture was mediaeval. Given the nature of the new philosophy the second and basic task absorbed all its strength, both quantitatively and qualitatively. For "didactic" reasons the new philosophy developed in a cultural form only slightly higher than the popular average (which was very low), and as such was absolutely inadequate for overcoming the ideology of the educated classes, despite the fact that the new philosophy had been expressly created to supersede the highest cultural manifestation of the period, classical German philosophy, and in order to recruit into the new social class whose world view it was a group of intellectuals of its own. On the other hand modern culture, particularly the idealist, has been unable to elaborate a popular culture and has failed to provide a moral and scientific content to its own educational programmes, which still remain abstract and theoretical schemes. It is still the culture of a narrow intellectual aristocracy which is able to attract the youth only when it becomes immediately and topically political.

Marxism assumes this whole cultural past—the Renaissance and the Reformation, German Philosophy, the French Revolution, Calvinism and English classical political economy, lay liberalism and the historical thinking which rests at the foundation of the whole modern conception of life. Marxism crowns the whole movement for intellectual and moral reform dialecticised in the contrast between popular and higher culture. It corresponds to the nexus of Protestant Reformation plus French Revolution. It is philosophy which is also politics, and it is politics which is also philosophy. It is still passing through its popularising stage; to develop a core of independent intellectuals is no simple task but a long process with actions and reactions, agreements and dissolutions and new formations, both numerous and complex; it is the creation of a subordinate social group, without historical initiative, which is constantly growing but in a disorganised manner, never being able to pass beyond a qualitative stage which always lies this side of the possession of State power, of real hegemony over all of society which alone permits a certain organic equilibrium in the development of the intellectual group. Marxism itself has become "prejudice" and "superstition"; as it is, it is the popular aspect of modern historical thinking, but it contains within itself the principle for overcoming this. In the history of culture, which is broader by far than that of philosophy, whenever popular culture has flowered because there was a period of revolt and the metal of a new class was being selected out of the popular mass, there has always been a flowering of "materialism," while conversely the traditional classes have clung to spiritualism. Hegel, astride the French Revolution and the Restoration, dialecticised the two streams in the history of thought: materialism and spiritualism, but his synthesis was "a man standing on his head." Those who followed after Hegel destroyed this unity and a return was made to materialist systems of thought on the one hand and on the other, to the spiritual. Marxism, through its founder, relived this whole experience from Hegel to Feuerbach and French materialism in order to reconstitute the synthesis of the dialectical unity—"man on his feet." The mutilation suffered by Hegelian thought was also inflicted on Marxism; on the one hand there has been a return to philosophical materialism and on the other, modern idealist thought has tried to incorporate into itself elements from Marxism which were indispensable to it in its search for a new elixir.

THE SCIENCE OF POLITICS

The fundamental innovation introduced by Marxism into the science of politics and history is the proof that there does not exist an abstract, fixed and immutable "human nature" (a concept which certainly derives from religious thought and transcendentalism); but that human nature is the totality of historically determined social relations, that is, an historical fact, ascertainable, within certain limits, by the methods of philology and criticism. Therefore, political science must be conceived in its concrete content (and also in its logical formulation) as an organism in development.

Mao Tse-tung
(1893–   )

Mao Tse-tung was born in Shaoshan, Hunan Province, Central China, on December 26, 1893. His father was a "middle" peasant, owning his own land. Mao began work in the fields when he was six years old, and from eight to thirteen went to the local primary school for part of each day. Famine was endemic in China, but Mao wanted further schooling and attended Hunan Normal School. He later went to Peking, where he joined the Communist Party and led

*the struggle against the Kuomintang under Chiang Kai-shek.
Mao took 100,000 men on the Long March starting on October 16, 1934, from Kiangsi to escape from Chiang and the Japanese, and in one year they marched 8,000 miles, "the biggest armed propaganda tour in history."[1] By January 1949 the Red Army had occupied Peking, and on October 1, 1949, Mao became the first Chairman of the People's Republic of China, a post he held until 1959.*

Excerpts from Mao Tse-tung's Writings

PERIOD OF THE FIRST REVOLUTIONARY WAR

ANALYSIS OF THE CLASSES IN CHINESE SOCIETY

This article was written in 1926 to combat two deviations then existing in the Party—"Right" opportunism represented by Ch'en Tu-hsiu and "Left" opportunism represented by Chang Kuo-t'ao. One paid attention only to the Kuomintang-Communist cooperation and the other only to the labour movement, but both forgot the peasants. Although both brands of opportunists were keenly aware of the insufficiency of the revolutionary forces, neither knew where to look for reinforcements and for broad masses of allies. Comrade Mao Tse-tung pointed out that the Chinese proletariat had in the peasantry its staunchest and most numerous ally, and thus solved the problem concerning the chief ally in the Chinese revolution. At the same time he foresaw that the national bourgeoisie, as a wavering class, would split up during a revolutionary upsurge, with its right wing going over to the imperialist camp. The events of 1927 confirmed his judgment.

Who are our enemies, and who are our friends? This question is one of primary importance in the revolution. All past revolutionary struggles in China achieved very little, basically because the revolutionaries were unable to unite

[1] Edgar Snow, *Red Star Over China*, New York, 1961.
From: *Mao Tse-tung: An Anthology of His Writings*, edited by Anne Fremantle, New York, 1962.

their real friends to attack their real enemies. A revolutionary party is the guide of the masses, and no revolution ever succeeds when the revolutionary party leads it astray. To make sure that we will not lead our revolution astray but will achieve positive success, we must pay attention to uniting our real friends to attack our real enemies. To distinguish real friends from real enemies, we must make a general analysis of the economic status of the various classes in Chinese society and of their respective attitudes towards the revolution.

What are the conditions of the various classes in Chinese society?

The landlord and comprador classes. In economically backward and semi-colonial China the landlords and compradors are completely the vassals of the international bourgeoisie, depending upon imperialism for their existence and development. These classes represent the most backward and the most reactionary relations of production in China and hinder the development of her productive forces. Their existence is incompatible with the objectives of the Chinese revolution. This is especially true of the big landlords and big compradors who always side with imperialism and form the extreme counter-revolutionary group. They are politically represented by the *Etatistes*[2] and the right wing of the Kuomintang.

The middle class. This class represents China's capitalist relations of production in town and country. The middle class, by which is chiefly meant the national bourgeoisie, is contradictory in its attitudes towards the Chinese revolution: when it suffers from the blows of foreign capital and the oppression of the warlords, it feels the need of a revolution and favours the revolutionary movement against imperialism and the warlords; but when the proletariat at home takes a militant part in the revolution and the international proletariat abroad gives its active support, so that it senses the threat to the realisation of its desire to develop as a class into the status of a big bourgeoisie, it becomes sceptical about the revolution. Politically it stands for the

[2] A group of unscrupulous fascist-minded politicians who formed the Chinese *Etatiste* Youth League, later renamed the Chinese Youth Party. Subsidised by the imperialists and the reactionary cliques in power, these counter-revolutionaries made a career out of opposing the Communist Party and the Soviet Union. *Etatism* is used to translate "*Kuochia-ism*" to distinguish it from the usual English rendering of Kuomintang which is the *Nationalist* Party. In theory the Chinese *Etatistes* also laid more emphasis on the state than on the people.

establishment of a state under the rule of a single class, the national bourgeoisie.

A self-styled "true disciple" of Tai Chi-t'ao[2a] wrote in the *Chen Pao*,[3] Peking: "Raise your left fist to knock down imperialism and your right fist to knock down the Communist Party." This remark depicts the dilemma and quandary of this class. This class objects to the Kuomintang's Principle of the People's Welfare being interpreted according to the theory of the class struggle, and objects to the Kuomintang's alliance with Russia and inclusion of Communists[4] and left-wingers. But its aim of establishing a state under its own rule is impracticable, because the present world situation is one in which the two big forces, revolution and counter-revolution, are engaged in the final struggle. Two huge banners have been raised by these two huge forces: One is the red banner of revolution which the Third International holds aloft, rallying all the oppressed classes of the world, and the other is the white banner of counter-revolution which the League of Nations holds aloft, rallying all the counter-revolutionary elements of the world. The intermediate class will beyond doubt rapidly fall apart, some sections turning left and joining the ranks of the revolution and others turning right and joining the ranks of the counter-revolution; there is no room for any to remain "independent." Therefore the idea cherished by the Chinese middle class of an "independent" revolution in which it would play the leading role is a mere illusion.

[2a] As a veteran member of the Kuomintang and Chiang Kai-shek's partner in commodity speculation in Shanghai, Tai carried on an anti-Communist agitation after Sun Yat-sen's death in 1925 and prepared the ground ideologically for Chiang Kai-shek's *coup d'état* in 1927. For years he served as Chiang's faithful jackal in counter-revolutionary activities. Driven to despair by the imminent doom of Chiang's régime, he committed suicide in February 1949.

[3] Organ of the Association for the Study of Constitutional Government, a political group then supporting the warlords of the Northern clique.

[4] With the help of the Chinese Communist Party, Sun Yat-sen decided in 1923 to reorganise the Kuomintang, bring about co-operation between the Kuomintang and the Communist Party, and admit the Communists into his party. Furthermore, in January 1924, he convened the Kuomintang's First National Congress in Canton, and laid down the three cardinal policies of alliance with Russia, co-operation with the Communists, and assistance to the peasants and workers. Comrades Mao Tse-tung, Li Ta-chao, Lin Po-ch'u and Ch'u Ch'iu-pai attended the Congress and played a great role in launching the Kuomintang on the revolutionary path. They were elected regular or alternate members of the Central Executive Committee of the Kuomintang.

The petty bourgeoisie. Owner-peasants,[5] master handicraftsmen and the petty intellectuals—students, primary and middle school teachers, lower government functionaries, office clerks, small lawyers and petty traders—all belong to this category. On account of its size and its class character, this class deserves great attention. The owner-peasants and the master handicraftsmen are both engaged in small-scale production. Although the various strata of this class have the same petty-bourgeois economic status, they nevertheless fall into three different groups.

The first group consists of those who have some surplus money and grain, i.e. people who, by their manual or mental labour, have an annual surplus over and above what they need for their own support. Such people are very eager about getting rich and worship Marshal Chao[6] most devotedly; though without any illusions about amassing a great fortune, they constantly desire to climb up to the position of the middle class. At the sight of small capitalists who command people's respect their mouths water copiously. They are timid, afraid of government officials, and also a bit afraid of the revolution. Since their economic status is quite close to that of the middle class, they more or less believe in the latter's propaganda and adopt a sceptical attitude towards the revolution. This group is a minority among the petty bourgeoisie and constitutes its right wing.

The second group consists of those who in the main are economically self-supporting. People of this group differ greatly from the people of the first group in that, though they also want to become rich, Marshal Chao never allows them to, and moreover in recent years, victimized by the oppression and exploitation of the imperialists, the warlords, the feudal landlords and the big comprador bourgeoisie, they feel that the world now is no longer what it was. They feel that if they put in now only the same amount of labour as before, they will be unable to maintain their standard of living. They can maintain their standard of living only by increasing their working hours, getting up earlier and finishing work later, and redoubling their efforts at their jobs. They begin to be somewhat abusive, calling the foreigners "foreign devils," the warlords "money-grabbing commanders," and the local bullies and bad gentry "the heartless rich." Merely feeling uncertain of the success of the movement against the imperialists and the warlords (the

---

[5] Here Comrade Mao refers to the middle peasants as later defined in *How to Analyse the Classes in the Rural Areas*.
[6] The God of Wealth in Chinese folklore.

reason being that the foreigners and the warlords have so much power behind them), they refuse to join it rashly and remain neutral, but they never oppose the revolution. This group is very numerous, making up about one-half of the petty bourgeoisie.

The third group consists of those whose standard of living is being reduced. Many of this group, who belonged on the whole to the so-called prosperous families in the past, are going through a gradual change in their condition— from that of being barely able to hold on to their wealth to that of living in more and more reduced circumstances. At the end of each year, on settling their accounts, they are horrified, exclaiming, "What! Another deficit!" Because such people have seen better days and are now going down-hill with every passing year, their debts mounting and their life becoming more and more miserable, they "shudder as if with cold" at the thought of the future. Spiritually they suffer very much because they have in mind the contrast between the past and the present. Such people are quite important in the revolutionary movement, constitute a mass following of no small number and form the left wing of the petty bourgeoisie. . . .

The semi-proletariat. What is called the semi-proletariat here consists of five categories: (1) the overwhelming majority of the semi-tenant peasants,[7] (2) poor peasants, (3) handicraftsmen, (4) shop assistants[8] and (5) pedlars. The overwhelming majority of the semi-tenant peasants, together with the poor peasants, constitute a very large section of the masses in the countryside. The "peasant problem" is essentially their problem. The semi-tenant peasants, the poor peasants and the handicraftsmen are all engaged in production on yet a smaller scale than the petty bourgeoisie. Although both the overwhelming majority of the semi-tenant peasants and the poor peasants belong to the semi-proletariat, yet according to their economic conditions they can be further divided into three grades, upper, middle and lower.

The life of the semi-tenant peasants is harder than that of the owner-peasants because every year they are short of about half the food they need, and must rent land from

---

[7] By the overwhelming majority of the semi-tenant peasants, Comrade Mao here refers to the poor peasants who work partly on their own land and partly on land they rent from others.

[8] Shop assistants in China belong to different strata. Here Comrade Mao refers to the largest stratum. Another stratum, whose economic status is even lower, lead the life of the proletariat.

others, sell part of their labour power, or engage in petty trading to make up the shortage. Between spring and summer, before the green corn grows and after the white crop is consumed, they borrow money at exorbitant interest and buy grain at high prices; compared with the lot of the owner-peasants who need no help from others, theirs is of course harder, though still better than that of the poor peasants. For the poor peasants own no land, and, for their year's ploughing and sowing, receive only half the harvest or even less, while the semi-tenant peasants, though they receive only half or less than half of the harvest of the land rented from others, can nevertheless keep the entire crop from the land owned by themselves. The revolutionary qualities of the semi-tenant peasants are therefore superior to those of the owner-peasants, but inferior to those of the poor peasants.

The poor peasants are tenant-peasants in the countryside, exploited by the landlords. According to their economic status, they can again be divided into two sections. One section of the poor peasants owns comparatively adequate farm implements and a proportional amount of funds. Such peasants can get half the product of their year's toil; to make up the deficit they can cultivate side-crops, catch fish and crayfish, raise chickens and pigs, or sell part of their labour power, thus eking out a living and hoping to tide over the year amid want and hardships. Therefore their life is harder than that of the semi-tenant peasants, but better than that of the other section of the poor peasants. Their revolutionary qualities are superior to those of the semi-tenant peasants, but inferior to those of the other section of the poor peasants. As to the other section of the poor peasants, they possess neither adequate farm implements nor funds; they have not enough manure, reap but a poor harvest from their land, and, with little left after the payment of the land rent, have even greater need to sell part of their labour power. During lean seasons and hard times they appeal to relatives and friends, borrowing a few *tou* or *sheng*[9] of grain to tide over three or five days, and their debts pile up like the load on the backs of draught oxen. They are among the most hard-pressed of the peasants, and very receptive to revolutionary agitation.

The handicraftsmen are classed with the semi-proletariat because, though they possess some simple means of production and moreover follow a sort of liberal profession, they

[9] *Tou*, a Chinese measure of capacity. A standard (market) *tou* is equivalent to 0.285 bushel; a *sheng* is 1/10 of a *tou*.

are often forced to sell part of their labour power and are somewhat similar in economic status to the poor peasants in the countryside. As a result of their heavy family burdens and the disparity between their earnings and the cost of living, they also on the whole resemble the poor peasants in constantly feeling the pressure of poverty and threat of unemployment.

Shop assistants are employees in commercial establishments, who have to defray their family expenses with their meagre pay; while prices rise with every passing year, their pay is raised usually once in several years, and any casual conversation with them is an occasion for them to ventilate their endless grievances. They are not much different in status from the poor peasants and handicraftsmen and are very receptive to revolutionary agitation.

The pedlars, whether carrying their wares around on a pole or setting up stalls along the street, have but small capital, make but a meagre profit, and do not earn enough to feed and clothe themselves. They are not much different in status from the poor peasants and likewise need a revolution that will change the existing state of affairs.

The proletariat. The modern industrial proletariat in China numbers about two million. As China is economically backward the number of her modern industrial proletariat is not large. The majority of the approximately two million industrial workers are engaged in five industries—railways, mining, maritime transport, textiles and shipbuilding—and are enslaved in large numbers in enterprises owned by foreign capital. The industrial proletariat, though small in number, is nevertheless the representative of China's new productive forces and the most progressive class in modern China, and has become the leading force in the revolutionary movement. If we look at the strength it showed in the strike movements of the last four years, such as the seamen's strike,[10] the railway strike,[11] the strikes in the Kailan and

[10] In early 1922, seamen at Hongkong and the crews of the Yangtze river steamships went on strike. The seamen held out stubbornly for eight weeks. After a bitter struggle in which much blood was shed, the British imperialist authorities in Hongkong were forced to agree to increase wages, lift the ban on the seamen's union, release the strikers under arrest, and indemnify the families of the martyrs. Shortly afterwards the crews of the Yangtze steamships began a strike, which lasted two weeks and also ended in victory.

[11] Immediately after its founding in 1921 the Chinese Communist Party set about organising the railway workers. In 1922–23 strikes took place under the Party's leadership on all the main lines. The best known is the great strike on the Peking-Hongkong railway which began on February 4, 1923, and was a fight for the right to organise

Tsiaotso coal-mines,[12] the Shameen strike[13] and the general strikes in Shanghai and Hongkong after the May 30 Movement,[14] we can immediately realise the importance of the position of the industrial proletariat in the Chinese revolution. The first reason why the industrial workers can hold such a position is their concentration. No other section of the people is so concentrated. The second reason is their low economic status. They are particularly able to fight because, deprived of all means of production and left with nothing but their hands, they have despaired of ever becoming rich and are subjected to the most ruthless treatment by the imperialists, the warlords and the bourgeoisie. The strength of the city coolies is also well worth attention. They are mostly stevedores and rickshawmen, but with them belong also sewage carters and street cleaners. Having nothing but their hands, they are similar in economic status to the industrial workers, but they are less concentrated and play a less important role in production.

There is as yet little modern capitalist farming in China. What is called the rural proletariat consists of farm labourers hired by the year, the month or the day. Having neither land nor farm implements, nor even the least

---

a general union for the whole line. On February 7 Wu P'ei-fu and Hsiao Yao-nan, warlords of the Northern clique supported by British imperialism, carried out a ruthless slaughter of the strikers. This is known as the February 7 Massacre.

[12] The Kailan strike took place in October 1922. The "Kailan coal mines," an inclusive name for the Kaiping and Lwanchow (Lanchow) coalfields in Hopeh province, form a large, contiguous coal-mining area where over fifty thousand workers were employed at that time. During the Boxer Movement of 1900 the British imperialists wrested the Kaiping mines from China, and the Chinese subsequently organised the Lwanchow Coal Mining Company. Later, when the British secured control of both coalfields, they formed the Kailan Mining Administration by consolidating the two companies.

The Tsiaotso miners struck from July 1 to August 9, 1925. The well-known coal mines of Tsiaotso are in the northwestern section of Honan province.

[13] Shameen, a section of the city of Canton, was held on lease by the British imperialists. In July 1924 the British imperialist authorities there issued a police decree requiring all Chinese to present passes bearing their photos on leaving or entering the area, while foreigners could move in and out freely. The workers in Shameen struck in protest on July 15 and the British were forced to annul the decree.

[14] The general strikes broke out on June 1, 1925, in Shanghai and on June 19 in Hongkong. More than 200,000 workers took part in Shanghai and 250,000 in Hongkong. With the support of the people throughout the country the Hongkong strikers held out for sixteen months and staged the longest strike in the history of the world labour movement.

amount of funds, they can only sell their labour power to make a living. Compared with other workers, they work the longest hours, on the lowest pay, and under the worst conditions, and with the least security of employment. Such people find themselves the most hard-pressed in the villages, and hold a position in the peasant movement as important as the poor peasants.

In addition to these, there is a fairly large number of *lumpen*-proletarians, that is, peasants who have lost their land and handicraftsmen who have lost all opportunity of employment. They lead the most precarious kind of life. They have formed secret societies in various places—for instance, the Triune Society in Fukien and Kwangtung; the Society of Brothers in Hunan, Hupeh, Kweichow and Szechwan; the Society of Big Swords in Anhwei, Honan and Shantung; the Society of Rational Life in Chihli and the three north-eastern provinces;[15] and the Blue Band in Shanghai and elsewhere—all these have been their mutual-aid organisations in political and economic struggle. To assign these people to their proper role is one of China's difficult problems. Able to fight very bravely but apt to be destructive, they can become a revolutionary force when properly guided.

From the above it can be seen that all those in league with imperialism—the warlords, the bureaucrats, the compradors, the big landlords and the reactionary section of the intelligentsia dependent on them—are our enemies. The industrial proletariat is the leading force in our revolution. All sections of the semi-proletariat and the petty bourgeoisie are our closest friends. As to the vacillating middle class, its right wing may become our enemy and its left wing may become our friend, but we must be constantly on our guard towards the latter and not allow it to create confusion in our front.

March 1926

PROCLAMATION OF THE CHINESE PEOPLE'S LIBERATION ARMY

The Kuomintang reactionaries have rejected the terms for peace and persist in their stand of waging a criminal war

[15] Chihli was the name of the present Hopeh province. The then three north-eastern provinces, Fengtien, Kirin and Heilungkiang now form China's North-east.

against the nation and the people. The people all over the country hope that the People's Liberation Army will speedily wipe out the Kuomintang reactionaries. We have ordered the People's Liberation Army to advance courageously, wipe out all reactionary Kuomintang troops who dare to resist, arrest all the incorrigible war criminals, liberate the people of the whole country, safeguard the independence and integrity of China's territory and sovereignty and bring about the genuine unification of the country, which the whole people long for. We earnestly hope that people in all walks of life will assist the People's Liberation Army wherever it goes. We hereby proclaim the following eight-point covenant by which we, together with the whole people, shall abide.

1. Protect the lives and property of all the people. People in all walks of life, irrespective of class, belief or occupation, are expected to maintain order and adopt a co-operative attitude towards the People's Liberation Army. The People's Liberation Army on its part will adopt a co-operative attitude towards people in all walks of life. Counter-revolutionaries or other saboteurs who seize the opportunity to create disturbances, loot or sabotage shall be severely dealt with.

2. Protect the industrial, commercial, agricultural and livestock enterprises of the national bourgeoisie. All privately owned factories, shops, banks, warehouses, vessels, wharves, farms, livestock farms and other enterprises will without exception be protected against any encroachment. It is hoped that workers and employees in all occupations will maintain production as usual and that all shops will remain open as usual.

3. Confiscate bureaucrat-capital. All factories, shops, banks and warehouses, all vessels, wharves and railways, all postal, telegraph, electric light, telephone and water supply services, and all farms, livestock farms and other enterprises operated by the reactionary Kuomintang government and the big bureaucrats shall be taken over by the People's Government. In such enterprises the private shares held by national capitalists engaged in industry, commerce, agriculture or livestock raising shall be recognized, after their ownership is verified. All personnel working in bureaucrat-capitalist enterprises must remain at their posts pending the take-over by the People's Government and must assume responsibility for the safekeeping of all assets, machinery, charts, account books, records, etc., in preparation for the check-up and take-over. Those who render useful service in

this connection will be rewarded; those who obstruct or sabotage will be punished. Those desiring to go on working after the take-over by the People's Government will be given employment commensurate with their abilities so that they will not become destitute and homeless.

4. Protect all public and private schools, hospitals, cultural and educational institutions, athletic fields and other public welfare establishments. It is hoped that all personnel in these institutions will remain at their posts; the People's Liberation Army will protect them from molestation.

5. Except for the incorrigible war criminals and counter-revolutionaries who have committed the most heinous crimes, the People's Liberation Army and the People's Government will not hold captive, arrest or subject to indignity any officials, whether high or low, in the Kuomintang's central, provincial, municipal and county governments, deputies to the "National Assembly," members of the Legislative and Control Yuans, members of the political consultative councils, police officers and district, township, village and *pao-chia* officials, so long as they do not offer armed resistance or plot sabotage. All these persons are enjoined, pending the take-over, to stay at their posts, abide by the orders and decrees of the People's Liberation Army and the People's Government and assume responsibility for the safekeeping of all the assets and records of their offices. The People's Government will permit the employment of those among them who can make themselves useful in some kind of work and have not committed any grave reactionary act or other flagrant misdeed. Punishment shall be meted out to those who seize the opportunity to engage in sabotage, theft or embezzlement, or abscond with public funds, assets or records, or refuse to give an accounting.

6. In order to ensure peace and security in both cities and rural areas and to maintain public order, all stragglers and disbanded soldiers are required to report and surrender to the People's Liberation Army or the People's Government in their localities. No action will be taken against those who voluntarily do so and hand over their arms. Those who refuse to report or who conceal their arms shall be arrested and investigated. Persons who shelter stragglers and disbanded soldiers and do not report them to the authorities shall be duly punished.

7. The feudal system of landownership in the rural areas is irrational and should be abolished. To abolish it, however, preparations must be made and the necessary steps taken. Generally speaking, the reduction of rent and interest

should come first and land distribution later; only after the People's Liberation Army has arrived at a place and worked there for a considerable time will it be possible to speak of solving the land problem in earnest. The peasant masses should organize themselves and help the People's Liberation Army to carry out the various initial reforms. They should also work hard at their farming so as to prevent the present level of agricultural production from falling and should then raise it step by step to improve their own livelihood and supply the people of the cities with commodity grain. Urban land and buildings cannot be dealt with in the same way as the problem of rural land.

8. Protect the lives and property of foreign nationals. It is hoped that all foreign nationals will follow their usual pursuits and observe order. All foreign nationals must abide by the orders and decrees of the People's Liberation Army and the People's Government and must not engage in espionage, act against the cause of China's national independence and the people's liberation, or harbour Chinese war criminals, counter-revolutionaries or other law-breakers. Otherwise, they shall be dealt with according to law by the People's Liberation Army and the People's Government.

The People's Liberation Army is highly disciplined; it is fair in buying and selling and is not allowed to take even a needle or a piece of thread from the people. It is hoped that the people throughout the country will live and work in peace and will not give credence to rumours or raise false alarms. This proclamation is hereby issued in all sincerity and earnestness.

Mao Tse-tung

Chairman of the Chinese People's
Revolutionary Military Commission

Chu Teh

Commander-in-Chief of the Chinese
People's Liberation Army

April 25, 1949

ON THE PEOPLE'S DEMOCRATIC DICTATORSHIP

IN COMMEMORATION OF THE TWENTY-FIFTH
ANNIVERSARY OF THE COMMUNIST PARTY OF CHINA

The first of July 1949 marks the fact that the Communist Party of China has already lived through twenty-eight years. Like a man, a political party has its childhood, youth, manhood and old age. The Communist Party of China is no longer a child or a lad in his teens but has become an adult. When a man reaches old age, he will die; the same is true of a party. When classes disappear, all instruments of class struggle—parties and the state machinery—will lose their function, cease to be necessary, therefore gradually wither away and end their historical mission; and human society will move to a higher stage. We are the opposite of the political parties of the bourgeoisie. They are afraid to speak of the extinction of classes, state power and parties. We, on the contrary, declare openly that we are striving hard to create the very conditions which will bring about their extinction. The leadership of the Communist Party and the state power of the people's dictatorship are such conditions. Anyone who does not recognize this truth is no Communist. Young comrades who have not studied Marxism-Leninism and have only recently joined the Party may not yet understand this truth. They must understand it—only then can they have a correct world outlook. They must understand that the road to the abolition of classes, to the abolition of state power and to the abolition of parties is the road all mankind must take; it is only a question of time and conditions. Communists the world over are wiser than the bourgeoisie, they understand the laws governing the existence and development of things, they understand dialectics and they can see farther. The bourgeoisie does not welcome this truth because it does not want to be overthrown. To be overthrown is painful and is unbearable to contemplate for those overthrown, for example, for the Kuomintang reactionaries whom we are now overthrowing and for Japanese imperialism which we together with other peoples overthrew some time ago. But for the working class, the labouring

278

people and the Communist Party the question is not one of being overthrown, but of working hard to create the conditions in which classes, state power and political parties will die out very naturally and mankind will enter the realm of Great Harmony.[1] We have mentioned in passing the long-range perspective of human progress in order to explain clearly the problems we are about to discuss.

As everyone knows, our Party passed through these twenty-eight years not in peace but amid hardships, for we had to fight enemies, both foreign and domestic, both inside and outside the Party. We thank Marx, Engels, Lenin and Stalin for giving us a weapon. This weapon is not a machine-gun, but Marxism-Leninism. . . .

From the time of China's defeat in the Opium War of 1840,[2] Chinese progressives went through untold hardships in their quest for truth from the Western countries. Hung Hsiu-chuan,[3] Kang Yu-wei,[4] Yen Fu[5] and Sun Yat-sen were

[1] Also known as the world of Great Harmony. It refers to a society based on public ownership, free from class exploitation and oppression—a lofty ideal long cherished by the Chinese people. Here the realm of Great Harmony means communist society.

[2] Faced with the opposition of the Chinese people to her traffic in opium, Britain sent forces in 1840–42 to invade Kwangtung and other coastal regions of China under the pretext of protecting trade. The troops in Kwangtung, led by Lin Tse-hsu, fought a war of resistance.

[3] Hung Hsiu-chuan (1814–64), who was born in Kwangtung, was the leader of a peasant revolutionary war in the middle of the 19th century. In 1851 he led a mass uprising in Kwangsi and proclaimed the establishment of the Taiping Heavenly Kingdom, which held many provinces and fought the Ching Dynasty for fourteen years. In 1864 this revolutionary war failed and Hung Hsiu-chuan committed suicide by poison.

[4] Kang Yu-wei (1858–1927), of Nanhai County, Kwangtung Province. In 1895, after China had been defeated by Japanese imperialism in the previous year, he led thirteen hundred candidates for the third grade in the imperial examinations at Peking in submitting a "ten thousand word memorial" to Emperor Kuang Hsu, asking for "constitutional reform and modernization" and asking that the autocratic monarchy be changed into a constitutional monarchy. In 1898, in an attempt to introduce reforms, the emperor promoted Kang Yu-wei together with Tan Sze-tung, Liang Chi-chao and others to key posts in the government. Later, the Empress Dowager Tzu Hsi, representing the die-hards, again took power and the reform movement failed. Kang Yu-wei and Liang Chi-chao fled abroad and formed the Protect-the-Emperor Party, which became a reactionary political faction in opposition to the bourgeois and petty bourgeois revolutionaries represented by Sun Yat-sen. Among Kang's works were *Forgeries in the Classics of the Confucian Canon, Confucius as a Reformer,* and *Ta Tung Shu* or the *Book of Great Harmony.*

[5] Yen Fu (1853–1921), of Foochow, Fukien Province, studied at a naval academy in Britain. After the Sino-Japanese War of 1894, he

representative of those who had looked to the West for truth before the Communist Party of China was born. Chinese who then sought progress would read any book containing the new knowledge from the West. The number of students sent to Japan, Britain, the United States, France, and Germany was amazing. At home, the imperial examinations[6] were abolished and modern schools sprang up like bamboo shoots after a spring rain; every effort was made to learn from the West. In my youth, I too engaged in such studies. They represented the culture of Western bourgeois democracy, including the social theories and natural sciences of that period, and they were called "the new learning" in contrast to Chinese feudal culture, which was called "the old learning." For quite a long time, those who had acquired the new learning felt confident that it would save China, and very few of them had any doubts on this score, as the adherents of the old learning had. Only modernization could save China, only learning from foreign countries could modernize China. Among the foreign countries, only the Western capitalist countries were then progressive, as they had successfully built modern bourgeois states. The Japanese had been successful in learning from the West, and the Chinese also wished to learn from the Japanese. The Chinese in those days regarded Russia as backward, and few wanted to learn from her. That was how the Chinese tried to learn from foreign countries in the period from the 1840s to the beginning of the 20th century.

Imperialist aggression shattered the fond dreams of the Chinese about learning from the West. It was very odd—why were the teachers always committing aggression against their pupil? The Chinese learned a good deal from the West, but they could not make it work and were never able to realize their ideals. Their repeated struggles, including such a country-wide movement as the Revolution of 1911,[7] all

---

advocated constitutional monarchy and reforms to modernize China. His translations of T. H. Huxley's *Evolution and Ethics*, Adam Smith's *The Wealth of Nations*, J. S. Mill's *System of Logic*, Montesquieu's *L'Esprit des Lois*, and other works were vehicles for the spread of European bourgeois thought in China.

[6] A system of examinations adopted by China's autocratic dynasties. It was a method used by the feudal ruling class for selecting personnel to govern the people and also for enticing the intellectuals. The system, dating from the 7th century, persisted into the early 20th century.

[7] The Revolution of 1911 overthrew the autocratic regime of the Ching Dynasty. On October 10 of that year, a section of the New Army, at the urging of the revolutionary societies of the bourgeoisie and petty bourgeoisie, staged an uprising in Wuchang. This was fol-

ended in failure. Day by day, conditions in the country got worse, and life was made impossible. Doubts arose, increased and deepened. World War I shook the whole globe. The Russians made the October Revolution and created the world's first socialist state. Under the leadership of Lenin and Stalin, the revolutionary energy of the great proletariat and labouring people of Russia, hitherto latent and unseen by foreigners, suddenly erupted like a volcano, and the Chinese and all mankind began to see the Russians in a new light. Then, and only then, did the Chinese enter an entirely new era in their thinking and their life. They found Marxism-Leninism, the universally applicable truth, and the face of China began to change.

It was through the Russians that the Chinese found Marxism. Before the October Revolution, the Chinese were not only ignorant of Lenin and Stalin, they did not even know of Marx and Engels. The salvoes of the October Revolution brought us Marxism-Leninism. The October Revolution helped progressives in China, as throughout the world, to adopt the proletarian world outlook as the instrument for studying a nation's destiny and considering anew their own problems. Follow the path of the Russians—that was their conclusion. In 1919, the May 4th Movement took place in China. In 1921, the Communist Party of China was founded. Sun Yat-sen, in the depths of despair, came across the October Revolution and the Communist Party of China. He welcomed the October Revolution, welcomed Russian help to the Chinese and welcomed co-operation with the Communist Party of China. Then Sun Yat-sen died and Chiang Kai-shek rose to power. Over a long period of twenty-two years, Chiang Kai-shek dragged China into ever more hopeless straits. In this period, during the anti-fascist Second World War in which the Soviet Union was the main force, three big imperialist powers were knocked out, while two others were weakened. In the whole world only one big imperialist power, the United States of America, remained uninjured. But the United States faced a grave domestic

---

lowed by uprisings in other provinces, and very soon the rule of the Ching Dynasty crumbled. On January 1, 1912, the Provisional Government of the Republic of China was set up in Nanking, and Sun Yat-sen was elected Provisional President. The revolution achieved victory through the alliance of the bourgeoisie, peasants, workers and urban petty bourgeoisie. But because the group which led the revolution was compromising in nature, failed to bring real benefits to the peasants and yielded to the pressure of imperialism and the feudal forces, state power fell into the hands of the Northern warlord Yuan Shih-kai, and the revolution failed.

crisis. It wanted to enslave the whole world; it supplied arms to help Chiang Kai-shek slaughter several million Chinese. Under the leadership of the Communist Party of China, the Chinese people, after driving out Japanese imperialism, waged the People's War of Liberation for three years and have basically won victory.

Thus Western bourgeois civilization, bourgeois democracy and the plan for a bourgeois republic have all gone bankrupt in the eyes of the Chinese people. Bourgeois democracy has given way to people's democracy under the leadership of the working class and the bourgeois republic to the people's republic. This has made it possible to achieve socialism and communism through the people's republic, to abolish classes and enter a world of Great Harmony. Kang Yu-wei wrote *Ta Tung Shu*, or the *Book of Great Harmony*, but he did not and could not find the way to achieve Great Harmony. There are bourgeois republics in foreign lands, but China cannot have a bourgeois republic because she is a country suffering under imperialist oppression. The only way is through a people's republic led by the working class. . . .

Twenty-four years have passed since Sun Yat-sen's death, and the Chinese revolution, led by the Communist Party of China, has made tremendous advances both in theory and practice and has radically changed the face of China. Up to now the principal and fundamental experience the Chinese people have gained is twofold:

> (1) Internally, arouse the masses of the people. That is, unite the working class, the peasantry, the urban petty bourgeoisie and the national bourgeoisie, form a domestic united front under the leadership of the working class, and advance from this to the establishment of a state which is a people's democratic dictatorship under the leadership of the working class and based on the alliance of workers and peasants.
> (2) Externally, unite in a common struggle with those nations of the world which treat us as equals and unite with the people of all countries. That is, ally ourselves with the Soviet Union, with the People's Democracies and with the proletariat and the broad masses of the people in all other countries, and form an international united front.

"You are leaning to one side." Exactly. The forty years' experience of Sun Yat-sen and the twenty-eight years' experience of the Communist Party have taught us to lean to one side, and we are firmly convinced that in order to win victory and consolidate it we must lean to one side. In the light of the experiences accumulated in these forty years and these twenty-eight years, all Chinese without exception must lean either to the side of imperialism or to the side of socialism. Sitting on the fence will not do, nor is there a third road. We oppose the Chiang Kai-shek reactionaries who lean to the side of imperialism, and we also oppose the illusions about a third road.

"You are too irritating." We are talking about how to deal with domestic and foreign reactionaries, the imperialists and their running dogs, not about how to deal with anyone else. With regard to such reactionaries, the question of irritating them or not does not arise. Irritated or not irritated, they will remain the same because they are reactionaries. Only if we draw a clear line between reactionaries and revolutionaries, expose the intrigues and plots of the reactionaries, arouse the vigilance and attention of the revolutionary ranks, heighten our will to fight and crush the enemy's arrogance can we isolate the reactionaries, vanquish them or supersede them. We must not show the slightest timidity before a wild beast. We must learn from Wu Sung[8] on the Chingyang Ridge. As Wu Sung saw it, the tiger on Chingyang Ridge was a man-eater, whether irritated or not. Either kill the tiger or be eaten by him—one or the other.

"We want to do business." Quite right, business will be done. We are against no one except the domestic and foreign reactionaries who hinder us from doing business. Everybody should know that it is none other than the imperialists and their running dogs, the Chiang Kai-shek reactionaries, who hinder us from doing business and also from establishing diplomatic relations with foreign countries. When we have beaten the internal and external reactionaries by uniting all domestic and international forces, we shall be able to do business and establish diplomatic relations with all foreign countries on the basis of equality, mutual benefit and mutual respect for territorial integrity and sovereignty.

"Victory is possible even without international help." This is a mistaken idea. In the epoch in which imperialism exists, it is impossible for a genuine people's revolution to win victory in any country without various forms of help from the international revolutionary forces, and even if victory were won, it could not be consolidated. This was the case with the victory and consolidation of the great October

---

[8] A hero in the novel, *Shui Hu Chuan* (*Heroes of the Marshes*), who killed a tiger with his bare hands on the Chingyang Ridge. This is one of the most popular episodes in that famous novel.

Revolution, as Lenin and Stalin told us long ago. This was also the case with the overthrow of the three imperialist powers in World War II and the establishment of the People's Democracies. And this is also the case with the present and the future of People's China. Just imagine! If the Soviet Union had not existed, if there had been no victory in the anti-fascist Second World War, if Japanese imperialism had not been defeated, if the People's Democracies had not come into being, if the oppressed nations of the East were not rising in struggle and if there were no struggle of the masses of the people against their reactionary rulers in the United States, Britain, France, Germany, Italy, Japan and other capitalist countries—if not for all these in combination, the international reactionary forces bearing down upon us would certainly be many times greater than now. In such circumstances, could we have won victory? Obviously not. And even with victory, there could be no consolidation. The Chinese people have had more than enough experience of this kind. This experience was reflected long ago in Sun Yat-sen's death-bed statement on the necessity of uniting with the international revolutionary forces.

"We need help from the British and U.S. governments." This, too, is a naive idea in these times. Would the present rulers of Britain and the United States, who are imperialists, help a people's state? Why do these countries do business with us and, supposing they might be willing to lend us money on terms of mutual benefit in the future, why would they do so? Because their capitalists want to make money and their bankers want to earn interest to extricate themselves from their own crisis—it is not a matter of helping the Chinese people. The Communist Parties and progressive groups in these countries are urging their governments to establish trade and even diplomatic relations with us. This is goodwill, this is help, this cannot be mentioned in the same breath with the conduct of the bourgeoisie in the same countries. Throughout his life, Sun Yat-sen appealed countless times to the capitalist countries for help and got nothing but heartless rebuffs. Only once in his whole life did Sun Yat-sen receive foreign help, and that was Soviet help. Let readers refer to Dr. Sun Yat-sen's testament; his earnest advice was not to look for help from the imperialist countries but to "unite with those nations of the world which treat us as equals." Dr. Sun had experience; he had suffered, he had been deceived. We should remember his words and not allow ourselves to be deceived again. Internationally, we belong to the side of the anti-imperialist front headed by the Soviet Union, and so we can turn only to this side for genuine and friendly help, not to the side of the imperialist front.

"You are dictatorial." My dear sirs, you are right, that is just what we are. All the experience the Chinese people have accumulated through several decades teaches us to enforce the people's democratic dictatorship, that is, to deprive the reactionaries of the right to speak and let the people alone have that right.

Who are the people? At the present stage in China, they are the working class, the peasantry, the urban petty bourgeoisie and the national bourgeoisie. These classes, led by the working class and the Communist Party, unite to form their own state and elect their own government; they enforce their dictatorship over the running dogs of imperialism—the landlord class and bureaucrat-bourgeoisie, as well as the representatives of those classes, the Kuomintang reactionaries and their accomplices—suppress them, allow them only to behave themselves and not to be unruly in word or deed. If they speak or act in an unruly way, they will be promptly stopped and punished. Democracy is practised within the ranks of the people, who enjoy the rights of freedom of speech, assembly, association and so on. The right to vote belongs only to the people, not to the reactionaries. The combination of these two aspects, democracy for the people and dictatorship over the reactionaries, is the people's democratic dictatorship.

Why must things be done this way? The reason is quite clear to everybody. If things were not done this way, the revolution would fail, the people would suffer, the country would be conquered.

"Don't you want to abolish state power?" Yes, we do, but not right now; we cannot do it yet. Why? Because imperialism still exists, because domestic reaction still exists, because classes still exist in our country. Our present task is to strengthen the people's state apparatus—mainly the people's army, the people's police and the people's courts—in order to consolidate national defence and protect the people's interests. Given this condition, China can develop steadily, under the leadership of the working class and the Communist Party, from an agricultural into an industrial country and from a new-democratic into a socialist and communist society, can abolish classes and realize the Great Harmony. The state apparatus, including the army, the police and the courts, is the instrument by which one class oppresses another. It is an instrument for the oppression of antagonistic classes; it is violence and not "benevolence." "You are not benevolent!" Quite so. We definitely do not apply a policy of benevolence to the reactionaries and towards the reactionary activities of the reactionary classes. Our policy of benevolence is applied only within the ranks of the people, not beyond them to the reactionaries or to the reactionary activities of reactionary classes.

The people's state protects the people. Only when the people have such a state can they educate and remould themselves on a country-wide scale by democratic methods and, with everyone taking part, shake off the influence of domestic and foreign reactionaries (which is still very strong, will survive for a long time and cannot be quickly destroyed), rid themselves of the bad habits and ideas acquired in the old society, not allow themselves to be led astray by the reactionaries, and continue to advance—to advance towards a socialist and communist society.

Here, the method we employ is democratic, the method of persuasion, not of compulsion. When anyone among the people breaks the law, he too should be punished, imprisoned or even sentenced to death; but this is a matter of a few individual cases, and it differs in principle from the dictatorship exercised over the reactionaries as a class.

As for the members of the reactionary classes and individual reactionaries, so long as they do not rebel, sabotage or create trouble after their political power has been overthrown, land and work will be given to them as well in order to allow them to live and remould themselves through labour into new people. If they are not willing to work, the people's state will compel them to work. Propaganda and educational work will be done among them too and will be done, moreover, with as much care and thoroughness as among the captured army officers in the past. This, too, may be called a "policy of benevolence" if you like, but it is imposed by us on the members of the enemy classes and cannot be mentioned in the same breath with the work of self-education which we carry on within the ranks of the revolutionary people.

Such remoulding of members of the reactionary classes can be accomplished only by a state of the people's democratic dictatorship under the leadership of the Communist Party. When it is well done, China's major exploiting classes, the landlord class and the bureaucrat-bourgeoisie (the monopoly capitalist class), will be eliminated for good. There remain the national bourgeoisie; at the present stage, we can already do a good deal of suitable educational work with many of them. When the time comes to realize socialism, that is, to nationalize private enterprise, we shall carry the work of educating and remoulding them a step further. The people have a powerful state apparatus in their hands —there is no need to fear rebellion by the national bourgeoisie.

The serious problem is the education of the peasantry. The peasant economy is scattered, and the socialization of agriculture, judging by the Soviet Union's experience, will require a long time and painstaking work. Without socialization of agriculture, there can be no complete, consolidated socialism. The steps to socialize agriculture must be co-ordinated with the development of a powerful industry having state enterprise as its backbone. The state of the people's democratic dictatorship must systematically solve the problems of industrialization. . . .

We must overcome difficulties, we must learn what we do not know. We must learn to do economic work from all who know how, no matter who they are. We must esteem them as teachers, learning from them respectfully and conscientiously. We must not pretend to know when we do not know. We must not put on bureaucratic airs. If we dig into a subject for several months, for a year or two, for three or five years, we shall eventually master it. At first some of the Soviet Communists also were not very good at handling economic matters and the imperialists awaited their failure too. But the Communist Party of the Soviet Union emerged victorious and, under the leadership of Lenin and Stalin, it learned not only how to make the revolution but also how to carry on construction. It has built a great and splendid socialist state. The Communist Party of the Soviet Union is our best teacher and we must learn from it. The situation both at home and abroad is in our favour, we can rely fully on the weapon of the people's democratic dictatorship, unite the people throughout the country, the reactionaries excepted, and advance steadily to our goal.

June 30, 1949

ON THE CORRECT HANDLING OF CONTRADICTIONS AMONG THE PEOPLE

This is the text of a speech made on February 27, 1957, at the Eleventh Session (Enlarged) of the Supreme State Conference. The author has gone over the text based on the verbatim record and made certain additions.

Many people seem to think that the proposal to use democratic methods to resolve contradictions among the people raises a new question. But actually that is not so. Marxists have always held that the cause of the proletariat can only be promoted by relying on the masses of the people; that Communists must use democratic methods of persuasion and education when working among the working people and must on no account resort to commandism or coercion. The Chinese Communist Party faithfully adheres to this Marxist-Leninist principle. We have always maintained that, under the people's democratic dictatorship, two different methods—dictatorial and democratic—should be used to resolve the two kinds of contradictions—those between ourselves and the enemy and those among the people. . . .

Quite a few people fail to make a clear distinction between these two different types of contradictions—those between ourselves and the enemy and those among the people—and are prone to confuse the two. It must be admitted that it is sometimes easy to confuse them. We had instances of such confusion in our past work. In the suppression of counter-revolution, good people were sometimes mistaken for bad. Such things have happened before, and still happen today. We have been able to keep our mistakes within bounds because it has been our policy to draw a sharp line between our own people and our enemies and where mistakes have been made, to take suitable measures of rehabilitation. . . .

Contradictions in a socialist society are fundamentally different from contradictions in old societies, such as capitalist society. Contradictions in capitalist society find expression in acute antagonisms and conflicts, in sharp class struggle, which cannot be resolved by the capitalist system itself and can only be resolved by socialist revolution. Contradictions in socialist society are, on the contrary, not antagonistic and can be resolved one after the other by the socialist system itself.

The basic contradictions in socialist society are still those between the relations of production and the productive forces, and between the superstructure and the economic base. These contradictions, however, are fundamentally different in character and have different features from contradictions between the relations of production and the productive forces and between the superstructure and the economic base in the old societies. The present social system of our country is far superior to that of the old days. If this were not so, the old system would not have been overthrown and the new system could not have been set up. When we say that socialist relations of production are better suited than the old relations of production to the development of the productive forces, we mean that the former permits the productive forces to develop at a speed unparalleled in the old society, so that production can expand steadily and the constantly growing needs of the people can be met step by step. Under the rule of imperialism, feudalism and bureaucrat-capitalism, production in old China developed very slowly. For more than fifty years before liberation, China produced only a few score thousand tons of steel a year, not counting the output of the northeastern provinces. If we include these provinces, the peak annual output of steel of our country was only something over nine hundred thousand tons. In 1949, the country's output of steel was only something over one hundred thousand tons. Now, only seven years after liberation of the country, our steel output already exceeds four million tons. In old China, there was hardly any engineering industry to speak of; motor-car and aircraft industries were non-existent; now, we have them. When the rule of imperialism, feudalism and bureaucrat-capitalism was overthrown by the people, many were not clear as to where China was headed —to capitalism or socialism. Facts give the answer: Only socialism can save China. The socialist system has promoted the rapid development of the productive forces of our country—this is a fact that even our enemies abroad have had to acknowledge. . . .

THE SUPPRESSION OF COUNTER-REVOLUTION

The question of suppressing counter-revolutionaries is a question of the struggle of opposites in the contradiction between ourselves and the enemy. Within the ranks of the people, there are some who hold somewhat different views on this question. There are two kinds of persons whose views differ from ours. Those with a rightist way of thinking make no distinction between ourselves and the enemy and mistake our enemies for our own people. They regard as friends the very people the broad masses regard as enemies. Those with a "leftist" way of thinking so magnify contradictions between ourselves and the enemy that they mistake certain contradictions among the people for contradictions between ourselves and the enemy, and regard as counter-revolutionaries persons who really aren't. Both these views are wrong. Neither of them will enable us to handle properly the question of suppressing counter-revolution, or to correctly assess the results in this work. . . .

The consolidation of our state is due to the fact that our economic measures are basically sound, that the people's livelihood is secure and is steadily being improved, that our policies towards the national bourgeoisie and other classes are also correct, and so on. Nevertheless, our success in suppressing counter-revolution is undoubtedly an important reason for the consolidation of our state. Because of all this, although many of our college students come from families other than those of the working people, all of them, with few exceptions, are patriotic and support socialism; they didn't give way to unrest during the Hungarian events. The same was true of the national bourgeoisie, to say nothing of the basic masses—the workers and peasants.

After liberation, we rooted out a number of counter-revolutionaries. Some were sentenced to death because they had committed serious crimes. This was absolutely necessary; it was the demand of the people; it was done to free the masses from long years of oppression by counter-revolutionaries and all kinds of local tyrants; in other words, to set free the productive forces. If we had not done so, the masses would not have been able to lift their heads.

Since 1956, however, there has been a radical change in the situation. Taking the country as a whole, the main force of counter-revolution has been rooted out. Our basic task is no longer to set free the productive forces but to protect and expand them in the context of the new relations of production. Some people do not understand that our present policy fits the present situation and our past policy fitted the past situation; they want to make use of the present policy to reverse decisions on past cases and to deny the great success we achieved in suppressing counter-revolution. This is quite wrong, and the people will not permit it.

As regards the suppression of counter-revolution, the main thing is that we have achieved successes, but mistakes have also been made. There were excesses in some cases and in other cases counter-revolutionaries were overlooked. Our policy is: "Counter-revolutionaries must be suppressed whenever they are found, mistakes must be corrected whenever they are discovered." The line we adopted in this work was the mass line, that is, the suppression of counter-revolution by the people themselves. Of course, even with the adoption of this line, mistakes will still occur in our work, but they will be fewer and easier to correct. The masses have gained experience through this struggle. From what was done correctly they learned how things should be done. From what was done wrong they learned useful lessons as to why mistakes were made.

Steps have been or are being taken to correct mistakes which have already been discovered in the work of suppressing counter-revolutionaries. Those not yet discovered will be corrected as soon as they come to light. Decisions on exoneration and rehabilitation should receive the same measure of publicity as the original mistaken decisions. I propose that a comprehensive review of the work of suppressing counter-revolution be made this year or next to sum up experience, foster a spirit of righteousness and combat unhealthy tendencies. . . .

The present situation with regard to counter-revolutionaries can be stated in these words: There still are counter-revolutionaries, but not many. In the first place, there still are counter-revolutionaries. Some people say that there aren't any and that all is at peace; that we can pile up our pillows and just go to sleep. But this is not the way things are. The fact is that there still are counter-revolutionaries (this, of course, is not to say you'll find them everywhere and in every organization), and we must continue to fight them. It must be understood that the hidden counter-revolutionaries still at large will not take it lying down, but will certainly seize every opportunity to make trouble, and that the United States imperialists and the Chiang Kai-shek clique are constantly sending in secret agents to carry on wrecking activities. Even when all the counter-revolutionaries in existence have been rooted out, new ones may emerge. If we drop our guard we shall be badly fooled and suffer for it severely. Wherever counter-revolutionaries are found making trouble, they should be rooted out with a firm hand. But, of course, taking the country as a whole, there are certainly not many counter-revolutionaries. It would be wrong to say that there are still large numbers of counter-revolutionaries at large. Acceptance of that view will also breed confusion. . . .

THE QUESTION OF INDUSTRIALISTS AND
BUSINESS MEN

The year 1956 saw the transformation of privately owned industrial and commercial enterprises into joint state-private enterprises as well as the organization of co-operatives in agriculture and handicrafts as part of the transformation of our social system. The speed and smoothness with which this was carried out are closely related to the fact that we treated the contradiction between the working class and the national bourgeoisie as a contradiction among the people. Has this class contradiction been resolved completely? No, not yet. A considerable period of time is still required to do so. However, some people say that the capitalists have been so remoulded that they are now not much different from the workers, and that further remoulding is unnecessary. Others go so far as to say that the capitalists are even a bit better than the workers. Still others ask, if remoulding is necessary, why doesn't the working class undergo remoulding? Are these opinions correct? Of course not.

In building a socialist society, all need remoulding, the exploiters as well as the working people. Who says the working class doesn't need it? Of course, remoulding of the exploiters and that of the working people are two different types of remoulding. The two must not be confused. In the class struggle and the struggle against nature, the working class remoulds the whole of society, and at the same time remoulds itself. It must continue to learn in the process of its work and step by step overcome its shortcomings. It must never stop doing so. Take us who are present here, for example. Many of us make some progress each year; that is to say, we are being remoulded each year. I myself had all sorts of non-Marxist ideas before. It was only later that I embraced Marxism. I learned a little Marxism from books and so made an initial remoulding of my ideas, but it was mainly through taking part in the class struggle over the years that I came to be remoulded. And I must continue to study if I am to make further progress, otherwise I shall lag behind. Can the capitalists be so clever as to need no more remoulding?

Some contend that the Chinese bourgeoisie no longer has two sides to its character, but only one side. Is this true? No. On the one hand, members of the bourgeoisie have already become managerial personnel in joint state-private enterprises and are being transformed from exploiters into working people living by their own labour. On the other hand, they still receive a fixed rate of interest on their investments in the joint enterprises, that is, they have not yet cut themselves loose from the roots of exploitation. Between them and the working class there is still a considerable gap in ideology, sentiments and habits of life. How can it be said that they no longer have two sides to their character? Even when they stop receiving their fixed interest payments and rid themselves of the label "bourgeoisie," they will still need ideological remoulding for quite some time. If it were held that the bourgeoisie no longer has a dual character, then such study and remoulding for the capitalists would no longer be needed.

But it must be said that such a view doesn't tally with the actual circumstances of our industrialists and business men, nor with what most of them want. During the past few years, most of them have been willing to study and have made marked progress. Our industrialists and business men can be thoroughly remoulded only in the course of work; they should work together with the staff and workers in the enterprises, and make the enterprises the chief centres for remoulding themselves. It is also important for them to change certain of their old views through study. Study for them should be optional. After they have attended study groups for some weeks, many industrialists and business men, on returning to their enterprises, find they speak more of a common language with the workers and the representatives of state shareholdings, and so work better together. They know from personal experience that it is good for them to keep on studying and remoulding themselves. The idea just referred to that study and remoulding are not necessary does not reflect the views of the majority of industrialists and business men. Only a small number of them think that way.

THE QUESTION OF INTELLECTUALS

Contradictions within the ranks of the people in our country also find expression among our intellectuals. Several million intellectuals who worked for the old society have come to serve the new society. The question that now arises is how they can best meet the needs of the new society and how we can help them do so. This is also a contradiction among the people.

Most of our intellectuals have made marked progress during the past seven years. They express themselves in favour of the socialist system. Many of them are diligently studying Marxism, and some have become Communists. Their number, though small, is growing steadily. There are, of course, still some intellectuals who are sceptical of socialism or who do not approve of it, but they are in a minority.

China needs as many intellectuals as she can get to carry through the colossal task of socialist construction. We should trust intellectuals who are really willing to serve the cause of socialism, radically improve our relations with them and help them solve whatever problems that have to be solved, so that they can give full play to their talents. Many of our comrades are not good at getting along with intellectuals. They are stiff with them, lack respect for their work, and interfere in scientific and cultural matters in a way that is uncalled for. We must do away with all such shortcomings.

Our intellectuals have made some progress, but they should not be complacent. They must continue to remould themselves, gradually shed their bourgeois world outlook and acquire a proletarian, Communist world outlook so that they can fully meet the needs of the new society and closely unite with the workers and peasants. This change in world outlook is a fundamental one, and up till now it cannot yet be said that most of our intellectuals have accomplished it. We hope that they will continue making progress, and, in the course of work and study, gradually acquire a Communist world outlook, get a better grasp of Marxism-Leninism, and identify themselves with the workers and peasants. We hope they will not stop halfway, or, what is worse, slip back; for if they do they will find themselves in a blind alley.

Since the social system of our country has changed and the economic basis of bourgeois ideology has in the main been destroyed, it is not only necessary but also possible for large numbers of our intellectuals to change their world outlook. But a thorough change in world outlook takes quite a long time, and we should go about it patiently and not be impetuous. Actually there are bound to be some who are all along reluctant, ideologically, to accept Marxism-Leninism and communism. We should not be too exacting in what we expect of them; as long as they comply with the requirements of the state and engage in legitimate pursuits, we should give them opportunities for suitable work.

There has been a falling off recently in ideological and political work among students and intellectuals, and some unhealthy tendencies have appeared. Some people apparently think that there is no longer any need to concern themselves about politics, the future of their motherland and the ideals of mankind. It seems as if Marxism that was once all the rage is not so much in fashion now. This being the case, we must improve our ideological and political work. Both students and intellectuals should study hard. In addition to specialized subjects, they should study Marxism-Leninism, current events and political affairs in order to progress both ideologically and politically. Not to have a correct political point of view is like having no soul. Ideological remoulding in the past was necessary and has yielded positive results. But it was carried on in a somewhat rough and ready way and the feelings of some people were hurt—this was not good. We must avoid such shortcomings in future. All departments and organizations concerned should take up their responsibilities with regard to ideological and political work. This applies to the Communist Party, the Youth League, government departments responsible for this work, and especially heads of educational institutions and teachers. Our educational policy must enable everyone who gets an education, to develop morally, intellectually and physically and become a cultured, socialist-minded worker. We must spread the idea of building our country through hard work and thrift. We must see to it that all our young people understand that ours is still a very poor country, that we can't change this situation radically in a short time, and that only through the united efforts of our younger generation and all our people working with their own hands can our country be made strong and prosperous. . . .

ON "LETTING A HUNDRED FLOWERS BLOSSOM," AND "LETTING A HUNDRED SCHOOLS OF THOUGHT CONTEND,"* AND "LONG-TERM CO-EXISTENCE AND MUTUAL SUPERVISION"

"Let a hundred flowers blossom," and "let a hundred schools of thought contend," "long-term co-existence and mutual supervision"—how did these slogans come to be put forward?

They were put forward in the light of the specific conditions existing in China, on the basis of the recognition that various kinds of contradictions still exist in a socialist society, and in response to the country's urgent need to speed up its economic and cultural development.

The policy of letting a hundred flowers blossom and a hundred schools of thought contend is designed to promote the flourishing of the arts and the progress of science; it is designed to enable a socialist culture to thrive in our land. Different forms and styles in art can develop freely and different schools in science can contend freely. We think that it is harmful to the growth of art and science if administrative measures are used to impose one particular style of art or school of thought and to ban another. Questions of right and wrong in the arts and sciences should be settled through free discussion in artistic and scientific circles and in the course of practical work in the arts and sciences. They should not be settled in summary fashion. A period of trial is often needed to determine whether something is right or wrong. In the past, new and correct things often failed at the outset to win recognition from the majority of people and had to develop by twists and turns in struggle. Correct and good things have often at first been looked upon not as fragrant flowers but as poisonous weeds. Copernicus' theory of the solar system and Darwin's theory of evolution were once dismissed as erroneous and had to win through over bitter opposition. Chinese history

* "Let a hundred flowers blossom," and "let a hundred schools of thought contend" are two old Chinese sayings. The word "hundred" does not mean literally the number as such, but simply "numerous." —Translator.

offers many similar examples. In socialist society, conditions for the growth of new things are radically different from and far superior to those in the old society. Nevertheless, it still often happens that new, rising forces are held back and reasonable suggestions smothered.

The growth of new things can also be hindered, not because of deliberate suppression, but because of lack of discernment. That is why we should take a cautious attitude in regard to questions of right and wrong in the arts and sciences, encourage free discussion, and avoid hasty conclusions. We believe that this attitude will facilitate the growth of the arts and sciences.

Marxism has also developed through struggle. At the beginning, Marxism was subjected to all kinds of attacks and regarded as a poisonous weed. It is still being attacked and regarded as a poisonous weed in many parts of the world. However, it enjoys a different position in the socialist countries. But even in these countries, there are non-Marxist as well as anti-Marxist ideologies. It is true that in China, socialist transformation, in so far as a change in the system of ownership is concerned, has in the main been completed, and the turbulent, large-scale, mass class struggles characteristic of the revolutionary periods have in the main concluded. But remnants of the overthrown landlord and comprador classes still exist, the bourgeoisie still exists, and the petty bourgeoisie has only just begun to remould itself. Class struggle is not yet over. The class struggle between the proletariat and the bourgeoisie, the class struggle between various political forces, and the class struggle in the ideological field between the proletariat and the bourgeoisie will still be long and devious and at times may even become very acute. The proletariat seeks to transform the world according to its own world outlook, so does the bourgeoisie. In this respect, the question whether socialism or capitalism will win is still not really settled. Marxists are still a minority of the entire population as well as of the intellectuals. Marxism therefore must still develop through struggle. Marxism can only develop through struggle—this is true not only in the past and present, it is necessarily true in the future also. What is correct always develops in the course of struggle with what is wrong. The true, the good and the beautiful always exist in comparison with the false, the evil and the ugly, and grow in struggle with the latter. As mankind in general rejects an untruth and accepts a truth, a new truth will begin struggling with new erroneous ideas. Such struggles

will never end. This is the law of development of truth
and it is certainly also the law of development of Marxism.

It will take a considerable time to decide the issue in the
ideological struggle between socialism and capitalism in
our country. This is because the influence of the bourgeoisie and of the intellectuals who come from the old
society will remain in our country as the ideology of a
class for a long time to come. Failure to grasp this, or still
worse, failure to understand it at all, can lead to the gravest
mistakes—to ignoring the necessity of waging the struggle
in the ideological field. Ideological struggle is not like other
forms of struggle. Crude, coercive methods should not be
used in this struggle, but only the method of painstaking
reasoning. Today, socialism enjoys favourable conditions
in the ideological struggle. The main power of the state is
in the hands of the working people led by the proletariat.
The Communist Party is strong and its prestige stands high.
Although there are defects and mistakes in our work, every
fair-minded person can see that we are loyal to the people,
that we are both determined and able to build up our
country together with the people, and that we have achieved
great successes and will achieve still greater ones. The vast
majority of the bourgeoisie and intellectuals who come
from the old society are patriotic; they are willing to serve
their flourishing socialist motherland, and they know that
if they turn away from the socialist cause and the working
people led by the Communist Party, they will have no one
to rely on and no bright future to look forward to.

People may ask: Since Marxism is accepted by the
majority of the people in our country as the guiding ideology, can it be criticized? Certainly it can. As a scientific
truth, Marxism fears no criticism. If it did, and could be
defeated in argument, it would be worthless. In fact, aren't
the idealists criticizing Marxism every day and in all sorts
of ways? As for those who harbour bourgeois and petty
bourgeois ideas and do not wish to change, aren't they also
criticizing Marxism in all sorts of ways? Marxists should
not be afraid of criticism from any quarter. Quite the contrary, they need to steel and improve themselves and win
new positions in the teeth of criticism and the storm and
stress of struggle. Fighting against wrong ideas is like
being vaccinated—a man develops greater immunity from
disease after the vaccine takes effect. Plants raised in hot-
houses are not likely to be robust. Carrying out the policy
of letting a hundred flowers blossom and a hundred schools

of thought contend will not weaken but strengthen the leading position of Marxism in the ideological field.

What should our policy be towards non-Marxist ideas? As far as unmistakable counter-revolutionaries and wreckers of the socialist cause are concerned, the matter is easy: we simply deprive them of their freedom of speech. But it is quite a different matter when we are faced with incorrect ideas among the people. Will it do to ban such ideas and give them no opportunity to express themselves? Certainly not. It is not only futile but very harmful to use crude and summary methods to deal with ideological questions among the people, with questions relating to the spiritual life of man. You may ban the expression of wrong ideas, but the ideas will still be there. On the other hand, correct ideas, if pampered in hot-houses without being exposed to the elements or immunized from disease, will not win out against wrong ones. That is why it is only by employing methods of discussion, criticism and reasoning that we can really foster correct ideas, overcome wrong ideas, and really settle issues.

The bourgeoisie and petty bourgeoisie are bound to give expression to their ideologies. It is inevitable that they should stubbornly persist in expressing themselves in every way possible on political and ideological questions. You can't expect them not to do so. We should not use methods of suppression to prevent them from expressing themselves, but should allow them to do so and at the same time argue with them and direct well-considered criticism at them.

There can be no doubt that we should criticize all kinds of wrong ideas. It certainly would not do to refrain from criticism and look on while wrong ideas spread unchecked and acquire their market. Mistakes should be criticized and poisonous weeds fought against wherever they crop up. But such criticism should not be doctrinaire. We should not use the metaphysical method, but strive to employ the dialectical method. What is needed is scientific analysis and fully convincing arguments. Doctrinaire criticism settles nothing. We don't want any kind of poisonous weeds, but we should carefully distinguish between what is really a poisonous weed and what is really a fragrant flower. We must learn together with the masses of the people how to make this careful distinction, and use the correct methods to fight poisonous weeds.

While criticizing doctrinairism, we should at the same time direct our attention to criticizing revisionism. Revisionism, or rightist opportunism, is a bourgeois trend of thought which is even more dangerous than doctrinairism. The revisionists, or right opportunists, pay lip-service to Marxism and also attack "doctrinairism." But the real target of their attack is actually the most fundamental elements of Marxism. They oppose or distort materialism and dialectics, oppose or try to weaken the people's democratic dictatorship and the leading role of the Communist Party, oppose or try to weaken socialist transformation and socialist construction. Even after the basic victory of the socialist revolution in our country, there are still a number of people who vainly hope for a restoration of the capitalist system. They wage a struggle against the working class on every front, including the ideological front. In this struggle, their right-hand men are the revisionists.

On the surface, these two slogans—let a hundred flowers blossom and a hundred schools of thought contend—have no class character: the proletariat can turn them to account, so can the bourgeoisie and other people. But different classes, strata and social groups each have their own views on what are fragrant flowers and what are poisonous weeds. So what, from the point of view of the broad masses of the people, should be the criteria today for distinguishing between fragrant flowers and poisonous weeds?

In the political life of our country, how are our people to determine what is right and what is wrong in our words and actions? Basing ourselves on the principles of our Constitution, the will of the overwhelming majority of our people and the political programmes jointly proclaimed on various occasions by our political parties and groups, we believe that, broadly speaking, words and actions can be judged right if they:

(1) Help to unite the people of our various nationalities, and do not divide them;

(2) Are beneficial, not harmful, to socialist transformation and socialist construction;

(3) Help to consolidate, not undermine or weaken, the people's democratic dictatorship;

(4) Help to consolidate, not undermine or weaken, democratic centralism;

(5) Tend to strengthen, not to cast off or weaken, the leadership of the Communist Party;

(6) Are beneficial, not harmful, to international socialist solidarity and the solidarity of the peace-loving peoples of the world.

Of these six criteria, the most important are the socialist

path and the leadership of the Party. These criteria are put forward in order to foster, and not hinder, the free discussion of various questions among the people. Those who do not approve of these criteria can still put forward their own views and argue their case. When the majority of the people have clear-cut criteria to go by, criticism and self-criticism can be conducted along proper lines, and these criteria can be applied to people's words and actions to determine whether they are fragrant flowers or poisonous weeds. These are political criteria. Naturally, in judging the truthfulness of scientific theories or assessing the aesthetic value of works of art, other pertinent criteria are needed, but these six political criteria are also applicable to all activities in the arts or sciences. In a socialist country like ours, can there possibly be any useful scientific or artistic activity which runs counter to these political criteria?

All that is set out above stems from the specific historical conditions in our country. Since conditions vary in different socialist countries and with different Communist Parties, we do not think that other countries and Parties must or need to follow the Chinese way.

The slogan "long-term co-existence and mutual supervision" is also a product of specific historical conditions in our country. It wasn't put forward all of a sudden, but had been in the making for several years. The idea of long-term co-existence had been in existence for a long time, but last year when the socialist system was basically established, the slogan was set out in clear terms.

Why should the democratic parties of the bourgeoisie and petty bourgeoisie be allowed to exist side by side with the party of the working class over a long period of time? Because we have no reason not to adopt the policy of long-term co-existence with all other democratic parties which are truly devoted to the task of uniting the people for the cause of socialism and which enjoy the trust of the people. . . .

Mutual supervision among the various parties has also been a long-established fact, in the sense that they advise and criticize each other. Mutual supervision, which is obviously not a one-sided matter, means that the Communist Party should exercise supervision over the other democratic parties, and the other democratic parties should exercise supervision over the Communist Party. Why should the other democratic parties be allowed to exercise supervision over the Communist Party? This is because for a party as much as for an individual there is great need to hear opinions different from its own. We all know that supervision over the Communist Party is mainly exercised by the working people and Party membership. But we will benefit even more if the other democratic parties do this as well. Of course, advice and criticism exchanged between the Communist Party and the other democratic parties will play a positive role in mutual supervision only when they conform to the six political criteria given above. That is why we hope that the other democratic parties will all pay attention to ideological remoulding, and strive for long-term co-existence and mutual supervision with the Communist Party so as to meet the needs of the new society.

IV.

CONTEMPORARY
COMMUNISM

Communism, like any other living faith, is riven by heresies. And just as, for example, in Christianity, Catholics and Protestants each claim to be the sole bearers of the true Scripture, so also in communism, Moscow accuses Peking of revisionism, and vice versa. What is more interesting than these family squabbles is the large number of contemporary thinkers who, while influenced by classical communism, are not, or are no longer in the strictest sense, communists. Even those who are still Communist Party members have developed on their own, sometimes in directions divergent from orthodox Marxism. Such men as Ernst Bloch and Roger Garaudy among the old guard, or Leo Labedz among the younger writers, are not adherents to the Party line but seminal thinkers in their own right. In the following section, examples have been chosen from many parts of the world.

Ho Chi Minh
(1890–1969)

Vietnamese leader and head of state, Ho Chi Minh was in France, where he became a founding member of the French Communist Party. He took an active part in the Chinese Revolution in 1925–1927 and was saved from death by a western family after his imprisonment in Hong Kong in 1931. He led the struggle for Indochinese independence in World War II and became president of the Democratic Republic of Vietnam in 1945. Following the 1954 armistice he became president and prime minister of North Vietnam. He was reelected in 1960 and received the Order of Lenin in 1967.

On Revolution

THE PATH WHICH LED ME TO LENINISM*

After World War I, I made my living in Paris, now as a retoucher at a photographer's, now as painter of "Chinese antiquities" (made in France!). I would distribute leaflets denouncing the crimes committed by the French colonialists in Viet-Nam.

From: *On Revolution*, by Ho Chi Minh, edited by B. B. Fall, New York, 1967.

 * Article written in April, 1960, for the Soviet review *Problems of the East*, for the ninetieth anniversary of Lenin's birth. (*This is by far the most candid statement made by Ho about his reasons for joining the Communist Party, and amply demonstrates his pragmatic approach to ideological commitments.*—ED.)

At that time, I supported the October Revolution only instinctively, not yet grasping all its historic importance. I loved and admired Lenin because he was a great patriot who liberated his compatriots; until then, I had read none of his books.

The reason for my joining the French Socialist Party was that these "ladies and gentlemen"—as I called my comrades at that moment—had shown their sympathy toward me, toward the struggle of the oppressed peoples. But I understood neither what was a party, a trade-union, nor what was Socialism or Communism.

Heated discussions were then taking place in the branches of the Socialist Party, about the question of whether the Socialist Party should remain in the Second International, should a Second-and-a-half International be founded, or should the Socialist Party join Lenin's Third International? I attended the meetings regularly, twice or thrice a week, and attentively listened to the discussions. First, I could not understand thoroughly. Why were the discussions so heated? Either with the Second, Second-and-a-half, or Third International, the revolution could be waged. What was the use of arguing then? As for the First International, what had become of it?

What I wanted most to know—and this precisely was not debated in the meetings—was: Which International sides with the peoples of colonial countries?

I raised this question—the most important in my opinion—in a meeting. Some comrades answered: It is the Third, not the Second, International. And a comrade gave me Lenin's "Thesis on the National and Colonial Questions," published by *l'Humanité,* to read.

There were political terms difficult to understand in this thesis. But by dint of reading it again and again, finally I could grasp the main part of it. What emotion, enthusiasm, clear-sightedness, and confidence it instilled into me! I was overjoyed to tears. Though sitting alone in my room, I shouted aloud as if addressing large crowds: "Dear martyrs, compatriots! This is what we need, this is the path to our liberation!"

After then, I had entire confidence in Lenin, in the Third International.

Formerly, during the meetings of the Party branch, I only listened to the discussion; I had a vague belief that all were logical, and could not differentiate as to who were right and who were wrong. But from then on, I also plunged into the debates and discussed with fervor. Though I was still lacking French words to express all my thoughts, I smashed the allegations attacking Lenin and the Third International with no less vigor. My only argument was: "If you do not condemn colonialism, if you do not side with the colonial people, what kind of revolution are you waging?"

Not only did I take part in the meetings of my own Party branch, but I also went to other Party branches to lay down "my position." Now I must tell again that Comrades Marcel Cachin, Vaillant Couturier, Munmousseau, and many others helped me to broaden my knowledge. Finally, at the Tours Congress, I voted with them for our joining the Third International.

At first, patriotism, not yet Communism, led me to have confidence in Lenin, in the Third International. Step by step, along the struggle, by studying Marxism-Leninism parallel with participation in practical activities, I gradually came upon the fact that only Socialism and Communism can liberate the oppressed nations and the working people throughout the world from slavery.

There is a legend, in our country as well as in China, on the miraculous "Book of the Wise." When facing great difficulties, one opens it and finds a way out. Leninism is not only a miraculous "book of the wise," a compass for us Vietnamese revolutionaries and people: it is also the radiant sun illuminating our path to final victory, to Socialism and Communism.

SOME CONSIDERATIONS ON THE COLONIAL QUESTION*

Since the French Party has accepted Moscow's "twenty-one conditions" and joined the Third International, among the problems which it has set itself is a particularly ticklish one—colonial policy. Unlike the First and Second Internationals, it cannot be satisfied with purely sentimental expressions of position leading to nothing at all, but must have a well-defined working program, an effective and practical policy.

* Printed in *l'Humanité*, May 25, 1922.

On this point, more than on others, the Party faces many difficulties, the greatest of which are the following:

THE GREAT SIZE OF THE COLONIES

Not counting the new "trusteeships" acquired after the war, France possesses:

In Asia, 450,000 square kilometers; in Africa, 3,541,000 square kilometers; in America, 108,000 square kilometers; and in Oceania, 21,600 square kilometers—a total area of 4,120,000 square kilometers (eight times its own territory), with a population of 48,000,000 souls. These people speak over twenty different languages. This diversity of tongues does not make propaganda easy, for, except in a few old colonies, a French propagandist can make himself understood only through an interpreter. However, translations are of limited value, and in these countries of administrative despotism, it is rather difficult to find an interpreter to translate revolutionary speeches.

There are other drawbacks: Though the natives of all the colonies are equally oppressed and exploited, their intellectual, economic, and political development differs greatly from one region to another. Between Annam and the Congo, Martinique and New Caledonia, there is absolutely nothing in common, except poverty.

THE INDIFFERENCE OF THE PROLETARIAT OF THE MOTHER COUNTRY TOWARD THE COLONIES

In his theses on the colonial question, Lenin clearly stated that "the workers of colonizing countries are bound to give the most active assistance to the liberation movements in subject countries." To this end, the workers of the mother country must know what a colony really is, they must be acquainted with what is going on there, and with the suffering—a thousand times more acute than theirs—endured by their brothers, the proletarians in the colonies. In a word, they must take an interest in this question.

Unfortunately, there are many militants who still think that a colony is nothing but a country with plenty of sand underfoot and of sun overhead, a few green coconut palms and colored folk, that is all. And they take not the slightest interest in the matter.

INDOCHINA AND THE PACIFIC*

At first sight, it seems that the question of Indochina and the Pacific is of no concern to European workers. But it must be remembered that:

1. During the revolution, the Allies, not having succeeded in their attack on Russia from the West, tried to attack it from the East. And the Pacific powers, the United States and Japan, landed their troops in Vladivostock, while France sent Indochinese regiments to Siberia to support the Whites.

2. At present, international capitalism draws all its vital force from the colonial countries. It finds there raw materials for its factories, investments for its capital, markets for its products, cheap replenishments for its labor army, and above all, native soldiers for its counterrevolutionary army. One day, revolutionary Russia will have to cope with this capitalism. It is thus necessary for the Russian comrades to realize the full strength and all the immediate and long-term maneuvers of their adversary.

3. Having become the center of attraction for imperialist ambitions, the Pacific area and the neighboring colonies are likely in the future to become the seat of a new world conflagration, whose proletariat will have to bear the burden.

These statements of fact prove that the Pacific problem will concern all proletarians in general.

Therefore, to reconstruct France ruined by an imperialist war, the French Minister of Colonies has worked out a plan for developing the colonies. The plan aims to exploit the resources of colonized countries for the benefit of the colonizing country. This plan states that Indochina must help the other colonies in the Pacific to intensify their production so that, in their turn, they too can be useful to the mother country. If the plan were carried out, it would necessarily lead to the depopulation and impoverishment of Indochina.

Lately, however, the Government Council of Indochina, despite the resistance of Annamese opinion, unanimously voted for the carrying out of the plan. To understand the importance of this unanimity, it is useful to know that this Council is composed of the Governor General of Indochina, the General Commander-in-Chief of the troops in Indochina, and about thirty high-ranking French civil servants, as well as five native mandarins, tools of the Governor.

* Printed in *La Correspondance Internationale*, No. 18, 1924.

And all these gentlemen pretend to act for Indochina and in the interests of the Annamese people. Imagine Eskimos or Zulus deciding the fate of a European people.

According to an official avowal, the colonies in the Pacific are afflicted with debility, and are living—if we can call it living—at a slower and slower rate. The truth is that populous islands are being entirely depopulated, in a short time, by alcohol and forced labor. Fifty years ago, the Marquesas had more than 20,000 souls, but now have only 1,500 weak and debilitated inhabitants. Tahiti had its population reduced by 25 per cent in ten years. From these declining populations, French imperialism has further taken more than 1,500 men to serve as cannon fodder during the war. This rapid extinction of a race seems unbelievable. However, it is a fact to be observed in many colonies. (In the regions of the Congo, populations of 40,000 inhabitants fell to 30,000 in the space of twenty years. Saint-Pierre et Miquelon islands had 6,500 inhabitants in 1902; in 1922 this colony had only 3,900, etc.)

Most islands in the French Pacific have been yielded to concessionary companies which rob the natives of their land and make them work as slaves. Here is an example showing how the native workers are treated. Two hundred mother-of-pearl divers were sent by force by the French Company of Oceania to plantations 800 miles from their native districts. (It is as if tailors were sent to work in mines.) They were penned up in a small schooner fitted up for ten passengers and lacking any life-saving equipment, and embarked without being allowed to see their wives and children. For two years, these unfortunate toilers were kept prisoner in the company's jail. Many were harshly treated. Others died.

Add to this inhuman exploitation the immorality of the rascals to whom French imperialism entrusts the administration of these islands, and you will see in all its beauty the regime of exploitation and oppression which is leading the colonized countries in the Pacific to death and extinction.

Imperialism has now reached a degree of almost scientific perfection. It uses white proletarians to conquer the proletarians of the colonies. Then it hurls the proletarians of one colony against those of another. Finally, it relies on the proletarians of the colonies to rule white proletarians. Senegalese had the sad distinction of having helped French militarism to massacre their brothers of the Congo, the Sudan, Dahomey, and Madagascar. Algerians fought in

Indochina. Annamese were garrisoned in Africa. And so on. During the great slaughter, more than 1 million colonial peasants and workers were brought to Europe to massacre white peasants and workers. Only recently, French soldiers in the Ruhr were surrounded by native soldiers, and native light infantry were sent against German strikers. Almost half of the French army is composed of natives, to the number of about 300,000.

Beyond this military usefulness, capitalism uses these colonies for the most skillful economic exploitation. It is often noticed that a decrease in wages in some regions in France and in some trades is always preceded by an increase in the proportion of colonial labor. The natives are employed as strikebreakers. Capitalism now uses one colony as a tool for exploiting another; this is the case of Indochina and the Pacific area. Indochina, despite the noisy untruths of the officials, is exhausted. During 1914–18, almost 100,000 Annamese (official number: 97,903 men) were dragged from their homes to be sent to Europe. Although deprived of so many hands for production, Indochina was obliged to send, for the defense of its oppressors, more than 500,000 tons of edible grains. Hundreds of millions of francs were raked off in "victory loans." Each year, the Annamese sweat blood to yield up about 450,000 francs, a sum which is almost entirely used to fatten spongers. Moreover, Indochina is responsible for big military expenses, elegantly called a "filial contribution" by the Minister of Colonies.

It is from this oppressed, weakened, and emaciated country that millions of piasters and several thousand men (40,000 to begin with) are further going to be wrung to satisfy the insatiable appetites of the concessionaires and the personal ambitions of a gang of unscrupulous politicians.

It is not enough to demoralize the whole Annamese race with alcohol and opium. It is not enough to take 40,000 "volunteers" yearly for the glory of militarism. It is not enough to have turned a people of 20 million souls into one big sponge to be squeezed by money-grubbers. We are, on top of all this, to be endowed with slavery.

It is not only the fate of the proletariat in Indochina and the Pacific area, but also that of the international proletariat, which is threatened by these imperialist actions. Japan commands the telegraphic stations on Yap Island. The United States is spending millions of dollars on improving the turret guns of its warships in the Pacific. England will turn Singapore into a naval base. France finds it necessary to build a Pacific Empire.

Since the Washington Conference,* colonial rivalries have become sharper and sharper, imperialist follies greater and greater, and political conflicts more and more unavoidable. Wars have been launched over India, Africa, and Morocco. Other wars may break out over the Pacific area if the proletariat is not watchful.

LYNCHING†

A LITTLE-KNOWN ASPECT OF AMERICAN CIVILIZATION

It is well known that the black race is the most oppressed and most exploited of the human family. It is well known that the spread of capitalism and the discovery of the New World had as an immediate result the rebirth of slavery which was, for centuries, a scourge for the Negroes and a bitter disgrace for mankind. What everyone does not perhaps know, is that after sixty-five years of so-called emancipation, American Negroes still endure atrocious moral and material sufferings, of which the most cruel and horrible is the custom of lynching.

The word "lynching" comes from Lynch. Lynch was the name of a planter in Virginia, a landlord and judge. Availing himself of the troubles of the War of Independence, he took the control of the whole district into his hands. He inflicted the most savage punishment, without trial or process of law, on Loyalists and Tories. Thanks to the slave-traders, the Ku Klux Klan, and other secret societies, the illegal and barbarous practice of lynching is spreading and continuing widely in the States of the American Union. It has become more inhuman since the emancipation of the Blacks, and is especially directed at the latter.

Imagine a furious horde. Fists clenched, eyes bloodshot, mouths foaming, yells, insults, curses. . . . This horde is transported with the wild delight of a crime to be committed without risk. They are armed with sticks, torches,

* The conference held from November 12, 1921, to February 6, 1922, and attended by the United States, the United Kingdom, Japan, France, Italy, China, Belgium, Portugal, and the Netherlands.
† Printed in *La Correspondance Internationale*, No. 59, 1924.

revolvers, ropes, knives, scissors, vitriol, daggers; in a word, with all that can be used to kill or wound.

Imagine in this human sea a flotsam of black flesh pushed about, beaten, trampled underfoot, torn, slashed, insulted, tossed hither and thither, bloodstained, dead.

The horde are the lynchers. The human rag is the Black, the victim.

In a wave of hatred and bestiality, the lynchers drag the Black to a wood or a public place. They tie him to a tree, pour kerosene over him, cover him with inflammable material. While waiting for the fire to be kindled, they smash his teeth, one by one. Then they gouge out his eyes. Little tufts of crinkly hair are torn from his head, carrying away with them bits of skin, baring a bloody skull. Little pieces of flesh come off his body, already contused from the blows.

The Black can no longer shout: his tongue has been swollen by a red hot iron. His whole body ripples, trembling, like a half-crushed snake. A slash with a knife: one of his ears falls to the ground. . . . Oh! How black he is! How awful! And the ladies tear at his face. . . .

"Light up," shouts someone. "Just enough to cook him slowly," adds another.

The Black is roasted, browned, burned. But he deserves to die twice instead of once. He is therefore hanged, or more exactly, what is left of his corpse is hanged. And all those who were not able to help with the cooking applaud now.

Hurrah!

When everybody has had enough, the corpse is brought down. The rope is cut into small pieces which will be sold for three or five dollars each. Souvenirs and lucky charms quarreled over by ladies.

"Popular justice," as they say over there, has been done. Calmed down, the crowd congratulate the "organizers," then stream away slowly and cheerfully, as if after a feast, make appointments with one another for the next time.

While on the ground, stinking of fat and smoke, a black head, mutilated, roasted, deformed, grins horribly and seems to ask the setting sun, "Is this civilization?"

SOME STATISTICS

From 1889 to 1919, 2,600 Blacks were lynched, including 51 women and girls and ten former Great War soldiers.

Among 78 Blacks lynched in 1919, 11 were burned alive, three burned after having been killed, 31 shot, three tortured to death, one cut into pieces, one drowned, and 11 put to death by various means.

Georgia heads the list with 22 victims, Mississippi follows with 12. Both have also three lynched soldiers to their credit. Of 11 burned alive, the first State has four and the second two. Out of 34 cases of systematic, premeditated and organized lynching, it is still Georgia that holds first place with five. Mississippi comes second with three.

Among the charges brought against the victims of 1919, we note: one of having been a member of the League of Non-Partisans (independent farmers); one of having distributed revolutionary publications; one of expressing his opinion on lynchings too freely; one of having criticized the clashes between Whites and Blacks in Chicago; one of having been known as a leader of the cause of the Blacks; one for not getting out of the way and thus frightening a white child who was in a motorcar. In 1920, there were fifty lynchings, and in 1923, twenty-eight.

These crimes were all motivated by economic jealousy. Either the Negroes in the area were more prosperous than the Whites, or the black workers would not let themselves be exploited thoroughly. In all cases, the principal culprits were never troubled, for the simple reason that they were always incited, encouraged, spurred on, then protected, by the politicians, financiers, and authorities, and above all, by the reactionary press.

When a lynching was to take place or had taken place, the press seized upon it as a good occasion to increase the number of copies printed. It related the affair with a wealth of detail. Not the slightest reproach to the criminals. Not a word of pity for the victims. Not a commentary.

The *New Orleans States* of June 26, 1919, published a headline running right across the front page in letters five inches high: "Today a Negro Will Be Burned by 3,000 Citizens." And immediately underneath, in very small print: "Under a strong escort, the Kaiser has taken flight with the Crown Prince."

The *Jackson Daily News* of the same date published across the first two columns of its front page in big letters: "Negro J. H. to Be Burned by the Crowd at Ellistown This Afternoon at 5 P.M."

The newspaper only neglected to add: "The whole population is earnestly invited to attend." But the spirit is there.

APPEAL MADE ON THE OCCASION OF THE FOUNDING OF THE COMMUNIST PARTY OF INDOCHINA*
(February 18, 1930)

Workers, peasants, soldiers, youth, and pupils!
Oppressed and exploited compatriots!
Sisters and brothers! Comrades!
Imperialist contradictions were the cause of the 1914–18 World War. After this horrible slaughter, the world was divided into two camps: One is the revolutionary camp including the oppressed colonies and the exploited working class throughout the world. The vanguard force of this camp is the Soviet Union. The other is the counterrevolutionary camp of international capitalism and imperialism whose general staff is the League of Nations.

During this World War, various nations suffered untold losses in property and human lives. The French imperialists were the hardest hit. Therefore, in order to restore the capitalist forces in France, the French imperialists have resorted to every underhand scheme to intensify their capitalist exploitation in Indochina. They set up new factories to exploit the workers with low wages. They plundered the peasants' land to establish plantations and drive them to utter poverty. They levied many heavy taxes. They imposed public loans upon our people. In short, they reduced us to wretchedness. They increased their military forces, firstly to strangle the Vietnamese revolution, secondly to prepare for a new imperialist war in the Pacific aimed at capturing new colonies, thirdly to suppress the Chinese revolution, fourthly to attack the Soviet Union because the latter helps the revolution of the oppressed nations and the exploited working class. World War II will break out.

* The Communist Party of Indochina, founded on February 3, 1930, was the outcome of the conference convened in Hong Kong by the Communist International. This historic conference merged the three Communist groups in the three parts of Viet-Nam (North, Center, and South) into a single Communist Party. Comrade Nguyen Ai Quoc was charged by the Communist International to attend the conference. Basing itself on Nguyen Ai Quoc's proposals, the conference approved of the general political thesis on the revolutionary line in Viet-Nam at that stage and decided to unify the Party under the name of the Communist Party of Indochina, to draft the Party's political program, its constitution, and the statutes of various mass organizations, and to appoint the Party's Provisional Central Committee.

When it breaks, the French imperialists will certainly drive our people to a more horrible slaughter. If we give them a free hand to prepare for this war, suppress the Chinese revolution, and attack the Soviet Union, if we give them a free hand to stifle the Vietnamese revolution, it is tantamount to giving them a free hand to wipe our race off the earth and drown our nation in the Pacific.

However the French imperialists' barbarous oppression and ruthless exploitation have awakened our compatriots, who have all realized that revolution is the only road to life, without it they will die out piecemeal. This is the reason why the Vietnamese revolutionary movement has grown even stronger with each passing day. The workers refuse to work, the peasants demand land, the pupils strike, the traders boycott. Everywhere the masses have risen to oppose the French imperialists.

The Vietnamese revolution has made the French imperialists tremble with fear. On the one hand, they utilize the feudalists and comprador bourgeois in our country to oppress and exploit our people. On the other, they terrorize, arrest, jail, deport, and kill a great number of Vietnamese revolutionaries. If the French imperialists think that they can suppress the Vietnamese revolution by means of terrorist acts, they are utterly mistaken. Firstly, it is because the Vietnamese revolution is not isolated but enjoys the assistance of the world proletarian class in general and of the French working class in particular. Secondly, while the French imperialists are frenziedly carrying out terrorist acts, the Vietnamese Communists, formerly working separately, have now united into a single party, the Communist Party of Indochina, to lead our entire people in their revolution.

Workers, peasants, soldiers, youth, pupils!

Oppressed and exploited compatriots!

The Communist Party of Indochina is founded. It is the party of the working class. It will help the proletarian class to lead the revolution in order to struggle for all the oppressed and exploited people. From now on we must join the Party, help it and follow it in order to implement the following slogans:

1. To overthrow French imperialism, feudalism, and the reactionary Vietnamese capitalist class.

2. To make Indochina completely independent.

3. To establish a worker-peasant and soldier government.

4. To confiscate the banks and other enterprises belonging to the imperialists and put them under the control of the worker-peasant and soldier government.

5. To confiscate the whole of the plantations and property belonging to the imperialists and the Vietnamese reactionary capitalist class and distribute them to poor peasants.

6. To implement the eight-hour working day.

7. To abolish public loans and poll tax. To waive unjust taxes hitting the poor people.

8. To bring back all freedoms to the masses.

9. To carry out universal education.

10. To implement equality between man and woman.

DECLARATION OF INDEPENDENCE OF THE DEMOCRATIC REPUBLIC OF VIET-NAM*
(September 2, 1945)

All men are created equal; they are endowed by their Creator with certain unalienable Rights; among these are Life, Liberty, and the pursuit of Happiness.

This immortal statement was made in the Declaration of Independence of the United States of America in 1776. In a broader sense, this means: All the peoples on the earth are equal from birth, all the peoples have a right to live, to be happy and free.

The Declaration of the French Revolution made in 1791 on the Rights of Man and the Citizen also states: "All men are born free and with equal rights, and must always remain free and have equal rights."

Those are undeniable truths.

Nevertheless, for more than eighty years, the French imperialists, abusing the standard of Liberty, Equality, and Fraternity, have violated our Fatherland and oppressed our fellow citizens. They have acted contrary to the ideals of humanity and justice.

In the field of politics, they have deprived our people of every democratic liberty.

They have enforced inhuman laws; they have set up three

* *The borrowing from the United States Declaration of Independence was open and intended. American members of the OSS mission parachuted to Ho in the summer of 1945 recall several of Ho's attempts to obtain a copy of the Declaration, or, failing this, a close approximation of its essential passages.*—ED.

distinct political regimes in the North, the Center, and the South of Viet-Nam in order to wreck our national unity and prevent our people from being united.

They have built more prisons than schools. They have mercilessly slain our patriots; they have drowned our uprisings in rivers of blood.

They have fettered public opinion; they have practiced obscurantism against our people.

To weaken our race they have forced us to use opium and alcohol.

In the field of economics, they have fleeced us to the backbone, impoverished our people and devastated our land.

They have robbed us of our rice fields, our mines, our forests, and our raw materials. They have monopolized the issuing of bank notes and the export trade.

They have invented numerous unjustifiable taxes and reduced our people, especially our peasantry, to a state of extreme poverty.

They have hampered the prospering of our national bourgeoisie; they have mercilessly exploited our workers.

In the autumn of 1940, when the Japanese fascists violated Indochina's territory to establish new bases in their fight against the Allies, the French imperialists went down on their bended knees and handed over our country to them.

Thus, from that date, our people were subjected to the double yoke of the French and the Japanese. Their sufferings and miseries increased. The result was that, from the end of last year to the beginning of this year, from Quang Tri Province to the North of Viet-Nam, more than two million of our fellow citizens died from starvation. On March 9 [1945], the French troops were disarmed by the Japanese. The French colonialists either fled or surrendered, showing that not only were they incapable of "protecting" us, but that, in the span of five years, they had twice sold our country to the Japanese.

On several occasions before March 9, the Viet Minh League urged the French to ally themselves with it against the Japanese. Instead of agreeing to this proposal, the French colonialists so intensified their terrorist activities against the Viet Minh members that before fleeing they massacred a great number of our political prisoners detained at Yen Bay and Cao Bang.

Notwithstanding all this, our fellow citizens have always manifested toward the French a tolerant and humane attitude. Even after the Japanese *Putsch* of March, 1945, the Viet Minh League helped many Frenchmen to cross the frontier, rescued some of them from Japanese jails, and protected French lives and property.

From the autumn of 1940, our country had in fact ceased to be a French colony and had become a Japanese possession.

After the Japanese had surrendered to the Allies, our whole people rose to regain our national sovereignty and to found the Democratic Republic of Viet-Nam.

The truth is that we have wrested our independence from the Japanese and not from the French.

The French have fled, the Japanese have capitulated, Emperor Bao Dai has abdicated. Our people have broken the chains which for nearly a century have fettered them and have won independence for the Fatherland. Our people at the same time have overthrown the monarchic regime that has reigned supreme for dozens of centuries. In its place has been established the present Democratic Republic.

For these reasons, we, members of the Provisional Government, representing the whole Vietnamese people, declare that from now on we break off all relations of a colonial character with France; we repeal all the international obligation that France has so far subscribed to on behalf of Viet-Nam, and we abolish all the special rights the French have unlawfully acquired in our Fatherland.

The whole Vietnamese people, animated by a common purpose, are determined to fight to the bitter end against any attempt by the French colonialists to reconquer their country.

We are convinced that the Allied nations, which at Teheran and San Francisco have acknowledged the principles of self-determination and equality of nations, will not refuse to acknowledge the independence of Viet-Nam.

A people who have courageously opposed French domination for more than eighty years, a people who have fought side by side with the Allies against the fascists during these last years, such a people must be free and independent.

For these reasons, we, members of the Provisional Government of the Democratic Republic of Viet-Nam, solemnly declare to the world that Viet-Nam has the right to be a free and independent country—and in fact it is so already. The entire Vietnamese people are determined to mobilize all their physical and mental strength, to sacrifice their lives and property in order to safeguard their independence and liberty.

TWELVE RECOMMENDATIONS
(April 5, 1948)

The nation has its root in the people.

In the Resistance War and national reconstruction, the main force lies in the people. Therefore, all the people in the army, administration, and mass organizations who are in contact or live with the people must remember and carry out the following twelve recommendations.

Six forbiddances:

1. Not to do what is likely to damage the land and crops or spoil the houses and belongings of the people.

2. Not to insist on buying or borrowing what the people are not willing to sell or lend.

3. Not to bring living hens into the mountain people's houses.

4. Never to break your word.

5. Not to give offense to people's faith and customs (such as to lie down before the altar, to raise the feet over the hearth, to play music in the house, etc.).

6. Not to do or speak what is likely to make people believe that we hold them in contempt.

Six permissibles:

1. To help the people in their daily work (harvesting, fetching firewood, carrying water, sewing, etc.).

2. Whenever possible, to buy commodities for those who live far from markets (knives, salt, needles, thread, pen, paper, etc.).

3. In spare time, to tell amusing, simple, and short stories useful to the Resistance, but not betraying secrets.

4. To teach the population the national script and elementary hygiene.

5. To study the customs of each region so as to be acquainted with them in order to create an atmosphere of sympathy first, then gradually to explain to the people to abate their superstitions.

6. To show to the people that you are correct, diligent, and disciplined.

STIMULATING POEM

The above-mentioned twelve recommendations
Are feasible to all.
He who loves his country,

Will never forget them.
When the people have a habit,
All are like one man.
With good armymen and good people,
Everything will be crowned with success.
Only when the root is firm, can the tree live long,
And victory is built with the people as foundation.

Herbert Marcuse
(1898–   )

*Born and educated in Berlin, Herbert Marcuse later spent
ten years with the United States Office of Intelligence Research (State Department) in Washington; Marcuse was a
Research Fellow at Columbia and is currently professor of
political thought at the University of California.*

On Humanism

Socialism cannot be made humanistic by committing socialist policy to the traditional humanistic values. In the
situation of coexistence (which must be the framework for
any nonideological analysis), such humanization is bound
to be ideological and self-defeating. Here, a distinction
must be made between capitalist and socialist humanism.
In the capitalist world, the fight for the rights of man, for
freedom of speech and assembly, for equality before the
law, which marked the beginning of the liberal era, is again
a desperate concern at its end, when it becomes evident to
what extent these liberties have remained restricted and

From *Socialist Humanism*, edited by Eric Fromm, New York,
1965.

denied. And this fight is hampered to the degree to which it respects, in its own action and suffering, the liberal values and the legality which the adversary meets with unpunished violence. In the communist world, the assertion of individual rights and liberties and of the initiative of the laboring classes would promote (and should promote) radical dissent and opposition to the economic and political repression on which the established regime depends, and which it considers as prerequisite for defense and growth in competitive coexistence. According to this logic, effective dissent and opposition within the communist societies would alter the precarious international balance in favor of capitalism—which would not necessarily brighten the prospects of socialist humanism. For the laboring classes are no longer those to whom the revolution once appealed, and their initiative is not likely to revive international socialist solidarity.

These are the given historical conditions which a discussion of the failures and chances of socialist humanism must face if it does not want to deal with mere ideologies. Advanced industrial society can take care of humanistic values while continuing to pursue its inhuman goals: it promotes culture and personalities together with toil, injustice, nuclear armament, total indoctrination, self-propelling productivity. The intensity with which the powers that be mobilize the underlying population against their liberation goes hand in hand with the growing capabilities of society to accomplish this liberation. In as much as these capabilities are utilized (or suppressed) in the interest of domination, of the defense of the status quo, they remain technical capabilities, barred from their humanistic realization. As technical capabilities, they define the prospects of socialist humanism. Severance of the fatal link between technical progress and progress in domination and exploitation is the precondition. Humanism must remain ideology as long as society depends on continued poverty, arrested automation, mass media, prevented birth control, and on the creation and re-creation of masses, of noise and pollution, of planned obsolescence and waste, and of mental and physical rearmament. These conditions and institutions are the social controls which sustain and extend the prevailing state of affairs. Consequently, their abrogation on behalf of humanism would be revolutionary subversion, and this subversion would also subvert the very needs and necessities of human existence. What appeared, in the pre-totalitarian era, as the precondition of freedom may well turn out to be its substance, its historical content. For the substance of freedom as well as humanism must be defined in terms of the human beings in their society, and in terms of their capabilities. Advanced industrial society is a society in which the technical apparatus of production and distribution has become a totalitarian political apparatus, coordinating and managing all dimensions of life, free time as well as working time, negative as well as positive thinking. To the victims, beneficiaries, and heirs of such a society, the realm of freedom has lost its classical content, its qualitative difference from the realm of necessity. It is the work world, the technical world which they must first make their own: the realm of necessity must become the realm of their freedom. The technical apparatus of production, distribution, and consumption must be reconstructed. Technological rationality must be redirected to make the work world a place for human beings who one day may perhaps be willing to live in peace and do away with the masters who guide them to desist from this effort. This means not "humanization" of labor but its mechanization and planned production for the emergence of new needs—those of pacification of the struggle for existence. Some aspects of the new technology can be delineated: the complete rebuilding of cities and towns, the reconstruction of the countryside after the ravages of repressive industrialization, the institution of truly public services, the care for the sick and the aged.

The failure of humanism seems to be due to overdevelopment rather than backwardness; once the productive apparatus, under repressive direction, has grown into an apparatus of ubiquitous controls, democratic or authoritarian, the chances of a humanistic reconstruction are very poor. This situation accentuates the historical truth of the Marxian conception. The humanistic chance of socialism is objectively grounded neither in the socialization of the means of production nor in their control by the "immediate producers"—although these are necessary prerequisites —but rather in the existence, *prior* to these changes, of social classes whose life is the very negation of humanity, and whose consciousness and practice are determined by the need to abnegate this condition. The totalitarian-technological stage has not altered this truth: no matter how "technical" the basis of socialism has become, no matter how much it is a matter of the redirection and even reversal of technical progress and technological rationality—these are political tasks, involving radical changes in the society as a whole. Technical progress occurs as political progress in domination; thus it is progress in the suppression of the alternatives. The fact that, in the most advanced areas of industrial civilization, this suppression is no longer terroristic but democratic, introjected, productive, and even satisfying does not change this condition. If suppression is compatible with individual autonomy and operates through individual autonomy, then the *Nomos* (norm) which the individual gives himself is that of servitude. This *Nomos,* which is the law of our time, outlaws the pacification of the struggle for existence, national and international, among societies and among individuals. Competition must go on—for profit and power, for work and fun, for the bigger and better deterrent, and it increases the productivity of the whole, which in turn perpetuates this sort of competition and promises the transformation of its victims into its beneficiaries, who will then do their best to make their contribution. And to the degree to which the other societies are forced into the same circle, the qualitative difference between socialism and capitalism is being obliterated by the sweep of a productivity which improves the standard of living through improved exploitation.

Socialist theory has no right to denounce, in the name of other historical possibilities, growing social productivity which allows a better life for more sections of the population. But the question here is not that of future possibilities; it is the present reality which is at stake. In this reality, the denial of humanity spreads through all achievements: it is the daily preparedness for annihilation, in the equipment for a subterranean existence, in the ever more ingenious planning of waste, in the inescapable inanities of the Media, in the abolition of privacy, and—perhaps the most effective denial of all—in the helpless awareness of all this, in public acknowledgment and criticism, which are impotent and contribute to the power of the whole, if they are not crushed and silenced by force. Thus the need for liberation exists: it exists as universal need far beyond that of one particular class—but it exists only "in itself," not *for* the individuals in need. Socialism appears again as an abstract idea; loyalty to its idea excludes the fostering of illusions. Its new abstractness does not signify falsification. The proletariat which was to validate the equation of socialism and humanism pertained to a past stage in the development of industrial society. Socialist theory, no matter how true, can neither prescribe nor predict the future agents of a historical transformation which is more than ever before the specter that haunts the established societies. But socialist theory can show that this specter is the image of a vital need; it can develop and protect the consciousness of this need and thus lay the groundwork for the dissolution of the false unity in defense of the status quo.

Interview

Q. You have been bracketed with Marx and Mao. When people talk of the "Three M's" what is your reaction?

Marcuse I do not understand. Marx? I have studied his work deeply. But Mao? Certainly today every Marxist who is not a communist of strict obedience is a Maoist. I have always thought there was an alternative, and in my books I have not kept to the old Marxist ideology. Socialist societies as they are set up today do not seem to me what I call "qualitatively different" from other capitalist societies. They allow one type of domination to exist instead of another; that is all. True socialism is something else again. I am convinced that it is possible from now on to construct a truly socialist society without going through a Stalinist type period. A socialist society must be founded on true solidarity, on true cooperation: the Cuban revolution seems to me to be moving in that direction. As for "Che," he was the symbol of it, very far from the Stalinist bureaucrats, very near to socialist man.

Q. Are you only trying to explain the world we live in, or are you also trying to change it?

Marcuse That is a big question. Every real explanation must lead to the search for a transformation, and there is evidently an interior relation between the explanation and the transformation. For myself, it is true that for a long time now I have not been a militant activist. I write, I teach, I give lectures, I talk to the students: these are normal activities of an intellectual in the United States because in that country the situation is in no sense revolu-

From interview with Pierre Viansson-Ponte, translated by Anne Fremantle, *Le Monde*, Paris, June 1969.

tionary, it is not even pre-revolutionary. Therefore an intellectual's duty is first of all a mission of radical education. We are, in America, entering into a new "period of illumination."

Q. And in Europe?

Marcuse In Europe, the situation is different because there politics are still largely determined by the working class. Also, there are big differences between one country and another: West Germany is very close to the American "model," Italy is fairly close, France is much further away. I know Rudi Dutschke and his friends well, and the boys of the SDS, the left-wing student organisation. He is very kind, very sensitive, not at all a demagogue. And he is someone who has done a lot of work and thought a lot; for him and his comrades, the link between theory and action is solidly established. It is said that they took months to forge it. This is not true: they took eight years. In France, have your angry students also worked? Have they also established solid ideological bases? I do not have the impression that they have.

Q. Have you sometimes the feeling of having been overtaken by those who proclaim your theses?

Marcuse Perhaps. If they are violent, it is because they are desperate. And despair powers effective political action. Take the inhabitants of the black ghettoes in the US; they set fire to their own areas, they burn their own houses. This is not a revolutionary action, but it is an act of despair, and a political act. Moreover, in the USA, the uneasiness is not limited to students. The students are not in revolt against a poor and badly organized society, but against a quite rich society quite well organized in its luxury and waste, while 25% of the population live in the poverty of the ghettoes. Their revolt is not directed against the misery which this society provokes, but against its benefits. This is a new phenomenon, belonging only to what is called "the opulent society." In Germany, the process is the same. In France, I do not think it is, because French society is not yet an affluent society.

Q. What do you think about what has been called, by analogy with "Black Power," "Student Power"?

Marcuse That slogan seems dangerous to me. Everywhere, always, the great majority of students is conservative, even reactionary. Therefore "student power," if it were democratic, would be conservative, even reactionary. "Student power" means that the left in no way opposes the

University administration, but opposes the students themselves. Otherwise it would be necessary for it to outflank the democratic process. There is here a fundamental contradiction.

Q. What is, in your opinion, the basic reason for these violent student demonstrations in so many countries?

Marcuse For American and West German students, whom I know better, it is a requirement that is not merely intellectual, but "instinctual." They want an entirely different kind of existence. They reject a life that is simply a struggle for existence, they refuse to enter what the English call the Establishment, because they think it is no longer necessary. They feel their whole life will be overwhelmed by the requirements of the industrial society and exclusively in the interests of big business, the military and the politicians. Take the hippies. Their rebellion is directed against puritan morality, against American society where one washes ten times a day, and at the same time burns and kills in Vietnam purely and simply. So they methodically protest against this hypocrisy by keeping their hair long, growing beards, not washing and refusing to go to war. To them the contradictions are blinding. But, as with the students, this is true only of a very small minority. The students know that society absorbs opposition and offers the irrational as rational. They feel more or less clearly that the "one dimensional" man has lost his power of negation, his possibility of saying no. So they refuse to let themselves become integrated in this society.

Q. What reply would you give to students if they came to you and asked whether their manifestations make sense and could help to transform society?

Marcuse I would tell them first that one cannot expect anything but big manifestations like those which are taking place pretty well everywhere, even in France, in a situation which is not even pre- or counter-revolutionary. But I am not a defeatist, ever. In the US, the growing opposition to the Vietnam war has already succeeded in provoking, at least in part, change in American policy. One must not have illusions; but one must not be defeatist, either. It is useless to expect, in such a confrontation, that the masses should join the movement and participate in the process. Something of the kind can be seen, it seems to me, in the present student revolts. Yet they are completely spontaneous revolts. In the United States there is no coordination, no organization acting on a national scale, nor even on a statewide scale, and one is very far from any kind of international organization. This kind of revolt certainly does not lead to the creation of a revolutionary force. But it converges with the movements of the "Third World" and with activity in the ghettoes. It is a powerful force for disintegration.

Milovan Djilas
(1911–   )

Yugoslav writer and politician, Milovan Djilas became a member of the Communist Party in 1932, was imprisoned 1932–1935, and became a member of the Politburo in 1940. Djilas fought with the Resistance against the Germans (1939–1945). He was vice-president of Yugoslavia 1945–1954. In 1954 he was expelled from the Communist Party. Djilas wrote The New Class *and* Conversations with Stalin *while in jail from 1956 to 1962.*

The New Class

1.

Everything happened differently in the U.S.S.R. and other communist countries from what the leaders—even such prominent ones as Lenin, Stalin, Trotsky, and Bukharin—anticipated. They expected that the state would rapidly wither away, that democracy would be strengthened. The reverse happened. They expected a rapid improvement in

From *Essential Works of Marxism*, edited by Arthur P. Mendel, New York, 1965.

the standard of living—there has been scarcely any change in this respect and, in the subjugated East European countries, the standard has even declined. In every instance, the standard of living has failed to rise in proportion to the rate of industrialization, which was much more rapid. It was believed that the differences between cities and villages, between intellectual and physical labor, would slowly disappear; instead these differences have increased. Communist anticipations in other areas—including their expectations for developments in the noncommunist world—have also failed to materialize.

The greatest illusion was that industrialization and collectivization in the U.S.S.R., and destruction of capitalist ownership, would result in a classless society. In 1936, when the new Constitution was promulgated, Stalin announced that the "exploiting class" had ceased to exist. The capitalist and other classes of ancient origin had in fact been destroyed, but a new class, previously unknown to history, had been formed.

It is understandable that this class, like those before it, should believe that the establishment of its power would result in happiness and freedom for all men. The only difference between this and other classes was that it treated the delay in the realization of its illusions more crudely. It thus affirmed that its power was more complete than the power of any other class before in history, and its class illusions and prejudices were proportionally greater.

This new class, the bureaucracy, or more accurately the political bureaucracy, has all the characteristics of earlier ones as well as some new characteristics of its own. Its origin had its special characteristics also, even though in essence it was similar to the beginnings of other classes.

Other classes, too, obtained their strength and power by the revolutionary path, destroying the political, social, and other orders they met in their way. However, almost without exception, these classes attained power *after* new economic patterns had taken shape in the old society. The case was the reverse with the new class in the communist systems. It did not come to power to *complete* a new economic order but to *establish* its own and, in so doing, to establish its power over society. . . .

2.

The social origin of the new class lies in the proletariat just as the aristocracy arose in a peasant society, and the bourgeoisie in a commercial and artisans' society. There are exceptions, depending on national conditions, but the proletariat in economically underdeveloped countries, being backward, constitutes the raw material from which the new class arises.

There are other reasons why the new class always acts as the champion of the working class. The new class is anticapitalistic and, consequently, logically dependent upon the working strata. The new class is supported by the proletarian struggle and the traditional faith of the proletariat in a socialist, communist society where there is no brutal exploitation. It is vitally important for the new class to assure a normal flow of production, hence it cannot ever lose its connection with the proletariat. Most important of all, the new class cannot achieve industrialization and consolidate its power without the help of the working class. On the other hand, the working class sees in expanded industry the salvation from its poverty and despair. Over a long period of time, the interests, ideas, faith, and hope of the new class, and of parts of the working class and of the poor peasants, coincide and unite. Such mergers have occurred in the past among other widely different classes. Did not the bourgeoisie represent the peasantry in the struggle against the feudal lords?

The movement of the new class toward power comes as a result of the efforts of the proletariat and the poor. These are the masses upon which the party or the new class must lean and with which its interests are most closely allied. This is true until the new class finally establishes its power and authority. Over and above this, the new class is interested in the proletariat and the poor only to the extent necessary for developing production and for maintaining in subjugation the most aggressive and rebellious social forces.

The monopoly which the new class establishes in the name of the working class over the whole of society is, primarily, a monopoly over the working class itself. This monopoly is first intellectual, over the so-called *avant-garde* proletariat, and then over the whole proletariat. This is the biggest deception the class must accomplish, but it shows that the power and interests of the new class lie primarily in industry. Without industry the new class cannot consolidate its position or authority.

Former sons of the working class are the most steadfast members of the new class. It has always been the fate of slaves to provide for their masters the most clever and gifted representatives. In this case a new exploiting and governing class is born from the exploited class.

3.

When communist systems are being critically analyzed, it is considered that their fundamental distinction lies in the fact that a bureaucracy, organized in a special stratum, rules over the people. This is generally true. However, a more detailed analysis will show that only a special stratum of bureaucrats, those who are not administrative officials, makes up the core of the governing bureaucracy, or, in my terminology, of the new class. This is actually a party or political bureaucracy. Other officials are only the apparatus under the control of the new class; the apparatus may be clumsy and slow but, no matter what, it must exist in every socialist society. It is sociologically possible to draw the borderline between the different types of officials, but in practice they are practically indistinguishable. This is true not only because the communist system by its very nature is bureaucratic, but because communists handle the various important administrative functions. In addition, the stratum of political bureaucrats cannot enjoy their privileges if they do not give crumbs from their tables to other bureaucratic categories. . . .

. . . The bureaucrats in a noncommunist state are officials in modern capitalist economy, while the communists are something different and new: a new class.

As in other owning classes, the proof that it is a special class lies in its ownership and its special relations to other classes. In the same way, the class to which a member belongs is indicated by the material and other privileges which ownership brings to him.

As defined by Roman law, property constitutes the use, enjoyment, and disposition of material goods. The communist political bureaucracy uses, enjoys, and disposes of nationalized property.

If we assume that membership in this bureaucracy or new

owning class is predicated on the use of privileges inherent in ownership—in this instance nationalized material goods —then membership in the new party class, or political bureaucracy, is reflected in a larger income in material goods and privileges than society should normally grant for such functions. In practice, the ownership privilege of the new class manifests itself as an exclusive right, as a party monopoly, for the political bureaucracy to distribute the national income, to set wages, direct economic development, and dispose of nationalized and other property. This is the way it appears to the ordinary man who considers the communist functionary as being very rich and as a man who does not have to work.

The ownership of private property has, for many reasons, proved to be unfavorable for the establishment of the new class's authority. Besides, the destruction of private ownership was necessary for the economic transformation of nations. The new class obtains its power, privileges, ideology, and its customs from one specific form of ownership—collective ownership—which the class administers and distributes in the name of the nation and society.

The new class maintains that ownership derives from a designated social relationship. This is the relationship between the monopolists of administration, who constitute a narrow and closed stratum, and the mass of producers (farmers, workers, and intelligentsia) who have no rights. But that is not all, since the communist bureaucracy also has complete monopolistic control over material assets.

Every substantive change in the social relationship between those who monopolize administration and those who work is inevitably reflected in the ownership relationship. . . .

4.

The development of modern communism, and the emergence of the new class, is evident in the character and roles of those who inspired it.

The leaders and their methods, from Marx to Khrushchev, have been varied and changing. It never occurred to Marx to prevent others from voicing their ideas. Lenin tolerated free discussion in his party and did not think that party forums, let alone the party head, should regulate the expression of "proper" or "improper" ideas. Stalin abolished every type of intraparty discussion, and made the expression of ideology solely the right of the central forum—or of himself. Other communist movements were different. For instance, Marx's International Workers' Union (the so-called First International) was not Marxist in ideology, but a union of varied groups which adopted only the resolutions on which its members agreed. Lenin's party was an *avant-garde* group combining an internal revolutionary morality and ideological monolithic structure with democracy of a kind. Under Stalin the party became a mass of ideologically disinterested men, who got their ideas from above, but were wholehearted and unanimous in the defense of a system that assured them unquestionable privileges. Marx actually never created a party; Lenin destroyed all parties except his own, including the Socialist Party. Stalin relegated even the Bolshevik Party to second rank, transforming its core into the core of the new class, and transforming the party into a privileged impersonal and colorless group.

Marx created a system of the roles of classes, and of class war in society, even though he did not discover them, and he saw that mankind is mostly made up of members of discernible classes, although he was only restating Terence's Stoic philosophy: *"Humani nihil a me alienum puto."* Lenin viewed men as sharing ideas rather than as being members of discernible classes. Stalin saw in men only obedient subjects or enemies. Marx died a poor emigrant in London, but was valued by learned men and valued in the movement; Lenin died as the leader of one of the greatest revolutions, but died as a dictator about whom a cult had already begun to form; when Stalin died, he had already transformed himself into a god.

These changes in personalities are only the reflection of changes which had already taken place and were the very soul of the communist movement.

Although he did not realize it, Lenin started the organization of the new class. He established the party along Bolshevik lines and developed the theories of its unique and leading role in the building of a new society. This is but one aspect of his many-sided and gigantic work; it is the aspect which came about from his actions rather than his wishes. It is also the aspect which led the new class to revere him.

The real and direct originator of the new class, however, was Stalin. He was a man of quick reflexes and a tendency to coarse humor, not very educated nor a good speaker.

But he was a relentless dogmatician and a great administrator, a Georgian who knew better than anyone else whither the new powers of Greater Russia were taking her. He created the new class by the use of the most barbaric means, not even sparing the class itself. It was inevitable that the new class which placed him at the top would later submit to his unbridled and brutal nature. He was the true leader of that class as long as the class was building itself up, and attaining power.

The new class was born in the revolutionary struggle in the Communist Party, but was developed in the industrial revolution. Without the revolution, without industry, the class's position would not have been secure and its power would have been limited.

While the country was being industrialized, Stalin began to introduce considerable variations in wages, at the same time allowing the development toward various privileges to proceed. He thought that industrialization would come to nothing if the new class were not made materially interested in the process, by acquisition of some property for itself. Without industrialization the new class would find it difficult to hold its position, for it would have neither historical justification nor the material resources for its continued existence.

The increase in the membership of the party, or of the bureaucracy, was closely connected with this. In 1927, on the eve of industrialization, the Soviet Communist Party had 887,233 members. In 1934, at the end of the First Five Year Plan, the membership had increased to 1,874,488. This was a phenomenon obviously connected with industrialization: the prospects for the new class and privileges for its members were improving. What is more, the privileges and the class were expanding more rapidly than industrialization itself. It is difficult to cite any statistics on this point, but the conclusion is self-evident for anyone who bears in mind that the standard of living has not kept pace with industrial production, while the new class actually seized the lion's share of the economic and other progress earned by the sacrifices and efforts of the masses.

The establishment of the new class did not proceed smoothly. It encountered bitter opposition from existing classes and from those revolutionaries who could not reconcile reality with the ideals of their struggle. In the U.S.S.R. the opposition of revolutionaries was most evident in the Trotsky–Stalin conflict. The conflict between Trotsky and Stalin, or between oppositionists in the party and

Stalin, as well as the conflict between the regime and the peasantry, became more intense as industrialization advanced and the power and authority of the new class increased.

Trotsky, an excellent speaker, brilliant stylist, and skilled polemicist, a man cultured and of excellent intelligence, was deficient in only one quality: a sense of reality. He wanted to be a revolutionary in a period when life imposed the commonplace. He wished to revive a revolutionary party which was being transformed into something completely different, into a new class unconcerned with great ideals and interested only in the everyday pleasures of life. He expected action from a mass already tired by war, hunger, and death, at a time when the new class already strongly held the reins and had begun to experience the sweetness of privilege. Trotsky's fireworks lit up the distant heavens; but he could not rekindle fires in weary men. He sharply noted the sorry aspect of the new phenomena but he did not grasp their meaning. In addition, he had never been a Bolshevik. This was his vice and his virtue. Attacking the party bureaucracy in the name of the revolution, he attacked the cult of the party and, although he was not conscious of it, the new class.

Stalin looked neither far ahead nor far behind. He had seated himself at the head of the new power which was being born—the new class, the political bureaucracy, and bureaucratism—and became its leader and organizer. He did not preach—he made decisions. He too promised a shining future, but one which bureaucracy could visualize as being real because its life was improving from day to day and its position was being strengthened. He spoke without ardor and color, but the new class was better able to understand this kind of realistic language. Trotsky wished to extend the revolution to Europe; Stalin was not opposed to the idea but this hazardous undertaking did not prevent him from worrying about Mother Russia or, specifically, about ways of strengthening the new system and increasing the power and reputation of the Russian state. Trotsky was a man of the revolution of the past; Stalin was a man of today and, thus, of the future.

In Stalin's victory Trotsky saw the Thermidorian reaction against the revolution, actually the bureaucratic corruption of the Soviet government and the revolutionary cause. Consequently, he understood and was deeply hurt by the amorality of Stalin's methods. Trotsky was the first, although he was not aware of it, who in the attempt to save the

communist movement discovered the essence of contemporary communism. But he was not capable of seeing it
through to the end. He supposed that this was only a
momentary cropping up of bureaucracy, corrupting the
party and the revolution, and concluded that the solution
was in a change at the top, in a "palace revolution." . . .

Roger Garaudy
(1909–   )

*Roger Garaudy is a member of the Politburo of the French
Communist Party; former senator and vice-president of the
French National Assembly; director of the Center for
Marxist Studies and Research in Paris; Professor of philosophy at Poitiers University. In 1965 he lectured at Louvain
on Catholic-Communist Dialogue. The same year he lectured at Harvard, St. Louis, and Temple Universities, and
and in Canada at Toronto. In 1968 Garaudy published a
book of Czech texts by Alexander Dubcek, Ota Sik, Jiri
Hayek, et al., entitled* La Liberté en Sursis.

Twentieth Century Marxism

Marxist materialism is in principle anti-dogmatic.
　　Marx, in his *Thesis on Feuerbach*, pointed out the principal defeat of all former forms of materialism: that of
not having seen the *active moment* of knowledge, the act
by which man, in order to know things, goes ahead of
them, projecting schemes for their perception, hypotheses
for their conception, and then verifies in practise the cor-

From *Twentieth Century Marxism*, by Roger Garaudy, translated
by Renée Hague, Scribners, New York, 1970.

rectness of his schemes, of his hypotheses, of his models. Knowledge is a construct of models and practical experience is the only criterion of the value of these models.

Marxist materialism is a call to modesty: by affirming that the world exists outside of myself and without me and that it has no need of me in order to exist, but, at the same time, by never confounding the world with the more or less complex "model" which science makes of it at every historical epoch, the knowledge which we have of it, and that every scientific conception is always a provisional construction, waiting for richer, more practical, truer constructs.

Marxist materialism—a critical philosophy because it never forgets in all the things I say about things that it is a man who says them and not a god—forbids us, as materialists, the idealistic illusion which consists in confounding, as Hegel did, our conceptual reproduction of the world, by means of models that are always approximate, with its production. . . .

The materialist moment of knowledge, according to Marx and Lenin, is subject to the criterion of practical experience, that of the experimental verification of our hypotheses, of our models, which alone can guarantee us, in the last resort, that our conceptual construction corresponds to an objective reality. As Marx wrote in his second *Thesis on Feuerbach*, "the question of knowing whether human thought can arrive at objective truth is not a theoretical question, but a practical one. It is by practical experience that man proves the truth, the power, the thusness of his thought."

Dialectical materialism is particularly distinguished from all previous forms of materialism by the fact that it takes into account the dialectical relationships between relative and absolute truths. For a Marxist every truth is at the same time both relative and absolute. Every scientific theory taking into account the phenomena of its field, is a relative truth in that sooner or later it will be overtaken by a more comprehensive and wider theory, which will reduce it to being nothing more than a particular instance of a more general truth. Further, it is an absolute truth in the sense that the theory which will go beyond it will necessarily integrate everything that it explains and on which it has given us a grasp. This "relativity," as Lenin underlined in *Materialism and Empirocriticism*, does not in any way lead to relativism. For every scientific discovery and every theory which takes it into account, constitutes a definite step forward for science and cannot be queried again and again as it has given us, and for ever, an effective ability in the handling of nature and, consequently, a reflection, an approximate reflection, of its reality.

This dialectic of the relationships between relative and absolute truth is of primary importance, because, in order not to give a false—and fatalistic—idea of scientific socialism, it is necessary to have a clear idea of what a scientific truth is. And one should not think that one can escape from scepticism and eclecticism only by taking refuge in a dogmatic rationalism, by opposing ideology to science, as the Cartesians opposed truth and error. To think that one can, once and for all, install oneself in a concept, possess all first principles, immutable and complete, and from then on progress from concept to concept, is to place oneself outside of the true forward march of science.

There exists a kernel of absolute truth, won by science, which can never be called into question, but this kernel of absolute truth—that is, the totality of the real powers we possess and the resemblance which that totality implies between the scientific models we have constructed and reality:

1.   is never complete.
2.   is present within concepts, theories and models that are constantly revisible, totally relative.

Scientific socialism, as its name suggests, lays claims to the same kind of truth as does science itself. It is a science, in fact, and like every science:

1.   it contains a kernel of absolute truth in the sense that it gives us a grasp on the phenomena it studies, which are those of history. And this authority implies a certain resemblance between the theory and the level of reality of which it is the theory.
2.   The kernel of truth is always growing.
3.   This growth does not come about by mechanical addition, but by an organic development requiring at each stage a global reorganization of concepts.

The property of dialectical reason is to formulate a reason which guides action, without determining it, and to formulate a responsible decision. Reason is not transcendant order but the continuous creation of human order.

Dialectical reason is a moment in the rational construction of reality. It is not the contemplation of an order but rather its construction. The moment of negativity, of the refusal of an already constituted order, of the rejection of the illusion of a world already entirely made outside of and without us, is an essential moment: that which affirms the increasing unity of the history of nature and of man.

It has been said that the rational is more and more the operational. For if nature is humanized, man is initially a natural being, and, consequently, the accord of his thought with the nature from which he issued and from which thought itself was born, is neither a mystery nor a miracle. Man, in one and the same movement, thinks reality and achieves his thought.

But then a problem arises: how was this dialectical reason itself constructed? Man's thought was only compelled to become dialectical in order to integrate into reality aspects of nature which rebelled against any other logic. The primacy of practical experience is again affirmed as the criterion of the truth of thought and of its adequacy, approximately at least, to reality.

Dialectic is not an *a priori* scheme to be stuck on to and imposed on things, obliging them to enter a Procustean bed. The laws of dialectic are not a closed system of thought like Aristotle's logical forms, the categories of Kant or Hegel's logic. The very principles of Marxism require that the laws of dialectic be studied, not as defining the immovable structure of an absolute Reason, but, we repeat, like a still tentative balance-sheet, for each great historical period, of the victories of reason.

It is in this critical perspective that one can speak of a dialectic of nature, but not in a dogmatic sense which would imply an arbitrary belief in the possibility of an absolute spectator outside of history.

One can speak of a dialectic of nature, for I cannot simply affirm the bare existence of original nature, as agnostics and pragmatists do.

Materiality is not only negation, limit, shock or resistance with regard to the action of thought or of practical human experience. For this negation is not arbitrary, anonymous, abstract, always identical with itself: the "thing in itself" says *no* to such a hypothesis. Sometimes also *yes*. This reply has a *practical* character: nature allows herself to be handled, or else she refuses. Acting upon one hypothesis, my action fails. Acting upon such another, I gain power over nature. It is true that hypotheses destroy each other and that no one of them can claim to reveal a final structure of being. But each dead hypothesis, simply by having been alive, has bequeathed to us a new power over nature. This power and this knowledge have survived it. The new hypothesis is heir to the one it replaced and which it has destroyed. So these powers have accumulated and my gestures of today, using these powers to handle nature, sketch in the void at least an outline of its structure, more and more subtly known. . . .

To speak of a dialectic of nature implies no arbitrary dogmatic—that is, no precritical (short-cut) extrapolation from knowledge to being. To say that there is a dialectic of nature is not to claim to know in advance, and to admit of no change in, the fundamental laws of the development of nature; on the contrary, it is, driven by irrefutable scientific discoveries only, to see in Aristotelian logic, the Euclidean postulates or the principles of classical mechanics a particular case and a moment of rationality within a dialectical rationality far more general and in constant metamorphosis.

To say that there is a dialectic of nature is to say that the structure and the movement of reality are such that only dialectical thought renders phenomena intelligible and manageable. That is an inference only.

But it is an inference based on practical human experience as a whole. . . .

An inference to be constantly revised in function of the progress of this practical experience. This is not presented as a dogma, but as a working hypothesis. . . .

Scientific laws are not the copy of some archetypal reason, like Plato's ideas, nor are they the copy of absolute laws of nature as such, of which who knows what god would be the primordial legislator. Scientific laws are not a copy of anything; they are constructions of our mind, always approximate and provisional, which allow us to understand a reality we have not created and of which practical experience alone and methodical experiment, guarantee us that our model corresponds in some measure with their structure, and are at least "isomorphs" from a certain point of view. . . .

The perspectives opened to Marxist research by structuralism and cybernetics rule out dogmatic, mechanistic interpretations of materialism and equally dogmatic, speculative, theological interpretations of dialectic.

MARXISM AND MORALITY

"To be radical is to take things by their roots, and the root, for man, is man himself."[1] . . .

The moral problem, like the problem of knowledge, is found to be inverted: when we ask ourselves what must be done to act well, we do not seek to conform ourselves to a preexisting law or an already given being. We ask ourselves what we must bring into existence which does not yet exist. This morality which is history in the making, a strictly human history, whose scenario has not been written by any god or destiny, nor by any abstract dialectic—whether the absolute spirit of Hegel or the "ineluctable progress" of the eighteenth-century materialists—this morality is the continuous creation of man by man. This creation is at no moment arbitrary and at no moment determinate. Man at one and the same time is totally responsible for becoming, not what he is but what he is not yet, which has not yet been written anywhere; and he is also obligated to be aware of the historic conditions created by man's previous creations which obey necessary laws, misunderstanding or contempt for which leads to hazard and impotence.

Marx's essential discovery, in morals, is firstly by his . . . historical and militant conception of alienation, then by his demonstration in *Kapital*, to have unfrozen into human actions what had been crystalized in things and in historical situations, thus showing man the possibility of a right to make over his own destiny.

To show, as Marx did, how man's action in pursuing his own creation in history, is at the same time and indivisibly necessary and free, was to postulate the theoretical foundation of all morality and of every revolutionary act while sacrificing neither objective necessity to personal responsibility, nor the moment of subjectivity to an awareness of the stern laws of development.

In this Marxist perspective of man and his history, the moral problem cannot be avoided: nor can it be replaced by the scientific and technical problem of truth, of search for, and discovery of, a *true* order of things and of nature which would give moral conduct a basis outside of man.

The study of the laws of social development, even the possibility of plotting, at least in its essentials, the trajectory

[1] Karl Marx: *Contribution to the Criticism of Hegel's Philosophy of Law*, I, p. 91.

of a near, or far, future more or less probable, does not at any moment excuse us from the awareness of our own responsibility as *subjects* acting and creating our own history, and not as the *objects* of history in a conception which would reduce us to being only the resultant or the sum of the conditions, of our existence.

The moral problem is not a simple one, neither as simple as the blind acceptance of rules of conduct given us from outside ready-made, nor as the affirmation of a radical liberty to postulate, for ourselves and alone, our values and our aims.

The moral problem, in a man's life, is made up of contradictions, lived and constantly recurring, between the demands of a discipline necessary to the efficacy of our fight, and the sense of the personal responsibility of every one of us in the elaboration as in the application of the very laws of our struggle. . . .

A man does not reduce himself to the totality of the conditions which have engendered him: he exists, as a man, by surpassing them.

Frantz Fanon
(1925–1961)

Frantz Fanon was born in Martinique, studied medicine in France, and became a psychiatrist. His first book, Black Skin, White Masks, *described his experiences as a Negro doctor in the Antilles. Working in an Algerian hospital during the French-Algerian war, Fanon found his sympathies with the rebels. He traveled to the USSR at the end of the war and developed cancer. Brought to Washington at his own request by the CIA, he died there in December 1961, aged thirty-six.*

Jean-Paul Sartre
(1905–   )

French philosopher, novelist, essayist, and playwright, Jean-Paul Sartre was born in Paris. The theoretician of existen-

tialism, he developed his premises in L'Etre et le néant
(1943), and also in novels such as Nausea *(1938) and plays
such as* No Exit *(1944). In 1964 he refused the Nobel Prize
for Literature.*

Wretched of the Earth

PREFACE
(by Jean-Paul Sartre)

Not so very long ago, the earth numbered two thousand
million inhabitants: five hundred million men, and one
thousand five hundred million natives. The former had
the Word; the others had the use of it. Between the two
there were hired kinglets, overlords, and a bourgeoisie,
sham from beginning to end, which served as go-betweens.
In the colonies the truth stood naked, but the citizens of
the mother country preferred it with clothes on: the native
had to love them, something in the way mothers are loved.
The European elite undertook to manufacture a native
elite. They picked out promising adolescents; they branded
them, as with a red-hot iron, with the principles of Western
culture; they stuffed their mouths full with high-sounding
phrases, grand glutinous words that stuck to the teeth.
After a short stay in the mother country they were sent
home, whitewashed. These walking lies had nothing left
to say to their brothers; they only echoed. From Paris,
from London, from Amsterdam we would utter the words
"Parthenon! Brotherhood!" and somewhere in Africa or
Asia lips would open ". . . thenon! . . . therhood!" It was
the golden age.

It came to an end; the mouths opened by themselves;
the yellow and black voices still spoke of our humanism
but only to reproach us with our inhumanity. We listened
without displeasure to these polite statements of resent-
ment, at first with proud amazement. What? They are

From *Wretched of the Earth*, by Frantz Fanon, translated by
Constance Farrington, Preface by Jean-Paul Sartre, New York, 1968.

able to talk by themselves? Just look at what we have
made of them! We did not doubt but that they would
accept our ideals, since they accused us of not being faithful to them. Then, indeed, Europe could believe in her
mission; she had hellenized the Asians; she had created
a new breed, the Greco-Latin Negroes. We might add,
quite between ourselves, as men of the world: "After all,
let them bawl their heads off, it relieves their feelings; dogs
that bark don't bite." . . .

A new generation came on the scene, which changed the
issue. With unbelievable patience, its writers and poets tried
to explain to us that our values and the true facts of their
lives did not hang together, and that they could neither
reject them completely nor yet assimilate them. By and
large, what they were saying was this: "You are making us
into monstrosities; your humanism claims we are at one
with the rest of humanity but your racist methods set us
apart." Very much at our ease, we listened to them all;
colonial adminstrators are not paid to read Hegel, and for
that matter they do not read much of him, but they do not
need a philosopher to tell them that uneasy consciences are
caught up in their own contradictions. They will not get
anywhere; so, let us perpetuate their discomfort; nothing
will come of it but talk. If they were, the experts told us,
asking for anything at all precise in their wailing, it would
be integration. Of course, there is no question of granting
that; the system, which depends on over-exploitation, as you
know, would be ruined. But it's enough to hold the carrot in
front of their noses, they'll gallop all right. As to a revolt,
we need not worry at all; what native in his senses would go
off to massacre the fair sons of Europe simply to become
European as they are? . . .

During the last century, the middle classes looked on the
workers as covetous creatures, made lawless by their greedy
desires; but they took care to include these great brutes in
our own species, or at least they considered that they were
free men—that is to say, free to sell their labor. . . .

In the case of forced labor, it is quite the contrary. There
is no contract; moreover, there must be intimidation and
thus oppression grows. Our soldiers overseas, rejecting the
universalism of the mother country, apply the "numerus
clausus" to the human race: since none may enslave, rob,
or kill his fellow man without committing a crime, they lay
down the principle that the native is not one of our fellow
men. Our striking power has been given the mission of
changing this abstract certainty into reality: the order is

given to reduce the inhabitants of the annexed country to the level of superior monkeys in order to justify the settler's treatment of them as beasts of burden. Violence in the colonies does not only have for its aim the keeping of these enslaved men at arm's length; it seeks to dehumanize them. Everything will be done to wipe out their traditions, to substitute our language for theirs and to destroy their culture without giving them ours. Sheer physical fatigue will stupefy them. Starved and ill, if they have any spirit left, fear will finish the job; guns are leveled at the peasant; civilians come to take over his land and force him by dint of flogging to till the land for them. If he shows fight, the soldiers fire and he's a dead man; if he gives in, he degrades himself and he is no longer a man at all; shame and fear will split up his character and make his inmost self fall to pieces. The business is conducted with flying colors and by experts; the "psychological services" weren't established yesterday; nor was brainwashing. And yet, in spite of all these efforts, their ends are nowhere achieved: neither in the Congo, where Negroes' hands were cut off, nor in Angola, where until very recently malcontents' lips were pierced in order to shut them with padlocks. I do not say that it is impossible to change a man into an animal: I simply say that you won't get there without weakening him considerably. Blows will never suffice; you have to push the starvation further, and that's the trouble with slavery.

For when you domesticate a member of our own species, you reduce his output, and however little you may give him, a farmyard man finishes by costing more than he brings in. For this reason the settlers are obliged to stop the breaking-in halfway; the result, neither man nor animal, is the native. Beaten, undernourished, ill, terrified—but only up to a certain point—he has, whether he's black, yellow, or white, always the same traits of character: he's a sly-boots, a lazybones, and a thief, who lives on nothing, and who understands only violence.

Poor settler; here is his contradiction naked, shorn of its trappings. He ought to kill those he plunders, as they say djinns do. Now, this is not possible, because he must exploit them as well. Because he can't carry massacre on to genocide, and slavery to animal-like degradation, he loses control, the machine goes into reverse, and a relentless logic leads him on to decolonization.

But it does not happen immediately. At first the European's reign continues. He has already lost the battle, but this is not obvious; he does not yet know that the natives are only half native; to hear him talk, it would seem that he ill-treats them in order to destroy or to repress the evil that they have rooted in them; and after three generations their pernicious instincts will reappear no more. What instincts does he mean? The instincts that urge slaves on to massacre their master? Can he not here recognize his own cruelty turned against himself? In the savagery of these oppressed peasants, does he not find his own settler's savagery, which they have absorbed through every pore and for which there is no cure? The reason is simple; this imperious being, crazed by his absolute power and by the fear of losing it, no longer remembers clearly that he was once a man; he takes himself for a horsewhip or a gun; he has come to believe that the domestication of the "inferior races" will come about by the conditioning of their reflexes. But in this he leaves out of account the human memory and the ineffaceable marks left upon it; and then, above all there is something which perhaps he has never known: we only become what we are by the radical and deep-seated refusal of that which others have made of us. Three generations did we say? Hardly has the second generation opened their eyes than from then on they've seen their fathers being flogged. In psychiatric terms, they are "traumatized" for life. But these constantly renewed aggressions, far from bringing them to submission, thrust them into an unbearable contradiction which the European will pay for sooner or later. After that, when it is their turn to be broken in, when they are taught what shame and hunger and pain are, all that is stirred up in them is a volcanic fury whose force is equal to that of the pressure put upon them. You said they understand nothing but violence? Of course; first, the only violence is the settler's; but soon they will make it their own; that is to say, the same violence is thrown back upon us as when our reflection comes forward to meet us when we go toward a mirror.

Make no mistake about it; by this mad fury, by this bitterness and spleen, by their ever-present desire to kill us, by the permanent tensing of powerful muscles which are afraid to relax, they have become men: men *because of* the settler, who wants to make beasts of burden of them— because of him, and against him. Hatred, blind hatred which is as yet an abstraction, is their only wealth; the Master calls it forth because he seeks to reduce them to animals, but he fails to break it down because his interests stop him halfway. Thus the "half natives" are still humans, through the power and the weakness of the oppressor which is transformed within them into a stubborn refusal of the animal condition. We realize what follows; they're lazy: of course—it's a form of sabotage. They're sly and thieving; just imagine! But their petty thefts mark the beginning of a resistance which is still unorganized. That is not enough; there are those among them who assert themselves by throwing themselves barehanded against the guns; these are their heroes. Others make men of themselves by murdering Europeans, and these are shot down; brigands or martyrs, their agony exalts the terrified masses.

Yes, terrified; at this fresh stage, colonial aggression turns inward in a current of terror among the natives. By this I do not only mean the fear that they experience when faced with our inexhaustible means of repression but also that which their own fury produces in them. They are cornered between our guns pointed at them and those terrifying compulsions, those desires for murder which spring from the depth of their spirits and which they do not always recognize; for at first it is not *their* violence, it is ours, which turns back on itself and rends them; and the first action of these oppressed creatures is to bury deep down that hidden anger which their and our moralities condemn and which is however only the last refuge of their humanity . . . their mad impulse to murder is the expression of the natives' collective unconscious.

If this suppressed fury fails to find an outlet, it turns in a vacuum and devastates the oppressed creatures themselves. In order to free themselves they even massacre each other. The different tribes fight between themselves since they cannot face the real enemy—and you can count on colonial policy to keep up their rivalries; the man who raises his knife against his brother thinks that he has destroyed once and for all the detested image of their common degradation, even though these expiatory victims don't quench their thirst for blood. They can only stop themselves from marching against the machine-guns by doing our work for us; of their own accord they will speed up the dehumanization they reject. . . .

There is one duty to be done, one end to achieve: to thrust out colonialism by *every* means in their power. The more farseeing among us will be, in the last resort, ready to admit this duty and this end; but we cannot help seeing in this ordeal by force the altogether inhuman means that these less-than-men make use of to win the concession of a charter of humanity. Accord it to them at once, then, and let them endeavor by peaceful undertakings to deserve it. Our worthiest souls contain racial prejudice. . . .

CONCERNING VIOLENCE

National liberation, national renaissance, the restoration of nationhood to the people, commonwealth: whatever may be the headings used or the new formulas introduced, decolonization is always a violent phenomenon. At whatever level we study it—relationships between individuals, new names for sports clubs, the human admixture at cocktail parties, in the police, on the directing boards of national or private banks—decolonization is quite simply the replacing of a certain "species" of men by another "species" of men. Without any period of transition, there is a total, complete, and absolute substitution. It is true that we could equally well stress the rise of a new nation, the setting up of a new state, its diplomatic relations, and its economic and political trends. But we have precisely chosen to speak of that kind of *tabula rasa* which characterizes at the outset all decolonization. Its unusual importance is that it constitutes, from the very first day, the minimum demands of the colonized. To tell the truth, the proof of success lies in a whole social structure being changed from the bottom up. The extraordinary importance of this change is that it is willed, called for, demanded. The need for this change exists in its crude state, impetuous and compelling, in the consciousness and in the lives of the men and women who are colonized. But the possibility of this change is equally experienced in the form of a terrifying future in the consciousness of another "species" of men and women: the colonizers.

Decolonization, which sets out to change the order of the world, is, obviously, a program of complete disorder. But it cannot come as a result of magical practices, nor of a natural shock, nor of a friendly understanding. Decolonization, as we know, is a historical process: that is to say that it cannot be understood, it cannot become intelligible nor clear to itself except in the exact measure that we can discern the movements which give it historical form and content. Decolonization is the meeting of two forces, opposed to each other by their very nature, which in fact owe their originality to that sort of substantification which results from and is nourished by the situation in the colonies. Their first encounter was marked by violence and their existence together—that is to say the exploitation of the native by the settler—was carried on by dint of a great array of bayonets and cannons. The settler and the native are old acquaintances. In fact, the settler is right when he speaks of knowing "them" well. For it is the settler who has brought the native into existence and who perpetuates his existence. The settler owes the fact of his very existence, that is to say, his property, to the colonial system.

Decolonization never takes place unnoticed, for it influences individuals and modifies them fundamentally. It transforms spectators crushed with their inessentiality into privileged actors, with the grandiose glare of history's floodlights upon them. It brings a natural rhythm into existence, introduced by new men, and with it a new language and a new humanity. Decolonization is the veritable creation of new men. But this creation owes nothing of its legitimacy to any supernatural power; the "thing" which has been colonized becomes man during the same process by which it frees itself.

In decolonization, there is therefore the need of a complete calling in question of the colonial situation. If we wish to describe it precisely, we might find it in the well-known words: "The last shall be first and the first last." *
Decolonization is the putting into practice of this sentence. That is why, if we try to describe it, all decolonization is successful. . . .

The colonial world is a world cut in two. The dividing line, the frontiers are shown by barracks and police stations. In the colonies it is the policeman and the soldier who are the official, instituted go-betweens, the spokesmen of the settler and his rule of oppression. In capitalist societies the educational system, whether lay or clerical, the structure of moral reflexes handed down from father to son, the exemplary honesty of workers who are given a medal after fifty years of good and loyal service, and the affection which springs from harmonious relations and good behavior—all these aesthetic expressions of respect for the established order serve to create around the exploited person an atmosphere of submission and of inhibition which lightens the task of policing considerably. In the capitalist countries a multitude of moral teachers, counselors and "bewilderers" separate the exploited from those in power. In the colonial countries, on the contrary, the policeman and the soldier, by their immediate presence and their frequent and direct action, maintain contact with the native and advise him by means of rifle butts and napalm not to budge. It is obvious here that the agents of government speak the language of pure force. The intermediary does not lighten the oppression, nor seek to hide the domination; he shows them up and puts them into practice with the clear conscience of an upholder of the peace; yet he is the bringer of violence into the home and into the mind of the native.

The zone where the natives live is not complementary to the zone inhabited by the settlers. The two zones are opposed, but not in the service of a higher unity. Obedient to the rules of pure Aristotelian logic, they both follow the principle of reciprocal exclusivity. No conciliation is possible, for of the two terms, one is superfluous. The settlers' town is a strongly built town, all made of stone and steel. It is a brightly lit town; the streets are covered with asphalt, and the garbage cans swallow all the leavings, unseen, unknown and hardly thought about. The settler's feet are never visible, except perhaps in the sea; but there you're never close enough to see them. His feet are protected by strong shoes although the streets of his town are clean and even, with no holes or stones. The settler's town is a well-fed town, an easygoing town; its belly is always full of good things. The settlers' town is a town of white people, of foreigners.

The town belonging to the colonized people, or at least the native town, the Negro village, the medina, the reservation, is a place of ill fame, peopled by men of evil repute. They are born there, it matters little where or how; they die there, it matters not where, nor how. It is a world without spaciousness; men live there on top of each other, and their huts are built one on top of the other. The native town is a hungry town, starved of bread, of meat, of shoes, of coal, of light. The native town is a crouching village, a town on its knees, a town wallowing in the mire. It is a town of niggers and dirty Arabs. The look that the native turns on the settler's town is a look of lust, a look of envy; it expresses his dreams of possession—all manner of possession: to sit at the settler's table, to sleep in the settler's bed, with his wife if possible. The colonized man is an envious man. And this the settler knows very well; when their glances meet he ascertains bitterly, always on the defensive, "They want to take our place." It is true, for there is no native who does not dream at least once a day of setting himself up in the settler's place.

This world divided into compartments, this world cut in two is inhabited by two different species. The originality of the colonial context is that economic reality, inequality, and the immense difference of ways of life never come to mask the human realities. When you examine at close quarters the colonial context, it is evident that what parcels out the world is to begin with the fact of belonging to or not belonging to a given race, a given species. In the colonies the economic substructure is also a superstructure. The cause is the consequence; you are rich because you are white, you are white because you are rich. This is why Marxist analysis should always be slightly stretched every time we have to do with the colonial problem.

Everything up to and including the very nature of pre-capitalist society, so well explained by Marx, must here be thought out again. The serf is in essence different from the knight, but a reference to divine right is necessary to legitimize this statutory difference. In the colonies, the foreigner coming from another country imposed his rule by means of guns and machines. In defiance of his successful transplantation, in spite of his appropriation, the settler still remains a foreigner. It is neither the act of owning factories, nor estates, nor a bank balance which distinguishes the governing classes. The governing race is first and foremost those who come from elsewhere, those who are unlike the original inhabitants, "the others." . . .

Nowadays a theoretical problem of prime importance is being set, on the historical plane as well as on the level of political tactics, by the liberation of the colonies: when can one affirm that the situation is ripe for a movement of national liberation? In what form should it first be manifested? Because the various means whereby decolonization has been carried out have appeared in many different aspects, reason hesitates and refuses to say which is a true decolonization, and which a false. We shall see that for a man who is in the thick of the fight it is an urgent matter to decide on the means and the tactics to employ: that is to say, how to conduct and organize the movement. If this coherence is not present there is only a blind will toward freedom, with the terrible reactionary risks which it entails.

What are the forces which in the colonial period open up new outlets and engender new aims for the violence of colonized peoples? In the first place there are the political parties and the intellectual or commercial elites. Now, the characteristic feature of certain political structures is that they proclaim abstract principles but refrain from issuing definite commands. The entire action of the nationalist political parties during the colonial period is action of the electoral type: a string of philosophico-political dissertations on the themes of the rights of peoples to self-determination, the rights of man to freedom from hunger and human dignity, and the unceasing affirmation of the principle: "One man, one vote." The national political parties never lay stress upon the necessity of a trial of armed strength, for the good reason that their objective is not the radical overthrowing of the system. Pacifists and legalists, they are in fact partisans of order, the new order—but to the colonialist bourgeoisie they put bluntly enough the demand which to them is the main one: "Give us more power." On the specific question of violence, the elite are ambiguous. They are violent in their words and reformist in their attitudes. When the nationalist political leaders *say* something, they make quite clear that they do not really *think* it.

This characteristic on the part of the nationalist political parties should be interpreted in the light both of the make-up of their leaders and the nature of their followings. The rank-and-file of a nationalist party is urban. The workers, primary schoolteachers, artisans, and small shopkeepers who have begun to profit—at a discount, to be sure—from the colonial setup, have special interests at heart. What this sort of following demands is the betterment of their particular lot: increased salaries, for example. The dialogue between these political parties and colonialism is never broken off. Improvements are discussed, such as full electoral representation, the liberty of the press, and liberty of association. Reforms are debated. Thus it need not astonish anyone to notice that a large number of natives are militant members of the branches of political parties which stem from the mother country. These natives fight under an abstract watchword: "Government by the workers," and they forget that in their country it should be *nationalist* watchwords which are first in the field. The native intellectual has clothed his aggressiveness in his barely veiled desire to assimilate himself to the colonial world. He has used his aggressiveness to serve his own individual interests. . . .

The peasantry is systematically disregarded for the most part by the propaganda put out by the nationalist parties. And it is clear that in the colonial countries the peasants alone are revolutionary, for they have nothing to lose and everything to gain. The starving peasant, outside the class

system, is the first among the exploited to discover that only
violence pays. For him there is no compromise, no possible
coming to terms; colonization and decolonization are simply
a question of relative strength. The exploited man sees that
his liberation implies the use of all means, and that of force
first and foremost. . . .

NB

At the decisive moment, the colonialist bourgeoisie which
up till then has remained inactive, comes into the field. It
introduces that new idea which is in proper parlance a
creation of the colonial situation: non-violence. In its sim-
plest form this non-violence signifies to the intellectual and
economic elite of the colonized country that the bourgeoisie
has the same interests as they and that it is therefore urgent
and indispensable to come to terms for the public good.
Non-violence is an attempt to settle the colonial problem
around a green baize table, before any regrettable act has
been performed or irreparable gesture made, before any
blood has been shed. But if the masses, without waiting for
the chairs to be arranged around the baize table, listen to
their own voice and begin committing outrages and setting
fire to buildings, the elite and the nationalist bourgeois
parties will be seen rushing to the colonialists to exclaim,
"This is very serious! We do not know how it will end; we
must find a solution—some sort of compromise."

This idea of compromise is very important in the phenomenon of decolonization, for it is very far from being
a simple one. Compromise involves the colonial system
and the young nationalist bourgeoisie at one and the same
time. The partisans of the colonial system discover that
the masses may destroy everything. Blown-up bridges,
ravaged farms, repressions, and fighting harshly disrupt the
economy. Compromise is equally attractive to the nationalist bourgeoisie, who, since they are not clearly aware of
the possible consequences of the rising storm, are genuinely
afraid of being swept away by this huge hurricane and
never stop saying to the settlers: "We are still capable of
stopping the slaughter; the masses still have confidence in
us; act quickly if you do not want to put everything in jeop-
ardy." One step more, and the leader of the nationalist
party keeps his distance with regard to that violence. He
loudly proclaims that he has nothing to do with these
Mau-Mau, these terrorists, these throat-slitters. At best, he
shuts himself off in a no man's land between the terrorists
and the settlers and willingly offers his services as go-
between; that is to say, that as the settlers cannot discuss
terms with these Mau-Mau, he himself will be quite willing

to begin negotiations. Thus it is that the rear guard of the national struggle, that very party of people who have never ceased to be on the other side in the fight, find themselves somersaulted into the van of negotiations and compromise —precisely because that party has taken very good care never to break contact with colonialism. . . .

Private companies, when asked to invest in independent countries, lay down conditions which are shown in practice to be inacceptable or unrealizable. Faithful to the principle of immediate returns which is theirs as soon as they go "overseas," the capitalists are very chary concerning all long-term investments. They are unamenable and often openly hostile to the prospective programs of planning laid down by the young teams which form the new government. At a pinch they willingly agree to lend money to the young states, but only on condition that this money is used to buy manufactured products and machines: in other words, that it serves to keep the factories in the mother country going.

In fact the cautiousness of the Western financial groups may be explained by their fear of taking any risk. They also demand political stability and a calm social climate which are impossible to obtain when account is taken of the appalling state of the population as a whole immediately after independence. Therefore, vainly looking for some guarantee which the former colony cannot give they insist on garrisons being maintained or the inclusion of the young state in military or economic pacts. The private companies put pressure on their own government to at least set up military bases in these countries for the purpose of assuming the protection of their interests. In the last resort these companies ask their government to guarantee the investments which they decide to make in such-and-such an underdeveloped region.

It happens that few countries fulfill the conditions demanded by the trusts and monopolies. Thus capital, failing to find a safe outlet, remains blocked in Europe and is frozen. It is all the more frozen because the capitalists refuse to invest in their own countries. The returns in this case are in fact negligible and treasury control is the despair of even the boldest spirits.

In the long run the situation is catastrophic. Capital no longer circulates, or else its circulation is considerably diminished. In spite of the huge sums swallowed up by military budgets, international capitalism is in desperate straits.

But another danger threatens it as well. Insofar as the

Third World is in fact abandoned and condemned to regression or at least to stagnation by the selfishness and wickedness of Western nations, the underdeveloped peoples will decide to continue their evolution inside a collective autarky. Thus the Western industries will quickly be deprived of their overseas markets. The machines will pile up their products in the warehouses and a merciless struggle will ensue on the European market between the trusts and the financial groups. The closing of factories, the paying off of workers and unemployment will force the European working class to engage in an open struggle against the capitalist regime. Then the monopolies will realize that their true interests lie in giving aid to the underdeveloped countries—unstinted aid with not too many conditions. So we see that the young nations of the Third World are wrong in trying to make up to the capitalist countries. We are strong in our own right, and in the justice of our point of view. We ought on the contrary to emphasize and explain to the capitalist countries that the fundamental problem of our time is not the struggle between the socialist regime and them. The Cold War must be ended, for it leads nowhere. The plans for nuclearizing the world must stop, and large-scale investments and technical aid must be given to underdeveloped regions. The fate of the world depends on the answer that is given to this question. . . .

. . . Let us decide not to imitate Europe; let us combine our muscles and our brains in a new direction. Let us try to create the whole man, whom Europe has been incapable of bringing to triumphant birth.

Two centuries ago, a former European colony decided to catch up with Europe. It succeeded so well that the United States of America became a monster, in which the taints, the sickness, and the inhumanity of Europe have grown to appalling dimensions.

Comrades, have we not other work to do than to create a third Europe? The West saw itself as a spiritual adventure. It is in the name of the spirit of Europe, that Europe has made her encroachments, that she has justified her crimes and legitimized the slavery in which she holds the four-fifths of humanity.

Yes, the European spirit has strange roots. All European thought has unfolded in places which were increasingly more deserted and more encircled by precipices; and thus it was that the custom grew up in those places of very seldom meeting man.

A permanent dialogue with oneself and an increasingly

obscene narcissism never ceased to prepare the way for a half delirious state, where intellectual work became suffering and the reality was not at all that of a living man, working and creating himself, but rather words, different combinations of words, and the tensions springing from the meanings contained in words. Yet some Europeans were found to urge the European workers to shatter this narcissism and to break with this unreality.

But in general, the workers of Europe have not replied to these calls; for the workers believe, too, that they are part of the prodigious adventure of the European spirit.

So, comrades, let us not pay tribute to Europe by creating states, institutions, and societies which drew their inspiration from her.

Humanity is waiting for something from us other than such an imitation, which would be almost an obscene caricature.

If we want to turn Africa into a new Europe, and America into a new Europe, then let us leave the destiny of our countries to Europeans. They will know how to do it better than the most gifted among us.

But if we want humanity to advance a step further, if we want to bring it up to a different level than that which Europe has shown it, then we must invent and we must make discoveries.

If we wish to live up to our peoples' expectations, we must seek the response elsewhere than in Europe.

Moreover, if we wish to reply to the expectations of the people of Europe, it is no good sending them back a reflection, even an ideal reflection, of their society and their thought with which from time to time they feel immeasurably sickened.

For Europe, for ourselves, and for humanity, comrades, we must turn over a new leaf, we must work out new concepts, and try to set afoot a new man.

Fidel Castro
(1926–   )

Fidel Castro is the son of Angel Castro, a Spanish immigrant from Galicia, and his second wife, Lina Ruiz Gonzales.

Castro was educated at the Belen Jesuit School in Havana and the University of Havana. In 1947 he joined with 3,000 men attempting to overthrow the late Rafael Trujillo, then dictator of the Dominican Republic. In 1950 Castro began to practice law; in 1952 he was a congressional candidate. After Batista came to power in Cuba, Castro initiated a plan to attack the Moncada fortress on July 26, 1953. The plan failed and Batista killed thousands in reprisal. On September 1, 1953, 122 prisoners, including Fidel Castro, were brought to trial. Castro was condemned to fifteen years of imprisonment. He was later amnestied and fled to Mexico, where he organized a small band of revolutionaries who landed in Oriente Province, Cuba, in 1956. From there he carried on an armed struggle until Batista fled Cuba in 1959. Castro has been prime minister of Cuba since 1959. He was awarded the Lenin prize in 1961.

La historia me absolverá

On September 21, 1953, and after 76 days in solitary confinement in the courthouse at Santiago, Cuba, 122 prisoners, including many persons who had had nothing to do with the attack on Moncada, were brought to trial. All the approaches to the courthouse were blocked by armored cars. Lining both sides of the road from Boniato prison to the courthouse, a distance of six miles, were 1,000 soldiers with automatic weapons at the ready. All the prisoners except Fidel Castro were transported in buses; he was taken in a jeep, handcuffed, escorted by heavily-armed soldiers on every side.

On the stand Fidel was asked whether he had participated in the attack on Moncada. He proudly admitted that he had. Then he was asked why he hadn't used "civil means" to accomplish his purpose. His answer was sharp and to the point:

> Simply because there is no freedom in Cuba, because since the 10th of March nobody can talk. I already said that efforts were made but the government, always intransigent, did not want to give ground.

From speech made after unsuccessful assault on the Moncada Barracks, 1953, later published in *Monthly Review*, New York, July–August 1960.

Given the opportunity, at long last, to take the stand in his own defense, Fidel spoke for five hours. His speech was not a plea for mercy; on the contrary, it was an indictment of the Batista regime. The argument was bolstered with citations from law, political science, economics, history, and philosophy. It was as learned as it was long; as eloquent as only a dedicated person burning with a vision of glory for his country could be. It was one of the greatest speeches in the history of the fight for freedom anywhere in the world. . . .

These are the words of a man just turned 27 years of age, speaking extemporaneously, after being held incommunicado for 76 days in solitary confinement.

. . . An unheard-of situation had arisen, Honorable Magistrates. Here was a regime afraid to bring an accused before the courts; a regime of blood and terror which shrank in fear at the moral conviction of a defenseless man —unarmed, slandered, and isolated. Thus, having deprived me of all else, they finally deprived me of the trial in which I was the principal accused.

Bear in mind that this was during a period of suspension of rights of the individual and while there was in full force the Law of Public Order as well as censorship of radio and press. What dreadful crimes this regime must have committed, to so fear the voice of one accused man!

As a result of so many obscure and illegal machinations, due to the *will* of those who govern and the *weakness* of those who judge, I find myself here in this little room of the Civil Hospital—to which I have been brought to be tried in secret; so that my voice may be stifled and so that no one may learn of the things I am going to say. Why, then, do we need that imposing Palace of Justice which the Honorable Magistrates would without doubt find rather more comfortable? I must warn you: it is unwise to administer justice from a hospital room, surrounded by sentinels with bayonets fixed; the citizens might suppose that our justice is sick—and that it is captive.

I remind you, your laws of procedure provide that trials shall be "both audible and public"; however, the people have been barred altogether from this session of court. The only civilians admitted here have been two attorneys and six reporters, whose newspapers censorship will prevent from printing a word that I say. I see, as my sole audience, in this chamber and in the corridors, nearly a hundred soldiers and officers. I am grateful for the polite and serious attention they give me. I only wish I could have the whole army before me! I know, one day this army will seethe with rage to wash away the awful, the shameful bloodstains splattered across the uniform by the present ruthless clique in their lust for power. On that day, oh, what a fall awaits those mounted, in arrogance, on the backs of the noble soldiers!—provided, that is, that the people have not pulled them down long before!

Finally, I should like to add that no treatise on penal law was allowed to be brought to my cell. I have at my disposal just this tiny code of law lent to me by my learned counsel, Dr. Baudilio Castellanos, the courageous defender of my comrades. In the same way they prohibited me from receiving the books of Martí; it seems the prison censorship considered them too subversive. Or is it because I named Martí as the instigator of the 26th of July?

I was also prevented from bringing to this trial reference books on any other subject. It makes no difference whatsoever! I carry in my heart the teachings of the *Maestro* and in my mind the noble ideas of all men who have defended the freedom of the peoples of the world! . . .

It was never our intention to engage the soldiers of the regiment in combat, but to seize control and weapons by surprise, to arouse the people and then call the soldiers together. We would have invited them to abandon the flag of tyranny and to embrace the banner of Liberty; to defend the supreme interests of the nation and not the petty interests of a small group; to turn their guns around and fire on the enemies of the people and not fire on the people, among whom are their own sons and fathers; to join with the people themselves, brothers of ours that they are, instead of opposing the people as the enemies the government tried to make of them; to march behind the only beautiful ideal worthy of the sacrifice of one's life—the greatness and the happiness of one's country. To those who doubt that many soldiers would have followed us, I ask: What Cuban does not cherish glory? What heart is not set aflame by the dawn of freedom? . . .

The Honorable Prosecutor was very much interested in knowing our chances for success. These chances were based on considerations of technical, military, and social orders. There has been an attempt to establish the myth that modern arms render the people helpless to overthrow tyrants. Military parades and the pompous display of the machines of war are utilized to perpetuate this myth and to create in the people a complex of absolute impotence. But no weapon, no violence can vanquish the people once they have decided to win back their rights. Both past and present are full of examples. . . .

Here I will pause to consider the facts. The Government itself has said the attack was carried on with such precision and perfection that it proved the presence of military experts in the preparation of the plan. Nothing is more absurd! The plan was drawn up by a group of young men, none of whom had any military experience and I will tell you who they were—except for two of them who are neither dead nor jailed and he who now speaks to you. Half of them are dead, and in just tribute to their memory, they were not military experts, but they had enough patriotism to give, under equal conditions, a sound hiding to all the generals of 10 March who were neither soldiers nor patriots. It was more difficult to organize, to train, and to mobilize men and arms under a repressive regime which wasted millions of pesos in espionage, bribery and denunciation. These young people and many others accomplished their tasks with a reliability, a discretion and a constancy that were truly incredible. It is still more meritorious to give to an ideal everything one has—including life itself.

The final mobilization of the men who came to this province from the most remote villages of the whole island, was carried out with admirable precision and absolute secrecy. And the attack was effected with magnificent co-ordination. It began at 5.15 A.M. simultaneously in Bayano and in Santiago de Cuba, and one after another, with the exactness of minutes and seconds calculated in advance, the buildings that surrounded the camp fell. Indeed, I will reveal another grave blunder. One half of the bulk of our forces, and the best armed, by a lamentable error went astray at the entrance of the city and was missing at the decisive moment. Abel Santamaría, with twenty-one men, had occupied the Civil Hospital; a doctor and two of our people had gone with him to attend to our wounded. Raul Castro with ten men occupied the Palace of Lustue, and I attacked the camp with those who were left, ninety-five men. I arrived with a first group of forty-five, preceded by a vanguard of eight, who captured post 3. And it was there that the battle began—by the encounter of my car with a reconnaissance patrol armed with machine guns. The reserve group which had almost all the heavy arms (since the small arms had been given to the vanguard), took a wrong turning and lost themselves completely in a city they did not know. I must make it clear that I have not the slightest doubt about the courage of these men who suffered, in these circumstances, great anxiety and even despair. It happened as a result of the type of action which was developing, and since the uniforms of the combatants on both sides were identical in color, it was not easy to reestablish contact. Many of these men, later taken prisoner, met death with real heroism.

Everyone had received precise instructions to be, above all, humane in the fight. Never has a group of armed men been more generous to their adversaries. From the first moment about twenty prisoners were taken, and at the outset three of our men, of those who took the post, succeeded in penetrating into a barracks and arresting and holding for a time, about fifty soldiers. These prisoners declared before the tribunal that they were treated with absolute respect, without having to suffer even an insulting word. On this point I wish most sincerely to thank the public prosecutor: in the judgment meted out to my companions he had the justice to recognize in his report, as an indubitable fact, the high spirit of chivalry we maintained in the struggle. The discipline on the part of the army was quite poor. They finally won because of their numbers which gave them a superiority of 15 to 1, and because of the protection given them by the defenses of the fortress. Our men shot much better, and they themselves admitted this. Courage was equally high on both sides. . . .

It is not my intention to entertain the tribunal with epic stories. All I have said is necessary in order to understand more clearly what I will state later, but I wish to point out two important facts in order that our attitude should be fairly judged. First, we could have facilitated the taking of the regiment we took prisoner simply by arresting all the high officials in their homes, a possibility we rejected because we wished to avoid scenes of tragedy and struggle in the presence of their families. Secondly, it was agreed not to take any radio station until the camp had been taken. This gallant and noble attitude of ours prevented a bloodbath of citizens. With only ten men I could have occupied a radio station and issued an appeal to the people to fight: of their courage it is not possible to doubt. Take the recent case of Bolivia, for instance, when the miners, with dynamite cartridges, put to flight and smashed regiments of the regular army. Luckily for us, we do not need to find examples from other countries, for none is so eloquent or fine as that of our own. During the war of '95 there were in Cuba about half a million Spanish soldiers under arms, far more than the dictatorship could have opposed to a population now five times greater. The weapons of the Spanish army were incomparably heavier and more modern than those of the *mambises;* the army was in many cases equipped with campaign artillery and its infantry used breech-loading rifles similar to those still used by modern infantry. In general, the Cubans had nothing but their *machetes,* because their cartridge cases were almost always empty. There is an unforgettable description of our civil war, by General Miro Argenter, chief of General Antonio Maceo's general staff, which without exaggeration on my part, could apply in this present context:

> The green troops commanded by Pedro Delgado, for the most part provided only with *machetes,* were decimated by their charge on the Spanish soldiers to such an extent that out of fifty men half fell. They attacked the Spanish with their fists, without pistols, without *machetes,* without knives. Searching the thickets edging the Hondo River, another fifteen dead of the Cuban contingent were found, without it being possible at the time to discover to what corps they belonged. They did not appear to be armed, were fully clothed, and hanging from their belts nothing but tin mugs. Two feet from them was a lifeless horseman with his equipment intact. The last phase of this tragedy was reconstructed: these men, following their chief, Colonel Pedro Delgado, had obtained the palm of heroism. They threw themselves on the bayonets with their bare hands, the noise of metal which sounded around them was the clash of their drinking mugs against the horses' accoutrements. Maceo was moved and he, so accustomed to viewing death in all its aspects, murmured: "I have never seen such a thing, inexperienced men attacking the Spaniards unarmed, with their drinking mugs for their sole weapons. And I had called them a liability."

That is how the people fight when they wish to gain their liberty: they throw stones at airplanes, and turn tanks upside down. . . .

I stated that the second consideration on which we based our chances for success was one of social order because we were assured of the people's support. When we speak of the people we do not mean the comfortable ones, the conservative elements of the nation, who welcome any regime of oppression, any dictatorship, any despotism, prostrating themselves before the master of the moment until they grind their foreheads into the ground. When we speak of struggle, the *people* means the vast unredeemed masses, to whom all make promises and whom all deceive; we mean the people who yearn for a better, more dignified and more just nation; who are moved by ancestral aspirations of justice, for they have suffered injustice and mockery, generation after generation; who long for great and wise changes in all aspects of their life; people, who, to attain these changes, are ready to give even the very last breath of their lives—when they believe in something or in someone, especially when they believe in themselves. In stating a purpose, the first condition of sincerity and good faith, is to do precisely what nobody else ever does, that is, to speak with absolute clarity, without fear. The demagogues and professional politicians who manage to perform the miracle of being right in everything and in pleasing everyone, are, of necessity, deceiving everyone about everything. The revolutionaries must proclaim their ideas courageously, define their principles and express their intentions so that no one is deceived, neither friend nor foe.

The people we counted on in our struggle were these:

Seven hundred thousand Cubans without work, who desire to earn their daily bread honestly without having to emigrate in search of livelihood.

Five hundred thousand farm laborers inhabiting miserable shacks, who work four months of the year and starve for the rest of the year, sharing their misery with their children, who have not an inch of land to cultivate, and whose existence inspires compassion in any heart not made of stone.

Four hundred thousand industrial laborers and stevedores whose retirement funds have been embezzled, whose benefits are being taken away, whose homes are wretched quarters, whose salaries pass from the hands of the boss to those of the usurer, whose future is a pay reduction and dismissal, whose life is eternal work and whose only rest is the tomb.

One hundred thousand small farmers who live and die working on land that is not theirs, looking at it with sadness as Moses did the promised land, to die without possessing it; who, like feudal serfs, have to pay for the use of their parcel of land by giving up a portion of their products; who cannot love it, improve it, beautify it or plant a lemon or an orange tree on it, because they never know when a sheriff will come with the rural guard to evict them from it.

Thirty thousand teachers and professors who are so devoted, dedicated and necessary to the better destiny of future generations and who are so badly treated and paid.

Twenty thousand small business men weighted down by

debts, ruined by the crisis and harangued by a plague of filibusters and venal officials.

Ten thousand young professionals: doctors, engineers, lawyers, veterinarians, school teachers, dentists, pharmacists, newspapermen, painters, sculptors, etc., who come forth from school with their degrees, anxious to work and full of hope, only to find themselves at a dead end with all doors closed, and where no ear hears their clamor or supplication.

These are the people, the ones who know misfortune and, therefore, are capable of fighting with limitless courage!

To the people whose desperate roads through life have been paved with the brick of betrayals and false promises, we were not going to say: "We will eventually give you what you need," but rather—"There you have it, fight with all your might so that liberty and happiness may be yours!" . . .

THE PROBLEMS WE MUST RESOLVE

The problems concerning land, the problem of industrialization, the problem of housing, the problem of unemployment, the problem of education, and the problem of the health of the people; these are the six problems we would take immediate steps to resolve, along with the restoration of public liberties and political democracy.

Perhaps this exposition appears cold and theoretical if one does not know the shocking and tragic conditions of the country with regard to these six problems, to say nothing of the most humiliating political oppression.

Eighty-five percent of the small farmers in Cuba pay rent and live under the constant threat of being dispossessed from the land that they cultivate. More than half the best cultivated land belongs to foreigners. In Oriente, the largest province, the lands of the United Fruit Company and West Indian Company join the north coast to the southern one. There are two hundred thousand peasant families who do not have a single acre of land to cultivate to provide food for their starving children. On the other hand, nearly three hundred thousand *caballerías** of pro-

* A *cabellería* is equal to about 33 acres.

ductive land owned by powerful interests remain uncultivated.

Cuba is above all an agricultural state. Its population is largely rural. The city depends on these rural areas. The rural people won the Independence. The greatness and prosperity of our country depends on a healthy and vigorous rural population that loves the land and knows how to cultivate it, within the framework of a state that protects and guides them. Considering all this, how can the present state of affairs be tolerated any longer? . . .

Just as serious or even worse is the housing problem. There are two hundred thousand huts and hovels in Cuba; four hundred thousand families in the country and in the cities live cramped into barracks and tenements without even the minimum sanitary requirements; two million two hundred thousand of our urban population pay rents which absorb between one-fifth and one-third of their income; and two million eight hundred thousand of our rural and suburban population lack electricity. If the state proposes lowering rents, landlords threaten to freeze all construction; if the state does not interfere, construction goes on so long as the landlords get high rents, otherwise they would not lay a single brick even though the rest of the population should have to live exposed to the elements. The utilities monopoly is no better: they extend lines as far as it is profitable, and beyond that point they don't care if the people have to live in darkness for the rest of their lives. The state folds its arms and the people have neither homes nor electricity.

Our educational system is perfectly compatible with the rest of our national situation. Where the peasant is not the owner of his land, what need is there for agricultural schools? Where there are no industries what need is there for technical or industrial schools? Everything falls within the same absurd logic: there is neither one thing nor the other. In any small European country there are more than 200 technical and industrial art schools; in Cuba, there are only six such schools, and the boys graduate without having anywhere to use their skills. The little rural schools are attended by only half the school-age children—barefoot, half-naked, and undernourished—and frequently the teacher must buy necessary materials—from his own salary. Is this the way to make a nation great?

Only death can liberate one from so much misery. In this, however—early death—the state is most helpful. Ninety percent of rural children are consumed by parasites which filter through their bare feet from the earth. Society is moved to compassion upon hearing of the kidnapping or murder of one child, but they are criminally indifferent to the mass murder of so many thousands of children who die every year from lack of facilities, agonizing with pain. Their innocent eyes—death already shining in them—seem to look into infinity as if entreating forgiveness for human selfishness, as if asking God to stay his wrath. When the head of a family works only four months a year, with what can he purchase clothing and medicine for his children? They will grow up with rickets, with not a single good tooth in their mouths by the time they reach thirty; they will have heard ten million speeches and will finally die of misery and deception. Public hospitals, which are always full, accept only patients recommended by some powerful politician who, in turn, demands the electoral votes of the unfortunate one and his family so that Cuba may continue forever the same or worse. . . .

A revolutionary government with the backing of the people and the respect of the nation, after cleansing the various institutions of all venal and corrupt officials, would proceed immediately to industrialize the country, mobilizing all inactive capital, currently estimated at about 1500 million dollars, through the National Bank, the Agricultural and Industrial Bank, and the Development Bank, and submitting this mammoth task to experts and men of absolute competence, completely removed from all political machinations, for study, direction, planning, and realization.

After settling the one hundred thousand small farmers as owners on land which they previously rented, a revolutionary government would proceed immediately to solve the land problem. First, as the Constitution orders, we would establish the maximum amount of land to be held by each type of agricultural enterprise and would acquire the excess acres by: expropriation, recovery of the lands stolen from the state, improvement of swampland, planting of large nurseries, and reserving of zones for reforestation. Secondly, we would distribute the remaining land among peasant families with priority given to the larger ones, and would promote agricultural cooperatives with a single technical, professional direction in farming and cattle raising. Finally, we would provide resources, equipment, protection, and useful guidance to the peasants.

A revolutionary government would solve the housing problem by cutting all rents in half, by providing tax exemptions on homes inhabited by the owners; by tripling taxes on rented homes; by tearing down hovels and replacing them with modern multiple-dwelling buildings; and by financing housing all over the island on a scale heretofore unheard of; with the criterion that, just as each rural family should possess its own tract of land, each city family should own its home or apartment. There is plenty of building material and more than enough manpower to make a decent home for every Cuban. But if we continue to wait for the miracle of the golden calf, a thousand years will have gone by and the problem will still be the same. On the other hand, today there are greater than ever possibilities of bringing electricity to the remotest corner of the island. The use of nuclear energy in this field is now a reality and will greatly reduce the cost of producing electricity.

With these three projects and reforms, the problem of unemployment would automatically disappear and the work to improve public health and to fight against disease would be made much less difficult.

Finally, a revolutionary government would undertake the integral reform of the educational system, bringing it in line with the foregoing projects with the idea of educating those generations who will have the privilege of living in a happy land. Do not forget the words of the *Apóstol**: "A serious error is being made in Latin America: where the inhabitants depend almost exclusively on the products of the soil for their livelihood, the education stress, contradictorily, is on urban rather than farm life." "The happiest people are the ones whose children are well-educated and instructed in philosophy; whose sentiments are directed into noble channels." "A well-educated people will always be strong and free." . . .

WHERE WILL THE MONEY COME FROM?

Where the money will be found for all this? When there is an end to rife embezzlement of government funds, when public officials stop taking graft from the large companies who owe taxes to the state, when the enormous resources of the country are brought into full use, when we no longer buy tanks, bombers, and guns for this country (which has

* I.e. José Martí.

no frontiers to defend and where these instruments of war, now being purchased, are used against the people), when there is more interest in educating the people than in killing them—then there will be more than enough money.

Cuba could easily provide for a population three times as great as it now has, so there is no excuse for the abject poverty of a single one of its present inhabitants. The markets should be overflowing with produce, pantries should be full, all hands should be working. This is not an inconceivable thought. What is inconceivable is that anyone should go to bed hungry, that children should die for lack of medical attention; what is inconceivable is that 30 percent of our farm people cannot write their names and that 99 percent of them know nothing of Cuba's history. What is inconceivable is that the majority of our rural people are now living in worse circumstances than were the Indians Columbus discovered living in the fairest land that human eyes had ever seen.

To those who would call me a dreamer, I quote the words of Martí: "A true man does not seek the path where advantage lies, but rather, the path where duty lies, and this is the only practical man, whose dream of today will be the law of tomorrow, because he who has looked back on the upheavals of history and has seen civilizations going up in flames, crying out in bloody struggle, throughout the centuries, knows that the future well-being of man, without exception, lies on the side of duty."

THIS MOVEMENT IS A NEW GENERATION

Only when we understand that such high ideals inspired them, can we conceive the heroism of the young men who fell in Santiago.

The meager material means at our disposal was all that prevented our certain success. When the soldiers were told that Prío had given a million dollars to us, they were told this in the regime's attempt to distort the most serious fact —the fact that our movement had no link with past politicians. The regime was trying to prevent the soldiers from learning that this movement is a new Cuban generation with its own ideas, rising up against tyranny; that this movement is made up of young men who were barely seven years old when Batista committed the first of his crimes in 1934. . . .

"WITH DEATH, LIFE BEGINS"

For my dear friends, I claim no vengeance. Since their lives were priceless, the murderers could not pay for them with their own lives. It is not by blood that we can redeem the lives of those who died for their country. The happiness of their people is the only tribute worthy of them.

My comrades, furthermore, are neither dead nor forgotten; they live today, more than ever, and their murderers will view with dismay the immortality of the victorious spirit of their ideas. . . .

THE RIGHT TO REBELLION AGAINST TYRANNY

. . . The right to revolt, established in Article 40 of the Constitution, is still valid. Was it established to function while the Republic was enjoying normal conditions? No. This provision is, in relation to the Constitution, what a lifeboat is to a ship on high sea. The lifeboat is lowered only when, for example, the boat is torpedoed by enemies in ambush along its course. With our Constitution betrayed and the people deprived of all their prerogatives, there was only one right left, one right which no power may abolish —the right to resist oppression and injustice. . . .

The right of rebellion against tyranny, Honorable Magistrates, has been recognized from the most ancient times to the present day by men of all creeds, ideas, and doctrines.

In the theocratic monarchies of remote antiquity, in China, it was in effect a constitutional principle that when a king governed rudely and despotically he should be deposed and replaced by a virtuous prince.

The philosophers of ancient India upheld the principle of active resistance to arbitrary authority. They justified revolution and very often put their theories into practice. One of their spiritual leaders used to say that "An opinion held by the majority is stronger than the king himself. A rope weaved of many strands is strong enough to drag a lion."

The city states of Greece and republican Rome not only admitted but defended the meting-out of violent death to tyrants.

In the Middle Ages, John of Salisbury in his *Book of the Statesman* says that when a prince does not govern according to law and degenerates into a tyrant, violent overthrow is legitimate and justifiable. He recommends for tyrants the dagger rather than poison.

Saint Thomas Aquinas, in the *Summa Theologica*, rejects the doctrine of tyrannicide, and yet upholds the thesis that tyrants should be overthrown by the people.

Martin Luther proclaimed that when a government degenerates into a tyranny violating the laws, the subjects are released from their obligation to obey. His disciple, Philippe Melancthon, upholds the right of resistance when governments become despotic. Calvin, the most outstanding thinker of the Reformation, with regard to political ideas, postulates that people are entitled to take up arms to oppose any usurpation.

No less a man than Juan Mariana, a Spanish Jesuit during the reign of Philip II, asserts in his book, *De Rege et Regis Institutione*, that when a governor usurps power, or even if he were elected, when he governs in a tyrannical manner, it is licit for a private citizen to exercise tyrannicide, either directly or through subterfuge, with the least possible disturbance.

The French writer, François Hotman, maintained that between the government and its subjects there is a bond or contract, and that the people may rise in rebellion against the tyranny of governments when the latter violate said agreement. . . .

John Althus, a German jurist of the early seventeenth century, states, in his *Treatise on Politics,* that sovereignty, as the supreme authority of the state, is born from the voluntary concourse of all its members; that governmental authority stems from the people and that its unjust, illegal, or tyrannical function exempts them from the duty of obedience and justifies their resistance or rebellion.

Thus far, Honorable Magistrates, I have mentioned examples from antiquity, from the Middle Ages and from the beginnings of the modern age. I selected these examples from writers of all creeds.

Moreover, as you can see, the right to rebellion is at the

very roots of Cuba's existence as a nation. By virtue of a rebellion fifty years ago you are today able to appear in the robes of Cuban magistrates. Would that those garments served the cause of justice!

La historia me absolverá.

Speech on Education

Each year the historical fact which unites us here on the University steps has been the central theme of our meeting. This year we wish to speak of what cannot fail to be an important theme this 13 March: the University. We will not pretend to make an exhaustive or definitive exposition of what the university institution should be in a revolutionary context, because even our own ideas on the subject, our own concepts, during the process of unfolding them, will also become developed in practice, and they will become enriched by daily experience.

On what a university should be in a revolutionary context, we all thought we held rather clear ideas. Yet in reality, we all held ideas that were somewhat vague. We used to speak of university reform, as we used to speak of agrarian reform. The agrarian revolution that is developing in our country has almost nothing in common with our original ideas of what an agrarian revolution should be. We had called it a reform when we did not understand that the problem of the land could not be resolved by reforms, but only by means of fundamental revolutionary changes.

And with the university exactly the same thing has happened. Nor was it possible that it should happen differently, because the ideas of those original times were weighted down by the conceptions which had been forged in the system of the society in which we lived. And within that system arose—as an important aspiration of our people—

From speech by Fidel Castro, first minister of the Revolutionary Government, at the University of Havana 1969, at a celebration in honor of the martyrs of 13 March 1957, translated by Anne Fremantle.

the will to effect a series of changes which, in the compass of any society, in reality were not possible.

The aim of the agrarian reform can be considered an aim within a revolution which needs to be reformed, or, more precisely, within a society which requires to be revolutionized. And when the society is really revolutionized, then all the ideas which could be considered reforming, conceived as they were, now appear completely outmoded. We must also say that this transformation of ideas relative to the university takes some time.

However, in the whole revolutionary process, one could always count on the enthusiastic participation of the students. It is also necessary to recognize with satisfaction that never, in the whole intimacy of the revolutionary process, did a single contradiction arise between the development of the Revolution and the students. To this fact belongs an especial merit of a political character, for the composition of the university students was heterogeneous. But even in the midst of this heterogeneous and complete mass something else could be said of them: that the majority came from those sectors classically called lower middle and middle classes. Thus, logically, the students of the university to a large extent brought with them an important part of the habits, ideas and customs of this social milieu.

I wish to point out here that a remarkable change in the way of thinking and of acting of this group took place, and that this constitutes a good example of the importance of ideological and of moral factors in man's behaviour. This group moved along with the university and was radicalized and its conceptions were deepened to the extent which the Revolution deepened and to the extent to which the Revolution was radicalized. And today we can proclaim with satisfaction that in the hierarchy of ideas, and in the hierarchy of political positions, in the hierarchy of attitudes, the students of our universities occupy, without any doubt, a vanguard position in the revolutionary process.

Nevertheless, a vanguard position in this case cannot be merely a political vanguard. It must correspond at the same time to a vanguard position in the technical and in the scientific fields, it must correspond to a vanguard position along the road which one day the whole society must take. WE CANNOT HAVE ANY IDEA OF THE DEVELOPMENT OF A PEOPLE UNLESS THIS IDEA CORRESPONDS TO THE DEVELOPMENT OF THE WHOLE INTELLIGENCE QUOTIENT OF THIS PEOPLE.

As you know all ideas produce an impact, and all new

ideas produce a shock. New ideas are often not easily comprehensible. And thus, when on some occasions it has been said that one day the university would become universal, and that when the university became universal it would disappear as a university, these words—which are not a play upon words nor a riddle nor said for the sake of style —express an idea: an idea that not everyone will easily accept at first sight, because they cannot conceive, they don't know how to conceive of university education becoming universal and of a whole people one day reaching the level of what we today call university education. This arises in part from the whole outlook and the whole schema which we bear, which is of that we have always known, it comes from the old schema of the old society, it is the product of a society in which knowledge, the domain of technics and of science, was the patrimony of an insignificant minority. And who knows what terrible vices and habits engendered this circumstance that knowledge should be the patrimony of a minority.

But without doubt, it is difficult to conciliate the idea of a revolution with the idea that always, in the future, there shall be in the heart of this society a minority possessing these technical and scientific skills and the majority not understanding them. Firstly, it is not possible to conceive how the problems of the future can be resolved unless such knowledge becomes universal; secondly, it is not possible to conceive how there could be a real communist society without the universalization of scientific and technical knowledge. Some people believe that there will always be a part of mankind doing intellectual work and only intellectual work and another part of humanity doing heavy labor. But this work which occupies long and interminable hours, this work which uses up enormous energies—physical energies, energies of man that are almost animal—this old work, lifted man from his primitive condition. In the same measure as his force becomes more intelligent in time, this work, when it shall acquire the character of completely intelligent work, work dominated by the intelligence, will disappear as that heavy labor, as that animal work.

It is for this reason that we cannot have any other idea of the development of the education of a people unless that idea includes, whatever its ultimate consequences, the development of all people's potential faculties.

And, in fact, the Revolution began, practically, from zero. It began by fighting against illiteracy. After the battle against illiteracy, began the battle for general education, for general primary education. The problems which it involved of professors, teachers, scholars, were enormous, and many of these problems are still with us. After, there was the battle for the sixth grade, which has also produced remarkable results in the number of workers in our country who have completed the whole of primary education and have passed the sixth grade. In the near future the whole people must discuss the problem of obligatory general education up to pre-university level. That is to say, not only up to the sixth grade, not only to the basic secondary school, not only or temporarily only up to pre-university standard. The last leap must be more progressive—that is to say, by stages.

I repeat, the rhythm of the leap from the primary school to the pre-university won't be maintained. We need much time before we arrive at the final leap which will be general university education. And then it will not be a leap, but clearly the result of previous leaps. Because once we have made general education up to pre-university standard a reality, the step to the universalization of university education will flow from this in a normal way.

In fact, to a certain extent it is already happening in the case of thousands of students from the technical institutes, who have acquired the pre-university grade level, and have passed to work at production and there are raising the level of university studies, and are themselves succeeding in their examinations, succeeding in their studies, succeeding in their tests. In spite of the fact that today this is still very difficult, because in very few places in the country do the conditions exist which facilitate this type of study. So that our next fundamental step will be the establishment by a law of the whole people, for the participation and understanding of the whole people, on universal education for all children and for all young people in corresponding grades up to pre-university.

This will require of all of us an enormous effort: this will require from all our students in the higher grades an enormous effort, because we do not have, and for many years we will not have, many additional classrooms, many additional professors to go ahead with this program, than these very students of the higher grades who today already are being used on a fairly wide scale. This will help us to resolve our many contradictions: the contradiction between defense and study, which is one of the most obvious contradictions in the revolutionary process . . . let us say that there are three contradictions in the conditions in which our Revolution is evolving: the enormous requirements of development, the enormous demands of the country's defense, and the enormous needs of study. We have to overcome these contradictions, we have to resolve these contradictions.

THERE CAN BE NO ONE, NOT ONE OF YOU, WHO CAN ESCAPE OR CAN HAVE HOPES OF ESCAPING STUDY, FOR THE WHOLE OF YOUR LIFETIME.

Here can be said certain words related to study as a necessity, to study as a duty. Yet truly we should speak to students of study as a pleasure. Logically, this could not have been said fifteen years ago in a university.

And what was the university in the past?

Many times we have described a certain university as a kindergarten for adults. And, truly, the majority of us who came to these universities, came because we were sent, and because we could be sent to these universities. And what was the content? What was the objective? And who would easily believe that study under such conditions would be a pleasure? The best that could be hoped was that in some cases it was a great necessity for some people in order to resolve an individual problem.

And most of the students at that time arranged to see how little studying that could do and how they could best amuse themselves. Every thing was good, except study. And thus were we all, one way and another . . . there were some exceptionally honorable: it was said that Carlos Rafael was first in the Law School and some other of my companions possibly were first-class students. But, disgracefully, I cannot count myself among them. And I recall perfectly the whole atmosphere and the whole feeling in that university and when we contrast it with the university of today and above all with the ideas of what a university can and should be, there *is* no comparison.

And, since then, life has obliged us to study continually. The realities oblige us to study all our lives. And there can be no one in the future, not one of you, who will not be obliged by the realities to study all your life. And you will do it. And you will do it with the more pleasure the more you feel the necessity, the more you see and understand that nothing else is possible, that there is no other alternative. And this will help to make you all members of the society. And you will have much more time for this, because to the same extent that man dominates technology and applies the productive processes and elevates the productivity of his work, to the same extent in which the whole of society shares in these productive processes, each member of society will dispose of much more time for activities of a recreative type, for cultural and intellectual activities.

To the point that these ideas of which I speak, these ideas which were of the essence of Marxist thought: the combination of study and work, the combination of manual labor and intellectual labor, are not simple phrases—they are ideas which contain the essence of the society of the future.

Another phenomenon which has been observed, is the fact that intellectual work, and nothing but intellectual work, also becomes painful activity for man: and now the possibility for many people who have always developed intellectual tasks, is to realize that to undertake some manual type tasks, has constituted for countless people a kind of pleasure, even though some of these manual activities were hard, and were ones to which they were not accustomed. This type of activity, like cutting the sugar cane, we have decided will not be offered in the future, but there are many other activities of a manual kind—or manual or mechanical or what you will—but it will entail passing from a purely intellectual work to work with machines, to work in crews, or to some work of another kind.

THE UNIVERSITY WILL HAVE IN THE SUGAR CROP OF 1970 A GREAT TASK.

The students will participate, will give what help they can as part of the university, as part of the university they will go to work where the necessities of the country require it, and not where the smartest administrator or vice-minister has decided to produce a greater output than the others. That is no way to resolve the problem correctly, that is a sectional way which could never be a solution of any problem. Thanks to this resolve there are a great number, and thanks to this they can provide many services.

And the university will have, next year, in the sugar crop of 1970, a great task. The technical students will go during the sugar crop of ten millions, to the province of Camagüey to work and to lend their technical assistance in the collecting centers and in the sugar centers. Members of other faculties will go to other activities during this period. The civil engineers, the architects, have hundreds of thousands of kilometers to map, of roads, of highways, of fire-prevention trails in the woods; the architecture students have much physical planning to do, many many industrial installations, of services and dwellings, to locate, and many projects to carry out; in the same way those working in biology are all registered in the pine groves of Piñar del Río, fourteen thousand knights of the pines, choosing the bonus pines: female pines, male pines, bonus pines. This appears to be a social category of pines, in virtue of which they are considered the best examples of the species and from which the seeds must be taken for genetic work in connection with reafforestation. The efforts the biology students have made in this activity is admirable, and it has been admirable for the pine forests, for the mountains, working for weeks at a time and collecting information which is valid for the country, at times living under difficult conditions.

Also the experience of the political science students in the Center Camillo Cienfuegos is interesting. Because there is a center of work, with all the problems of different kinds, that is where theory is completed, where the knowledge of how to distinguish the essential and the fundamental is acquired. It is hard to find a political cadre or a specialist in sociological or political questions who ignores the problems of the productive process and who ignores the conditions in which the work of a human agglomeration develops. And we can be sure that this will give them an extraordinary experience.

In our opinion, the country will benefit greatly. It will benefit from the contribution which this injection of intelligence to the activities of the country's development, and it will also benefit from the quality of the technicians who will come out of our universities armed with this type of knowledge. It has been possible to provide the university with means to undertake these tasks, and we recognize that the means are not yet sufficient. But the enthusiasm with which the university has undertaken these missions, the success which has accompanied this work, has stimulated the country to make efforts towards giving the university the means with which to complete this work.

Another new experiment is a group of thirty alumni specialists in the engineering of hill terraces, in the Cayarjabos zone of Piñar del Río, who have their university there and there, in country stores, they receive their classes and there prepare themselves. A good example of a university which begins to move from its original emplacement. . . .

The old idea, the classic idea of a university will disappear in so far as it is the sort of idea, will disappear in so far as it is the sort of concept, will disappear in so far as it is the kind of institution that belongs to a long-ago, by-passed society.

And this production itself, these productive activities, these productive processes, will constitute the material base, the laboratory, in which all the workers of the future will receive their higher studies. . . .

And this will be the means, the most important, unique, true and legitimate means, by which this country will advance. Because almost all the rest, all our future progress, will be a subproduct of whatever advances our country will be capable of in the way of study, in the way of the technical and scientific concepts.

Ernesto "Che" Guevara
(1928–1967)

Ernesto "Che" Guevara was born in Argentina, the son of a civilian engineer of Irish descent. During his youth, as a result of Guevara's severe asthma, the family moved several times. At the age of twenty-five, Guevara graduated from medical school and, for a time, practiced in a leper colony. Following this, he set out for Guatemala and then Mexico, where he joined Fidel Castro. With Castro and his band, Guevara landed in Cuba in November, 1956, serving both as a doctor and a soldier. A revolutionary activist and theoretician with few equals in history, "Che" Guevara was killed in Bolivia in 1967.

Notes for the Study of the Ideology of the Cuban Revolution

This is a unique Revolution which some people maintain contradicts one of the most orthodox premises of the rev-

From *Studies on the Left*, Madison, Wisconsin, 1960.

olutionary movement, expressed by Lenin: "Without a revolutionary theory there is no revolutionary movement." It would be suitable to say that revolutionary theory, as the expression of a social truth, surpasses any declaration of it; that is to say, even if the theory is not known, the revolution can succeed if historical reality is interpreted correctly and if the forces involved are utilized correctly. Every revolution always incorporates elements of very different tendencies which, nevertheless, coincide in action and in the revolution's most immediate objectives.

It is clear that if the leaders have an adequate theoretical knowledge prior to the action, they can avoid trial and error whenever the adopted theory corresponds to the reality. The principal actors of this revolution had no coherent theoretical criteria; but it cannot be said that they were ignorant of the various concepts of history, society, economics, and revolution which are being discussed in the world today. Profound knowledge of reality, a close relationship with the people, the firmness of the liberator's objective and the practical revolutionary experience gave to those leaders the chance to form a more complete theoretical concept.

The foregoing should be considered an introduction to the explication of this curious phenomenon which has intrigued the entire world: the Cuban Revolution. It is a deed worthy of study in contemporary world history; the how and the why of a group of men who, shattered by an army enormously superior in technique and equipment, managed first to survive, soon became strong, later became stronger than the enemy in the battle zones, still later moved into new zones of combat, and finally defeated that enemy on the battlefield even though their troops were still very inferior in number. . . .

Naturally, we who often do not show the requisite concern for theory, will not run the risk of expounding the truth of the Cuban Revolution as though we were its masters. We will simply try to give the bases from which one can interpret this truth. In fact, the Cuban Revolution must be separated into two absolutely distinct stages: that of the armed action up to January 1, 1959, and the political, economic and social transformations since then.

Even these two stages deserve further subdivisions; however, we will not take them from the viewpoint of historical exposition, but from the viewpoint of the evolution of the revolutionary thought of its leaders through their contact with the people. Incidentally, here one must introduce a general attitude toward one of the most controversial terms of the modern world: Marxism. When asked whether or not we are Marxists, our position is the same as that of a physicist or a biologist when asked if he is a "Newtonian," or if he is a "Pasteurian."

There are truths so evident, so much a part of people's knowledge, that it is now useless to discuss them. One ought to be "Marxist" with the same naturalness with which one is "Newtonian" in physics, or "Pasteurian" in biology, considering that if facts determine new concepts, these new concepts will never divest themselves of that portion of truth possessed by the older concepts they have outdated. Such is the case, for example, of Einsteinian relativity or of Planck's "quantum" theory with respect to the discoveries of Newton; they take nothing at all away from the greatness of the learned Englishman. Thanks to Newton, physics was able to advance until it had achieved new concepts of space. The learned Englishman provided the necessary steppingstone for them.

The advances in social and political science, as in other fields, belong to a long historical process whose links are connecting, adding up, molding and constantly perfecting themselves. In the field of social and political sciences, from Democritus to Marx, a long series of thinkers added their original investigations and accumulated a body of experience and of doctrines. The merit of Marx is that he suddenly produces a qualitative change in the history of social thought. He interprets history, understands its dynamics, predicts the future, but in addition to predicting it (which would satisfy his scientific obligation), he expresses a revolutionary concept: the world must not only be interpreted, it must be transformed. Man ceases to be the slave and tool of his environment and converts himself into the architect of his own destiny. At that moment, Marx puts himself in a position where he becomes the necessary target of all who have a special interest in maintaining the old—similar to Democritus before him, whose work was burned by Plato and his disciples, the ideologues of Athenian slave aristocracy. Beginning with the revolutionary Marx, a political group with concrete ideas establishes itself. Basing itself on the giants, Marx and Engels, and developing through sucessive steps with personalities like Lenin, Stalin, Mao Tsetung and the new Soviet and Chinese rulers, it establishes a body of doctrine and, let us say, examples to follow.

The Cuban Revolution takes up Marx at the point where he himself left science to shoulder his revolutionary rifle. And it takes him up at that point, not in a revisionist spirit of struggling against that which follows Marx, of reviving "pure" Marx, but simply because up to that point Marx, the scientist, placed himself outside of the History he studied and predicted. From then on Marx the revolutionary could fight within History. We, practical revolutionaries, initiating our own struggle, simply fulfill laws foreseen by Marx the scientist. We are simply adjusting ourselves to the predictions of the scientific Marx as we travel this road of rebellion, struggling against the old structure of power, supporting ourselves in the people for the destruction of this structure, and having the happiness of this people as the basis of our struggle. That is to say, and it is well to emphasize this once again: the laws of Marxism are present in the events of the Cuban Revolution, independently of what its leaders profess or fully know of those laws from a theoretical point of view....

Each of those brief historical moments in the guerrilla warfare framed distinct social concepts and distinct appreciations of the Cuban reality; they outlined the thought of the military leaders of the Revolution—those who in time would also take their position as political leaders.

Before the landing of the *Granma,* a mentality predominated that, to some degree, might be called "subjectivist"; blind confidence in a rapid popular explosion, enthusiasm and faith in the power to liquidate the Batista regime by a swift, armed uprising combined with spontaneous revolutionary strikes, and the subsequent fall of the dictator....

After the landing comes the defeat, the almost total destruction of the forces and their regrouping and integration as guerrillas. Characteristic of those few survivors, imbued with the spirit of struggle, was the understanding that to count upon spontaneous outbursts throughout the island was a falsehood, an illusion. They understood also that the fight would have to be a long one and that it would need vast *campesino* participation. At this point, the *campesinos* entered the guerrilla war for the first time. Two events— hardly important in terms of the number of combatants, but of great psychological value—were unleashed. First, antagonism that the city people, who comprised the central guerrilla group, felt toward the *campesinos* was erased. The *campesinos,* in turn, distrusted the group and, above all, feared barbarous reprisals of the government. Two things demonstrated themselves at this stage, both very important for the interrelated factors: to the *campesinos,* the bestialities of the army and all the persecution would not be sufficient to put an end to the guerrilla war, even though the army was certainly capable of liquidating the *campesinos'* homes, crops, and families. To take refuge with those in hiding was a good solution. In turn, the guerrilla fighters learned the necessity, each time more pointed, of winning the *campesino* masses. . . .

Here ends the insurrection. But the men who arrive in Havana after two years of arduous struggle in the mountains and plains of Oriente, in the plains of Camagüey, and in the mountains, plains, and cities of La Villas, are not the same men, ideologically, that landed on the beaches of Las Coloradas, or who took part in the first phase of the struggle. Their distrust of the *campesino* has been converted into affection and respect for his virtues; their total ignorance of life in the country has been converted into a knowledge of the needs of our peasants; their flirtations with statistics and with theory have been fixed by the cement which is practice.

With the banner of Agrarian Reform, the execution of which begins in the Sierra Maestra, these men confront imperialism. They know that the Agrarian Reform is the basis upon which the new Cuba must build itself. They know also that the Agrarian Reform will give land to all the dispossessed, but that it will dispossess its unjust possessors; and they know that the greatest of the unjust possessors are also influential men in the State Department or in the Government of the United States of America. But they have learned to conquer difficulties with bravery, with audacity, and above all, with the support of the people; and they have now seen the future of liberation which awaits us on the other side of our sufferings. . . .

More than a year has passed now since the flight of the dictator, corollary to a long civil and armed struggle of the Cuban people. The achievements of the Government in the social, economic and political fields are enormous; nevertheless, we need to analyze, to give to each term its proper meaning; and to show the people the exact dimensions of our Cuban revolution. This is because our national revolution (fundamentally agrarian, but with the enthusiastic participation of workers, people of the middle class, and today even with the support of industrialists) has acquired continental and even world importance, sheltered as it is by the unshakable decision of its people and the peculiar features which animate it.

We are not attempting a synthesis, however much one may be needed, of the sum total of laws passed, all of them of undeniable popular benefit. It will suffice to place upon some of them the needed emphasis, showing at the same time the logical sequence which from first to last leads us, in a progressive and necessary scale, from affairs of state to the necessities of the Cuban people.

Attention was first directed against the hopes of the parasitic classes of our country, when there were decreed, in rapid succession, the rent regulation law, the lowering of electrical rates, and the intervention of the telephone company with the subsequent lowering of rates. Those who hoped to see in Fidel Castro and in the men who made this revolution only some politicians of the old school, or some manageable dolts whose beards were their only distinctive trait, began to suspect that there was something deeper emerging from the depths of the Cuban people and that their prerogatives were in danger of disappearing. The word Communism began to hover about the figures of the leaders, the figures of the triumphant guerrillas, and as a consequence, the word Anticommunism as the dialectically contrary position began to nuclearize all those whose unjust sinecures were hampered or taken away. . . .

Of all the characteristics which differentiate the Cuban from the other three great agrarian reforms in America (Mexico, Guatemala and Bolivia), that which appears most important is the decision to carry it through to the end, without leniencies or concessions of any sort. This integral Agrarian Reform respects no right which is not the right of the people, nor is it directed against any particular class or nationality; the scales of the law tip alike for the United Fruit Company or the King Ranch, and for the Creole *latifundistas*.

Under these conditions, the production of the materials most important for the country, such as rice, oleaginous grains and cotton, is being developed intensively and is being made central in the planning process; but the Nation is not satisfied and it is going to redeem all its wealth. Its rich subsoil, the site of monopolists' struggle and pasture for their voracity, has for all practical purposes been rescued by the petroleum law. This law, like the Agrarian Reform and all the others dictated by the revolution, responds to the undeniable needs of Cuba, to the inescapable urgencies of a people which wants to be free, which wants to be master of its economy, which wants to prosper and to achieve progressively higher goals of social development. But for this very reason it is a continental example which is feared by the petroleum monopolies. It is not that

Cuba harms the petroleum monopoly substantially or directly, for there is no reason to consider our country an emporium of that precious combustible, although there are reasonable hopes of obtaining a sufficient amount to satisfy internal needs. On the other hand, the palpable example of Cuba's law is seen by the sister nations of America, many of whom are the grazing-land of those monopolies, while others are impelled to internal wars in order to satisfy the necessities or appetites of competing trusts. It shows to them what is possible, indicating likewise the exact hour when one may think of carrying it out. . . .

By a simple law of gravity, the small island of 114,000 square kilometers and 6,500,000 inhabitants is assuming the leadership of the anti-colonial struggle in America, for there are important conditions which permit it to take the glorious, heroic and dangerous lead. The nations of colonial America which are economically less weak, those which are developing their national capitalism by fits and starts in a continual struggle, at times violent and without quarter, against the foreign monopolies, are gradually relinquishing their place to this small new power for liberty, since their governments do not find themselves with sufficient strength to carry the struggle to the finish. This is because the struggle is no simple matter, nor is it free of dangers nor exempt from difficulties. It is essential to have the backing of an entire people, and an enormous amount of idealism and the spirit of sacrifice, to carry it out to the end under the almost isolated conditions in which we are doing it in America. . . .

Cuba knows the previous examples, it knows the failures and the difficulties, but it knows also that it stands at the dawn of a new era in the world; the colonial pillars have been swept away before the impulse of the national and popular struggle, in Asia as in Africa. Now the tendencies to unification of the peoples are no longer given by their religions, by their customs, by their appetites, by their racial affinities or lack of them; it is given by the economic similarities of their social conditions and by the similarity of their desire for progress and recovery. Asia and Africa have shaken hands at Bandung, Asia and Africa are coming to shake hands with colonial and indigenous America by means of Cuba, here in Havana.

On the other hand, the great colonial powers have given ground before the struggle of the peoples. Belgium and Holland are but two caricatures of empire; Germany and Italy have lost their colonies. France debates in the midst of a war she has lost, and England, diplomatic and skilled, liquidates her political power while maintaining economic connections. North American capitalism has replaced some of the old colonial capitalisms in those countries which have initiated their independent life; but it knows that this is transitory and that there is no real rest to be found in the new territory of its financial speculations. The claws of the imperial eagle have been blunted. Colonialism has died in all those places of the world or is in process of natural death.

America is another matter. It was some time ago that the English lion removed his greedy paws from our America, and the nice young Yankee capitalists installed the "democratic" version of the English clubs and imposed their sovereign domination in every one of the twenty republics.

These nations are the colonial feudal-estate of North American monopoly, "right in its own backyard"; at the present moment this is their *raison d'être* and the only possibility they have. If all the Latin American peoples were to raise the banner of dignity, as has Cuba, monopoly would tremble; it would have to accommodate itself to a new politico-economic situation and to substantial cuts in its profits. But monopoly does not like to cut its profits and the Cuban example—this "bad example" of national and international dignity—is spreading among the American countries. Every time that an upstart people sets up a cry of liberation, Cuba is accused; somehow or other Cuba is guilty, guilty because it has shown a way, the way of armed popular struggle against the supposedly invincible armies, the way of struggle in difficult terrain in order to exhaust and destroy the enemy away from his bases; in short, the way of dignity.

Leszek Kolakowski
(1927–   )

Polish philosopher and former professor at the University of Warsaw, Kolakowski received international recognition in the days of the "thaw" after Stalin's death in 1953. He has

*published a book on medieval scholastic thought and many
other studies in Polish. His* Toward a Marxist Humanism
*was published in an English translation in 1969. He is pres-
ently teaching at All Soul's College, Oxford.*

The Concept of the Left

Every work of man is a compromise between the material
and the tool. Tools are never quite equal to their tasks, and
none is beyond improvement. Aside from differences in
human skill, the tool's imperfection and the material's resistance together set the limits that determine the end product. But the tool must fit the material, no matter how
remotely, if it isn't to produce a monstrosity. You cannot
properly clean teeth with an oil drill or perform brain
operations with a pencil. Whenever such attempts have been
made the results have always been less than satisfactory.

THE LEFT AS NEGATION

Social revolutions are a compromise between utopia and
historical reality. The tool of the revolution is utopia, and
the material is the social reality on which one wants to impose a new form. And the tool must to some degree fit the
substance if the results are not to become ludicrous.

There is, however, an essential difference between work
on physical objects and work on history; for the latter,
which is the substance, also creates the tools used to give
this substance shape. Utopias which try to give history a
new form are themselves a product of history, while history
itself remains anonymous. That is why even when the tools
turn out to be grossly unsuited to the material, no one is to
blame, and it would be senseless to hold anyone responsible.

On the other hand, history is a human product. Although

From *Toward a Marxist Humanism*, by Leszek Kolakowski,
translated by Jane Peel, New York, 1969.

no individual is responsible for the results of the historical process, still each is responsible for his personal involvement in it. Therefore each is also responsible for his role in fashioning the intellectual tools used upon reality in order to change it—for accepting or rejecting a given utopia and the means employed to realize it.

To construct a utopia is always an act of negation toward an existing reality, a desire to transform it. But *negation is not the opposite of construction—it is only the opposite of affirming existing conditions.* That is why it makes little sense to reproach someone for committing a destructive rather than a constructive act because every act of destruction is necessarily a negation of the existing order. At most, you may reproach him for not supporting the reality that exists and for wanting to change it; or, on the other hand, for accepting it without qualification, without seeking change; or, finally, for seeking harmful changes. But a negative position is only the opposite of a conservative attitude toward the world, negation in itself being merely a desire for change. The difference between destructive and constructive work lies in a verbal mystification stemming from the adjectives used to describe the changes, which are considered either good or bad. Every change is, in fact, an act both negative and positive at one and the same time, and the opposite only of an affirmation of things as they are. To blow up a house is just as constructive as to build one—and at the same time just as negative. Of course, this does not mean that it is all the same whether one destroys or builds a house. The difference between the two acts is that the first, in most instances, works to the detriment of the people involved, and the second is almost always to their benefit. The opposite of blowing up a house is not to build a new house but to retain the existing one.

This observation will serve to lead to conclusions whose aim is to define more closely the meaning we give to the concept of the social Left.

The Left—and this is its unchangeable and indispensable quality, though by no means its only one—is a movement of negation toward the existent world. For this very reason it is, as we have seen, a constructive force. It is, simply, a quest for change.

That is why *the Left rejects the objection that its program is only a negative and not a constructive one.*

The Left can cope with reproaches directed at the potential harm or utility that may arise from its negations. It can also contend with the conservative attitude that wants to perpetuate things as they are. It will not defend itself, however, against the accusation of being purely negative, because every constructive program is negative, and vice versa. A Left without a constructive program cannot, by that token, have a negative one, since these two terms are synonymous. If there is no program, there is at the same time no negation, that is, no opposite of the Left—in other words, conservativism.

UTOPIA AND THE LEFT

But the act of negation does not in itself define the Left, for there are movements with retrogressive goals. Hitlerism was the negation of the Weimar Republic, but this does not make it leftist. In countries not controlled by the Right, an extreme counterrevolutionary movement is always a negation of the existing order. Thus the Left is defined by its negation, *but not only by this;* it is also defined by the direction of this negation, in fact, by the nature of its utopia.

I use the word "utopia" deliberately and not in the derogatory sense that expresses the absurd notion that all social changes are pipe dreams. By utopia I mean a state of social consciousness, a mental counterpart to the social movement striving for radical change in the world—a counterpart itself inadequate to these changes and merely reflecting them in an idealized and obscure form. It endows the real movement with the sense of realizing an ideal born in the realm of pure spirit and not in *current* historical experience. Utopia is, therefore, a mysterious consciousness of an actual historical tendency. As long as this tendency lives only a clandestine existence, without finding expression in mass social movements, it gives birth to utopias in the narrower sense, that is, to individually constructed models of the world, as it *should* be. But in time utopia becomes actual social consciousness; it invades the consciousness of a mass movement and becomes one of its essential driving forces. Utopia, then, crosses over from the domain of theoretical and moral thought into the field of practical thinking, and itself begins to govern human action.

Still, this does not make it realizable. Utopia always remains a phenomenon of the world of thought; even when backed by the power of a social movement and more importantly, even when it enters its consciousness, it is inadequate, going far beyond the movement's potentials. It is, in a way, "pathological" (in a loose sense of the word, for utopian consciousness is in fact a natural social phenomenon). It is a warped attempt to impose upon a historically realistic movement goals that are beyond history.

However—and this is fundamental to an understanding of the internal contradictions of left-wing movements—the Left cannot do without a utopia. The Left gives forth utopias just as the pancreas discharges insulin—by virtue of an innate law. Utopia is the striving for changes which "realistically" cannot be brought about by immediate action, which lie beyond the forseeable future and defy planning. Still, utopia is a tool of action upon reality and of planning social activity.

A utopia, if it proves so remote from reality that the wish to enforce it would be grotesque, would lead to a monstrous deformation, to socially harmful changes threatening the freedom of man. The Left, if it succeeds, would then turn into its opposite—the Right. But then, too, the utopia would cease to be a utopia and become a slogan justifying every current practice.

On the other hand, the Left cannot renounce utopia; it cannot give up goals that are, for the time being, unattainable, but that impart meaning to social changes. I am speaking of the social Left as a whole, for though the concept of the Left is relative—one is a leftist only in comparison with something, and not in absolute terms—still the extreme element of every Left is a revolutionary movement. The revolutionary movement is a catch-all for all the ultimate demands made upon existing society. It is a total negation of the existing system and, therefore, also a total program. A total program is, in fact, a utopia. A utopia is a necessary component of the revolutionary Left, and the latter is a necessary product of the social Left as a whole.

Yet why is a utopia a condition of all revolutionary movements? Because much historical experience, more or less buried in the social consciousness, tells us that goals unattainable now will never be reached unless they are articulated when they are still unattainable. It may well be that the impossible at a given moment can become possible only by being stated at a time when it is impossible. To cite an example, a series of reforms will never attain the goals of revolution, a consistent reform party will never imperceptibly be transformed into the fulfillment of a revolution. *The existence of a utopia as a utopia is the necessary prerequisite for its eventually ceasing to be a utopia.*

A revolutionary movement cannot be born simultaneously with the act of revolution, for without a revolutionary movement to precede it the revolution could never come about. As long as the revolutionary act has not been accomplished, or is not indisputably and clearly evident, it is a utopia. For today's Spanish proletariat a social revolution is a utopia; but the Spanish proletariat will never achieve a revolution if it does not proclaim it when it is impossible. This is why tradition plays such an important role in the revolutionary movement: the movement would never know any victories if it had not in previous phases suffered inevitable defeats—if it had not initiated revolutionary activity when the historical situation precluded success.

The desire for revolution cannot be born only when the situation is ripe, because among the conditions for this ripeness are the revolutionary demands made of an unripe reality. The continuous influence of social consciousness is one of the necessary conditions for the maturation of history to the point of radical change; utopia is a prerequisite of social upheavals, just as unrealistic efforts are the precondition of realistic ones. That is the reason why revolutionary consciousness cannot be satisfied with mere participation in changes already taking place; it cannot merely follow events, but must precede them at a time when they are neither planned nor anticipated.

Therefore—and this is an elementary practical conclusion—*the Left doesn't mind being reproached for striving for a utopia.* It may have to defend itself against the accusation that the content of its utopia is damaging to society, but it need not defend itself against the charge of being utopian.

The Right, as a conservative force, needs no utopia; its essence is the affirmation of existing conditions—a fact and not a utopia—or else the desire to revert to a state which was once an accomplished fact. The Right strives to idealize actual conditions, not to change them. What it needs is fraud, not utopia.

The Left cannot give up utopia because it is a real force even when it is merely a utopia. The sixteenth-century revolt of the German peasants, the Babouvist movement, and the Paris Commune were all utopian. As it turned out, without such utopian activities no nonutopian, progressive social changes would have taken place. Obviously, it does not follow that the task of the Left is to undertake extreme actions in every historical situation. All we are saying is that to condemn utopia for the mere fact that it is a utopia is rightist, conservative, and hampers the prospects of ever creating a utopia. In any event, we are not at the moment formulating social tasks. We are considering the concept of the Left completely in the abstract, trying to ascertain and not to postulate. Since the Left is as "normal" a social phenomenon as the Right, and progressive social movements are as normal as reactionary ones, it is equally normal for the Left, which is a minority, to be persecuted by the Right. . . .

THE LEFT AND SOCIAL CLASSES

We can set forth certain characteristics of the position of the Left in various social orders:

In capitalist countries the fight of the Left is to abolish all social privilege. In noncapitalist countries, it is to remove privileges that have grown out of noncapitalist conditions.

In capitalist countries the Left fights all forms of colonial oppression. In noncapitalist ones, it demands the abolition of inequalities, discrimination, and the exploitation of certain countries by others.

In capitalist countries the Left struggles against limitations on freedom of speech and expression. It does so also in noncapitalist lands. In one and the other the Left fights all the contradictions of freedom that arise in *both kinds* of social conditions: How far can one push the demand for tolerance without turning against the idea of tolerance itself? How can one guarantee that tolerance will not lead to the victory of forces that will strangle the principle of tolerance? This is the great problem of all leftist movements. It is also true, obviously, that the Left can make mistakes and act ineffectively, and thus engender a situation that is inimical to itself. However, it is not faulty tactics that are the distinguishing feature of the Left, for, as we have said, its criteria are established on an ideological plane.

In capitalist countries the Left strives to secularize social life. This is also true in noncapitalist countries.

In capitalist countries the destruction of all racism is an essential part of the Left's position. This is so in noncapitalist lands as well. . . .

All this time I have been describing the Left as a certain ideological and moral attitude. For the Left is not a single, defined political movement, or party, or group of parties.

The Left is a characteristic which to a greater or lesser degree can serve particular movements or parties, as well as given individuals or human activities, attitudes, and ideologies. One can be leftist from one point of view and not from another. There rarely occur political movements that are totally leftist in every aspect throughout the entire course of their existence. A man of the Left can participate in the political struggle and be a politician in a leftist party, but refuse to approve actions and opinions that are clearly inimical to a leftist attitude. Which does not mean, obviously, that the leftist position does not lead to internal conflicts and contradictions.

For these reasons the Left, as such and as a whole, cannot be an organized political movement. The Left is always to the left in certain respects with relation to some political movements. Every party has its left wing, a current which is farther to the left than the rest of the party in regard to some trait that can be cited as an example. Still, this does not mean that all the leftist elements of all parties taken together form a single movement, or that they are more closely allied to each other than they are to the party that gave birth to them. This would be so if they fulfilled all the requirements of being left in every aspect; but in that case they would not have been segments of so many diverse parties with such varied programs to begin with. The left wing of the Christian-democratic parties has, as a rule, infinitely more in common with them than with the socialist Left, yet it is the Christian-democratic Left on this very basis. Its "Leftness" may be shown by a stand on one or another actual political problem that, in the particular instance, brings it nearer the left of other parties—for example, a condemnation of colonialism or racism. On the other hand, the demands of the Left are met to varying degrees by different parties, which for this reason are called more or less leftist. . . .

Thus we profess the doctrine of total responsibility of the individual for his deeds and of the amorality of the historical process. In the latter we avail ourselves of Hegel; in the former of Descartes. It was he who formulated the famous principle, whose consequences are not always visible at first glance, "There is not a soul so weak that it cannot, with good guidance, gain an absolute mastery over its passions." This means that we cannot explain away any of our actions on the grounds of emotion, passion, or the moral impotence to act differently, and that we have no right to transfer the responsibility for our conscious acts to any factor which determines our behavior; because in every instance we have the power to choose freely.

This assumption—which, as I have mentioned, can be accepted without contradicting the deterministic interpretation of the world—must also be extended to all the justifications we find for ourselves in historical necessities and historical determinism. Neither our personal, supposedly invincible emotions ("I could not resist the desire"), nor anyone's command ("I was a soldier"), nor conformity with the customs of one's environment ("everybody did it"), nor theoretically deduced exigencies of the demiurge of history ("I judged I was acting for the sake of progress") —none of these four most typical and popular rationalizations has any validity. This is not to say that these four types of determination do not actually occur in life, but merely to state that none of them releases us from individual responsibility, because none of them destroys the freedom of individual choice. Individual action remains in the absolute power of the individual. We walk the main roads of our life on our own:

> Not I, not anyone else can travel that road for you
> You must travel it for yourself. . . .
>
> —WHITMAN

I stress that we are concerned with *moral* responsibility. The soldier who executes his commander's erroneous orders —orders which are inefficient as military tactics—is not thereby responsible for the loss of the battle. A soldier who, on orders, participates in the mass murder of civilians is responsible for homicide. His moral duty is to not carry out the command. Only on this basis were we able to try SS men.

That is why, regardless of what philosophy of history we may wish to accept, we will be rightly judged for everything subject to moral appraisal that we do in its name.

And it is not true that our philosophy of history decides our main choices in life. They are determined by our moral sense. We are not communists because we recognized communism to be a historical necessity. We are communists because we stand on the side of the oppressed against their oppressors, on the side of wretches against their masters, on the side of the persecuted against their persecutors. Although we know that a theoretically correct division of society is not between "rich" and "poor" or "persecuted" and "persecutors," still when we have to accompany our theories with an act of *practical* choice, which means a *pledge,* then we act out of moral motivations, not theoretical concerns. It cannot be otherwise, for the most convincing theory is unable to make us lift our little finger. Practical choice is a choice of values, that is, a moral act, and that means an act for which everyone bears his own, personal responsibility.

Gabriel Cohn-Bendit
(1936–   )

Daniel Cohn-Bendit
(1945–   )

Brothers, sons of German refugees, Gabriel teaches German in a French school and Daniel was expelled from France after the May student rebellion in 1968 in Paris.

Obsolete Communism: The Left-Wing Alternative
INTRODUCTION

. . . The world identifies the recent revolutionary movement with the student struggle, the barricades, the occupation of the universities, and finally the general strike and the occupation of the factories by the workers. For me, the revolutionary movement was born much earlier and took the form of unofficial strikes, student unrest, the activity of tiny left-wing splinter groups, the so-called *groupuscles*. The events of May and June were merely an intensification of what went before, albeit on so vast a scale that they opened up an

From *Obsolete Communism: The Left-Wing Alternative,* by Daniel and Gabriel Cohn-Bendit, London, 1969.

undreamt-of possibility: the prospect of a revolution. This book might, perhaps, be a brief moment of reflection in this great historical process.

That is why I do not address myself to a "reader" or to the "public," but only to those who were with us, might have been with us, or may be with us in the future, and quite particularly to the workers and peasants from whom the Establishment tried to separate us so assiduously. I know that the only chance of resuming the struggle is to put an end to the division between intellectuals, workers and peasants. Every revolution, every radical transformation of society, needs the conscious and creative participation of the working and peasant classes, and not simply their participation as a malleable mass whose only usefulness is their strength and numerical weight.

I know that there are many other ways of ending our division. However, since I happen to be writing a book, I shall try to use this particular method. Here, the problem of language becomes fundamental. The works of philosophers, sociologists, and professional politicians (sometimes quite outspoken, particularly after the elections . . .) are written in a style which is not intended for the workers and peasants and which, in any case, they cannot understand. This is a danger I shall do my best to avoid.

Stilted language is not, moreover, a monopoly of the bourgeoisie; it also creeps into the writings of those Leftists who see themselves as the leaders, the self-appointed vanguard, of a working-class movement whose language they have ceased to speak and which, once it has become revolutionary as it did in May and June, is only too happy to dispense with leaders and a vanguard altogether. . . .

"The ideas of the ruling class are in every epoch the ruling idea: i.e. the class which is the ruling material force of society is at the same time the ruling intellectual force. The class which has the means of material production at its disposal, has control at the same time over the means of mental production . . ." (Karl Marx: *The German Ideology*.)

The division of society into manual and intellectual workers is a fundamental aspect of all exploitative societies. Every revolutionary movement must try by its actions and also by its very structure to narrow this gulf, while remembering that only a socialist society can finally end it. It is only by working for a socialist revolution that the exploited masses can take control of their own future and that of society at large. No book can help them to achieve this;

they can only learn by their own revolutionary endeavours. "In a revolution, when the masses erupt on to the political stage, their class-consciousness becomes practical and active. Hence one year of revolution gave the Russian proletariat the kind of education that thirty years of parliamentary and trade union struggle failed to give the German proletariat." (Rosa Luxemburg: *The General Strike*.) . . .

For three or four years, the student movement has been recognized as a revolutionary force by all political observers, and it will therefore be part of my task to explain the history of this movement, to recount the major ideas proclaimed for more than ten years in the revolutionary study groups of Paris and elsewhere. These "clubs," which were derided as "splinter groups" by the official and patented representatives of the revolution (their letters patent were deposited by Maurice Thorez, the Son of the French People, with Joseph Stalin, the Father of all the Russias)—these groups, of which no one took the slightest notice, were nevertheless so effective that their ideas and revolutionary experience eventually spilled over into the streets and factories, and so helped to write a new chapter in the history of the revolutionary movement—the permanent struggle to end the exploitation of man by man.

This brings me to the question of the organization not only of capitalist or bureaucratic society—for this must be the starting point in any discussion of "productive relationships"—but also of a non-authoritarian and non-hierarchical socialist society: should the new society be organized along Bolshevik lines or along the non-Bolshevik lines of the 22 March Movement?

This introduces the larger problem of the relationship between the revolutionary minority and the so-called "masses." What precisely are these masses, and why are there masses in the first place? How can the masses transform themselves into something more than an amorphous mass? And what sort of minority organization is capable of challenging an exploitative society and unmasking its real nature? To that end, I shall try to show how the "masses" discovered the means of taking their own destiny in their hands, for example during the Paris Commune of 1871, during the Russian Revolutions of 1905 and 1917, during the Spanish Revolution of 1936, and finally during the Hungarian Revolution of 1956. These moments in the revolutionary struggle of the working class are more important than all the treatises that have been and will be written on this subject. This book, for one, does not try to do more than hold up to the working class the mirror of its own revolutionary experience, an experience that ran counter to all the tenets and practices of its would-be leaders. This experience and the chance that it may be widely copied are perhaps the most positive aspects of the May events as well. Thus while Lefort, Morin and Coudray are right to claim (*Mai 1968: la Brèche*) that the month of May saw a breach of modern capitalist society and also of the old authority of the Left, it did far more than that: it represented a return to a revolutionary tradition these parties have betrayed. Hence the 22 March Movement was no "brilliant invention" of a group of "naive prodigies," but the result of arduous research into revolutionary theory and practice.

It would be wrong to think that what happened in France could only have happened there, just as it is a mistaken idea that concentration camps could only have occurred in Hitler's Germany or in Stalin's Russia. Revolution as well as counter-revolution are international, and much as the student movements in Spain, America, Japan, Italy, etcetera influenced the French student movement, so the French student movement, which was the first to spill out from the university into the factories, can serve as an example elsewhere.

The events in France have proved that revolution is possible in even a highly industrialized capitalist society. Those who argued that the working class had outgrown revolution stood convicted of theoretical and practical incompetence, a fact that suggests it is high time to discover why the working class has remained so passive for so long. . . .

The history of "Leftism" is, in fact, the history of all that is truly revolutionary in the working class movement. Marx was to the left of Proudhon and Bakunin to the left of Marx. Lenin was a Leftist when he opposed social democratic reformism, and again when he opposed his own Central Committee and Politburo during the 1917 Revolution. After the Revolution, the "Workers' Opposition," a group of left-wing "deviationists" among the Bolsheviks, became the most revolutionary element inside the party, while the Ukrainian anarchist Makhno represented the most revolutionary movement outside. This struggle between its "Left" and "Right" wings continues to divide the working-class movement to this day.

"As Lenin never tired of repeating, the masses are greatly to the left of the Party, just as the Party is to the left of its Central Committee." (Trotsky: *History of the Russian Revolution*.)

The question of "Leftism" became a major issue during the events of May and June. Who is the authentic representative of the Left today: the Fourth International, the Situationist International or the Anarchist Federation? Leftism is everything that is new in Revolutionary history, and is forever being challenged by the old. This new factor is what we must firmly defend in the present, lest it be crushed by what is obsolete in Leftism itself. Let the dead bury their dead.

The transformation and development of Leftist ideas reflect not only the transformation and development of capitalist society, but also the transformation and development of the Russian Revolution into a bureaucratic counter-revolution, sustained and defended by Communist parties throughout the world. I, for one, do not think that the French Communist Party betrayed its own principles during May and June; it simply acted in defence of its bureaucratic interests as a party, and of the bureaucratic interests of the USSR as a state. . . .

Those who wish to be shown the royal road to socialism, or have a clear blueprint for the future, may take comfort from the words of Commandant Gaveau's indictment of the International Association in 1871, words which perfectly summarize my own point of view: "To raze the old and build the new from scratch—that is how the supporters of the International Association intend to construct a state that recognizes neither the government nor the army nor religion; that believes in legislation by the people for the people, in the collective ownership of all things, in the abolition of the right of inheritance and marriage; wants to disband the permanent army, and by breaking down all frontiers, to replace the Fatherland with the idea of international solidarity." . . .

1. THE STUDENT REVOLT

FROM BERKELEY TO BERLIN

A spectre is haunting Europe—the spectre of student revolt. All the powers of old Europe have entered into a holy alliance to exorcize this spectre: Pope and Central Committee, Kiesinger and de Gaulle, French Communists and German police-spies.

But now it has become world-wide: Berkeley, Berlin, Tokyo, Madrid, Warsaw—the student rebellion is spreading like wildfire, and authorities everywhere are frantically asking themselves what has hit them. The answer is really quite simple.

Let us take just one example: the student struggle at Berkeley in 1964—four years before the events in Paris. How much just reading the newspapers might have helped the French authorities!

At Berkeley in 1964—well in advance of Berlin or Paris —the students defended their right to participate in politics, and in particular to protest against the war in Vietnam, unhampered by internal rules and regulations.

It started with a decision by the administration to ban all fund-raising and propaganda for any political or social ideas of which they did not approve.

This inept move by the bureaucrats stung a small group of students into action, and their numbers rapidly increased as the administration tried with typical bluster to assert its authority. The students put their point of view in the bi-monthly *Free-Speech Movement News Letters;* which brought hundreds, and later thousands, of students without previous political experience into the movement. The ensuing struggle taught them a few fundamental truths about the nature of the State, and in particular about the relationship of the university with the world of business, local politics and the people.

This student struggle at Berkeley was significant in that it helped to underline the dilemma of a rich but increasingly bureaucratic society.

The Berkeley model was copied at Berlin University a few years later, with Paris following suit soon afterwards. Here we shall look, therefore, not so much at the specific causes of the violent protest of the SDS (the left-wing German student Union) but at the way it influenced events in France.

In Germany, the call for university reform became a rallying cry for students and a strong one, in the absence of an effective parliamentary opposition to West German capitalism. As a result, the German student movement became the standard bearer of resistance to both the German state and also to American atrocities in Vietnam.

While the German students were challenging the system, their French colleagues were becoming increasingly alive to the total failure of the reformist policies advocated by the UNEF (National Union of French Students). Unfortunately, the extreme Left was devoting all its energies to making scientific, Marxist analyses of the situation, which, despite their learned character, did little to mobilize the students for *their own* struggle.

However, as opposition to the Vietnam war assumed international proportions, French students, particularly in Paris, were increasingly involved in campus demonstrations, the more so as their hatred of this war went hand in hand with the dawning realization that their own universities were nothing but cogs in the capitalist machine.

STUDENTS AND SOCIETY

There are 600,000 of us; sometimes treated as mere children, sometimes as adults. We work, but produce nothing. Often we have no money, but few of us are really poor. Although most of us come from the bourgeoisie, we do not always behave like them. The girls among us look like boys but are not sure whether they really want to be boys. We look upon our professors as part father, part boss and part teacher, and can't quite make up our minds about them. Some of us are destined to control the nation, others will become poorly paid intellectual hacks—but every one of us is privileged for all that. There are 600,000 of us—the so-called "students" of the military academy at St. Cyr, the artists and the "arties," the technocrats of the faculty of political science (the École Nationale d'Administration), and the rigid Marxist "intellectuals" of the Sorbonne, of Nanterre and elsewhere. We include followers of *L'Humanité* and "militant" journals, assiduous readers of *Le Monde,* and devotees of the sporting press or the cinema, beatniks, crammers, spoilt rich kids who never graduate, girls who will marry during their first year, but meanwhile study law, languages and even psychology, dunces, duds, future mathematicians and doctors. How can one "understand" modern students? Only by trying to understand their place in society.

A modern university has two contradictory roles. To begin with, a university must churn out the trained personnel that is so essential for bureaucratic capitalism. The system needs an ever increasing number of engineers, technicians, scientists, teachers, administrators and sociologists to organize production, to "rationalize" industrial methods, to run the gigantic state machine, "to adjust the psychology of individuals and groups" and to preserve their sanity, even to "organize" leisure activities. Now, since the bourgeoisie itself cannot provide enough student material from among its own ranks, increasing numbers of bright lads are recruited from the lower middle classes and even the proletariat and the peasantry. The "right-thinking" Left concentrates its fire on the class structure of French higher education, but stressing that only 6 per cent of the students are the sons of workers, when, in fact, they should be attacking the social function of the university: the production of a managerial élite. If some self-destructive fit should seize the bourgeoisie overnight and persuade it to recruit students exclusively from among the sons of manual workers, the university would become more democratic only in its composition. To the extent that the development of new manufacturing techniques is increasingly eliminating the need for unskilled labour, it is inevitable that pseudo-democratization by the recruitment of working class children to the universities will increase. In the past, the economic depression of the working and lower middle classes meant that sending one child, let alone several children, to the university imposed an intolerable financial burden on the family, but higher wages and government grants now make it more and more possible. And what all the reformists—be they Communists, Social Democrats or left-wing Gaullists—really mean when they cry for the "democratization" of the universities, is that this process be speeded up.

But in any case it is obvious that, as capitalism increases its demands for graduates, not only the prize pigs, but more and more horses, sheep, even chickens, will all be pressed into the sausage machine. Now this is precisely where the contradiction in the system lies. The production of the maximum number of graduate workers in the minimum time calls for increasingly closer contacts between the universities and industry, for the ever greater adaptation of education to specific industrial needs. But at the same time, the university is supposed to be the supreme guardian of "culture," human reason and disinterested research, of unalloyed truth and objectivity. In brief, the university is supposed to be the temple and eternal repository of the spiritual values of society. Now if for "spiritual values" we read the "ideology and values of the ruling class," we are left with the role the university has played from the Middle Ages down to the First World War. We might say that during this period the "social" and "cultural" role of the universities more or less overlapped. Society needed a relatively small number of lawyers, doctors, philosophers and professors, and chose them almost exclusively from among the sons of the ruling class. These enjoyed a humanistic and liberal education and were prepared to condone the most glaring social contradictions, while comforting themselves with the thought that the bourgeoisie was a champion of liberalization, democracy, universal education, etcetera. Later, a measure of petty bourgeois radicalism began to filter into the university, but was contained at a purely theoretical level: the crisis of society had not yet really occupied the academies.

Today, it is the economic rather than the theoretical role of the university which is predominant. This explains why the universities have been split up into a set of technical high schools, so many appendages to the major industries. But the system is internally inconsistent—it can only function by trying to suppress its own logic. The "cultural" function of the university is constantly assailed and has constantly to be re-affirmed. After all, even an alienated society cannot allow itself to become alienated to the point of psychosis. Even a totalitarian society, with its determination to subjugate every part of life to the will of the ruling class, group or party, cannot in the long run afford to suppress scientific *objectivity*, and without it, would quickly perish. For the strictest utilitarian reasons, modern societies need fundamental and "disinterested" research— because advances in applied technology depend on them. This the American bourgeoisie has come to realize more and more clearly.

Hence the basic problem of higher education is, then, that, while it cannot completely ignore the old humanistic values, since, after all, scientists and research workers must be produced, only the fragmentation of knowledge can supply all the faceless managers and technicians that are needed.

We have seen that the students are a socially heterogeneous group. They are also a transitory one, and their variety of social expectations increases their heterogeneity. Depending on his subject and the importance of his family connexions, a student may end up with a job worth 30,000 francs a month, and quite a few students want nothing better than that.

Their studies take from three to seven years. Hence while the younger students are still irresponsible adolescents, their older colleagues are men with a profession. Nor do these extremes always understand one another.

And yet it was these very students, the most heterogeneous of all social groups, who succeeded in banding together for collective political action, as witness their resistance to war in Algeria and the events of May 1968. The student movement was, in fact, the only "hard" reaction against the war in Algeria, what with violent demonstrations, and constant propaganda campaigns during the later years. It was always given out that "only a minority" participated in these student protests, but this minority represented at least 25 per cent of the French student population. As for the rest of the country, their protests remained largely verbal. The absence of organized protest outside of the universities can be laid squarely at the door of the Communist Party—it was both unwilling and unable to organize effective opposition to the war and support for the Algerian revolutionaries. Only towards the very end, did the Communist Party see fit to hold a few demonstrations, including the one at Charonne Métro Station (Paris) where eight people were killed by the police.

The remarkable phenomenon of student opposition was due to several factors, chief among them what so many people call sneeringly "the revolt of modern youth." Now this revolt, which involves ever larger numbers of young people throughout the world, must not be confused with the old "conflict between the generations." The latter, as we know it, particularly in earlier forms of bourgeois society, reflected the impatience of the young to step into the shoes of the old. This impatience often took the form of an attack on the fossilized thinking of the older generation and sometimes crystallized into a liberal, radical or a reformist attitude. In the current revolt of youth, however, very much more is being questioned—the distaste is for the system itself. Modern youth is not so much envious of, as disgusted with, the dead, empty lives of their parents. This feeling began among bourgeois children but has now spread through all levels of society. Daniel Mothé (*Socialisme ou Barbarie* No. 33) has shown clearly how opposed young workers are to both the "values" that capitalist society has to offer them and also to working class values and traditional forms of organization (political parties and trade unions). Factory work, trade union "militancy," verbose party programmes, and the sad, colourless life of their elders are subjects only for their sarcasm and contempt.

The same sort of disdain is the reason why so many students have taken a radical stand, and have made common cause with young workers in the struggle against a repressive society.

Another factor in the student revolt was their own position in the system and the special problems it brings to light.

A minority of students accept the culture which is being dispensed to them, and the knowledge which is being ladled out, with the trust of small children. They have been completely taken in by what we have called the mythical secondary function of the modern university as the temple of values. They dutifully attend all their lectures, and try above all to pass off as their own their professor's ideas; their ambitions stop short at the coveted degree, or perhaps to become, if they are worthy of it, professors themselves. However, this fraction of student opinion is fast dwindling away—for reasons we shall examine below. Another fraction can see through the system, but keep their eyes firmly on the main chance: they are the opportunists, only concerned with their professional future. They realize that much of what they are taught is false, or at least inadequate, they have no illusions about the purely utilitarian function of their education, know that they will be fitted to hold down a "good" job, and are willing to accept the official bribes of privilege, a car, holidays abroad, money, a house in the country.

This section can always be mobilized in defence of the system. More often, however, they simply sit back and watch their more militant colleagues fight battles from which all students will benefit: for less overcrowding, better facilities, etcetera.

But for a third and constantly growing group, university life itself raises a series of fundamental questions. And once they start to analyse their own problems, the logic of their conclusions drives them on ultimately to reject the whole of contemporary society. This is because, as an essential part of the social system, the university necessarily contains all the contradictions, conflicts and paradoxes that characterize society itself.

We have said a university is supposed to be a seat of learning and rational inquiry. Now what young economist, for instance, can seriously believe in the rational character of the contemporary economic scene, whether planned or not? And only a few diehards among their teachers still pretend that the system is even capable of rationalization. How can an economist talk seriously about the rational distribution of goods in view of the glaring contradiction between the affluence of the highly industrialized countries and the misery of the Third World? How can a young industrial psychologist help being lead to self-questioning when he sees that the object of his discipline is to "fit the man to the job" and that the job itself is deadly and quite futile? How can a young physicist ignore the theoretical crisis that is shaking the very foundations of contemporary physics and with it all its claims to be an exact science; how can he tell himself that his research is of benefit to humanity, in an age which has produced the H-bomb? Can he really avoid wondering about his personal responsibility when the greatest atomic scientists themselves are beginning to question the function of science and its role in society?

And how can students of social psychology possibly shut their eyes to their professional role: to help in the sacred interest of profit, to break in more workers to the conveyor belt, or to launch yet another useless product on the market?

If these doubts about the value of one's studies are examined, inevitably the system which organizes it is brought into question as well. Subjects for courses are picked out of the hat; there is no logic in the curriculum, other than keeping research subservient to the demands of industry or, perhaps, the professor's next book. . . .

For all that, we are not so much protesting that our education is out of touch with the needs of the future, nor complaining about the shortage of jobs. We totally reject the entire system. Our protest only turns into violent action because the structure of society cannot be smashed by talk or ballot papers. To dream of turning the university into an "island unto itself," where every man will be able to work in independence and peace, is in any case an empty dream because the future "intellectual worker" will not be able to accept the fragmented and alienated life which this dream entails. . . .

THE PATTERN FOR THE FUTURE

A society without exploitation is inconceivable where the management of production is controlled by one social class, in other words where the division of society into managers and workers is not totally abolished. Now, the workers are told day after day that they are incapable of managing their own factory, let alone society, and they have come to believe this fairy tale. This is precisely what leads to their alienation in a capitalist society, and this is precisely why socialists must do their utmost to restore the people's autonomy and not just doctor the economic ills of the West.

It is not by accident that liberals, Stalinist bureaucrats and reformists alike, all reduce the evils of capitalism to economic injustice, and exploitation to the unequal distribution of the national income. And when they extend their criticism of capitalism to other fields, they still imply that everything would be solved by a fairer distribution of wealth. The sexual problems of youth and the difficulties of family life are ignored—all that apparently needs to be solved is the problem of prostitution. Problems of culture come down to the material cost of dispensing it. Of course, this aspect is important, but a man is more than a mere consumer, he can not only get fed, he can get fed up as well. While most of man's problems are admittedly economic, man also demands the right to find fulfilment on every other possible level. If a social organization is repressive it will be so on the sexual and cultural no less than on the economic planes.

As our society becomes more highly industrialized, the workers' passive alienation turns into active hostility. To prevent this happening, there have been many attempts to "adapt the workers," "give them a stake in society," and quite a few technocrats now think this is the only hope of salvaging "the democratic way of life."

But however comfortable they may make the treadmill, they are determined never to give the worker control of the wheel. Hence many militants have come to ask themselves how they can teach the workers that their only hope lies in revolution. Now, this merely reintroduces the old concept of the vanguard of the proletariat, and so threatens to create a new division within society. The workers need no teachers; they will learn the correct tactics from the class struggle. And the class struggle is not an abstract conflict of ideas, it is people fighting in the street. Direct control can only be gained through the struggle itself. Any form of class struggle, over wages, hours, holidays, retirement, if it is pushed through to the end, will lead to a general strike, which in turn introduces a host of new organizational and social problems. For instance, there cannot be a total stoppage of hospitals, transport, provisions, etcetera, and the responsibility for organizing these falls on the strikers. The longer the strike continues, the greater the number of factories that have to be got going again. Finally the strikers will find themselves running the entire country.

This gradual restoration of the economy is not without its dangers, for a new managerial class may emerge to take over the factories if the workers are not constantly on their guard. They must ensure that they retain control over their delegated authorities at all times. Every function of social life—planning, liaison and coordination—must be taken up by the producers themselves, as and when the need arises.

It is certain that the managerial class will do everything they can to prevent a real revolution. There will be intimidation and violent repression, prophets both new and old of every shape and form will be held up to bamboozle the workers. There will be election campaigns, referenda, changes in the cabinet, electoral reforms, red herrings, bomb plots and what have you. At the same time, the experts will preach about the dire threat to the national economy and international prestige of the country. And should the workers turn a deaf ear to them, and persist in restarting production under their direct control, the managerial class will end up, as always, by calling in the army and police. This is precisely what happened in France in 1968, and not for the first time either.

What of the future? We cannot produce a blueprint—the future alone can evolve that. What we must agree on, rather, are the general principles of the society we want to create. The politicians tell us we live in an age of technological miracles. But it is up to us to apply them to a new society, to use the new media so as to gain greater mastery over the environment. While people today simply watch television as a surrogate for the lives they have ceased to live, in the new society they will use it as a means of widening their experience, of mastering the environment and of keeping in touch with the real lives of other people. If television programmes were to be put on for their social value and not solely because they induce the maximum hypnosis in the greatest numbers, they would enable us to extend the real democracy to the entire population. . . . Now, at the time, [May 1968] the politically conscious students were, in fact, still a minority, and they knew it. Hence they never set themselves up as champions of the "common interest of all students," but simply demanded the right to express political opinions within the campus and without police interference. They realized full well that the main body of students were far more interested in furthering their careers than in social justice.

It was because of this that the Communist Party has accused us of despising the students. In fact, we only despise the sons of the bourgeoisie who, not only content with belonging to a privileged class, clamour for its privileges and are ready to defend them. Students differ in their political opinions as in everything else. Moreover, they are not a class, and they have no objective interests to defend. In a truly democratic society, higher education will be open to all, and students will cease to be a group apart. We do not, therefore, despise students as such but only those who applaud the men with the whip, who move in against every revolution.

But let us return to the events themselves. It was the action of the authorities that opened the eyes of many previously uncommitted students. Our "provocation" daily brought the latent authoritarianism of the bureaucracy into the open. As soon as any real problems were brought up, dialogue gave place to the policeman's baton: in Berkeley and Berlin no less than in Paris. The pathetic excuses put forward by the university dignitaries, who thought every pussy cat was a tiger, have left many a liberal observer perplexed.

"Was it really necessary, on account of a handful of troublemakers, to suspend all lectures in two faculties? It seems that the authorities lacked sang-froid. It is certainly true that small groups of the extreme Left, or at least several among them, have turned provocation into a weapon of war. Loving absolute truths and even more the fear they arouse in the 'bourgeoisie,' they claim that examinations help to perpetuate an archaic and meaningless system of education. But do we really have to take them so seriously?" . . .

If lack of political understanding means the rejection of bureaucracies big (e.g. the Communists and the Social Democrats) and small (e.g. the Trotskyist splinter groups), and the denial that the workers must be led by a revolutionary élite; if lack of political interest means being bored with platform rhetoric, with theories that have no practical application, with resolutions, petitions, marches, congresses and annual dinners; if lack of political interest is the rejection of all the phoney alternatives (Communists vs. Social Democrats; London vs. Paris; Mendès-France vs. Mitterand; Mali vs. Guinea; gin and tonic vs. tonic and gin; the King in his palace vs. the palace in King Street; the Six vs. the Common Market)—if lack of political interest means all this, then indeed most young workers and working intellectuals have become eminently apolitical. The origins of our movement, the absence of officials in the district and factory Action Committees alone demonstrate that no professional agitator or theoretician was ever seen or ever needed. Better still, the Action Committees stopped such people meddling in practice. All that was most effective at Nanterre and in the fighting—our ability to rally where the action was hottest, and to take common decisions without consulting the "leadership" of the splinter groups— all this went into the creation of Action Committees. They were born for the purpose of solving concrete common problems and sharing life in battle, rendering aid to the strikers, and helping wherever help was most needed. All individuals and splinter groups involved in the student struggle or the strike movement felt the urgent need to unite for the sake of greater efficiency. Solidarity became not an ideological slogan but a necessity. Almost overnight, atomized individuals turned into vital groups, into genuine communities (for several weeks in Sorbonne, and at the new annex in the rue de Censier, members of various Action Committees lived together almost continuously).

The petty life of yesterday was left behind; gone the dingy office, the boredom in a tiny flat, with a tiny television and, outside, a tiny road with a tiny car; gone the repetition, the studied gestures, the regimentation and the lack of joy and desire. . . .

2. THE WORKERS

The students' movement triggered off that of the workers. The students went into the streets and, by their courage, they brought out the people, took the universities, and attacked the Stock Exchange. Faced with the combined forces of the government, the educational authorities, the police, and the trade union bureaucracies, they showed their ability to provoke errors and to exploit them. Moreover, they proved that it is possible to occupy factories— would the workers but realize it—without running the slightest risks. The student movement developed its radical critique of the authorities to a fine point but, in the absence of mass support, it was bound to fail in the long run.

The students were deeply disappointed when, on the morning after the "night of the barricades," the workers did not take to the streets, but limited their sympathy to going on a twenty-four-hour general strike, which had been called by the trade unions and was political only in its choice of date: 13 May—the day on which de Gaulle had assumed power in 1958. Then, on Tuesday, 14th, late in the evening, the students holding the Sorbonne learned that some workers had gone much further than their trade union bosses intended: they occupied the Sud-Aviation works in Nantes. This movement spread rapidly and spontaneously—from 14 to 17 May, a host of other factories fell to the workers.

In this wave of strikes, which were illegal because no advance notice was given, it was the young workers, most of whom were not members of the trade unions, who proved the most militant and tenacious. These strikes, unlike the official ones, were not for any precise wage claims, but simply, as several strikers put it, because "we've had a bellyful." A bellyful of low wages, true, but beyond that, a bellyful of futility and the boredom of the daily round, of a life that stamped them, like everyone else, a hollow replica of their fathers and grandfathers, perhaps slightly more comfortable, but no less vacuous. What they felt was something they had not learned from any books, something so primitive and deep that it did not give way before the power of the state or the threats of the bosses, or even before the cajoling of the unions.

To accuse the CGT of treachery in May and June is nonsense—it had shown its hand long before. The trade unions, in France as elsewhere in the West, play the part of the "loyal opposition," and in May 1968, the workers simply turned down their thumbs not only on the contestants but also on the game itself.

Unfortunately most of them failed to take that final and decisive step beyond bourgeois legality: the actual running of the factories by and for themselves. The extraordinary scope of the movement is not any the less remarkable; it was both immense and spontaneous and it produced a degree of awareness and discussion that was often extremely high, and sometimes exemplary. The workers had no time for abstract theories; at the beginning especially they were groping their way, and would sometimes, particularly when frustrated, turn back to their old ways of thinking. They acted often for the sake of action alone, with no conscious goal, neither knowing nor caring where their actions would lead. Their feelings are hard to explain to anyone who has not, like them, been left to his own devices at a time of crisis, and found it necessary to act first and look for what theories can be deduced from the practice, afterwards. But from their experiences perhaps we can learn something of the forces which are already constructing the future. Hence it is worth trying to understand, for example, the workers' feelings about the Grenelle agreement and other industrial negotiations by the trade unions. Most of them realized, albeit dimly, that they were being sold down the river once again. It was this very feeling that one worker expressed to his astonished trade union leaders, when he said: "It's not you who started the strike. It was the ones who were willing to use force. Afterwards you tried to take charge and fob us off with the usual claims. You threw a spanner in the works, and that's why we have washed our hands of you." What had emerged at last, and had hitherto been no more than the pious hope of some of the extreme-left groups, was the explicit demand for responsibility and control over production, and it sprang from the sense of brotherhood that had developed in the struggle itself, and pointed towards a new and better society. It was this that made our movement so truly revolutionary, it is because of this that we can be sure it will spring up again. Moreover, in several cases strikers did, in fact, start running the factories on their own account. In this action can be seen the essence, the highest achievement, of the movement. Elsewhere the strikers organized their own food supplies with the help of students, small farmers and lorry drivers. Others again did try to apply radical solutions but grew more and more frightened as the general return to work speeded up and the traditional forces re-established their hold. The vision of the bolder among them acted as a leaven in the passive mass of the general consciousness, and deserves credit for that fact alone. . . .

II
THE STRATEGY OF THE STATE

INTRODUCTION

The Empire, with the coup d'état for its certificate of birth, universal suffrage for its sanction, and the sword for its sceptre, professed to rest upon the peasantry, the large mass of producers not directly involved in the struggle of capital and labour. It professed to save the working class by breaking down Parliamentarism and, with it, the undisguised subserviency of Government to the propertied classes. It professed to save the propertied classes. It professed to save the propertied classes by upholding their economic supremacy over the working class; and, finally, it professed to unite all classes by reviving for all the chimera of national glory. (Karl Marx: *The Civil War in France.*)

All "democratic" bourgeois authority is supposed to represent the interests of the nation as a whole. Since it ostensibly places itself above the conflicts within society, it can use the "will of the majority" to remove the cause of these conflicts. It is in the name of this principle that it justifies its actions during periods of overt class struggle. At times of crisis, the machinery, strategy and true nature of authority are brought into the open. Indeed, to provoke this is one of the primary and fundamental tasks of the revolutionary movement. To make the workers accept the ideology of, and repression by, the State the bourgeoisie has brought in a whole system of control and enslavement—a system that becomes more and more complex with increased industrialization and automation. Now, this very complexity renders the State less and less capable of decisive action in an emergency. It must therefore do its utmost to stop such emergencies from arising in the first place.

The French crisis was, at first, a crisis within a single institution—the university. We shall therefore begin by looking at the strategy of the State, or rather its nonstrategy, against the revolutionary student movement. . . .

THE AUTHORITY OF THE STATE AND THE
VULNERABILITY OF SOCIETY

The State has an army, a police force, and judges, to fight its battles. The State is above the law because it makes the law, and it will not hesitate to use all its power to defend itself. This could be seen in its reactions to the demonstrations at the Place de la Concorde and l'Étoile—when pained incomprehension gave way to panic. The liberal mask was dropped, and overnight the State resorted to naked force. The authorities had no overall strategy but acted pragmatically from day to day, issuing order after contradictory order. And, of course, neither the police, universities nor judiciary could take any action without a decision at ministerial level—an ironic example of the split between the executive and administrative arms.

The initial strategy of the authorities was to try intimidation. Manipulating justice and the parliamentary machine, they went into business on a grand scale. There were sermons and sentences in the courts (and they even managed to stage a hearing on a Sunday!); the law played its part as obediently as any policeman. Those who were suspected of having participated in the demonstrations were held up to public ridicule, like so many drunkards in the stocks. But in fact the victims attracted more sympathy than disgust. It is generally agreed now that most of the police evidence was trumped up. Sentence did not depend on the part played by the accused, but on the violence of the general demonstration.

"At a time when Paris has been chosen as the site for negotiations on Vietnam, and is showing the whole world that it has no peer as a capital of peace, we cannot allow a handful of agitators to abuse the tradition of French hospitality, to commit acts of violence in the plain light of day, not even sparing passers-by. These acts call down severe punishment upon the heads of those responsible, the more so as all of us know that the great majority of young people have no desire to cause trouble." (M. Caldaquès, Chairman of the Paris Council.)

"What do they study, these young students? They would be more at home in gaol than in a university. It is disappointing to discover that a handful of young people in revolt can stop the entire university system." (*Figaro*, 4 May.)

But hard though they tried to slander the movement, to put it outside of the law—they even went to the length of sentencing the noted Catholic student leader M. Clément (President of the Richelieu Student Centre)—their efforts all came to nothing. No one in his right senses paid the slightest attention to, for instance, such diatribes as the one mouthed by M. Peyrefitte on 6 May: "What right does a union have to launch a strike which does not respect the legal formalities and, moreover, calls airily on teachers to abandon their mission, their students and their university tradition?" (Peyrefitte, 6 May.)

At this stage, as we saw, the authorities brought in the police and the army. It should be said in all fairness that the police were not ordered to shoot, but they nevertheless went into action with considerable relish. Their brutality is well documented: houses were broken into; young people rounded up at gunpoint; and afterwards in the cells, there were beatings and sadistic tortures. It should also be noted that the authorities called in the police well before the students had taken to the streets—as soon as the administration felt they had lost the argument—and that once unleashed the police behaved in a manner that disgusted even their masters. Thus Pompidou felt impelled to disavow their atrocities, and his speech on 11 May brought a sharp reaction from the police: on 13 May, the Federal Police Union issued a press communiqué, the last lines of which ran: "The Union considers the declaration of the Prime Minister an endorsement of student violence and an attempt to disassociate himself from police actions the government itself had ordered. We find it astonishing that, in these circumstances, a dialogue with the students was not started before these regrettable riots occurred." . . .

The police traditionally hate French students, whom they see as the pampered offspring of the bourgeoisie—indeed, in their own Fascist way, they live out their part of the class struggle. But this time the new tactics and extreme mobility of the demonstrators took them completely by surprise. Moreover, in their hunt for students, the police had cordoned off certain districts at night, and then carried out house-to-house searches that antagonized the local population. Indoctrinated, regimented, bribed with special privileges and bonuses, they had undeniably developed a certain "flic" mentality. Usually, when called on, they respond with violence—but not always. In ordinary times, they are tolerated by the people, it is on this toleration that their power depends, and it only lasts so long as they are believed to be preserving the public peace. The Prime Minister's disavowal came when the country was in the throes of a crisis—the working class had entered the struggle. In these circumstances even the bulldogs in the police force began to wonder where their true loyalties lay. On 22 May, they issued what amounted to an ultimatum:

"We hope that the public authorities will bear in mind what we have said (wage claims for the whole force, a denunciation of the Prime Minister's speech, and expressions of regret that the police could not participate in the general protests), and that they will not try to use the police systematically to oppose the workers' demands for better conditions, lest the police find the performance of certain duties in conflict with their conscience." . . .

THE NATURE OF THE COMMUNIST BUREAUCRACY

The behaviour of the Communist Party throughout these critical months can only be understood in the context of international politics and the historical background. The present phase of capitalism is characterized by the concentration of economic and political power in the hands of the State, and by the parallel growth of a "workers'" bureaucracy in the industrial and political field. Now this bureaucracy, far from trying to represent the workers, endeavours to persuade them of the general benefits of capitalist production, while staking its own claim to a managerial say in the running of industry and the State. Internally, it is organized very much as is the capitalist system: it has a hierarchical structure in which the top becomes increasingly remote from the bottom. And as industries are becoming ever more complex and gigantic, the bourgeoisie and the capitalist State have discovered that they are quite unable to manage the vast problem of labour relations, and more than welcome the help of the new bureaucracy. In particular, they are quite willing to grant these bureaucrats privileges, to consult them during moments of crisis, or even to charge them with the conduct of public affairs, for only in that way are they able to find willing helpers in imposing their vital demands—greater productivity, wage-freezes, no strikes—on the mass of the workers, who would otherwise turn a deaf ear to them. But not content with this subservient role, the "workers" bureaucracy has been trying to wrest a seat in the very centres of economic power, on the boards of the increasingly important State industries, the latest offspring of the capitalist system. As a result, the "workers'" bureaucracy now consists of two strata: trade unionists and managers of industry. Their short-term interests do not always coincide: the trade unionists, unlike the managers, must preserve a semblance of concern with the proletariat for it is only inasmuch as they can claim to be "representative" of the workers that they have any power. However, their model of society—State, property, planning, specialist control of the economy, a social hierarchy based on ability, the subordination of man to the industrial machine, the improvement of living conditions through the production of more consumer goods, State control of all social and cultural activities—does not differ essentially from that of the economic bureaucracy. And that is precisely why both branches of the bureaucracy, in France no less than abroad,

have the same long-term interests as the bourgeoisie, and
why the Communist Party of France is so concerned with
what it chooses to call the "national interest."

This explains why the Communist Party is unable to
come out with a real analysis of modern French capitalism,
why it disguises the real issue with such red herrings as
"personal power," "a handful of multimillionaires" and
other twaddle—which only serves to disguise their community of interest with their so-called adversaries. In point
of fact, there is nothing to distinguish the theses of the
Communist Party from, say, those of the Gaullist Left,
albeit the Party dismisses them as utopian and confused.
It does not fight them as such, but simply argues that the
Gaullist movement is incapable of implementing them,
since it is the Gaullists' right and not the left wing that has
the greatest electoral appeal and hence the major say.

But this is only part of the picture. The Communist
Party, which once represented the revolutionary consciousness of the proletariat, has been subject to yet another
process of degeneration: it has become a mere appendage
of the Soviet bureaucracy. In that role it often comes into
open conflict with the Social Democratic or Gaullist
bureaucracies. Thus when the interests of the Soviet bureaucrats clash with those of their capitalist counterparts,
the Communist Party will invariably mobilize the workers
against the latter. Conversely, once the Soviet bureaucracy
has come to terms with the capitalists, the Party will go
out of its way to cement this agreement, and stop any
working-class activity that might jeopardize it. During periods of conflict the Communist bureaucrats bandy about
revolutionary phrases; during lulls they invariably adopt
a patriotic and reactionary tone. It is only by grasping these
two aspects of the Communist bureaucracy—self-interest
and subservience to the Soviet bureaucracy—that we can
hope to understand the political vagaries of the French
Communist Party from its beginnings to our day.

It is its attachment to the Soviet bureaucracy that causes
the Communist Party of France to adopt an ultra-national-
ist stance every so often, to be more patriotic than the
patriots, more flag-waving than even the Gaullists, the
better to deflect the working class from its true objective—
the struggle against the bourgeoisie and all forms of authority—and to mobilize them against the Soviet bugbear of
the moment, be it "Revanchist" Germany, American Imperialism, or "personal power." It is this double role that
dictates their day-to-day attitudes and language, and not

some temporary aberration or treachery, as so many good
socialists still like to believe. The Communist Party of
France defends its own interests and only betrays those who
fail to understand that these interests are not so much
unpatriotic—and who could blame them for that when
the workers have no country?—as unsocialist.

Unfortunately, the Party's links with the Soviet bureaucracy have yet another untoward result: they play directly
into the hands of bourgeois propagandists. When dealing
with Stalinist Russia, the capitalists do not have to resort
to lies or slander—they need only describe the "socialist
paradise" as it really was: a country of purges, concentration camps, forced collectivization and police terror
(Cheka, OGPU, NKVD, or whatever the successive names
of this permanent institution may be). There is not a
Gaullist candidate, particularly if he is on the left of the
Party or even an ex-Trotskyist militant like David Rousset,
who does not labour this point. As a result, the bourgeoisie
has an easy time in dismissing all working-class demands
as so many attempts to set up a totalitarian dictatorship.
This is precisely what the Gaullists tried to do throughout
the electoral campaign. The Communist Party therefore
allied itself with the authorities in two ways, firstly by
preventing the struggle from assuming revolutionary dimensions, and secondly by permitting the capitalists to
raise the bugbear of Stalinism.

It is only because of its authentic revolutionary origins,
because of memories of what the Russian Revolution was
before it became transformed into a hideous bureaucracy,
that the Communist Party of France has been able to keep
its hold on the French working class. Even today the Party
continues to publish the works of Marx and of Lenin and
of other revolutionaries, even though these writings have
ceased to have any bearing on the Party's practical policies.
It behaves like all reformist bodies, plays the electoral
game, adopts the practices of bourgeois democracy, is
deeply involved in the system, and makes pacts of all sorts
with capitalists. It participates in local government while
obeying the laws and principles of its class enemies; during
elections, it speaks with a thousand voices, defending small
holdings when it addresses the peasants, petty trade when
it speaks to the shopkeepers, and calling for better conditions in the army when it speaks to the soldiers. In short,
the Party has a theory for purely internal consumption,
and an electoral policy for external use, and the two cannot possibly be reconciled. Now, while the electoral policy

has turned the Party into a "big party," the theory helps to provide Party activists with an ideology—this is important to them, for in that way alone can they feel superior to the Social Democrats who differ from them only in overtly rejecting the Marxist-Leninist line. In short, this unsavoury mixture of theoretical rectitude and electoral compromise provides the Party itself with millions of voters, and its militants with a sense of purpose. This is the entire difference between Stalinist and Reformist organizations, and explains why Communist militants can defend the same policies as the Social Democrats, but with the added conviction that they alone are working for the revolution. This fact alone explains why the Party was so violently hostile to the student movement, because the May events brought the profound contradictions between the conviction of the militants and the policy of the bureaucrats into the open. During relatively peaceful periods —deliberately fostered by the Party—reformist practices can be justified by pointing to the impossibility of a truly revolutionary alternative, but how can this be done during revolutionary periods? That is why the Party does its utmost to ensure that no such situation arises, for only thus can it prevent its own militants from becoming "infected" with the Leftist virus. During peaceful periods, the Party bureaucrats can afford to dismiss Leftist propaganda as the ravings of splinter groups with no influence over the masses of workers. In other words they can claim that the workers will not heed the revolutionary message and that the Party therefore has every right to disguise its "true" revolutionary intentions. But this argument no longer holds during general strikes, when the Leftist message begins to "bite" and rank-and-file Party militants begin to realize that the workers are responding to the very truths the Party has been at such pains to conceal from them. No wonder then, that, in May 1968 for instance, the Party leaders were so bitter in their denunciations of Leftism! It also explains their peculiar tactics against the Left; ostensibly still members of a revolutionary and Leninist Party, they could not attack Leftism for what it was, and so had perforce to resort to lies and calumny. . . .

The Communist trade union bureaucracy cannot, of course, afford to use open violence against the workers whom, after all, they are supposed to represent, but must wheedle them into acting against their own interests, for instance in calling off a strike.

There are, admittedly, occasions when the trade union

bosses throw their normal caution to the wind and try to impose their will by force, but these are the exception: such methods invariably recoil and lose them the support of large numbers of militants. Hence the bureaucrats prefer to save their violence for individuals whom they first isolate from the mass of workers. For the rest they try to cow all opposition with a whole armoury of tricks and ruses. These they can play the more easily, as the workers are kept in complete ignorance of what is happening at the top.

Not that the workers themselves fully accept this situation. In periods of industrial peace, they simply stay away from union meetings and take no interest in a policy that is obviously not tailored to their needs, but during crises, they come up directly against the will of the bureaucracy. In fact, the class struggle continues at all times and expresses itself in a variety of forms ranging from passive resistance to wildcat strikes either against a particular employer or in solidarity with other workers. Now, once a group of workers wants to go on strike they are expected to pass through the normal trade union channels, and if the trade union does not approve—and it rarely approves of any strike that it has not called itself—it will try to put up every possible obstacle, with the result that, unless millions of workers are determined to strike at one time, the struggle remains purely local and generally fizzles out. To frustrate a strike, all the bureaucracy need normally do is to refuse to issue directives, and then sit back and watch it die. In a factory, the shop-steward faced with a demand for strike action will accordingly do nothing at all, hoping for the pressure to subside. If it does not, he will eventually call a meeting and adopt a completely passive attitude. This takes the workers, who are accustomed to instructions from above, completely by surprise and helps to shake those who are still undecided. ("The shop-steward is obviously not interested, so we are bound to fail.") If the "rabid" elements still persist, a secret vote is called for, and such votes invariably favour the most conservative elements. True, in a police state, the secret vote is a guarantee of democracy, but among comrades all it guarantees is anonymity for the weaklings.

Generally, at this stage, the bureaucracy carries the day —the workers do not feel strong enough to start a strike without the support of their union. But if even this tactic fails, the bureaucrats have yet another card up their sleeve:

they preach defeatism and try to undermine the workers' morale.

To begin with, they will try the trusted old policy of divide and rule: "You may go on strike, but the rest won't follow you, despite all their promises. They are sure to leave you in the lurch." Or: "It's easy for you to go on strike, but then you don't have any children to feed. . . ." Or again: "If you're so keen on this strike, why weren't you in the last one?" One group of workers is told that the rest have already gone back to work when, in fact, they have not—a tactic that, as we saw, proved most effective in breaking the strike of the Paris transport workers in June 1968. And what real chance have the workers of catching them out in time, when only the officials have the right to enter other factories, to see for themselves?

Financial pressure is brought to bear on the workers as well—everyone knows that, just when they are most needed, the solidarity funds are invariably at their lowest.

And once the workers have been brought to their knees by all these manoeuvres, the blame is thrown on them.

In fact, their demoralization is maintained by the bureaucrats who have a vested interest in relegating the workers to the role of mere puppets, a flock of trained sheep who bleat when they are told to do so, and at no other time. Under no circumstances must they be allowed to have any say in the affairs of "their" trade unions. . . .

The shop-stewards, for example, who, in principle, are supposed to be links not only between workers and management but also between workers and their trade unions, are, in fact, so many mouthpieces for the bureaucracy. In their dealings with their workers or the management, the shop-stewards never take their orders directly from the workers but from their trade union bosses. They are not chosen freely by the workers from the most militant among their own ranks, but from a list of names submitted by the union. It goes without saying that those on the list are never put there for their revolutionary ardour or for the trust their fellow-workers have in them. Nor do the candidates necessarily come from the shop-floor they are supposed to represent; some shops may have several shop stewards while others have complete strangers or none at all. This situation gives the trade union the strictest control over the shop-stewards, and prevents the workers from pressing their own claims. In effect, the shop-stewards represent their union rather than the workers.

Since he does not represent them, and does not have to

be their spokesman, the shop-steward does not have to tell them what has been agreed in the manager's office, let alone ask their opinion before he goes up.

And should he be foolish enough to go against the wishes of the bureaucrats and consult the workers all the same, his name is certain to be absent from the list of candidates at the next election.

The trade union bureaucrats take a similarly high-handed attitude when it comes to the publication of factory magazines. Most of the articles are general propaganda for the current policies of the CGT; for the rest they consist of tit-bits, interunion disputes, and personal recriminations. These papers in no way represent the interests or reflect the preoccupations of the workers; at best they reflect the quarrels of their self-appointed leaders. Thus, whenever the workers take independent action, for example by striking, holding spontaneous meetings, or by electing action committees, the factory press passes over the matter in complete silence. That is why a revolutionary movement must do everything it can to encourage the workers to express their own views on their own struggle and their own problems. We must create a workers' press that will be something more than a mouthpiece of the trade union bureaucracy.

It is during shop and factory meetings that the workers make their wishes known most clearly, especially when such meetings are called for the purpose of taking concrete action. Now since such meetings often arrive at conclusions that are opposed to trade union policy, and since the shop-stewards can rarely prevent them from being called, the leaders keep in reserve for such occasions a whole battery of outside speakers and demagogues, trade union specialists. Some of these men are well-known public figures (which did not prevent the Renault workers from booing Seguy), others are skilled politicians who know how to "handle the masses," that is, to browbeat them. In the presence of such men, the workers generally refuse to say anything; the meeting turns from a discussion into a monologue, the more so as the hall is generally arranged in such a way as to make it more difficult for anyone but the official speaker to make himself heard. The other "officials" on the platform can add their bit whenever they feel like it, but the worker in the body of the hall must first get up and move conspicuously and laboriously across the floor, before he can have his say—if the chairman lets him, that is. If he is known as a "trouble-maker" he will generally be called right at the end or right at the beginning of the meeting, only to be cut down by the professionals, and this in such scathing terms that few others will care to carry on where he left off. And at the earliest opportunity, the platform will generally see to it that the original purpose of the meeting is forgotten and treat the audience to a homily on general trade-union policy.

But it may happen that the speaker, eloquent though he is, fails to carry the men with him. In that case, the bureaucrats will call for another meeting, this time at Union headquarters. Now if the workers find it difficult enough to make themselves heard on the shop floor, they get no chance at all when faced with a whole bevy of yes-men, loudly applauding the official view, and shouting down any opposition. These meetings, moreover, take place after working hours, and many workers who live far away, or have families, cannot attend. . . .

In short, the trade unions have become completely alienated from the workers. As a result, the workers have also lost faith not only in the trade unions, which they are fully justified to do, but have grown sceptical of all working-class movements.

Now this situation will continue until such time as the workers decide to take charge of their own destiny, until they refuse to delegate their powers to any set of bureaucrats. The workers' struggle against the exploiters is automatically a struggle against the trade union bureaucracy, since the two invariably work hand in glove—this, as I have tried to show, became particularly obvious during May and June 1968. Inasmuch as the struggle against capitalism and the State is a struggle for freedom and self-government, its objectives can clearly not be achieved with the help of organizations whose very structure is designed to thwart them. Hence, if the workers want to run society, they must fight their own battles. . . .

BY WAY OF CONCLUSION

There is no such thing as an isolated revolutionary act. Acts that can transform society take place in association with others, and form part of a general movement that follows its own laws of growth. All revolutionary activity is collective, and hence involves a degree of organization.

What we challenge is not the need for this but the need for a revolutionary leadership, the need for a party.

Central to my thesis is an analysis of the bureaucratic phenomenon, which I have examined from various viewpoints. For example, I have looked at the French workers' unions and parties and shown that what is wrong with them is not so much their rigidity and treachery as the fact that they have become integrated into the overall bureaucratic system of the capitalist state.

The emergence of bureaucratic tendencies on a world scale, the continuous concentration of capital, and the increasing intervention of the State in economic and social matters, have produced a new managerial class whose fate is no longer bound up with that of the private ownership of the means of production.

It is in the light of this bureaucratization that the Bolshevik Party has been studied. Although its bureaucratic nature is not, of course, its only characteristic, it is true to say that Communists, and also Trotskyists, Maoists and the rest, no less than the capitalist State, all look upon the proletariat as a mass that needs to be directed from above. As a result, democracy degenerates into the ratification at the bottom of decisions taken at the top, and the class struggle is forgotten while the leaders jockey for power within the political hierarchy.

The objections to Bolshevism are not so much moral as sociological; what we attack is not the evil conduct of some of its leaders but an organizational set-up that has become its one and only justification.

The most forceful champion of a revolutionary party was Lenin, who in his *What is to be done?* argued that the proletariat is unable by itself to reach a "scientific" understanding of society, that it tends to adopt the prevailing, i.e. the bourgeois, ideology.

Hence it was the essential task of the party to rid the workers of this ideology by a process of political education which could only come to them *from without*. Moreover, Lenin tried to show that the party can only overcome the class enemy by turning itself into a professional revolutionary body in which everyone is allocated a fixed task. Certain of its infallibility, a Party appoints itself the natural spokesman and sole defender of the interests of the working class, and as such wields power on their behalf— i.e. acts as a bureaucracy.

We take quite a different view: far from having to teach the masses, the revolutionary's job is to try to understand

and express their common aspirations; far from being Lenin's "tribune of the people who uses every manifestation of tyranny and oppression . . . to explain his Socialist convictions and his Social Democratic demands," the real militant must encourage the workers to struggle on their own behalf, and show how their every struggle can be used to drive a wedge into capitalist society. If he does so, the militant acts as an agent of the people and no longer as their leader.

The setting up of any party inevitably reduces freedom of the people to freedom to agree with the party.

In other words, democracy is not suborned by bad leadership but by the very existence of leadership. Democracy cannot even exist within the Party, because the Party itself is not a democratic organization, i.e. it is based upon authority and not on representation. Lenin realized full well that the Party is an artificial creation, that it was imposed upon the working class "from without." Moral scruples have been swept aside: the party is "right" if it can impose its views upon the masses and wrong if it fails to do so. For Lenin, the whole matter ends there. In his *State and Revolution,* Lenin did not even raise the problem of the relationship between the people and the party. Revolutionary power was a matter of fact, based upon people who are prepared to fight for it; the paradox is that the party's programme, endorsed by these people, was precisely: All power to the Soviets! But whatever its programme, in retrospect we can see that the Party, because of its basic conception, is bound to bring in privilege and bureaucracy, and we must wash our hands of all organizations of this sort. To try and pretend that the Bolshevik Party is truly democratic is to deceive oneself, and this, at least, is an error that Lenin himself never committed.

What then is our conception of the role of the revolutionary? To begin with, we are convinced that the revolutionary cannot and must not be a leader. Revolutionaries are a militant minority drawn from various social strata, people who band together because they share an ideology, and who pledge themselves to struggle against oppression, to dispel the mystification of the ruling classes and the bureaucrats, to proclaim that the workers can only defend themselves and build a socialist society by taking their fate into their own hands, believing that political maturity comes only from revolutionary struggle and direct action.

By their action, militant minorities can do no more than support, encourage, and clarify the struggle. They must always guard against any tendency to become a pressure group outside the revolutionary movement to the masses. When they act, it must always be with the masses, and not as a faction.

For some time, the 22 March Movement was remarkable only for its radical political line, for its methods of attack—often spontaneous—and for its non-bureaucratic structure. Its objectives and the role it could play became clear only during the events of May and June, when it attracted the support of the working class. These militant students whose dynamic theories emerged from their practice, were imitated by others, who developed new forms of action appropriate to their own situation. The result was a mass movement unencumbered by the usual chains of command. By challenging the repressive nature of their own institution—the university—the revolutionary students forced the state to show its hand, and the brutality with which it did so caused a general revulsion and led to the occupation of the factories and the general strike. The mass intervention of the working class was the greatest achievement of our struggle; it was the first step on the path to a better society, a path that, alas, was not followed to the end. The militant minorities failed to get the masses to follow their example: to take collective charge of the running of society. We do not believe for a single moment that the workers are incapable of taking the next logical step beyond occupying the factories—which is to run them on their own. We are sure that they can do what we ourselves have done in the universities. The militant minorities must continue to wage their revolutionary struggle, to show the workers what their trade unions try to make them forget: their own gigantic strength. The distribution of petrol by the workers in the refineries and the local strike committees show clearly what the working class is capable of doing once it puts its mind to it.

During the recent struggle, many student militants became hero-worshippers of the working class, forgetting that every group has its own part to play in defending its own interests, and that, during a period of total confrontation, these interests converge.

The student movement must follow its own road—only thus can it contribute to the growth of militant minorities in the factories and workshops. We do not pretend that we can be leaders in the struggle, but it is a fact that small revolutionary groups can, at the right time and place, rupture the system decisively and irreversibly.

During May and June, 1968, the emergence of a vast chain of workers' committees and sub-committees bypassed the calcified structure of the trade unions, and tried to call together all workers in a struggle that was their own and not that of the various trade union bureaucracies. It was because of this that the struggle was carried to a higher stage. It is absurd and romantic to speak of revolution with a capital R and to think of it as resulting from a single, decisive action. The revolutionary process grows and is strengthened daily not only in revolt against the boredom of a system that prevents people from seeing the "beach under the paving stones" but also in our determination to make the beach open to all.

If a revolutionary movement is to succeed, no form of organization whatever must be allowed to dam its spontaneous flow. It must evolve its own forms and structures. . . .

How can anyone represent anyone else? All we can do is to involve them. We can try and get a few movements going, inject politics into all the structures of society, into the Youth Clubs, Youth Hostels, the YMCA and the Saturday Night dance, get out on to the streets, out on to all the streets of all the towns. To bring real politics into everyday life is to get rid of the politicians. We must pass from a critique of the university to the anti-university, open to all. Our challenge of the collective control of knowledge by the bourgeoisie must be radical and intransigent.

The multiplication of nuclei of confrontation decentralizes political life and neutralizes the repressive influence of the radio, television and party politics. Every time we beat back intimidation on the spot, we are striking a blow for freedom. To break out from isolation, we must carry the struggle to every market place and not create Messianic organizations to do the job for us. We reject the policy committee and the editorial board.

In the event, the students were defeated in their own struggle. The weakness of our movement is shown by the fact that we were unable to hold on to a single faculty—the recapture of the factories by the CRS (with the help of the CGT) might well have been halted by the working class, had there been a determined defence of a single "red base." But this is mere speculation. What is certain is that the movement must look carefully at its actions in May and June and draw the correct lessons for the future. The type of organization we must build can neither be a vanguard nor a rearguard, but must be right in the thick of the fight. What we need is not organization with a capital O, but a host of insurrectional cells, be they ideological groups, study groups—we can even use street gangs.

Effective revolutionary action does not spring from "individual" or "external" needs—it can only occur when the two coincide so that the distinction itself breaks down. Every group must find its own form, take its own action, and speak its own language. When all have learnt to express themselves, in harmony with the rest, we shall have a free society.

THE POSITION OF THE WORLD'S EIGHTY-EIGHT COMMUNIST PARTIES—1970

In Opposition			Ruling Party	Banned		
Afghanistan)U	Guadalupe)R	Netherlands #U	Albania *U	Algeria *U	Haiti)R	Portugal /R
Australia /R	Guyana /R	Reunion #R	Bulgaria)R	Argentina)R	Honduras)R	Singapore *U
Austria)R	Iceland)U	Sweden #O	China *O	Bolivia *U	Indonesia /R	S. Africa)U
Belgium /R	India /R	Switzerland /R	Cuba #R	Brazil /R	Iran /R	Spain)R
Canada)R	Ireland)R	U.S.A.)R	Czecho-slovakia)R	Burma /U	Iraq /R	Sudan)R
Ceylon /R	Israel /R	Uruguay)R	E. Germany)R	Cambodia /U	Lebanon /U	Syria /R
Chile)R	Italy /R	Laos /R	Jugoslavia #U	Costa Rica)R	Malaysia)R	Thailand *U
Colombia /R	Gt. Britain)R		N. Korea #U	Dominican Rep. /R	Nepal /R	Tunisia)R
Cyprus)R	Luxembourg)R		Hungary)R	Ecuador)R	Nicaragua)R	Turkey)R
Denmark)R	Martinique)R		Mongolia)R	San Salvador)R	Nigeria)R	Venezuela)R
Finland /R	Mexico /R		Poland)R	Philippines #U	Pakistan #U	S. Vietnam #U
France /R	Morocco #R		Rumania)R	Jordan)R	Panama)R	Peru /R
W.Germany /R	New Zealand /U		U.S.S.R.)R	Greece)R	Peru)R	
Japan #U	*Norway #U		N.Vietnam #U	Guatemala)R		

) supporting Moscow. * supporting Peking. / undecided. # neutral or independent.
R represented at Moscow summit meeting June 1969. U unrepresented at summit meeting.
O observer at summit meeting.
From Corriere della Sera, June 17, 1969.

INDEX

431

MENTOR Titles of Special Interest

☐ **CAPITALISM: THE UNKNOWN IDEAL by Ayn Rand.** A powerful advocacy of capitalism on the moral grounds that it is "the only system consonant with man's rational nature." By the best selling author and founder of Objectivism. Recommended Bibliography, Index.
(#Y4179—$1.25)

☐ **MAO TSE TUNG: AN ANTHOLOGY OF HIS WRITINGS.** The basic tenets of the influential Marxist philosopher and leader of the Chinese Communist Party. Selected Bibliography. (#MQ702—95¢)

☐ **LENIN by David Shub.** A fascinating biography of the man who led Russia into Communism and whose influence is still powerful. Appendix. (#M2988—95¢)

☐ **THE NATURE OF THE NON-WESTERN WORLD by Vera Micheles Dean.** A noted expert on foreign affairs throws new light on the conflict between East and West as she probes the beliefs, traditions, and emotions that motivate the people of the non-Western nations.
(#MQ862—95¢)

PLUME BOOKS are part of New American Library's trade paperback publishing program. The list includes important new books and carefully selected reprints ranging from art and the humanities to science. The high level of scholarship and writing that characterize Signet Classic and Mentor books will be continued and expanded in these editions.

℗ ℗ ℗ ℗ ℗

__Z5019 THE SCOTCH, Galbraith $2.95

__Z5020 EPIGRAMS OF MARTIAL, Bovie $3.95

__Z5021 MARTHA QUEST, Lessing..................$2.95

__Z5022 PRICKSONGS & DESCANTS, Coover $2.45

__Z5023 RIPPLE FROM THE STORM, Lessing $3.50

__Z5024 ROOTS OF APPEASEMENT, Gilbert $3.50

__Z5025 HERO ON A DONKEY, Bulatovic $2.75

__Z5026 LANDLOCKED, Lessing $2.95

__Z5027 EUROPEAN POWERS 1900-1945, Gilbert $3.50

__Z5028 A PROPER MARRIAGE, Lessing $3.50

__Z5029 CLIMAX OF ROME, Grant $3.95

__Z5030 HARD TRAVELLIN', Allsop $3.75

__Z5031 GARIBALDI & HIS ENEMIES, Hibbert $3.95
